Scala Machine Learning Projects

Build real-world machine learning and deep learning projects with Scala

Md. Rezaul Karim

BIRMINGHAM - MUMBAI

Scala Machine Learning Projects

Commissioning Editor: Sunith Shetty
Acquisition Editor: Tushar Gupta
Content Development Editor: Cheryl Dsa
Technical Editor: Sagar Sawant
Copy Editors: Vikrant Phadkay, Safis Editing
Project Coordinator: Nidhi Joshi
Proofreader: Safis Editing
Indexer: Aishwarya Gangawane
Graphics: Tania Dutta
Production Coordinator: Shantanu Zagade

First published: January 2018

Production reference: 1290118

Published by Packt Publishing Ltd.
Livery Place
35 Livery Street
Birmingham
B3 2PB, UK.

ISBN 978-1-78847-904-2

www.packtpub.com

`mapt.io`

Mapt is an online digital library that gives you full access to over 5,000 books and videos, as well as industry leading tools to help you plan your personal development and advance your career. For more information, please visit our website.

Why subscribe?

- Spend less time learning and more time coding with practical eBooks and Videos from over 4,000 industry professionals

- Improve your learning with Skill Plans built especially for you

- Get a free eBook or video every month

- Mapt is fully searchable

- Copy and paste, print, and bookmark content

PacktPub.com

Did you know that Packt offers eBook versions of every book published, with PDF and ePub files available? You can upgrade to the eBook version at `www.PacktPub.com` and as a print book customer, you are entitled to a discount on the eBook copy. Get in touch with us at `service@packtpub.com` for more details.

At `www.PacktPub.com`, you can also read a collection of free technical articles, sign up for a range of free newsletters, and receive exclusive discounts and offers on Packt books and eBooks.

Contributors

About the author

Md. Rezaul Karim is a Research Scientist at Fraunhofer FIT, Germany. He is also a PhD candidate at RWTH Aachen University, Germany. Before joining FIT, he worked as a Researcher at the Insight Centre for Data Analytics, Ireland. Before that, he worked as a Lead Engineer at Samsung Electronics, Korea.

He has 9 years of R&D experience with C++, Java, R, Scala, and Python. He has published several research papers concerning bioinformatics, big data, and deep learning. He has practical working experience with Spark, Zeppelin, Hadoop, Keras, Scikit-Learn, TensorFlow, DeepLearning4j, MXNet, and H2O.

About the reviewer

Dave Wentzel is the chief technology officer of Capax Global, a premier Microsoft consulting partner. Dave is responsible for setting the strategy and defining service offerings and capabilities for the data platform and Azure practice at Capax. He also works directly with clients to help them with their big data journeys. He is a frequent blogger and speaker on big data and data science topics.

Sumit Pal is a published author with Apress. He has more than 22 years of experience in software from startups to enterprises and is an independent consultant working with big data, data visualization, and data science. He builds end-to-end data-driven analytic systems.

Sumit has worked for Microsoft (SQLServer), Oracle (OLAP Kernel), and Verizon. He advises clients on their data architectures and build solutions in Spark and Scala. He has spoken at multiple conferences in North America and Europe and has developed a big data analyst training for Experfy. He has MS and BS in computer science.

Packt is searching for authors like you

If you're interested in becoming an author for Packt, please visit `authors.packtpub.com` and apply today. We have worked with thousands of developers and tech professionals, just like you, to help them share their insight with the global tech community. You can make a general application, apply for a specific hot topic that we are recruiting an author for, or submit your own idea.

Table of Contents

Preface

Machine learning has made a huge impact on academia and industry by turning data into actionable intelligence. Scala, on the other hand, has been observing a steady rise in its adoption over the last few years, especially in the field of data science and analytics. This book has been written for data scientists, data engineers, and deep learning enthusiasts who have a solid background with complex numerical computing and want to learn more hands-on machine learning application development.

So, if you're well-versed in machine learning concepts and want to expand your knowledge by delving into practical implementations using the power of Scala, then this book is what you need! Through 11 end-to-end projects, you will be acquainted with popular machine learning libraries such as Spark ML, H2O, Zeppelin, DeepLearning4j, and MXNet.

After reading this book and practicing all of the projects, you will be able to dominate numerical computing, deep learning, and functional programming to carry out complex numerical tasks. You can thus develop, build, and deploy research and commercial projects in a production-ready environment.

This book isn't meant to be read cover to cover. You can turn the pages to a chapter that looks like something you're trying to accomplish or that simply ignites your interest. But any kind of improvement feedback is welcome.

Happy reading!

Who this book is for

If you want to leverage the power of both Scala and open source libraries such as Spark ML, Deeplearning4j, H2O, MXNet, and Zeppelin to make sense of Big Data, then this book is for you. A strong understanding of Scala and the Scala Play Framework is recommended. Basic familiarity with ML techniques will be an added advantage.

What this book covers

Chapter 1, *Analyzing Insurance Severity Claims*, shows how to develop a predictive model for analyzing insurance severity claims using some widely used regression techniques. We will demonstrate how to deploy this model in a production-ready environment.

Chapter 2, *Analyzing and Predicting Telecommunication Churn*, uses the Orange Telecoms Churn dataset, consisting of cleaned customer activity and churn labels specifying whether customers canceled their subscription or not, to develop a real-life predictive model.

Chapter 3, *High-Frequency Bitcoin Price Prediction from Historical and Live Data*, shows how to develop a real-life project that collects historical and live data. We predict the Bitcoin price for the upcoming weeks, months, and so on. In addition, we demonstrate how to generate a simple signal for online trading in Bitcoin. Finally, this chapter wraps up the whole application as a web app using the Scala Play Framework.

Chapter 4, *Population-Scale Clustering and Ethnicity Prediction*, uses genomic variation data from the 1,000 Genome Project to apply the K-means clustering approach to scalable genomic data analysis. This is aimed at clustering genotypic variants at the population scale. Finally, we train deep neural network and random forest models to predict ethnicity.

Chapter 5, *Topic Modeling in NLP – A Better Insight into Large-Scale Texts*, shows how to develop a topic modeling application by utilizing the Spark-based LDA algorithm and Stanford NLP to handle large-scale raw texts.

Chapter 6, *Developing Model-Based Movie Recommendation Engines*, shows how to develop a scalable movie recommendation engine by inter-operating between singular value decomposition, ALS, and matrix factorization. The movie lens dataset will be used for this end-to-end project.

Chapter 7, *Options Trading using Q-Learning and the Scala Play Framework*, applies a reinforcement QLearning algorithm on real-life IBM stock datasets and designs a machine learning system driven by criticisms and rewards. The goal is to develop a real-life application called **options trading**. The chapter wraps up the whole application as a web app using the Scala Play Framework.

Chapter 8, *Clients Subscription Assessment for Bank Telemarketing using Deep Neural Networks* , is an end-to-end project that shows how to solve a real-life problem called **client subscription assessment**. An H2O deep neural network will be trained using a bank telemarketing dataset. Finally, the chapter evaluates the performance of this predictive model.

Chapter 9, *Fraud Analytics using Autoencoders and Anomaly Detection*, uses autoencoders and the anomaly detection technique for fraud analytics. The dataset used is a fraud detection dataset collected and analyzed during a research collaboration by Worldline and the Machine Learning Group of **ULB** (**Université Libre de Bruxelles**).

Chapter 10, *Human Activity Recognition using Recurrent Neural Networks*, includes another end-to-end project that shows how to use an RNN implementation called LSTM for human activity recognition using a smartphone sensor dataset.

Chapter 11, *Image Classification using Convolutional Neural Networks*, demonstrates how to develop predictive analytics applications such as image classification, using convolutional neural networks on a real image dataset called Yelp.

To get the most out of this book

This book is dedicated to developers, data analysts, and deep learning enthusiasts who do not have much background with complex numerical computations but want to know what deep learning is. A strong understanding of Scala and its functional programming concepts is recommended. Some basic understanding and high-level knowledge of Spark ML, H2O, Zeppelin, DeepLearning4j, and MXNet would act as an added advantage in order to grasp this book. Additionally, basic know-how of build tools such as Maven and SBT is assumed.

All the examples have been implemented using Scala on an Ubuntu 16.04 LTs 64-bit and Windows 10 64-bit. You will also need the following (preferably the latest versions):

- Apache Spark 2.0.0 (or higher)
- MXNet, Zeppelin, DeepLearning4j, and H2O (see the details in the chapter and in the supplied pom.xml files)
- Hadoop 2.7 (or higher)
- Java (JDK and JRE) 1.7+/1.8+
- Scala 2.11.x (or higher)
- Eclipse Mars or Luna (latest) with Maven plugin (2.9+), Maven compiler plugin (2.3.2+), and Maven assembly plugin (2.4.1+)
- IntelliJ IDE
- SBT plugin and Scala Play Framework installed

A computer with at least a Core i3 processor, Core i5 (recommended), or Core i7 (to get the best results) is needed. However, multicore processing will provide faster data processing and scalability. At least 8 GB RAM is recommended for standalone mode; use at least 32 GB RAM for a single VM and higher for a cluster. You should have enough storage for running heavy jobs (depending on the dataset size you will be handling); preferably, at least 50 GB of free disk storage (for standalone and for SQL Warehouse).

Linux distributions are preferable (including Debian, Ubuntu, Fedora, RHEL, CentOS, and many more). To be more specific, for example, for Ubuntu it is recommended to have a 14.04 (LTS) 64-bit (or later) complete installation, VMWare player 12, or VirtualBox. You can run Spark jobs on Windows (XP/7/8/10) or Mac OS X (10.4.7+).

Download the example code files

You can download the example code files for this book from your account at `www.packtpub.com`. If you purchased this book elsewhere, you can visit `www.packtpub.com/support` and register to have the files emailed directly to you.

You can download the code files by following these steps:

1. Log in or register at `www.packtpub.com`.
2. Select the **SUPPORT** tab.
3. Click on **Code Downloads & Errata**.
4. Enter the name of the book in the **Search** box and follow the onscreen instructions.

Once the file is downloaded, please make sure that you unzip or extract the folder using the latest version of:

- WinRAR/7-Zip for Windows
- Zipeg/iZip/UnRarX for Mac
- 7-Zip/PeaZip for Linux

The code bundle for the book is also hosted on GitHub at
`https://github.com/PacktPublishing/Scala-Machine-Learning-Projects`. We also have
other code bundles from our rich catalog of books and videos available at `https://github.com/PacktPublishing/`. Check them out!

Download the color images

We also provide a PDF file that has color images of the screenshots/diagrams used in this
book. You can download it here:
`http://www.packtpub.com/sites/default/files/downloads/ScalaMachineLearningProje cts_ColorImages.pdf`.

Conventions used

There are a number of text conventions used throughout this book.

`CodeInText`: Indicates code words in text, database table names, folder names, filenames,
file extensions, pathnames, dummy URLs, user input, and Twitter handles. Here is an
example: "Mount the downloaded `WebStorm-10*.dmg` disk image file as another disk in
your system."

A block of code is set as follows:

```
val cv = new CrossValidator()
      .setEstimator(pipeline)
      .setEvaluator(new RegressionEvaluator)
      .setEstimatorParamMaps(paramGrid)
      .setNumFolds(numFolds)
```

Scala functional code blocks look as follows:

```
def variantId(genotype: Genotype): String = {
    val name = genotype.getVariant.getContigName
    val start = genotype.getVariant.getStart
    val end = genotype.getVariant.getEnd
    s"$name:$start:$end"
}
```

When we wish to draw your attention to a particular part of a code block, the relevant lines or items are set in bold:

```
var paramGrid = new ParamGridBuilder()
      .addGrid(dTree.impurity, "gini" :: "entropy" :: Nil)
      .addGrid(dTree.maxBins, 3 :: 5 :: 9 :: 15 :: 23 :: 31 :: Nil)
      .addGrid(dTree.maxDepth, 5 :: 10 :: 15 :: 20 :: 25 :: 30 :: Nil)
      .build()
```

Any command-line input or output is written as follows:

```
$ sudo mkdir Bitcoin
$ cd Bitcoin
```

Bold: Indicates a new term, an important word, or words that you see onscreen. For example, words in menus or dialog boxes appear in the text like this. Here is an example: "Select **System info** from the **Administration** panel."

Warnings or important notes appear like this.

Tips and tricks appear like this.

Get in touch

Feedback from our readers is always welcome.

General feedback: Email feedback@packtpub.com and mention the book title in the subject of your message. If you have questions about any aspect of this book, please email us at questions@packtpub.com.

Errata: Although we have taken every care to ensure the accuracy of our content, mistakes do happen. If you have found a mistake in this book, we would be grateful if you would report this to us. Please visit www.packtpub.com/submit-errata, selecting your book, clicking on the Errata Submission Form link, and entering the details.

Piracy: If you come across any illegal copies of our works in any form on the Internet, we would be grateful if you would provide us with the location address or website name. Please contact us at copyright@packtpub.com with a link to the material.

If you are interested in becoming an author: If there is a topic that you have expertise in and you are interested in either writing or contributing to a book, please visit authors.packtpub.com.

Reviews

Please leave a review. Once you have read and used this book, why not leave a review on the site that you purchased it from? Potential readers can then see and use your unbiased opinion to make purchase decisions, we at Packt can understand what you think about our products, and our authors can see your feedback on their book. Thank you!

For more information about Packt, please visit packtpub.com.

1
Analyzing Insurance Severity Claims

Predicting the cost, and hence the severity, of claims in an insurance company is a real-life problem that needs to be solved in an accurate way. In this chapter, we will show you how to develop a predictive model for analyzing insurance severity claims using some of the most widely used regression algorithms.

We will start with simple **linear regression** (**LR**) and we will see how to improve the performance using some ensemble techniques, such as **gradient boosted tree** (**GBT**) regressors. Then we will look at how to boost the performance with Random Forest regressors. Finally, we will show you how to choose the best model and deploy it for a production-ready environment. Also, we will provide some background studies on machine learning workflow, hyperparameter tuning, and cross-validation.

For the implementation, we will use **Spark ML** API for faster computation and massive scalability. In a nutshell, we will learn the following topics throughout this end-to-end project:

- Machine learning and learning workflow
- Hyperparameter tuning and cross-validation of ML models
- LR for analyzing insurance severity claims
- Improving performance with gradient boosted regressors
- Boosting the performance with random forest regressors
- Model deployment

Machine learning and learning workflow

Machine learning (ML) is about using a set of statistical and mathematical algorithms to perform tasks such as concept learning, predictive modeling, clustering, and mining useful patterns can be performed. The ultimate goal is to improve the learning in such a way that it becomes automatic, so that no more human interactions are needed, or to reduce the level of human interaction as much as possible.

We now refer to a famous definition of ML by **Tom M. Mitchell** (*Machine Learning, Tom Mitchell*, McGraw Hill, 1997**)**, where he explained what learning really means from a computer science perspective:

> *"A computer program is said to learn from experience E with respect to some class of tasks T and performance measure P, if its performance at tasks in T, as measured by P, improves with experience E."*

Based on the preceding definition, we can conclude that a computer program or machine can do the following:

- Learn from data and histories
- Be improved with experience
- Interactively enhance a model that can be used to predict an outcome

A typical ML function can be formulated as a convex optimization problem for finding a minimizer of a convex function f that depends on a variable vector w (weights), which has d records. Formally, we can write this as the following optimization problem:

$$min_{w \in \mathbb{R}^d} f(w)$$

Here, the objective function is of the form:

$$f(w) := \lambda R(w) + \frac{1}{n} \sum_{i=1}^{n} L(w; x_i, y_i)$$

Here, the vectors $x_i \mathbb{R} \in^d$ are the training data points for *1≤i≤n,* and are their corresponding labels that we want to predict eventually. We call the method *linear* if *L(w;x,y)* can be expressed as a function of *wTx* and *y.*

The objective function *f* has two components:

- A regularizer that controls the complexity of the model
- The loss that measures the error of the model on the training data

The loss function *L(w;)* is typically a convex function in *w.* The fixed regularization parameter *λ≥0* defines the trade-off between the two goals of minimizing the loss on the training error and minimizing model complexity to avoid overfitting. Throughout the chapters, we will learn in details on different learning types and algorithms.

On the other hand, **deep neural networks (DNN)** form the core of **deep learning (DL)** by providing algorithms to model complex and high-level abstractions in data and can better exploit large-scale datasets to build complex models

There are some widely used deep learning architectures based on artificial neural networks: DNNs, Capsule Networks, Restricted Boltzmann Machines, deep belief networks, factorization machines and recurrent neural networks.

These architectures have been widely used in computer vision, speech recognition, natural language processing, audio recognition, social network filtering, machine translation, bioinformatics and drug design. Throughout the chapters, we will see several real-life examples using these architectures to achieve state-of-the art predictive accuracy.

Typical machine learning workflow

A typical ML application involves several processing steps, from the input to the output, forming a scientific workflow as shown in *Figure 1, ML workflow*. The following steps are involved in a typical ML application:

1. Load the data
2. Parse the data into the input format for the algorithm
3. Pre-process the data and handle the missing values
4. Split the data into three sets, for training, testing, and validation (train set and validation set respectively) and one for testing the model (test dataset)
5. Run the algorithm to build and train your ML model
6. Make predictions with the training data and observe the results
7. Test and evaluate the model with the test data or alternatively validate the model using some cross-validator technique using the third dataset called a **validation dataset**
8. Tune the model for better performance and accuracy
9. Scale up the model so that it can handle massive datasets in future
10. Deploy the ML model in production:

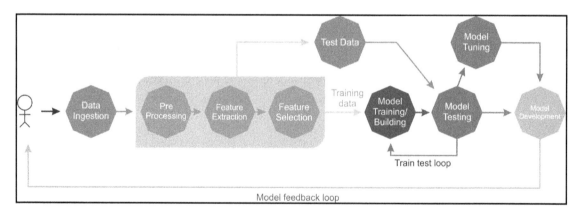

Figure 1: ML workflow

The preceding workflow is represent a few steps to solve ML problems. Where, ML tasks can be broadly categorized into supervised, unsupervised, semi-supervised, reinforcement, and recommendation systems. The following *Figure 2, Supervised learning in action*, shows the schematic diagram of supervised learning. After the algorithm has found the required patterns, those patterns can be used to make predictions for unlabeled test data:

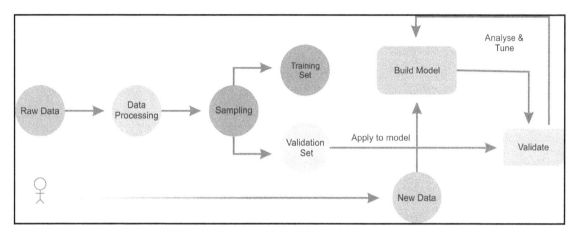

Figure 2: Supervised learning in action

Examples include classification and regression for solving supervised learning problems so that predictive models can be built for predictive analytics based on them. Throughout the upcoming chapters, we will provide several examples of supervised learning, such as LR, logistic regression, random forest, decision trees, Naive Bayes, multilayer perceptron, and so on.

A regression algorithm is meant to produce continuous output. The input is allowed to be either discrete or continuous:

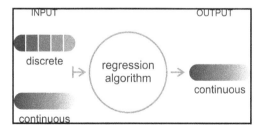

Figure 3: A regression algorithm is meant to produce continuous output

A classification algorithm, on the other hand, is meant to produce discrete output from an input of a set of discrete or continuous values. This distinction is important to know because discrete-valued outputs are handled better by classification, which will be discussed in upcoming chapters:

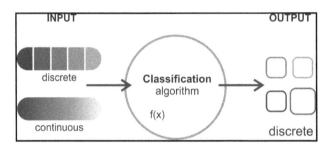

Figure 4: A classification algorithm is meant to produce discrete output

In this chapter, we will mainly focus on the supervised regression algorithms. We will start with describing the problem statement and then we move on to the very simple LR algorithm. Often, performance of these ML models is optimized using hyperparameter tuning and cross-validation techniques. So knowing them, in brief, is mandatory so that we can easily use them in future chapters.

Hyperparameter tuning and cross-validation

Tuning an algorithm is simply a process that one goes through in order to enable the algorithm to perform optimally in terms of runtime and memory usage. In Bayesian statistics, a hyperparameter is a parameter of a prior distribution. In terms of ML, the term hyperparameter refers to those parameters that cannot be directly learned from the regular training process.

Hyperparameters are usually fixed before the actual training process begins. This is done by setting different values for those hyperparameters, training different models, and deciding which ones work best by testing them. Here are some typical examples of such parameters:

- Number of leaves, bins, or depth of a tree
- Number of iterations
- Number of latent factors in a matrix factorization
- Learning rate

- Number of hidden layers in a deep neural network
- The number of clusters in k-means clustering and so on

In short, hyperparameter tuning is a technique for choosing the right combination of hyperparameters based on the performance of presented data. It is one of the fundamental requirements for obtaining meaningful and accurate results from ML algorithms in practice. The following figure shows the model tuning process, things to consider, and workflow:

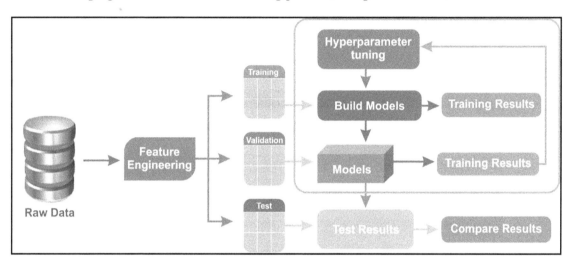

Figure 5: Model tuning process

Cross-validation (also known as **rotation estimation**) is a model validation technique for assessing the quality of the statistical analysis and results. The target is to make the model generalized toward an independent test set. It will help if you want to estimate how a predictive model will perform accurately in practice when you deploy it as an ML application. During the cross-validation process, a model is usually trained with a dataset of a known type.

Conversely, it is tested using a dataset of an unknown type. In this regard, cross-validation helps to describe a dataset to test the model in the training phase using the validation set. There are two types of cross-validation that can be typed as follows:

- **Exhaustive cross-validation**: This includes leave-p-out cross-validation and leave-one-out cross-validation
- **Non-exhaustive cross-validation**: This includes K-fold cross-validation and repeated random subsampling cross-validation

In most cases, the researcher/data scientist/data engineer uses 10-fold cross-validation instead of testing on a validation set (see more in *Figure 6, 10-fold cross-validation technique*). This is the most widely used cross-validation technique across all use cases and problem types, as explained by the following figure.

Basically, using this technique, your complete training data is split into a number of folds. This parameter can be specified. Then the whole pipeline is run once for every fold and one ML model is trained for each fold. Finally, the different ML models obtained are joined by a voting scheme for classifiers or by averaging for regression:

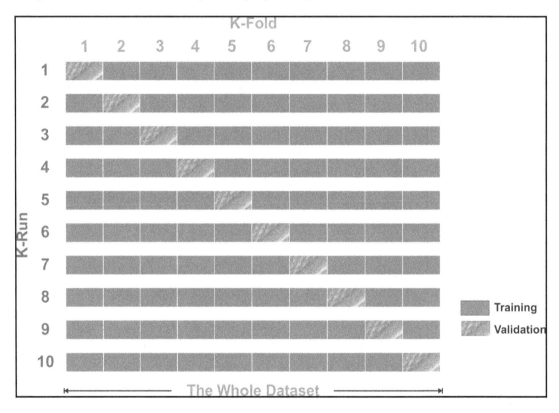

Figure 6: 10-fold cross-validation technique

Moreover, to reduce the variability, multiple iterations of cross-validation are performed using different partitions; finally, the validation results are averaged over the rounds.

Analyzing and predicting insurance severity claims

Predicting the cost, and hence the severity, of claims in an insurance company is a real-life problem that needs to be solved in a more accurate and automated way. We will do something similar in this example.

We will start with simple logistic regression and will learn how to improve the performance using some ensemble techniques, such as an random forest regressor. Then we will look at how to boost the performance with a gradient boosted regressor. Finally, we will show how to choose the best model and deploy it for a production-ready environment.

Motivation

When someone is devastated by a serious car accident, his focus is on his life, family, child, friends, and loved ones. However, once a file is submitted for the insurance claim, the overall paper-based process to calculate the severity claim is a tedious task to be completed.

This is why insurance companies are continually seeking fresh ideas to improve their claims service for their clients in an automated way. Therefore, predictive analytics is a viable solution to predicting the cost, and hence severity, of claims on the available and historical data.

Description of the dataset

A dataset from the **Allstate Insurance company** will be used, which consists of more than 300,000 examples with masked and anonymous data and consisting of more than 100 categorical and numerical attributes, thus being compliant with confidentiality constraints, more than enough for building and evaluating a variety of ML techniques.

The dataset is downloaded from the Kaggle website at `https://www.kaggle.com/c/allstate-claims-severity/data`. Each row in the dataset represents an insurance claim. Now, the task is to predict the value for the `loss` column. Variables prefaced with `cat` are categorical, while those prefaced with `cont` are continuous.

It is to be noted that the Allstate Corporation is the second largest insurance company in the United States, founded in 1931. We are trying to make the whole thing automated, to predict the cost, and hence the severity, of accident and damage claims.

Exploratory analysis of the dataset

Let's look at some data properties (use the `EDA.scala` file for this). At first, we need to read the training set to see the available properties. To begin with, let's place your training set in your project directory or somewhere else and point to it accordingly:

```
val train = "data/insurance_train.csv"
```

I hope you have Java, Scala and Spark installed and configured on your machine. If not, please do so. Anyway, I'm assuming they are. So let's create an active Spark session, which is the gateway for any Spark application:

```
val spark = SparkSessionCreate.createSession()
import spark.implicits._
```

Spark session alias on Scala REPL:
If you are inside Scala REPL, the Spark session alias `spark` is already defined, so just get going.

Here, I have a method called `createSession()` under the class `SparkSessionCreate` that goes as follows:

```
import org.apache.spark.sql.SparkSession

object SparkSessionCreate {
  def createSession(): SparkSession = {
    val spark = SparkSession
      .builder
      .master("local[*]") // adjust accordingly
      .config("spark.sql.warehouse.dir", "E:/Exp/") //change accordingly
      .appName("MySparkSession") //change accordingly
      .getOrCreate()
    return spark
    }
}
```

Since this will be used frequently throughout this book, I decided to create a dedicated method. So, let's load, parse, and create a DataFrame using the `read.csv` method but in Databricks `.csv` format (as known as `com.databricks.spark.csv`) since our dataset comes with `.csv` format.

At this point, I have to interrupt you to inform something very useful. Since we will be using Spark MLlib and ML APIs in upcoming chapters too. Therefore, it would be worth fixing some issues in prior. If you're a Windows user then let me tell you a very weired issue that you will be experiencing while working with Spark.

Well, the thing is that Spark works on **Windows**, **Mac OS**, and **Linux**. While using `Eclipse` or `IntelliJ IDEA` to develop your Spark applications (or through Spark local job sumit) on Windows, you might face an I/O exception error and consequently your application might not compile successfully or may be interrupted.

The reason is that Spark expects that there is a runtime environment for `Hadoop` on Windows. Unfortunately, the **binary** distribution of **Spark** (**v2.2.0 for example**) release does not contain some Windows native components (example, `winutils.exe`, `hadoop.dll`, and so on). However, these are required (not optional) to run `Hadoop` on Windows. Therefore, if you cannot ensure the runtime environment, an I/O exception saying the following:

```
24/01/2018 11:11:10
ERROR util.Shell: Failed to locate the winutils binary in the hadoop binary
path
java.io.IOException: Could not locate executable null\bin\winutils.exe in
the Hadoop binaries.
```

Now there are two ways to tackale this issue on Windows:

1. **From IDE such as Eclipse and IntelliJ IDEA**: Download the `winutls.exe` from `https://github.com/steveloughran/winutils/tree/master/hadoop-2.7.1/bin/`. Then download and copy it inside the `bin` folder in the Spark distribution—example, `spark-2.2.0-bin-hadoop2.7/bin/`. Then select the project | **Run Configurations...** | **Environment** | **New** | create a variable named `HADOOP_HOME` and put the path in the value field—example, `c:/spark-2.2.0-bin-hadoop2.7/bin/` | **OK** | **Apply** | **Run**. Then you're done!

2. **With local Spark job submit**: Add the `winutils.exe` file path to the hadoop home directory using System set properties—example, in the Spark code `System.setProperty("hadoop.home.dir", "c:\\\spark-2.2.0-bin-hadoop2.7\\bin\winutils.exe")`

Alright, let's come to your original discussion. If you see the preceding code block then we set to read the header of the CSV file, which is directly applied to the column names of the DataFrame created, and the `inferSchema` property is set to `true`. If you don't specify the `inferSchema` configuration explicitly, the float values will be treated as `strings`. This might cause `VectorAssembler` to raise an exception such as `java.lang.IllegalArgumentException: Data type StringType is not` supported:

```
val trainInput = spark.read
    .option("header", "true")
    .option("inferSchema", "true")
    .format("com.databricks.spark.csv")
    .load(train)
    .cache
```

Now let's print the schema of the DataFrame we just created. I have abridged the output and shown only a few columns:

```
Println(trainInput.printSchema())
root
  |-- id: integer (nullable = true)
  |-- cat1: string (nullable = true)
  |-- cat2: string (nullable = true)
  |-- cat3: string (nullable = true)
  . . .
  |-- cat115: string (nullable = true)
  |-- cat116: string (nullable = true)
  . . .
  |-- cont14: double (nullable = true)
  |-- loss: double (nullable = true)
```

You can see that there are 116 categorical columns for categorical features. Also, there are 14 numerical feature columns. Now let's see how many rows there are in the dataset using the `count()` method:

```
println(df.count())

>>>
 188318
```

The preceding number is pretty high for training an ML model. Alright, now let's see a snapshot of the dataset using the `show()` method but with only some selected columns so that it makes more sense. Feel free to use `df.show()` to see all columns:

```
df.select("id", "cat1", "cat2", "cat3", "cont1", "cont2", "cont3",
"loss").show()
>>>
```

```
+---+----+----+----+--------+--------+--------+-------+
| id|cat1|cat2|cat3|   cont1|   cont2|   cont3|   loss|
+---+----+----+----+--------+--------+--------+-------+
|  1|   A|   B|   A|  0.7263|0.245921|0.187583|2213.18|
|  2|   A|   B|   A|0.330514|0.737068|0.592681| 1283.6|
|  5|   A|   B|   A|0.261841|0.358319|0.484196|3005.09|
| 10|   B|   B|   A|0.321594|0.555782|0.527991| 939.85|
| 11|   A|   B|   A|0.273204| 0.15999|0.527991|2763.85|
| 13|   A|   B|   A| 0.54667|0.681761|0.634224|5142.87|
| 14|   A|   A|   A|0.471447|0.737068| 0.61366|1132.22|
| 20|   A|   B|   A|0.826591|0.488789| 0.26357|3585.75|
| 23|   A|   B|   B|0.330514|0.555782|0.440642|10280.2|
| 24|   A|   B|   A|  0.7263|0.358319|0.356819|6184.59|
| 25|   A|   B|   A|0.496063|0.358319| 0.65431|6396.85|
| 33|   A|   B|   A|0.520698|0.422197|0.634224|5965.73|
| 34|   B|   A|   A|0.321594|0.555782|0.527991|1193.05|
| 41|   B|   A|   A|0.351358|0.555782|0.440642|1071.77|
| 47|   A|   A|   A|0.894333|0.299102|0.094942| 585.18|
| 48|   A|   A|   A|0.472892|0.681761|0.484196|1395.45|
| 49|   A|   B|   B|0.424162|0.737068| 0.80643|6609.32|
| 51|   A|   A|   A|0.834747|0.488789|0.246911| 2658.7|
| 52|   A|   A|   B|0.488816|0.422197|0.592681|4167.32|
| 55|   A|   A|   A|0.391956| 0.15999| 0.26357|3797.89|
+---+----+----+----+--------+--------+--------+-------+
only showing top 20 rows
```

Nevertheless, if you look at all the rows using `df.show()`, you will see some categorical columns containing too many categories. To be more specific, category columns `cat109` to `cat116` contain too many categories, as follows:

```
df.select("cat109", "cat110", "cat112", "cat113", "cat116").show()
>>>
```

```
+------+------+------+------+------+
|cat109|cat110|cat112|cat113|cat116|
+------+------+------+------+------+
|    BU|    BC|    AS|     S|    LB|
|    BI|    CQ|    AV|    BM|    DP|
|    AB|    DK|     C|    AF|    GK|
|    BI|    CS|     N|    AE|    DJ|
|     H|     C|     Y|    BM|    CK|
|    BI|    CS|    AS|    AE|    DJ|
|    BI|    DK|     J|    AF|    DJ|
|    BI|    EB|    AH|     Y|    LO|
|    BI|    BC|     K|    AX|    IE|
|    BU|    DW|     U|     S|    LY|
|    BI|    AM|    AS|     H|    GS|
|    BI|    AI|     E|    AX|    HK|
|    BI|    CS|     E|    AE|    DJ|
|    AB|    EG|    AK|     K|    DC|
|    BI|    EG|    AH|     L|    MP|
|    BI|    CQ|    AI|    BM|    DS|
|    BI|    CL|    AE|     A|    DJ|
|    BU|    BC|     A|     S|    LE|
|    BI|    CS|    AV|     J|    HQ|
|    BI|    BS|     L|    BM|    HJ|
+------+------+------+------+------+
only showing top 20 rows
```

In later stages, it would be worth dropping these columns to remove the skewness in the dataset. It is to be noted that in statistics, skewness is a measure of the asymmetry of the probability distribution of a real-valued random variable with respect to the mean.

Now that we have seen a snapshot of the dataset, it is worth seeing some other statistics such as average claim or loss, minimum, maximum loss, and many more, using Spark SQL. But before that, let's rename the last column from `loss` to `label` since the ML model will complain about it. Even after using the `setLabelCol` on the regression model, it still looks for a column called `label`. This results in a disgusting error saying `org.apache.spark.sql.AnalysisException: cannot resolve 'label' given input columns:`

```
val newDF = df.withColumnRenamed("loss", "label")
```

Now, since we want to execute an SQL query, we need to create a temporary view so that the operation can be performed in-memory:

```
newDF.createOrReplaceTempView("insurance")
```

Now let's average the damage claimed by the clients:

```
spark.sql("SELECT avg(insurance.label) as AVG_LOSS FROM insurance").show()
>>>
+------------------+
|     AVG_LOSS     |
+------------------+
|3037.3376856699924|
+------------------+
```

Similarly, let's see the lowest claim made so far:

```
spark.sql("SELECT min(insurance.label) as MIN_LOSS FROM insurance").show()
>>>
+--------+
|MIN_LOSS|
+--------+
|    0.67|
+--------+
```

And let's see the highest claim made so far:

```
spark.sql("SELECT max(insurance.label) as MAX_LOSS FROM insurance").show()
>>>
+---------+
| MAX_LOSS|
+---------+
|121012.25|
+---------+
```

Since Scala or Java does not come with a handy visualization library, I could not something else but now let's focus on the data preprocessing before we prepare our training set.

Data preprocessing

Now that we have looked at some data properties, the next task is to do some preprocessing, such as cleaning, before getting the training set. For this part, use the `Preprocessing.scala` file. For this part, the following imports are required:

```
import org.apache.spark.ml.feature.{ StringIndexer, StringIndexerModel}
import org.apache.spark.ml.feature.VectorAssembler
```

Then we load both the training and the test set as shown in the following code:

```
var trainSample = 1.0
var testSample = 1.0
val train = "data/insurance_train.csv"
val test = "data/insurance_test.csv"
val spark = SparkSessionCreate.createSession()
import spark.implicits._
println("Reading data from " + train + " file")

    val trainInput = spark.read
        .option("header", "true")
        .option("inferSchema", "true")
        .format("com.databricks.spark.csv")
        .load(train)
        .cache
    val testInput = spark.read
        .option("header", "true")
        .option("inferSchema", "true")
        .format("com.databricks.spark.csv")
        .load(test)
        .cache
```

The next task is to prepare the training and test set for our ML model to be learned. In the preceding DataFrame out of the training dataset, we renamed the `loss` to `label`. Then the content of `train.csv` was split into training and (cross) validation data, 75% and 25%, respectively.

The content of `test.csv` is used for evaluating the ML model. Both original DataFrames are also sampled, which is particularly useful for running fast executions on your local machine:

```
println("Preparing data for training model")
var data = trainInput.withColumnRenamed("loss", "label").sample(false,
trainSample)
```

We also should do null checking. Here, I have used a naïve approach. The thing is that if the training DataFrame contains any null values, we completely drop those rows. This makes sense since a few rows out of 188,318 do no harm. However, feel free to adopt another approach such as null value imputation:

```
var DF = data.na.drop()
if (data == DF)
  println("No null values in the DataFrame")
else{
  println("Null values exist in the DataFrame")
  data = DF
}
val seed = 12345L
val splits = data.randomSplit(Array(0.75, 0.25), seed)
val (trainingData, validationData) = (splits(0), splits(1))
```

Then we cache both the sets for faster in-memory access:

```
trainingData.cache
validationData.cache
```

Additionally, we should perform the sampling of the test set that will be required in the evaluation step:

```
val testData = testInput.sample(false, testSample).cache
```

Since the training set contains both the numerical and categorical values, we need to identify and treat them separately. First, let's identify only the categorical column:

```
def isCateg(c: String): Boolean = c.startsWith("cat")
def categNewCol(c: String): String = if (isCateg(c)) s"idx_${c}" else c
```

Then, the following method is used to remove categorical columns with too many categories, which we already discussed in the preceding section:

```
def removeTooManyCategs(c: String): Boolean = !(c matches
"cat(109$|110$|112$|113$|116$)")
```

Now the following method is used to select only feature columns. So essentially, we should remove the ID (since the ID is just the identification number of the clients, it does not carry any non-trivial information) and the label column:

```
def onlyFeatureCols(c: String): Boolean = !(c matches "id|label")
```

Well, so far we have treated some bad columns that are either trivial or not needed at all. Now the next task is to construct the definitive set of feature columns:

```
val featureCols = trainingData.columns
    .filter(removeTooManyCategs)
    .filter(onlyFeatureCols)
    .map(categNewCol)
```

StringIndexer encodes a given string column of labels to a column of label indices. If the input column is numeric in nature, we cast it to string using the StringIndexer and index the string values. When downstream pipeline components such as Estimator or Transformer make use of this string-indexed label, you must set the input column of the component to this string-indexed column name. In many cases, you can set the input column with setInputCol.

Now we need to use the StringIndexer() for categorical columns:

```
val stringIndexerStages = trainingData.columns.filter(isCateg)
    .map(c => new StringIndexer()
    .setInputCol(c)
    .setOutputCol(categNewCol(c))
    .fit(trainInput.select(c).union(testInput.select(c))))
```

Note that this is not an efficient approach. An alternative approach would be using a OneHotEncoder estimator.

OneHotEncoder maps a column of label indices to a column of binary vectors, with a single one-value at most. This encoding permits algorithms that expect continuous features, such as logistic regression, to utilize categorical features.

Now let's use the VectorAssembler() to transform a given list of columns into a single vector column:

```
val assembler = new VectorAssembler()
    .setInputCols(featureCols)
    .setOutputCol("features")
```

`VectorAssembler` is a transformer. It combines a given list of columns into a single vector column. It is useful for combining the raw features and features generated by different feature transformers into one feature vector, in order to train ML models such as logistic regression and decision trees.

That's all we need before we start training the regression models. First, we start training the LR model and evaluate the performance.

LR for predicting insurance severity claims

As you have already seen, the loss to be predicted contains continuous values, that is, it will be a regression task. So in using regression analysis here, the goal is to predict a continuous target variable, whereas another area called classification predicts a label from a finite set.

Logistic regression (**LR**) belongs to the family of regression algorithms. The goal of regression is to find relationships and dependencies between variables. It models the relationship between a continuous scalar dependent variable y (that is, label or target) and one or more (a D-dimensional vector) explanatory variable (also independent variables, input variables, features, observed data, observations, attributes, dimensions, and data points) denoted as x using a linear function:

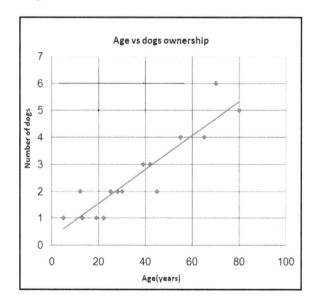

Figure 9: A regression graph separates data points (in red dots) and the blue line is regression

LR models the relationship between a dependent variable y, which involves a linear combination of interdependent variables x_i. The letters A and B represent constants that describe the y axis intercept and the slope of the line respectively:

$$y = A + Bx$$

Figure 9, Regression graph separates data points (in red dots) and the blue line is regression shows an example of simple LR with one independent variable—that is, a set of data points and a **best fit** line, which is the result of the regression analysis itself. It can be observed that the line does not actually pass through all of the points.

The distance between any data points (measured) and the line (predicted) is called the regression error. Smaller errors contribute to more accurate results in predicting unknown values. When the errors are reduced to their smallest levels possible, the line of best fit is created for the final regression error. Note that there are no single metrics in terms of regression errors; there are several as follows:

- **Mean Squared Error** (**MSE**): It is a measure of how close a fitted line is to data points. The smaller the MSE, the closer the fit is to the data.
- **Root Mean Squared Error** (**RMSE**): It is the square root of the MSE but probably the most easily interpreted statistic, since it has the same units as the quantity plotted on the vertical axis.
- **R-squared**: R-squared is a statistical measure of how close the data is to the fitted regression line. R-squared is always between 0 and 100%. The higher the R-squared, the better the model fits your data.
- **Mean Absolute Error** (**MAE**): MAE measures the average magnitude of the errors in a set of predictions without considering their direction. It's the average over the test sample of the absolute differences between prediction and actual observation where all individual differences have equal weight.
- **Explained variance**: In statistics, **explained** variation measures the proportion to which a mathematical model accounts for the variation of a given dataset.

Developing insurance severity claims predictive model using LR

In this sub-section, we will develop a predictive analytics model for predicting accidental loss against the severity claim by clients. We start with importing required libraries:

```
import org.apache.spark.ml.regression.{LinearRegression,
```

```
LinearRegressionModel}
import org.apache.spark.ml.{ Pipeline, PipelineModel }
import org.apache.spark.ml.evaluation.RegressionEvaluator
import org.apache.spark.ml.tuning.ParamGridBuilder
import org.apache.spark.ml.tuning.CrossValidator
import org.apache.spark.sql._
import org.apache.spark.sql.functions._
import org.apache.spark.mllib.evaluation.RegressionMetrics
```

Then we create an active Spark session as the entry point to the application. In addition, importing `implicits__` required for implicit conversions like converting RDDs to DataFrames.

```
val spark = SparkSessionCreate.createSession()
import spark.implicits._
```

Then we define some hyperparameters, such as the number of folds for cross-validation, the number of maximum iterations, the value of the regression parameter, the value of tolerance, and elastic network parameters, as follows:

```
val numFolds = 10
val MaxIter: Seq[Int] = Seq(1000)
val RegParam: Seq[Double] = Seq(0.001)
val Tol: Seq[Double] = Seq(1e-6)
val ElasticNetParam: Seq[Double] = Seq(0.001)
```

Well, now we create an LR estimator:

```
val model = new LinearRegression()
        .setFeaturesCol("features")
        .setLabelCol("label")
```

Now let's build a pipeline estimator by chaining the transformer and the LR estimator:

```
println("Building ML pipeline")
val pipeline = new Pipeline()
        .setStages((Preproessing.stringIndexerStages
        :+ Preproessing.assembler) :+ model)
```

Spark ML pipelines have the following components:

- **DataFrame**: Used as the central data store where all the original data and intermediate results are stored.

- **Transformer**: A transformer transforms one DataFrame into another by adding additional feature columns. Transformers are stateless, meaning that they don't have any internal memory and behave exactly the same each time they are used.

- **Estimator**: An estimator is some sort of ML model. In contrast to a transformer, an estimator contains an internal state representation and is highly dependent on the history of the data that it has already seen.

- **Pipeline**: Chains the preceding components, DataFrame, Transformer, and Estimator together.

- **Parameter**: ML algorithms have many knobs to tweak. These are called **hyperparameters**, and the values learned by a ML algorithm to fit data are called **parameters**.

Before we start performing the cross-validation, we need to have a paramgrid. So let's start creating the paramgrid by specifying the number of maximum iterations, the value of the regression parameter, the value of tolerance, and Elastic network parameters as follows:

```
val paramGrid = new ParamGridBuilder()
      .addGrid(model.maxIter, MaxIter)
      .addGrid(model.regParam, RegParam)
      .addGrid(model.tol, Tol)
      .addGrid(model.elasticNetParam, ElasticNetParam)
      .build()
```

Now, for a better and stable performance, let's prepare the K-fold cross-validation and grid search as a part of model tuning. As you can probably guess, I am going to perform 10-fold cross-validation. Feel free to adjust the number of folds based on your settings and dataset:

```
println("Preparing K-fold Cross Validation and Grid Search: Model tuning")
val cv = new CrossValidator()
      .setEstimator(pipeline)
      .setEvaluator(new RegressionEvaluator)
      .setEstimatorParamMaps(paramGrid)
      .setNumFolds(numFolds)
```

Fantastic - we have created the cross-validation estimator. Now it's time to train the LR model:

```
println("Training model with Linear Regression algorithm")
val cvModel = cv.fit(Preproessing.trainingData)
```

Now that we have the fitted model, that means it is now capable of making predictions. So let's start evaluating the model on the train and validation set and calculating RMSE, MSE, MAE, R-squared, and many more:

```
println("Evaluating model on train and validation set and calculating
RMSE")
val trainPredictionsAndLabels =
cvModel.transform(Preproessing.trainingData)
              .select("label", "prediction")
              .map { case Row(label: Double, prediction: Double)
              => (label, prediction) }.rdd

val validPredictionsAndLabels =
cvModel.transform(Preproessing.validationData)
                          .select("label", "prediction")
                          .map { case Row(label: Double, prediction:
Double)
                          => (label, prediction) }.rdd

val trainRegressionMetrics = new
RegressionMetrics(trainPredictionsAndLabels)
val validRegressionMetrics = new
RegressionMetrics(validPredictionsAndLabels)
```

Great! We have managed to compute the raw prediction on the train and the test set. Let's hunt for the best model:

```
val bestModel = cvModel.bestModel.asInstanceOf[PipelineModel]
```

Once we have the best fitted and cross-validated model, we can expect good prediction accuracy. Now let's observe the results on the train and the validation set:

```
val results =
"n==================================================================n" +
s"Param trainSample: ${Preproessing.trainSample}n" +
    s"Param testSample: ${Preproessing.testSample}n" +
    s"TrainingData count: ${Preproessing.trainingData.count}n" +
    s"ValidationData count: ${Preproessing.validationData.count}n" +
    s"TestData count: ${Preproessing.testData.count}n" +
"==================================================================n" +
s"Param maxIter = ${MaxIter.mkString(",")}n" +
```

```
        s"Param numFolds = ${numFolds}n" +
    "================================================================n" +
    s"Training data MSE = ${trainRegressionMetrics.meanSquaredError}n" +
        s"Training data RMSE =
${trainRegressionMetrics.rootMeanSquaredError}n" +
        s"Training data R-squared = ${trainRegressionMetrics.r2}n" +
        s"Training data MAE = ${trainRegressionMetrics.meanAbsoluteError}n" +
        s"Training data Explained variance =
${trainRegressionMetrics.explainedVariance}n" +
    "================================================================n" +
    s"Validation data MSE = ${validRegressionMetrics.meanSquaredError}n" +
        s"Validation data RMSE =
${validRegressionMetrics.rootMeanSquaredError}n" +
        s"Validation data R-squared = ${validRegressionMetrics.r2}n" +
        s"Validation data MAE = ${validRegressionMetrics.meanAbsoluteError}n"
+
        s"Validation data Explained variance =
${validRegressionMetrics.explainedVariance}n" +
        s"CV params explained: ${cvModel.explainParams}n" +
        s"LR params explained:
${bestModel.stages.last.asInstanceOf[LinearRegressionModel].explainParams}n
" +
    "================================================================n"
```

Now, we print the preceding results as follows:

```
println(results)
>>>

Building Machine Learning pipeline
Reading data from data/insurance_train.csv file
Null values exist in the DataFrame
Training model with Linear Regression algorithm
=======================================================================
Param trainSample: 1.0
Param testSample: 1.0
TrainingData count: 141194
ValidationData count: 47124
TestData count: 125546
=======================================================================
Param maxIter = 1000
Param numFolds = 10
=======================================================================
Training data MSE = 4460667.3666198505
Training data RMSE = 2112.0292059107164
Training data R-squared = -0.1514435541595276
Training data MAE = 1356.9375609756164
Training data Explained variance = 8336528.638733305
```

```
==========================================================================
Validation data MSE = 4839128.978963534
Validation data RMSE = 2199.802031766389
Validation data R-squared = -0.24922962724089603
Validation data MAE = 1356.419484419514
Validation data Explained variance = 8724661.329105612
CV params explained: estimator: estimator for selection (current:
pipeline_d5024480c670)
estimatorParamMaps: param maps for the estimator (current:
[Lorg.apache.spark.ml.param.ParamMap;@2f0c9855)
evaluator: evaluator used to select hyper-parameters that maximize the
validated metric (current: regEval_00c707fcaa06)
numFolds: number of folds for cross validation (>= 2) (default: 3, current:
10)
seed: random seed (default: -1191137437)
LR params explained: aggregationDepth: suggested depth for treeAggregate
(>= 2) (default: 2)
elasticNetParam: the ElasticNet mixing parameter, in range [0, 1]. For
alpha = 0, the penalty is an L2 penalty. For alpha = 1, it is an L1 penalty
(default: 0.0, current: 0.001)
featuresCol: features column name (default: features, current: features)
fitIntercept: whether to fit an intercept term (default: true)
labelCol: label column name (default: label, current: label)
maxIter: maximum number of iterations (>= 0) (default: 100, current: 1000)
predictionCol: prediction column name (default: prediction)
regParam: regularization parameter (>= 0) (default: 0.0, current: 0.001)
solver: the solver algorithm for optimization. If this is not set or empty,
default value is 'auto' (default: auto)
standardization: whether to standardize the training features before
fitting the model (default: true)
tol: the convergence tolerance for iterative algorithms (>= 0) (default:
1.0E-6, current: 1.0E-6)
weightCol: weight column name. If this is not set or empty, we treat all
instance weights as 1.0 (undefined)
==========================================================================
```

So our predictive model shows an MAE of about `1356.419484419514` for both the training and test set. However, the MAE is much lower on the Kaggle public and private leaderboard (go to: `https://www.kaggle.com/c/allstate-claims-severity/leaderboard`) with an MAE of 1096.92532 and 1109.70772 respectively.

Wait! We are not done yet. We still need to make a prediction on the test set:

```
println("Run prediction on the test set")
cvModel.transform(Preproessing.testData)
    .select("id", "prediction")
    .withColumnRenamed("prediction", "loss")
    .coalesce(1) // to get all the predictions in a single csv file
    .write.format("com.databricks.spark.csv")
    .option("header", "true")
    .save("output/result_LR.csv")
```

The preceding code should generate a CSV file named `result_LR.csv`. If we open the file, we should observe the loss against each ID, that is, claim. We will see the contents for both LR, RF, and GBT at the end of this chapter. Nevertheless, it is always a good idea to stop the Spark session by invoking the `spark.stop()` method.

An ensemble method is a learning algorithm that creates a model that is composed of a set of other base models. Spark ML supports two major ensemble algorithms called GBT and random forest based on decision trees. We will now see if we can improve the prediction accuracy by reducing the MAE error significantly using GBT.

GBT regressor for predicting insurance severity claims

In order to minimize a `loss` function, **Gradient Boosting Trees** (**GBTs**) iteratively train many decision trees. On each iteration, the algorithm uses the current ensemble to predict the label of each training instance.

Then the raw predictions are compared with the true labels. Thus, in the next iteration, the decision tree will help correct previous mistakes if the dataset is re-labeled to put more emphasis on training instances with poor predictions.

Since we are talking about regression, it would be more meaningful to discuss the regression strength of GBTs and its losses computation. Suppose we have the following settings:

- N data instances
- y_i = label of instance i
- x_i = features of instance i

Then the *F(x_i)* function is the model's predicted label; for instance, it tries to minimize the error, that is, loss:

Loss	Task	Formula	Description
Squared Error	Regression	$\sum_{i=1}^{N}(y_i - F(x_i))^2$	Also called L2 loss. Default loss for regression tasks
Absolute Error	Regression	$\sum_{i=1}^{N}|y_i - F(x_i)|$	Also called L1 loss. Can be more robust to outliers than Squared Error.

Now, similar to decision trees, GBTs also:

- Handle categorical features (and of course numerical features too)
- Extend to the multiclass classification setting
- Perform both the binary classification and regression (multiclass classification is not yet supported)
- Do not require feature scaling
- Capture non-linearity and feature interactions, which are greatly missing in LR, such as linear models

Validation while training: Gradient boosting can overfit, especially when you have trained your model with more trees. In order to prevent this issue, it is useful to validate while carrying out the training.

Since we have already prepared our dataset, we can directly jump into implementing a GBT-based predictive model for predicting insurance severity claims. Let's start with importing the necessary packages and libraries:

```
import org.apache.spark.ml.regression.{GBTRegressor, GBTRegressionModel}
import org.apache.spark.ml.{Pipeline, PipelineModel}
import org.apache.spark.ml.evaluation.RegressionEvaluator
import org.apache.spark.ml.tuning.ParamGridBuilder
import org.apache.spark.ml.tuning.CrossValidator
import org.apache.spark.sql._
import org.apache.spark.sql.functions._
import org.apache.spark.mllib.evaluation.RegressionMetrics
```

Now let's define and initialize the hyperparameters needed to train the GBTs, such as the number of trees, number of max bins, number of folds to be used during cross-validation, number of maximum iterations to iterate the training, and finally max tree depth:

```
val NumTrees = Seq(5, 10, 15)
val MaxBins = Seq(5, 7, 9)
val numFolds = 10
val MaxIter: Seq[Int] = Seq(10)
val MaxDepth: Seq[Int] = Seq(10)
```

Then, again we instantiate a Spark session and implicits as follows:

```
val spark = SparkSessionCreate.createSession()
import spark.implicits._
```

Now that we care an estimator algorithm, that is, GBT:

```
val model = new GBTRegressor()
                .setFeaturesCol("features")
                .setLabelCol("label")
```

Now, we build the pipeline by chaining the transformations and predictor together as follows:

```
val pipeline = new Pipeline().setStages((Preproessing.stringIndexerStages
:+ Preproessing.assembler) :+ model)
```

Before we start performing the cross-validation, we need to have a paramgrid. So let's start creating the paramgrid by specifying the number of maximum iteration, max tree depth, and max bins as follows:

```
val paramGrid = new ParamGridBuilder()
        .addGrid(model.maxIter, MaxIter)
        .addGrid(model.maxDepth, MaxDepth)
        .addGrid(model.maxBins, MaxBins)
        .build()
```

Now, for a better and stable performance, let's prepare the K-fold cross-validation and grid search as a part of model tuning. As you can guess, I am going to perform 10-fold cross-validation. Feel free to adjust the number of folds based on you settings and dataset:

```
println("Preparing K-fold Cross Validation and Grid Search")
val cv = new CrossValidator()
        .setEstimator(pipeline)
        .setEvaluator(new RegressionEvaluator)
        .setEstimatorParamMaps(paramGrid)
        .setNumFolds(numFolds)
```

Fantastic, we have created the cross-validation estimator. Now it's time to train the GBT model:

```
println("Training model with GradientBoostedTrees algorithm ")
val cvModel = cv.fit(Preproessing.trainingData)
```

Now that we have the fitted model, that means it is now capable of making predictions. So let's start evaluating the model on the train and validation set, and calculating RMSE, MSE, MAE, R-squared, and so on:

```
println("Evaluating model on train and test data and calculating RMSE")
val trainPredictionsAndLabels =
cvModel.transform(Preproessing.trainingData).select("label",
"prediction").map { case Row(label: Double, prediction: Double) => (label,
prediction) }.rdd

val validPredictionsAndLabels =
cvModel.transform(Preproessing.validationData).select("label",
"prediction").map { case Row(label: Double, prediction: Double) => (label,
prediction) }.rdd

val trainRegressionMetrics = new
RegressionMetrics(trainPredictionsAndLabels)
val validRegressionMetrics = new
RegressionMetrics(validPredictionsAndLabels)
```

Great! We have managed to compute the raw prediction on the train and the test set. Let's hunt for the best model:

```
val bestModel = cvModel.bestModel.asInstanceOf[PipelineModel]
```

As already stated, by using GBT it is possible to measure feature importance so that at a later stage we can decide which features are to be used and which ones are to be dropped from the DataFrame. Let's find the feature importance of the best model we just created previously, for all features in ascending order as follows:

```
val featureImportances =
bestModel.stages.last.asInstanceOf[GBTRegressionModel].featureImportances.t
oArray
val FI_to_List_sorted = featureImportances.toList.sorted.toArray
```

Once we have the best fitted and cross-validated model, we can expect good prediction accuracy. Now let's observe the results on the train and the validation set:

```
val output =
"n==================================================================n" +
s"Param trainSample: ${Preproessing.trainSample}n" +
```

```
        s"Param testSample: ${Preproessing.testSample}n" +
        s"TrainingData count: ${Preproessing.trainingData.count}n" +
        s"ValidationData count: ${Preproessing.validationData.count}n" +
        s"TestData count: ${Preproessing.testData.count}n" +
    "======================================================================n" +
s"Param maxIter = ${MaxIter.mkString(",")}n" +
        s"Param maxDepth = ${MaxDepth.mkString(",")}n" +
        s"Param numFolds = ${numFolds}n" +
    "======================================================================n" +
s"Training data MSE = ${trainRegressionMetrics.meanSquaredError}n" +
        s"Training data RMSE =
${trainRegressionMetrics.rootMeanSquaredError}n" +
        s"Training data R-squared = ${trainRegressionMetrics.r2}n" +
        s"Training data MAE = ${trainRegressionMetrics.meanAbsoluteError}n" +
        s"Training data Explained variance =
${trainRegressionMetrics.explainedVariance}n" +
    "======================================================================n" +
s"Validation data MSE = ${validRegressionMetrics.meanSquaredError}n" +
        s"Validation data RMSE =
${validRegressionMetrics.rootMeanSquaredError}n" +
        s"Validation data R-squared = ${validRegressionMetrics.r2}n" +
        s"Validation data MAE = ${validRegressionMetrics.meanAbsoluteError}n"
+
        s"Validation data Explained variance =
${validRegressionMetrics.explainedVariance}n" +
    "======================================================================n" +
s"CV params explained: ${cvModel.explainParams}n" +
        s"GBT params explained:
${bestModel.stages.last.asInstanceOf[GBTRegressionModel].explainParams}n" +
s"GBT features importances:n
${Preproessing.featureCols.zip(FI_to_List_sorted).map(t => s"t${t._1} =
${t._2}").mkString("n")}n" +
    "======================================================================n"
```

Now, we print the preceding results as follows:

```
println(results)
  >>>

======================================================================
Param trainSample: 1.0
Param testSample: 1.0
TrainingData count: 141194
ValidationData count: 47124
TestData count: 125546
======================================================================
Param maxIter = 10
Param maxDepth = 10
```

```
Param numFolds = 10
=====================================================================
Training data MSE = 2711134.460296872
Training data RMSE = 1646.5522950385973
Training data R-squared = 0.4979619968485668
Training data MAE = 1126.582534126603
Training data Explained variance = 8336528.638733303
=====================================================================
Validation data MSE = 4796065.983773314
Validation data RMSE = 2189.9922337244293
Validation data R-squared = 0.13708582379658474
Validation data MAE = 1289.9808960385383
Validation data Explained variance = 8724866.468978886
=====================================================================
CV params explained: estimator: estimator for selection (current:
pipeline_9889176c6eda)
estimatorParamMaps: param maps for the estimator (current:
[Lorg.apache.spark.ml.param.ParamMap;@87dc030)
evaluator: evaluator used to select hyper-parameters that maximize the
validated metric (current: regEval_ceb3437b3ac7)
numFolds: number of folds for cross validation (>= 2) (default: 3, current:
10)
seed: random seed (default: -1191137437)
GBT params explained: cacheNodeIds: If false, the algorithm will pass trees
to executors to match instances with nodes. If true, the algorithm will
cache node IDs for each instance. Caching can speed up training of deeper
trees. (default: false)
checkpointInterval: set checkpoint interval (>= 1) or disable checkpoint
(-1). E.g. 10 means that the cache will get checkpointed every 10
iterations (default: 10)
featuresCol: features column name (default: features, current: features)
impurity: Criterion used for information gain calculation (case-
insensitive). Supported options: variance (default: variance)
labelCol: label column name (default: label, current: label)
lossType: Loss function which GBT tries to minimize (case-insensitive).
Supported options: squared, absolute (default: squared)
maxBins: Max number of bins for discretizing continuous features. Must be
>=2 and >= number of categories for any categorical feature. (default: 32)
maxDepth: Maximum depth of the tree. (>= 0) E.g., depth 0 means 1 leaf
node; depth 1 means 1 internal node + 2 leaf nodes. (default: 5, current:
10)
maxIter: maximum number of iterations (>= 0) (default: 20, current: 10)
maxMemoryInMB: Maximum memory in MB allocated to histogram aggregation.
(default: 256)
minInfoGain: Minimum information gain for a split to be considered at a
tree node. (default: 0.0)
minInstancesPerNode: Minimum number of instances each child must have after
split. If a split causes the left or right child to have fewer than
```

```
minInstancesPerNode, the split will be discarded as invalid. Should be >=
1. (default: 1)
predictionCol: prediction column name (default: prediction)
seed: random seed (default: -131597770)
stepSize: Step size (a.k.a. learning rate) in interval (0, 1] for shrinking
the contribution of each estimator. (default: 0.1)
subsamplingRate: Fraction of the training data used for learning each
decision tree, in range (0, 1]. (default: 1.0)
GBT features importance:
    idx_cat1 = 0.0
    idx_cat2 = 0.0
    idx_cat3 = 0.0
    idx_cat4 = 3.167169394850417E-5
    idx_cat5 = 4.745749854188828E-5
...
    idx_cat111 = 0.018960701085054904
    idx_cat114 = 0.020609596772820878
    idx_cat115 = 0.02281267960792931
    cont1 = 0.023943087007850663
    cont2 = 0.028078353534251005
    ...
    cont13 = 0.06921704925937068
    cont14 = 0.07609111789104464
=======================================================================
```

So our predictive model shows an MAE of about `1126.582534126603` and `1289.9808960385383` for the training and test sets respectively. The last result is important for understanding the feature importance (the preceding list is abridged to save space but you should receive the full list). Especially, we can see that the first three features are not important at all so we can safely drop them from the DataFrame. We will provide more insight in the next section.

Now finally, let us run the prediction over the test set and generate the predicted loss for each claim from the clients:

```
println("Run prediction over test dataset")
cvModel.transform(Preproessing.testData)
        .select("id", "prediction")
        .withColumnRenamed("prediction", "loss")
        .coalesce(1)
        .write.format("com.databricks.spark.csv")
        .option("header", "true")
        .save("output/result_GBT.csv")
```

The preceding code should generate a CSV file named `result_GBT.csv`. If we open the file, we should observe the loss against each ID, that is, claim. We will see the contents for both LR, RF, and GBT at the end of this chapter. Nevertheless, it is always a good idea to stop the Spark session by invoking the `spark.stop()` method.

Boosting the performance using random forest regressor

In the previous sections, we did not experience the expected MAE value although we got predictions of the severity loss in each instance. In this section, we will develop a more robust predictive analytics model for the same purpose but use an random forest regressor. However, before diving into its formal implementation, a short overview of the random forest algorithm is needed.

Random Forest for classification and regression

Random Forest is an ensemble learning technique used for solving supervised learning tasks, such as classification and regression. An advantageous feature of Random Forest is that it can overcome the overfitting problem across its training dataset. A forest in Random Forest usually consists of hundreds of thousands of trees. These trees are actually trained on different parts of the same training set.

More technically, an individual tree that grows very deep tends to learn from highly unpredictable patterns. This creates overfitting problems on the training sets. Moreover, low biases make the classifier a low performer even if your dataset quality is good in terms of the features presented. On the other hand, an Random Forest helps to average multiple decision trees together with the goal of reducing the variance to ensure consistency by computing proximities between pairs of cases.

GBT or **Random Forest**? Although both GBT and Random Forest are ensembles of trees, the training processes are different. There are several practical trade-offs that exist, which often poses the dilemma of which one to choose. However, Random Forest would be the winner in most cases. Here are some justifications:

- GBTs train one tree at a time, but Random Forest can train multiple trees in parallel. So the training time is lower for RF. However, in some special cases, training and using a smaller number of trees with GBTs is easier and quicker.
- RFs are less prone to overfitting in most cases, so it reduces the likelihood of overfitting. In other words, Random Forest reduces variance with more trees, but GBTs reduce bias with more trees.
- Finally, Random Forest can be easier to tune since performance improves monotonically with the number of trees, but GBT performs badly with an increased number of trees.

However, this slightly increases bias and makes it harder to interpret the results. But eventually, the performance of the final model increases dramatically. While using the Random Forest as a classifier, there are some parameter settings:

- If the number of trees is 1, then no bootstrapping is used at all; however, if the number of trees is > 1, then bootstrapping is needed. The supported values are `auto`, `all`, `sqrt`, `log2`, and `onethird`.
- The supported numerical values are *(0.0-1.0)* and *[1-n]*. However, if `featureSubsetStrategy` is chosen as `auto`, the algorithm chooses the best feature subset strategy automatically.
- If the `numTrees == 1`, the `featureSubsetStrategy` is set to be `all`. However, if the `numTrees > 1` (that is, forest), the `featureSubsetStrategy` is set to be `sqrt` for classification.
- Moreover, if a real value n is set in the range of *(0, 1.0)*, `n*number_of_features` will be used. However, if an integer value n is in the range (1, the number of features) is set, only n features are used alternatively.
- The parameter `categoricalFeaturesInfo` is a map used for storing arbitrary or of categorical features. An entry *(n -> k)* indicates that feature n is categorical with I categories indexed from *0: (0, 1,...,k-1)*.

- The impurity criterion is used for information gain calculation. The supported values are `gini` and `variance` for classification and regression respectively.
- The `maxDepth` is the maximum depth of the tree (for example, depth 0 means one leaf node, depth 1 means one internal node plus two leaf nodes).
- The `maxBins` signifies the maximum number of bins used for splitting the features, where the suggested value is 100 to get better results.
- Finally, the random seed is used for bootstrapping and choosing feature subsets to avoid the random nature of the results.

As already mentioned, since Random Forest is fast and scalable enough for a large-scale dataset, Spark is a suitable technology to implement the RF, and to implement this massive scalability. However, if the proximities are calculated, storage requirements also grow exponentially.

Well, that's enough about RF. Now it's time to get our hands dirty, so let's get started. We begin with importing required libraries:

```
import org.apache.spark.ml.regression.{RandomForestRegressor,
RandomForestRegressionModel}
import org.apache.spark.ml.{ Pipeline, PipelineModel }
import org.apache.spark.ml.evaluation.RegressionEvaluator
import org.apache.spark.ml.tuning.ParamGridBuilder
import org.apache.spark.ml.tuning.CrossValidator
import org.apache.spark.sql._
import org.apache.spark.sql.functions._
import org.apache.spark.mllib.evaluation.RegressionMetrics
```

Then we create an active Spark session and import implicits:

```
val spark = SparkSessionCreate.createSession()
import spark.implicits._
```

Then we define some hyperparameters, such as the number of folds for cross-validation, number of maximum iterations, the value of regression parameters, value of tolerance, and elastic network parameters, as follows:

```
val NumTrees = Seq(5,10,15)
val MaxBins = Seq(23,27,30)
val numFolds = 10
val MaxIter: Seq[Int] = Seq(20)
val MaxDepth: Seq[Int] = Seq(20)
```

Note that for an Random Forest based on a decision tree, we require `maxBins` to be at least as large as the number of values in each categorical feature. In our dataset, we have 110 categorical features with 23 distinct values. Considering this, we have to set `MaxBins` to at least 23. Nevertheless, feel free to play with the previous parameters too. Alright, now it's time to create an LR estimator:

```
val model = new
RandomForestRegressor().setFeaturesCol("features").setLabelCol("label")
```

Now let's build a pipeline estimator by chaining the transformer and the LR estimator:

```
println("Building ML pipeline")
val pipeline = new Pipeline().setStages((Preproessing.stringIndexerStages
:+ Preproessing.assembler) :+ model)
```

Before we start performing the cross-validation, we need to have a paramgrid. So let's start creating the paramgrid by specifying the number of trees, a number for maximum tree depth, and the number of maximum bins parameters, as follows:

```
val paramGrid = new ParamGridBuilder()
        .addGrid(model.numTrees, NumTrees)
        .addGrid(model.maxDepth, MaxDepth)
        .addGrid(model.maxBins, MaxBins)
        .build()
```

Now, for better and stable performance, let's prepare the K-fold cross-validation and grid search as a part of model tuning. As you can probably guess, I am going to perform 10-fold cross-validation. Feel free to adjust the number of folds based on your settings and dataset:

```
println("Preparing K-fold Cross Validation and Grid Search: Model tuning")
val cv = new CrossValidator()
        .setEstimator(pipeline)
        .setEvaluator(new RegressionEvaluator)
        .setEstimatorParamMaps(paramGrid)
        .setNumFolds(numFolds)
```

Fantastic, we have created the cross-validation estimator. Now it's time to train the LR model:

```
println("Training model with Random Forest algorithm")
val cvModel = cv.fit(Preproessing.trainingData)
```

Now that we have the fitted model, that means it is now capable of making predictions. So let's start evaluating the model on the train and validation set, and calculating RMSE, MSE, MAE, R-squared, and many more:

```
println("Evaluating model on train and validation set and calculating
RMSE")
val trainPredictionsAndLabels =
cvModel.transform(Preproessing.trainingData).select("label",
"prediction").map { case Row(label: Double, prediction: Double) => (label,
prediction) }.rdd

val validPredictionsAndLabels =
cvModel.transform(Preproessing.validationData).select("label",
"prediction").map { case Row(label: Double, prediction: Double) => (label,
prediction) }.rdd

val trainRegressionMetrics = new
RegressionMetrics(trainPredictionsAndLabels)
val validRegressionMetrics = new
RegressionMetrics(validPredictionsAndLabels)
```

Great! We have managed to compute the raw prediction on the train and the test set. Let's hunt for the best model:

```
val bestModel = cvModel.bestModel.asInstanceOf[PipelineModel]
```

As already stated, by using RF, it is possible to measure the feature importance so that at a later stage, we can decide which features should be used and which ones are to be dropped from the DataFrame. Let's find the feature importance from the best model we just created for all features in ascending order, as follows:

```
val featureImportances =
bestModel.stages.last.asInstanceOf[RandomForestRegressionModel].featureImpo
rtances.toArray
val FI_to_List_sorted = featureImportances.toList.sorted.toArray
```

Once we have the best fitted and cross-validated model, we can expect a good prediction accuracy. Now let's observe the results on the train and the validation set:

```
val output =
"n=================================================================n" +
s"Param trainSample: ${Preproessing.trainSample}n" +
    s"Param testSample: ${Preproessing.testSample}n" +
    s"TrainingData count: ${Preproessing.trainingData.count}n" +
    s"ValidationData count: ${Preproessing.validationData.count}n" +
    s"TestData count: ${Preproessing.testData.count}n" +
"=================================================================n" +
s"Param maxIter = ${MaxIter.mkString(",")}n" +
    s"Param maxDepth = ${MaxDepth.mkString(",")}n" +
    s"Param numFolds = ${numFolds}n" +
"=================================================================n" +
s"Training data MSE = ${trainRegressionMetrics.meanSquaredError}n" +
    s"Training data RMSE =
${trainRegressionMetrics.rootMeanSquaredError}n" +
    s"Training data R-squared = ${trainRegressionMetrics.r2}n" +
    s"Training data MAE = ${trainRegressionMetrics.meanAbsoluteError}n" +
    s"Training data Explained variance =
${trainRegressionMetrics.explainedVariance}n" +
"=================================================================n" +
s"Validation data MSE = ${validRegressionMetrics.meanSquaredError}n" +
    s"Validation data RMSE =
${validRegressionMetrics.rootMeanSquaredError}n" +
    s"Validation data R-squared = ${validRegressionMetrics.r2}n" +
    s"Validation data MAE = ${validRegressionMetrics.meanAbsoluteError}n"
+
    s"Validation data Explained variance =
${validRegressionMetrics.explainedVariance}n" +
"=================================================================n" +
s"CV params explained: ${cvModel.explainParams}n" +
    s"RF params explained:
${bestModel.stages.last.asInstanceOf[RandomForestRegressionModel].explainPa
rams}n" +
    s"RF features importances:n
${Preproessing.featureCols.zip(FI_to_List_sorted).map(t => s"t${t._1} =
${t._2}").mkString("n")}n" +
"=================================================================n"
```

Now, we print the preceding results as follows:

```
println(results)
>>>
Param trainSample: 1.0
 Param testSample: 1.0
 TrainingData count: 141194
 ValidationData count: 47124
 TestData count: 125546
 Param maxIter = 20
 Param maxDepth = 20
 Param numFolds = 10
 Training data MSE = 1340574.3409399686
 Training data RMSE = 1157.8317412042081
 Training data R-squared = 0.7642745310548124
 Training data MAE = 809.5917285994619
 Training data Explained variance = 8337897.224852404
 Validation data MSE = 4312608.024875177
 Validation data RMSE = 2076.6819749001475
 Validation data R-squared = 0.1369507149716651"
 Validation data MAE = 1273.0714382935894
 Validation data Explained variance = 8737233.110450774
```

So our predictive model shows an MAE of about `809.5917285994619` and `1273.0714382935894` for the training and test set respectively. The last result is important for understanding the feature importance (the preceding list is abridged to save space but you should receive the full list).

I have drawn both the categorical and continuous features, and their respective importance in Python, so I will not show the code here but only the graph. Let's see the categorical features showing feature importance as well as the corresponding feature number:

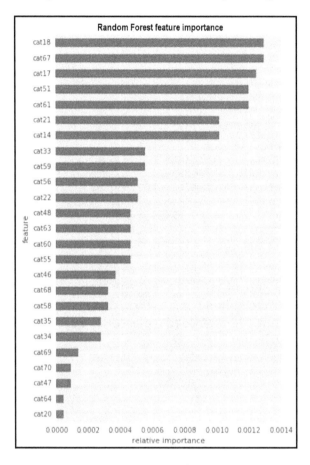

Figure 11: Random Forest categorical feature importance

From the preceding graph, it is clear that categorical features cat20, cat64, cat47, and cat69 are less important. Therefore, it would make sense to drop these features and retrain the Random Forest model to observe better performance.

Now let's see how the continuous features are correlated and contribute to the loss column. From the following figure, we can see that all continuous features are positively correlated with the loss column. This also signifies that these continuous features are not that important compared to the categorical ones we have seen in the preceding figure:

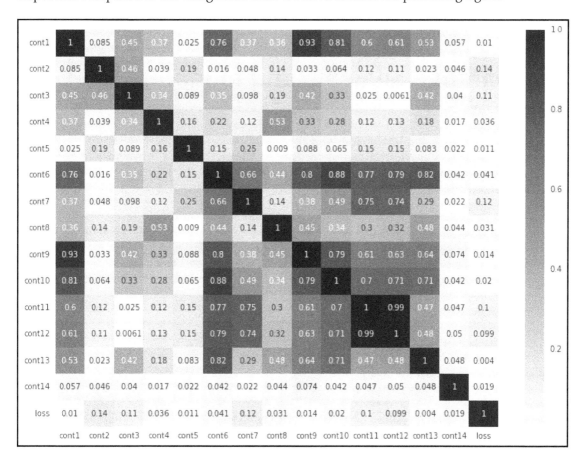

Figure 12: Correlations between the continuous features and the label

What we can learn from these two analyses is that we can naively drop some unimportant columns and train the Random Forest model to observe if there is any reduction in the MAE value for both the training and validation set. Finally, let's make a prediction on the test set:

```
println("Run prediction on the test set")
cvModel.transform(Preproessing.testData)
    .select("id", "prediction")
    .withColumnRenamed("prediction", "loss")
    .coalesce(1) // to get all the predictions in a single csv file
```

```
.write.format("com.databricks.spark.csv")
.option("header", "true")
.save("output/result_RF.csv")
```

Also, similar to LR, you can stop the Spark session by invoking the `stop()` method. Now the generated `result_RF.csv` file should contain the loss against each ID, that is, claim.

Comparative analysis and model deployment

You have already seen that the LR model is much easier to train for a small training dataset. However, we haven't experienced better accuracy compared to GBT and Random Forest models. However, the simplicity of the LR model is a very good starting point. On the other hand, we already argued that Random Forest would be the winner over GBT for several reasons, of course. Let's see the results in a table:

Training set			
Metrics	**Linear regression**	**Gradient Boosted Tree**	**Random Forest**
MSE	4460667.3666198505	2711134.460296872	1340574.3409399686
RMSE	2112.0292059107164	1646.5522950385973	1157.8317412042081
R^2	-0.1514435541595276	0.4979619968485668	0.7642745310548124
MAE	1356.9375609756164	1126.582534126603	809.5917285994619
Explained variance	8336528.638733305	8336528.638733303	8337897.224852404
Validation set			
Metrics	**Linear regression**	**Gradient Boosted Tree**	**Random Forest**
MSE	4839128.978963534	4796065.983773314	4312608.024875177
RMSE	2199.802031766389	2189.9922337244293	2076.6819749001475
R^2	-0.24922962724089603	0.13708582379658474	0.1369507149716651
MAE	1356.419484419514	1289.9808960385383	1273.0714382935894
Explained variance	8724661.329105612	8724866.468978886	8737233.110450774

Now let's see how the predictions went for each model for 20 accidents or damage claims:

id	loss	id	loss	id	loss
4	1205.818863	4	2118.753	4	2182.815
6	2124.032479	6	2425.418	6	1935.753
9	11466.34892	9	8967.434	9	11069.49
12	4671.905613	12	5772.11	12	6639.439
15	-29.56590485	15	907.1143	15	988.8615
17	2312.270982	17	2106.422	17	2061.888
21	2381.246045	21	2134.453	21	1982.437
28	199.0961342	28	1159.63	28	1977.683
32	2526.540265	32	2465.344	32	3138.645
43	5046.292227	43	4356.98	43	4143.904
46	3768.996872	46	2730.829	46	4423.25
50	1368.325947	50	971.0264	50	1075.983
54	1971.648909	54	1818.144	54	1552.547
62	2891.711648	62	1705.926	62	1759.637
70	2945.419087	70	1903.267	70	2543.034
71	5565.365742	71	6196.935	71	6566.392
75	2342.345313	75	2546.685	75	2426.998
77	3035.87975	77	2462.602	77	3329.786
81	3512.796204	81	2926.829	81	3685.368

Figure 13: Loss prediction by i) LR, ii) GBT, and iii) Random Forest models

Therefore, based on table 2, it is clear that we should go with the Random Forest regressor to not only predict the insurance claim loss but also its production. Now we will see a quick overview of how to take our best model, that is, an Random Forest regressor into production. The idea is, as a data scientist, you may have produced an ML model and handed it over to an engineering team in your company for deployment in a production-ready environment.

Here, I provide a naïve approach, though IT companies must have their own way to deploy the models. Nevertheless, there will be a dedicated section at the end of this topic. This scenario can easily become a reality by using model persistence—the ability to save and load models that come with Spark. Using Spark, you can either:

- Save and load a single model
- Save and load a full pipeline

A single model is pretty simple, but less effective and mainly works on Spark MLlib-based model persistence. Since we are more interested in saving the best model, that is, the Random Forest regressor model, at first we will fit an Random Forest regressor using Scala, save it, and then load the same model back using Scala:

```
// Estimator algorithm
val model = new RandomForestRegressor()
                    .setFeaturesCol("features")
                    .setLabelCol("label")
                    .setImpurity("gini")
                    .setMaxBins(20)
                    .setMaxDepth(20)
                    .setNumTrees(50)
fittedModel = rf.fit(trainingData)
```

We can now simply call the `write.overwrite().save()` method to save this model to local storage, HDFS, or S3, and the load method to load it right back for future use:

```
fittedModel.write.overwrite().save("model/RF_model")
val sameModel = CrossValidatorModel.load("model/RF_model")
```

Now the thing that we need to know is how to use the restored model for making predictions. Here's the answer:

```
sameModel.transform(Preproessing.testData)
    .select("id", "prediction")
    .withColumnRenamed("prediction", "loss")
    .coalesce(1)
    .write.format("com.databricks.spark.csv")
    .option("header", "true")
    .save("output/result_RF_reuse.csv")
```

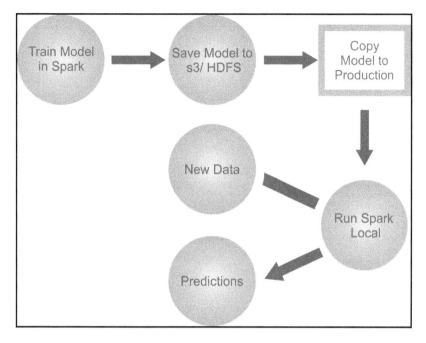

Figure 14: Spark model deployment for production

So far, we have only looked at saving and loading a single ML model but not a tuned or stable one. It might even provide you with many wrong predictions. Therefore, now the second approach might be more effective.

The reality is that, in practice, ML workflows consist of many stages, from feature extraction and transformation to model fitting and tuning. Spark ML provides pipelines to help users construct these workflows. Similarly, a pipeline with the cross-validated model can be saved and restored back the same way as we did in the first approach.

We fit the cross-validated model with the training set:

```
val cvModel = cv.fit(Preproessing.trainingData)
```

Then we save the workflow/pipeline:

```
cvModel.write.overwrite().save("model/RF_model")
```

Note that the preceding line of code will save the model in your preferred location with the following directory structure:

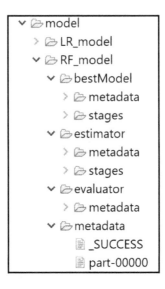

Figure 15: Saved model directory structure

```
//Then we restore the same model back:
val sameCV = CrossValidatorModel.load("model/RF_model")
Now when you try to restore the same model, Spark will automatically pick
the best one. Finally, we reuse this model for making a prediction as
follows:
sameCV.transform(Preproessing.testData)
      .select("id", "prediction")
      .withColumnRenamed("prediction", "loss")
      .coalesce(1)
      .write.format("com.databricks.spark.csv")
      .option("header", "true")
      .save("output/result_RF_reuse.csv")
```

Spark-based model deployment for large-scale dataset

In a production ready environment, we often need to deploy a pretrained models in scale. Especially, if we need to handle a massive amount of data. So our ML model has to face this scalability issue to perform continiously and with faster response. To overcome this issue, one of the main big data paradigms that Spark has brought for us is the introduction of in-memory computing (it supports dis based operation, though) and caching abstraction.

This makes Spark ideal for large-scale data processing and enables the computing nodes to perform multiple operations by accessing the same input data across multiple nodes in a computing cluster or cloud computing infrastructures (example, Amazon AWS, DigitalOcean, Microsoft Azure, or Google Cloud). For doing so, Spark supports four cluster managers (the last one is still experimental, though):

- **Standalone**: A simple cluster manager included with Spark that makes it easy to set up a cluster.
- **Apache Mesos**: A general cluster manager that can also run Hadoop MapReduce and service applications.
- **Hadoop YARN**: The resource manager in Hadoop 2.
- **Kubernetes (experimental)**: In addition to the above, there is experimental support for Kubernetes. Kubernetes is an open-source platform for providing container-centric infrastructure. See more at `https://spark.apache.org/docs/latest/cluster-overview.html`.

You can upload your input dataset on **Hadoop Distributed File System** (**HDFS**) or **S3** storage for efficient computing and storing big data cheaply. Then the `spark-submit` script in Spark's bin directory is used to launch applications on any of those cluster modes. It can use all of the cluster managers through a uniform interface so you don't have to configure your application specially for each one.

However, if your code depends on other projects, you will need to package them alongside your application in order to distribute the code to a Spark cluster. To do this, create an assembly jar (also called `fat` or `uber` jar) containing your code and its dependencies. Then ship the code where the data resides and execute your Spark jobs. Both the `SBT` and `Maven` have assembly plugins that should help you to prepare the jars.

When creating assembly jars, list Spark and Hadoop as dependencies as well. These need not be bundled since they are provided by the cluster manager at runtime. Once you have an assembled jar, you can call the script by passing your jar as follows:

```
./bin/spark-submit \
    --class <main-class> \
    --master <master-url> \
    --deploy-mode <deploy-mode> \
    --conf <key>=<value> \
    ... # other options
    <application-jar> \
    [application-arguments]
```

In the preceding command, some of the commonly used options are listed down as follows:

- `--class`: The entry point for your application (example, `org.apache.spark.examples.SparkPi`).
- `--master`: The master URL for the cluster (example, `spark://23.195.26.187:7077`).
- `--deploy-mode`: Whether to deploy your driver on the worker nodes (cluster) or locally as an external client.
- `--conf`: Arbitrary Spark configuration property in key=value format.
- `application-jar`: Path to a bundled jar including your application and all dependencies. The URL must be globally visible inside of your cluster, for instance, an `hdfs://` path or a `file://` path that is present on all nodes.
- `application-arguments`: Arguments passed to the main method of your main class, if any.

For example, you can run the `AllstateClaimsSeverityRandomForestRegressor` script on a Spark standalone cluster in client deploy mode as follows:

```
./bin/spark-submit \
    --class
com.packt.ScalaML.InsuranceSeverityClaim.AllstateClaimsSeverityRandomForest
Regressor\
    --master spark://207.184.161.138:7077 \
    --executor-memory 20G \
    --total-executor-cores 100 \
    /path/to/examples.jar
```

For more info see Spark website at `https://spark.apache.org/docs/latest/submitting-applications.html`. Nevertheless, you can find useful information from online blogs or books. By the way, I discussed this topic in details in one of my recently published books: Md. Rezaul Karim, Sridhar Alla, **Scala and Spark for Big Data Analytics**, Packt Publishing Ltd. 2017. See more at `https://www.packtpub.com/big-data-and-business-intelligence/scala-and-spark-big-data-analytics`.

Anyway, we will learn more on deploying ML models in production in upcoming chapters. Therefore, that's all I have to write for this chapter.

Summary

In this chapter, we have seen how to develop a predictive model for analyzing insurance severity claims using some of the most widely used regression algorithms. We started with simple LR. Then we saw how we can improve performance using a GBT regressor. Then we experienced improved performance using ensemble techniques, such as the Random Forest regressor. Finally, we looked at performance comparative analysis between these models and chose the best model to deploy for production-ready environment.

In the next chapter, we will look at a new end-to-end project called *Analyzing and Predicting Telecommunication Churn*. Churn prediction is essential for businesses as it helps you detect customers who are likely to cancel a subscription, product, or service. It also minimizes customer defection. It does so by predicting which customers are more likely to cancel a subscription to a service.

2
Analyzing and Predicting Telecommunication Churn

In this chapter, we will develop a **machine learning** (**ML**) project to analyze and predict whether a customer is likely to cancel the subscription to his telecommunication contract or not. In addition, we'll do some preliminary analysis of the data and take a closer look at what types of customer features are typically responsible for such a churn.

Widely used classification algorithms, such as decision trees, random forest, logistic regression, and **Support Vector Machines** (**SVMs**) will be used for analyzing and making the prediction. By the end, readers will be able to choose the best model to use for a production-ready environment.

In a nutshell, we will learn the following topics throughout this end-to-end project:

- Why, and how, do we do churn prediction?
- Logistic regression-based churn prediction
- SVM-based churn prediction
- Decision tree-based churn prediction
- Random forest-based churn prediction
- Selecting the best model for deployment

Why do we perform churn analysis, and how do we do it?

Customer churn is the loss of clients or customers (also known as **customer attrition**, customer turnover, or customer defection). This concept was initially used within the telecommunications industry when many subscribers switched to other service providers. However, it has become a very important issue in other areas of business, such as banks, internet service providers, insurance companies, and so on. Well, two of the primary reasons for churn are customer dissatisfaction and cheaper and/or better offers from the competition.

As you can see in *Figure 1*, there are four possible contracts with the customer in a business industry: contractual, non-contractual, voluntary, and involuntary. The full cost of customer churn includes both the lost revenue and the (tele-) marketing costs involved with replacing those customers with new ones. However, this type of loss can cause a huge loss to a business. Think back to a decade ago, when Nokia was the dominator of the cell phone market. All of a sudden, Apple announced iPhone 3G, and that was a revolution in the smartphone era. Then, around 10 to 12% of customers stopped using Nokia and switched to iPhone. Although later on, Nokia also tried to release a smartphone, eventually, they could not compete with Apple:

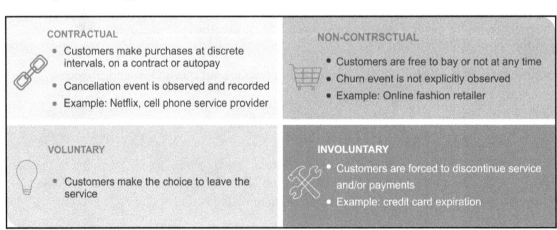

Figure 1: Four types of possible contracts with the customers

Churn prediction is fundamental to businesses, as it allows them to detect customers who are likely to cancel a subscription, product, or service. It can also minimize customer defection. It does so by predicting which customers are likely to cancel a subscription to a service. Then, the respective business can have a special offer or plan for those customers (who might cancel the subscription). This way, a business can reduce the churn ratio. This should be a key business goal of every online business.

When it comes to employee churn prediction, the typical task is to determine what factors predict an employee leaving his/her job. These types of prediction processes are heavily data-driven and are often required to utilize advanced ML techniques. In this chapter, however, we will mainly focus on customer churn prediction and analysis. For this, a number of factors should be analyzed in order to understand the customer's behavior, including but not limited to:

- Customer's demographic data, such as age, marital status, and so on
- Customer's sentiment analysis of social media
- Browsing behavior from clickstream logs
- Historical data that shows patterns of behavior that suggest churn
- Customer's usage patterns and geographical usage trends
- Calling-circle data and support call center statistics

Developing a churn analytics pipeline

In ML, we observe an algorithm's performance in two stages: learning and inference. The ultimate target of the learning stage is to prepare and describe the available data, also called the **feature vector**, which is used to train the model.

The learning stage is one of the most important stages, but it is also truly time-consuming. It involves preparing a list of vectors, also called **feature vectors** (vectors of numbers representing the value of each feature), from the training data after transformation so that we can feed them to the learning algorithms. On the other hand, training data also sometimes contains impure information that needs some pre-processing, such as cleaning.

Once we have the feature vectors, the next step in this stage is preparing (or writing/reusing) the learning algorithm. The next important step is training the algorithm to prepare the predictive model. Typically, (and of course based on data size), running an algorithm may take hours (or even days) so that the features converge into a useful model, as shown in the following figure:

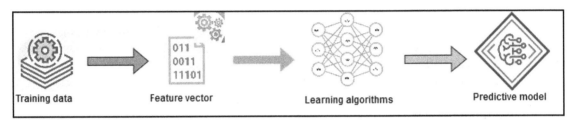

Figure 2: Learning and training a predictive model - it shows how to generate the feature vectors from the training data to train the learning algorithm that produces a predictive model

The second most important stage is the inference that is used for making an intelligent use of the model, such as predicting from the never-before-seen data, making recommendations, deducing future rules, and so on. Typically, it takes less time compared to the learning stage, and is sometimes even in real time. Thus, inferencing is all about testing the model against new (that is, unobserved) data and evaluating the performance of the model itself, as shown in the following figure:

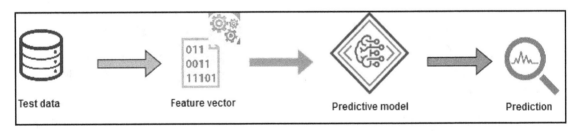

Figure 3: Inferencing from an existing model towards predictive analytics (feature vectors are generated from unknown data for making predictions)

However, during the whole process and for making the predictive model a successful one, data acts as the first-class citizen in all ML tasks. Keeping all this in mind, the following figure shows an analytics pipeline that can be used by telecommunication companies:

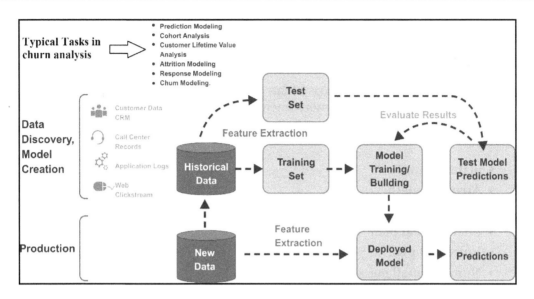

Figure 4: Churn analytics pipeline

With this kind of analysis, telecom companies can discern how to predict and enhance the customer experience, which can, in turn, prevent churn and tailor marketing campaigns. In practice, often these business assessments are used in order to retain the customers most likely to leave, as opposed to those who are likely to stay.

Thus, we need to develop a predictive model so that it ensures that our model is sensitive to the Churn = True samples—that is, a binary classification problem. We will see more details in upcoming sections.

Description of the dataset

The **Orange Telecom's Churn Dataset**, which consists of cleaned customer activity data (features), along with a churn label specifying whether a customer canceled the subscription, will be used to develop our predictive model. The churn-80 and churn-20 datasets can be downloaded from the following links, respectively:

- https://bml-data.s3.amazonaws.com/churn-bigml-80.csv
- https://bml-data.s3.amazonaws.com/churn-bigml-20.csv

However, as more data is often desirable for developing ML models, let's use the larger set (that is, churn-80) for training and cross-validation purposes, and the smaller set (that is, churn-20) for final testing and model performance evaluation.

Note that the latter set is only used to evaluate the model (that is for demonstration purposes). For a production ready environment, telecommunication companies can use their own dataset with necessary preprocessing and feature engineering. The dataset has the following schema:

- **State**: String
- **Account length**: Integer
- **Area code**: Integer
- **International plan**: String
- **Voicemail plan**: String
- **Number email messages**: Integer
- **Total day minutes**: Double
- **Total day calls**: Integer
- **Total day charge**: Double
- **Total eve minutes**: Double
- **Total eve calls**: Integer
- **Total eve charge**: Double
- **Total night minutes**: Double
- **Total night calls**: Integer
- **Total night charge**: Double
- **Total intl minutes**: Double
- **Total intl calls**: Integer
- **Total intl charge**: Double
- **Customer service calls**: Integer

Exploratory analysis and feature engineering

In this sub-section, we will see some EDA of the dataset before we start preprocessing and feature engineering. Only then creation of an analytics pipeline makes sense. At first, let's import necessary packages and libraries as follows:

```
import org.apache.spark._
import org.apache.spark.sql.functions._
import org.apache.spark.sql.types._
import org.apache.spark.sql._
import org.apache.spark.sql.Dataset
```

Then, let's specify the data source and schema for the dataset to be processed. When loading the data into a DataFrame, we can specify the schema. This specification provides optimized performance compared to the pre-Spark 2.x schema inference.

At first, let's create a Scala case class with all the fields specified. The variable names are self-explanatory:

```
case class CustomerAccount(state_code: String,
    account_length: Integer,
    area_code: String,
    international_plan: String,
    voice_mail_plan: String,
    num_voice_mail: Double,
    total_day_mins: Double,
    total_day_calls: Double,
    total_day_charge: Double,
    total_evening_mins: Double,
    total_evening_calls: Double,
    total_evening_charge: Double,
    total_night_mins: Double,
    total_night_calls: Double,
    total_night_charge: Double,
    total_international_mins: Double,
    total_international_calls: Double,
    total_international_charge: Double,
    total_international_num_calls: Double,
    churn: String)
```

Now, let's create a custom schema having a structure similar to our already created data source, as follows:

```
val schema = StructType(Array(
    StructField("state_code", StringType, true),
    StructField("account_length", IntegerType, true),
    StructField("area_code", StringType, true),
    StructField("international_plan", StringType, true),
    StructField("voice_mail_plan", StringType, true),
    StructField("num_voice_mail", DoubleType, true),
    StructField("total_day_mins", DoubleType, true),
    StructField("total_day_calls", DoubleType, true),
    StructField("total_day_charge", DoubleType, true),
    StructField("total_evening_mins", DoubleType, true),
    StructField("total_evening_calls", DoubleType, true),
    StructField("total_evening_charge", DoubleType, true),
    StructField("total_night_mins", DoubleType, true),
    StructField("total_night_calls", DoubleType, true),
    StructField("total_night_charge", DoubleType, true),
    StructField("total_international_mins", DoubleType, true),
    StructField("total_international_calls", DoubleType, true),
    StructField("total_international_charge", DoubleType, true),
    StructField("total_international_num_calls", DoubleType, true),
    StructField("churn", StringType, true)
))
```

Let's create a Spark session and import the `implicit._` that enables us to specify a DataFrame operation, as follows:

```
val spark: SparkSession = SparkSessionCreate.createSession("preprocessing")
import spark.implicits._
```

Now let's create the training set. We read the CSV file with Spark's recommended format, `com.databricks.spark.csv`. We don't need any explicit schema inference, making the infer Schema false, but instead, we need our own schema we just created previously. Then, we load the data file from our desired location, and finally, specify our data source so that our DataFrame looks exactly the same as we specified:

```
val trainSet: Dataset[CustomerAccount] = spark.read.
        option("inferSchema", "false")
        .format("com.databricks.spark.csv")
        .schema(schema)
        .load("data/churn-bigml-80.csv")
        .as[CustomerAccount]
```

Now, let's see what the schema looks like:

```
trainSet.printSchema()
>>>
```

```
root
 |-- state_code: string (nullable = true)
 |-- account_length: integer (nullable = true)
 |-- area_code: string (nullable = true)
 |-- international_plan: string (nullable = true)
 |-- voice_mail_plan: string (nullable = true)
 |-- num_voice_mail: double (nullable = true)
 |-- total_day_mins: double (nullable = true)
 |-- total_day_calls: double (nullable = true)
 |-- total_day_charge: double (nullable = true)
 |-- total_evening_mins: double (nullable = true)
 |-- total_evening_calls: double (nullable = true)
 |-- total_evening_charge: double (nullable = true)
 |-- total_night_mins: double (nullable = true)
 |-- total_night_calls: double (nullable = true)
 |-- total_night_charge: double (nullable = true)
 |-- total_international_mins: double (nullable = true)
 |-- total_international_calls: double (nullable = true)
 |-- total_international_charge: double (nullable = true)
 |-- total_international_num_calls: double (nullable = true)
 |-- churn: string (nullable = true)
```

Excellent! It looks exactly the same as the data structure. Now let's see some sample data using the `show()` method, as follows:

```
trainSet.show()
>>>
```

In the following figure, column names are made shorter for visibility on the picture:

```
+-----+---+-----+-------+-----+--------+------+-------+-------+------+------+--------+------+------+-------+------+-------+------+--------+-----+-----+
|state|len|acode|intlplan|vplan|numvmail|tdmins|tdcalls|tdcharge|temins|tecalls|techarge|tnmins|tncalls|tncharge|timins|ticalls|ticharge|numcs|churn|
+-----+---+-----+-------+-----+--------+------+-------+-------+------+------+--------+------+------+-------+------+-------+------+--------+-----+-----+
|   KS|128|  415|     No|  Yes|    25.0| 265.1|  110.0|  45.07| 197.4|  99.0|   16.78| 244.7|  91.0|  11.01|  10.0|    3.0|   2.7|     1.0|False|
|   OH|107|  415|     No|  Yes|    26.0| 161.6|  123.0|  27.47| 195.5| 103.0|   16.62| 254.4| 103.0|  11.45|  13.7|    3.0|   3.7|     1.0|False|
|   NJ|137|  415|     No|   No|     0.0| 243.4|  114.0|  41.38| 121.2| 110.0|    10.3| 162.6| 104.0|   7.32|  12.2|    5.0|  3.29|     0.0|False|
|   OH| 84|  408|    Yes|   No|     0.0| 299.4|   71.0|   50.9|  61.9|  88.0|    5.26| 196.9|  89.0|   8.86|   6.6|    7.0|  1.78|     2.0|False|
|   OK| 75|  415|    Yes|   No|     0.0| 166.7|  113.0|  28.34| 148.3| 122.0|   12.61| 186.9| 121.0|   8.41|  10.1|    3.0|  2.73|     3.0|False|
|   AL|118|  510|    Yes|   No|     0.0| 223.4|   98.0|  37.98| 220.6| 101.0|   18.75| 203.9| 118.0|   9.18|   6.3|    6.0|   1.7|     0.0|False|
|   MA|121|  510|     No|  Yes|    24.0| 218.2|   88.0|  37.09| 348.5| 108.0|   29.62| 212.6| 118.0|   9.57|   7.5|    7.0|  2.03|     3.0|False|
|   MO|147|  415|    Yes|   No|     0.0| 157.0|   79.0|  26.69| 103.1|  94.0|    8.76| 211.8|  96.0|   9.53|   7.1|    6.0|  1.92|     0.0|False|
|   WV|141|  415|    Yes|  Yes|    37.0| 258.6|   84.0|  43.96| 222.0| 111.0|   18.87| 326.4|  97.0|  14.69|  11.2|    5.0|  3.02|     0.0|False|
|   RI| 74|  415|     No|   No|     0.0| 187.7|  127.0|  31.91| 163.4| 148.0|   13.89| 196.0|  94.0|   8.82|   9.1|    5.0|  2.46|     0.0|False|
|   IA|168|  408|     No|   No|     0.0| 128.8|   96.0|   21.9| 104.9|  71.0|    8.92| 141.1| 128.0|   6.35|  11.2|    2.0|  3.02|     1.0|False|
|   MT| 95|  510|     No|   No|     0.0| 156.6|   88.0|  26.62| 247.6|  75.0|   21.05| 192.3| 115.0|   8.65|  12.3|    5.0|  3.32|     3.0|False|
|   IA| 62|  415|     No|   No|     0.0| 120.7|   70.0|  20.52| 307.2|  76.0|   26.11| 203.0|  99.0|   9.14|  13.1|    6.0|  3.54|     4.0|False|
|   ID| 85|  408|     No|  Yes|    27.0| 196.4|  139.0|  33.39| 280.9|  90.0|   23.88|  89.3|  75.0|   4.02|  13.8|    4.0|  3.73|     1.0|False|
|   VT| 93|  510|     No|   No|     0.0| 190.7|  114.0|  32.42| 218.2| 111.0|   18.55| 129.6| 121.0|   5.83|   8.1|    3.0|  2.19|     3.0|False|
|   VA| 76|  510|     No|  Yes|    33.0| 189.7|   66.0|  32.25| 212.8|  65.0|   18.09| 165.7| 108.0|   7.46|  10.0|    5.0|   2.7|     1.0|False|
|   TX| 73|  415|     No|   No|     0.0| 224.4|   90.0|  38.15| 159.5|  88.0|   13.56| 192.8|  74.0|   8.68|  13.0|    2.0|  3.51|     1.0|False|
|   FL|147|  415|     No|   No|     0.0| 155.1|  117.0|  26.37| 239.7|  93.0|   20.37| 208.8| 133.0|    9.4|  10.6|    4.0|  2.86|     0.0|False|
|   CO| 77|  408|     No|   No|     0.0|  62.4|   89.0|  10.61| 169.9| 121.0|   14.44| 209.6|  64.0|   9.43|   5.7|    6.0|  1.54|     5.0| True|
|   AZ|130|  415|     No|   No|     0.0| 183.0|  112.0|  31.11|  72.9|  99.0|     6.2| 181.8|  78.0|   8.18|   9.5|   19.0|  2.57|     0.0|False|
+-----+---+-----+-------+-----+--------+------+-------+-------+------+------+--------+------+------+-------+------+-------+------+--------+-----+-----+
only showing top 20 rows
```

We can also see related statistics of the training set using the `describe()` method from Spark:

> The `describe()` method is a Spark DataFrame's built-in method for statistical processing. It applies summary statistics calculations on all numeric columns. Finally, it returns the computed values as a single DataFrame.

```
val statsDF = trainSet.describe()
statsDF.show()
>>>
```

```
+-------+----------+-----------------+------------------+-----------------+---------------+
|summary|state_code|   account_length|         area_code|international_plan|voice_mail_plan|
+-------+----------+-----------------+------------------+-----------------+---------------+
|  count|      2666|             2666|              2666|             2666|           2666|
|   mean|      null|100.62040510127532|437.43885971492875|             null|           null|
| stddev|      null| 39.56397365334985|42.521018019427174|             null|           null|
|    min|        AK|                1|               408|               No|             No|
|    max|        WY|              243|               510|              Yes|            Yes|
+-------+----------+-----------------+------------------+-----------------+---------------+
```

If this dataset can be fit into RAM, we can cache it for quick and repeated access using the `cache()` method from Spark:

```
trainSet.cache()
```

Let's see some useful properties, such as variable correlation with churn. For example, let's see how the churn is related to the total number of international calls:

```
trainSet.groupBy("churn").sum("total_international_num_calls").show()
>>>
+-----+-----------------------------------+
|churn|sum(total_international_num_calls) |
+-----+-----------------------------------+
|False|  3310.0|
| True|  856.0|
+-----+-----------------------------------+
```

Let's see how the churn is related to the total international call charges:

```
trainSet.groupBy("churn").sum("total_international_charge").show()
  >>>
+-----+-------------------------------+
|churn|sum(total_international_charge)|
+-----+-------------------------------+
|False|  6236.499999999996|
| True|  1133.63|
+-----+-------------------------------+
```

Now that we also need to have the test set prepared to evaluate the model, let's prepare the same set, similar to the train set, as follows:

```
val testSet: Dataset[CustomerAccount] =
    spark.read.
    option("inferSchema", "false")
    .format("com.databricks.spark.csv")
    .schema(schema)
    .load("data/churn-bigml-20.csv")
    .as[CustomerAccount]
```

Now let's cache them for faster access for further manipulation:

```
testSet.cache()
```

Now, let's see some related properties of the training set to understand its suitableness for our purposes. At first, let's create a temp view for persistence for this session. We can create a catalog as an interface that can be used to create, drop, alter, or query underlying databases, tables, functions, and many more:

```
trainSet.createOrReplaceTempView("UserAccount")
spark.catalog.cacheTable("UserAccount")
```

Grouping the data by the churn label and calculating the number of instances in each group demonstrates that there are around six times more false churn samples as true churn samples. Let's verify this statement with the following line of code:

```
trainSet.groupBy("churn").count.show()
>>>
+-----+-----+
|churn|count|
+-----+-----+
|False| 2278|
| True| 388 |
+-----+-----+
```

We can also see the previous statement, verified using Apache Zeppelin (see more details on how to configure and getting started in Chapter 8, *Using Deep Belief Networks in Bank Marketing*), as follows:

```
spark.sqlContext.sql("SELECT churn,SUM(international_num_calls) as
Total_intl_call FROM UserAccount GROUP BY churn").show()
>>>
```

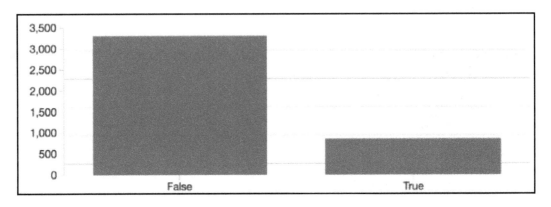

As we have already stated, in most cases the target is to retain the customers who are most likely to leave, as opposed to those who are likely to stay or are staying. This also signifies that we should prepare our training set such that it ensures that our ML model is sensitive to the true churn samples—that is, having churn label true.

We can also observe that the preceding training set is highly unbalanced. Therefore, it would be feasible to put two sample types on the same footing using stratified sampling. The sampleBy() method can be used to do so when provided with fractions of each sample type to be returned.

Here, we're keeping all instances of the True churn class, but downsampling the False churn class to a fraction of *388/2278*, which is about 0.1675:

```
val fractions = Map("False" -> 0.1675, "True" -> 1.0)
```

This way, we are also mapping only True churn samples. Now, let's create a new DataFrame for the training set containing only downsampled ones:

```
val churnDF = trainSet.stat.sampleBy("churn", fractions, 12345L)
```

The third parameter is the seed used for the reproducibility purpose. Now let's see:

```
churnDF.groupBy("churn").count.show()
>>>
+-----+-----+
|churn|count|
+-----+-----+
|False|  390|
| True|  388|
+-----+-----+
```

Now let's see how the variables are related to each other. Let's see how the day, night, evening, and international voice calls contribute to the churn class. Just execute the following line:

```
spark.sqlContext.sql("SELECT churn, SUM(total_day_charge) as TDC,
SUM(total_evening_charge) as TEC,
                   SUM(total_night_charge) as TNC,
SUM(total_international_charge) as TIC,
                   SUM(total_day_charge) + SUM(total_evening_charge) +
SUM(total_night_charge) +
                   SUM(total_international_charge) as Total_charge FROM
UserAccount GROUP BY churn
                   ORDER BY Total_charge DESC")
.show()
>>>
```

churn	TDC	TEC	TNC	TIC	Total_charge
False	67812.10999999997	38504.60000000002	20549.78	6236.499999999996	133102.99
True	13533.960000000005	6905.569999999997	3584.69	1133.63	25157.850000000002

On Apache Zeppelin, the preceding result can be seen as follows:

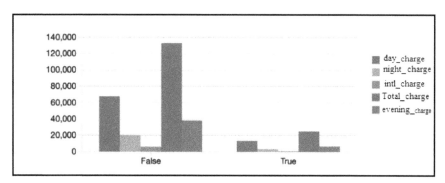

Now, let's see how many minutes of day, night, evening, and international voice calls have contributed to the preceding total charge to the churn class. Just execute the following line:

```
spark.sqlContext.sql("SELECT churn, SUM(total_day_mins)
                      + SUM(total_evening_mins) + SUM(total_night_mins)
                      + SUM(total_international_mins) as Total_minutes
                FROM UserAccount GROUP BY churn").show()
>>>
```

```
+-----+------------------+
|churn|     Total_minutes|
+-----+------------------+
|False| 1331626.900000002|
| True|244708.89999999994|
+-----+------------------+
```

On Apache Zeppelin, the preceding result can be seen as follows:

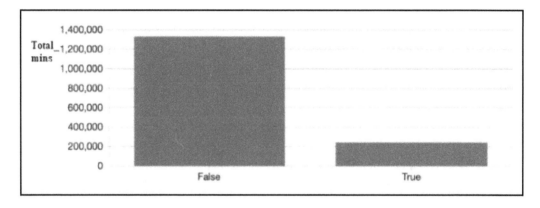

From the preceding two graphs and tables, it is clear that total day minutes and total day charge are a highly correlated feature in this training set, which is not beneficial for our ML model training. Therefore, it would be better to remove them altogether. Moreover, the following graph shows all possible correlations (plotted in PySpark, though):

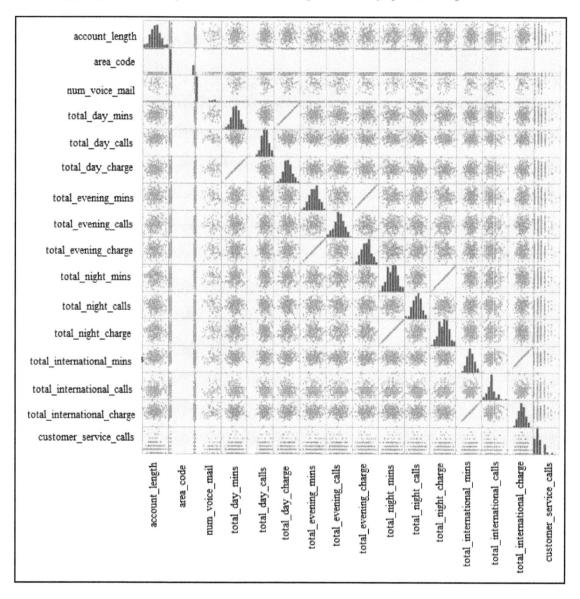

Figure 5: Correlation matrix, including all the features

Let's drop one column of each pair of correlated fields, along with the **State** and **Area code** columns, too, since those will not be used either:

```
val trainDF = churnDF
    .drop("state_code")
    .drop("area_code")
    .drop("voice_mail_plan")
    .drop("total_day_charge")
    .drop("total_evening_charge")
```

Excellent. Finally, we have our training DataFrame that can be used for better predictive modeling. Let's take a look at some columns of the resulting DataFrame:

```
trainDF.select("account_length", "international_plan", "num_voice_mail",
               "total_day_calls","total_international_num_calls", "churn")
.show(10)
>>>
```

account_length	international_plan	num_voice_mail	total_day_calls	total_international_num_calls	churn
84	Yes	0.0	71.0	2.0	False
74	No	0.0	127.0	0.0	False
95	No	0.0	88.0	3.0	False
62	No	0.0	70.0	4.0	False
147	No	0.0	117.0	0.0	False
77	No	0.0	89.0	5.0	True
130	No	0.0	112.0	0.0	False
142	No	0.0	95.0	2.0	False
12	No	0.0	118.0	1.0	True
57	No	25.0	94.0	0.0	False

only showing top 10 rows

However, we are not done yet; the current DataFrame cannot be fed to the model as an estimator. As we described, the Spark ML API needs our data to be converted in a Spark DataFrame format, consisting of a label (in Double) and features (in Vector).

Now, we need to create a pipeline to pass the data through and chain several transformers and estimators. The pipeline then works as a feature extractor. More specifically, we have prepared two `StringIndexer` transformers and a `VectorAssembler`.

`StringIndexer` encodes a categorical column of labels to a column of label indices (that is, numerical). If the input column is numeric, we have to cast it into a string and index the string values. Other Spark pipeline components, such as Estimator or Transformer, make use of this string-indexed label. In order to do this, the input column of the component must be set to this string-indexed column name. In many cases, you can set the input column with `setInputCol`. Interested readers should refer to this https://spark.apache.org/docs/latest/ml-features.html for more details.

The first `StringIndexer` converts the String categorical feature `international_plan` and labels into number indices. The second `StringIndexer` converts the categorical label (that is, `churn`) to numeric. This way, indexing categorical features enables decision trees and random forest-like classifiers to treat categorical features appropriately, hence improving performance.

Now, add the following lines of code, index labels, and metadata to the label column. Fit on the whole dataset to include all labels in the index:

```
val ipindexer = new StringIndexer()
    .setInputCol("international_plan")
    .setOutputCol("iplanIndex")

val labelindexer = new StringIndexer()
    .setInputCol("churn")
    .setOutputCol("label")
```

Now we need to extract the most important features that contribute to the classification. Since we have dropped some columns already, the resulting column set consists of the following fields:

```
* Label → churn: True or False
* Features → {("account_length", "iplanIndex", "num_voice_mail",
"total_day_mins", "total_day_calls", "total_evening_mins",
"total_evening_calls", "total_night_mins", "total_night_calls",
"total_international_mins", "total_international_calls",
"total_international_num_calls"}
```

As we have already converted categorical labels into numeric using `StringIndexer`, the next task is to extract the features:

```
val featureCols = Array("account_length", "iplanIndex",
                        "num_voice_mail", "total_day_mins",
                        "total_day_calls", "total_evening_mins",
                        "total_evening_calls", "total_night_mins",
                        "total_night_calls", "total_international_mins",
                        "total_international_calls",
  "total_international_num_calls")
```

Now, let's transform the features into feature vectors, which are vectors of numbers representing the value for each feature. In our case, we will use `VectorAssembler`. It takes all the `featureCols` and combines/transforms them into a single column called **features**:

```
val assembler = new VectorAssembler()
    .setInputCols(featureCols)
    .setOutputCol("features")
```

Now that we have the real training set consisting of labels and feature vectors ready, the next task is to create an estimator—the third element of a pipeline. We start with a very simple but powerful Logistic Regression classifier.

LR for churn prediction

LR is one of the most widely used classifiers to predict a binary response. It is a linear ML method, as described in `Chapter 1`, *Analyzing Insurance Severity Claim*. The `loss` function is the formulation given by the logistic loss:

$$L(w; x, y) := log(1 + exp(-yw^T x))$$

For the LR model, the `loss` function is the logistic loss. For a binary classification problem, the algorithm outputs a binary LR model such that, for a given new data point, denoted by x, the model makes predictions by applying the logistic function:

$$f(z) = \frac{1}{1 + e^{-z}}$$

In the preceding equation, z = $W^T X$ and if f(W^T X)>0.5, the outcome is positive; otherwise, it is negative.

Note that the raw output of the LR model, *f(z)*, has a probabilistic interpretation.

Note that compared to linear regression, logistic regression provides you with a higher classification accuracy. Moreover, it is a flexible way to regularize a model for custom adjustment, and overall, the model responses are measures of probability.

Most importantly, whereas linear regression can predict only continuous values, linear regression can still be generalized enough to make it predict discrete values:

```
import org.apache.spark._
import org.apache.spark.sql.SparkSession
import org.apache.spark.sql.functions._
import org.apache.spark.ml.classification.{BinaryLogisticRegressionSummary,
LogisticRegression, LogisticRegressionModel}
import org.apache.spark.ml.Pipeline
import org.apache.spark.ml.tuning.{ParamGridBuilder, CrossValidator}
import org.apache.spark.mllib.evaluation.BinaryClassificationMetrics
import org.apache.spark.ml.evaluation.BinaryClassificationEvaluator
```

Now that we already know linear regression's working principle, let's start using the Spark-based implementation of linear regression. Let's start by importing the required packages and libraries.

Now, let's create a Spark session and import implicit:

```
val spark: SparkSession =
SparkSessionCreate.createSession("ChurnPredictionLogisticRegression")
import spark.implicits._
```

We now need to define some hyperparameters to train an linear regression-based pipeline:

```
val numFolds = 10
val MaxIter: Seq[Int] = Seq(100)
val RegParam: Seq[Double] = Seq(1.0) // L2 regularization param, set 1.0
with L1 regularization
val Tol: Seq[Double] = Seq(1e-8)// for convergence tolerance for iterative
algorithms
val ElasticNetParam: Seq[Double] = Seq(0.0001) //Combination of L1 & L2
```

The `RegParam` is a scalar that helps adjust the strength of the constraints: a small value implies a soft margin, so naturally, a large value implies a hard margin, and being an infinity is the hardest margin.

By default, LR performs an L2 regularization with the regularization parameter set to 1.0. The same model performs an L1 regularized variant of LR with the regularization parameter (that is, `RegParam`) set to 0.10. Elastic Net is a combination of L1 and L2 regularization.

On the other hand, the `Tol` parameter is used for the convergence tolerance for iterative algorithms such as logistic regression or linear SVM. Now, once we have the hyperparameters defined and initialized, the next task is to instantiate an linear regression estimator, as follows:

```
val lr = new LogisticRegression()
    .setLabelCol("label")
    .setFeaturesCol("features")
```

Now that we have three transformers and an estimator ready, the next task is to chain in a single pipeline—that is, each of them acts as a stage:

```
val pipeline = new Pipeline()
    .setStages(Array(PipelineConstruction.ipindexer,
    PipelineConstruction.labelindexer,
    PipelineConstruction.assembler, lr))
```

In order to perform such a grid search over the hyperparameter space, we need to define it first. Here, the functional programming properties of Scala are quite handy, because we just add function pointers and the respective parameters to be evaluated to the parameter grid, where you set up the parameters to test, and a cross-validation evaluator, to construct a model selection workflow. This searches through linear regression's max iteration, regularization param, tolerance, and Elastic Net for the best model:

```
val paramGrid = new ParamGridBuilder()
    .addGrid(lr.maxIter, MaxIter)
    .addGrid(lr.regParam, RegParam)
    .addGrid(lr.tol, Tol)
    .addGrid(lr.elasticNetParam, ElasticNetParam)
    .build()
```

Note that the hyperparameters form an n-dimensional space where *n* is the number of hyperparameters. Every point in this space is one particular hyperparameter configuration, which is a hyperparameter vector. Of course, we can't explore every point in this space, so what we basically do is a grid search over a (hopefully evenly distributed) subset in that space.

We then need to define a `BinaryClassificationEvaluator` evaluator, since this is a binary classification problem. Using this evaluator, the model will be evaluated according to a precision metric by comparing the test label column with the test prediction column. The default metrics are an area under the precision-recall curve and an area under the **receiver operating characteristic (ROC)** curve:

```
val evaluator = new BinaryClassificationEvaluator()
    .setLabelCol("label")
    .setRawPredictionCol("prediction")
```

We use a `CrossValidator` for best model selection. The `CrossValidator` uses the Estimator Pipeline, the Parameter Grid, and the Classification Evaluator. The `CrossValidator` uses the `ParamGridBuilder` to iterate through the max iteration, regression param, and tolerance and Elastic Net parameters of linear regression, and then evaluates the models, repeating 10 times per parameter value for reliable results—that is, 10-fold cross-validation:

```
val crossval = new CrossValidator()
    .setEstimator(pipeline)
    .setEvaluator(evaluator)
    .setEstimatorParamMaps(paramGrid)
    .setNumFolds(numFolds)
```

The preceding code is meant to perform cross-validation. The validator itself uses the `BinaryClassificationEvaluator` estimator for evaluating the training in the progressive grid space on each fold and makes sure that there's no overfitting.

Although there is so much stuff going on behind the scenes, the interface to our `CrossValidator` object stays slim and well-known, as `CrossValidator` also extends from Estimator and supports the fit method. This means that, after calling fit, the complete predefined pipeline, including all feature preprocessing and the LR classifier, is executed multiple times—each time with a different hyperparameter vector:

```
val cvModel = crossval.fit(Preprocessing.trainDF)
```

Now it's time to evaluate the predictive power of the LR model we created using the test dataset, which has not been used for any training or cross-validation so far—that is, unseen data to the model. As a first step, we need to transform the test set to the model pipeline, which will map the features according to the same mechanism we described in the preceding feature engineering step:

```
val predictions = cvModel.transform(Preprocessing.testSet)
al result = predictions.select("label", "prediction", "probability")
val resutDF = result.withColumnRenamed("prediction", "Predicted_label")
resutDF.show(10)
>>>
```

```
+-----+---------------+--------------------+
|label|Predicted_label|         probability|
+-----+---------------+--------------------+
|  0.0|            0.0|[0.50128534704370...|
|  1.0|            0.0|[0.50128534704370...|
|  1.0|            0.0|[0.50128534704370...|
|  0.0|            0.0|[0.50128534704370...|
|  0.0|            0.0|[0.50128534704370...|
|  0.0|            0.0|[0.50128534704370...|
|  0.0|            0.0|[0.50128534704370...|
|  1.0|            0.0|[0.50128534704370...|
|  0.0|            0.0|[0.50128534704370...|
|  0.0|            0.0|[0.50128534704370...|
+-----+---------------+--------------------+
only showing top 10 rows
```

The prediction probabilities can also be very useful in ranking customers according to their likeliness to imperfection. This way, a limited number of resources can be utilized in a telecommunication business for withholding but can be focused to the most valuable customers.

However, seeing the previous prediction DataFrame, it is really difficult to guess the classification accuracy. In the second step, the evaluator evaluates itself using `BinaryClassificationEvaluator`, as follows:

```
val accuracy = evaluator.evaluate(predictions)
println("Classification accuracy: " + accuracy)
>>>
Classification accuracy: 0.7670592565329408
```

So, we get about 77% of classification accuracy from our binary classification model. Now using the accuracy for the binary classifier does not make enough sense.

Hence, researchers often recommend other performance metrics, such as area under the precision-recall curve and area under the ROC curve. However, for this we need to construct an RDD containing the raw scores on the test set:

```
val predictionAndLabels = predictions
    .select("prediction", "label")
    .rdd.map(x => (x(0).asInstanceOf[Double], x(1)
    .asInstanceOf[Double]))
```

Now, the preceding RDD can be used to compute the two previously-mentioned performance metrics:

```
val metrics = new BinaryClassificationMetrics(predictionAndLabels)
println("Area under the precision-recall curve: " + metrics.areaUnderPR)
println("Area under the receiver operating characteristic (ROC) curve : " +
metrics.areaUnderROC)
>>>
Area under the precision-recall curve: 0.5761887477313975
Area under the receiver operating characteristic (ROC) curve:
0.7670592565329408
```

In this case, the evaluation returns 77% accuracy, but only 58% precision. In the following, we calculate some more metrics; for example, false and true positive and negative predictions are also useful to evaluate the model's performance:

- **True positive**: How often the model correctly predicted subscription canceling
- **False positive**: How often the model incorrectly predicted subscription canceling
- **True negative**: How often the model correctly predicted no canceling at all
- **False negative**: How often the model incorrectly predicted no canceling

```
val lp = predictions.select("label", "prediction")
val counttotal = predictions.count()
val correct = lp.filter($"label" === $"prediction").count()

val wrong = lp.filter(not($"label" === $"prediction")).count()
val ratioWrong = wrong.toDouble / counttotal.toDouble
val ratioCorrect = correct.toDouble / counttotal.toDouble

val truep = lp.filter($"prediction" === 0.0).filter($"label" ===
$"prediction").count() / counttotal.toDouble

val truen = lp.filter($"prediction" === 1.0).filter($"label" ===
$"prediction").count() / counttotal.toDouble

val falsep = lp.filter($"prediction" === 1.0).filter(not($"label" ===
$"prediction")).count() / counttotal.toDouble
```

```
val falsen = lp.filter($"prediction" === 0.0).filter(not($"label" ===
$"prediction")).count() / counttotal.toDouble

println("Total Count : " + counttotal)
println("Correct : " + correct)
println("Wrong: " + wrong)
println("Ratio wrong: " + ratioWrong)
println("Ratio correct: " + ratioCorrect)
println("Ratio true positive : " + truep)
println("Ratio false positive : " + falsep)
println("Ratio true negative : " + truen)
println("Ratio false negative : " + falsen)
>>>
```

```
Markers  Properties  Servers  Data Source Explorer  Progress  JUnit  Console
<terminated> ChurnPredictionLR$ [Scala Application] C:\Program Files\Java\jdk1.8.0_131\bin\javaw.exe (Jan 1,
18/01/01 16:57:27 WARN NativeCodeLoader: Unable to load native-hadoop library for
18/01/01 16:57:30 WARN BLAS: Failed to load implementation from: com.github.fommil
18/01/01 16:57:30 WARN BLAS: Failed to load implementation from: com.github.fommil
18/01/01 16:57:30 WARN SparkSession$Builder: Using an existing SparkSession; some
18/01/01 16:57:32 WARN Utils: Truncated the string representation of a plan since
Total Count: 667
Correct: 534
Wrong: 133
Ratio wrong: 0.19940029985007496
Ratio correct: 0.800599700149925
Ratio true positive: 0.7136431784107946
Ratio false positive: 0.14392803598200898
Ratio true negative: 0.08695652173913043
Ratio false negative: 0.05547226386806597
```

Yet, we have not received good accuracy, so let's continue trying other classifiers, such as SMV. This time, we will use the linear SVM implementation from the Apache Spark ML package.

SVM for churn prediction

SVM is also used widely for large-scale classification (that is, binary as well as multinomial) tasks. Besides, it is also a linear ML method, as described in Chapter 1, *Analyzing Insurance Severity Claim*. The linear SVM algorithm outputs an SVM model, where the loss function used by SVM can be defined using the hinge loss, as follows:

$$L(\boldsymbol{w};\boldsymbol{x},y):=max\{0,1-y\boldsymbol{w}^T\boldsymbol{x}\}$$

The linear SVMs in Spark are trained with an L2 regularization, by default. However, it also supports L1 regularization, by which the problem itself becomes a linear program.

Now, suppose we have a set of new data points x; the model makes predictions based on the value of w^Tx. By default, if $w^Tx \geq 0$, then the outcome is positive, and negative otherwise.

Now that we already know the SVMs working principle, let's start using the Spark-based implementation of SVM. Let's start by importing the required packages and libraries:

```
import org.apache.spark._
import org.apache.spark.sql.SparkSession
import org.apache.spark.sql.functions._
import org.apache.spark.ml.classification.{LinearSVC, LinearSVCModel}
import org.apache.spark.sql.SparkSession
import org.apache.spark.sql.functions.max
import org.apache.spark.ml.Pipeline
import org.apache.spark.ml.tuning.{ParamGridBuilder, CrossValidator}
import org.apache.spark.mllib.evaluation.BinaryClassificationMetrics
import org.apache.spark.ml.evaluation.BinaryClassificationEvaluator
```

Now let's create a Spark session and import implicit:

```
val spark: SparkSession =
SparkSessionCreate.createSession("ChurnPredictionLogisticRegression")
import spark.implicits._
```

We now need to define some hyperparameters to train an LR-based pipeline:

```
val numFolds = 10
val MaxIter: Seq[Int] = Seq(100)
val RegParam: Seq[Double] = Seq(1.0) // L2 regularization param, set 0.10
with L1 reguarization
val Tol: Seq[Double] = Seq(1e-8)
val ElasticNetParam: Seq[Double] = Seq(1.0) // Combination of L1 and L2
```

Now, once we have the hyperparameters defined and initialized, the next task is to instantiate an LR estimator, as follows:

```
val svm = new LinearSVC()
```

Now that we have three transformers and an estimator ready, the next task is to chain in a single pipeline—that is, each of them acts as a stage:

```
val pipeline = new Pipeline()
    .setStages(Array(PipelineConstruction.ipindexer,
                     PipelineConstruction.labelindexer,
                     PipelineConstruction.assembler,svm)
                )
```

Let's define the `paramGrid` to perform such a grid search over the hyperparameter space. This searches through SVM's max iteration, regularization param, tolerance, and Elastic Net for the best model:

```
val paramGrid = new ParamGridBuilder()
    .addGrid(svm.maxIter, MaxIter)
    .addGrid(svm.regParam, RegParam)
    .addGrid(svm.tol, Tol)
    .addGrid(svm.elasticNetParam, ElasticNetParam)
    .build()
```

Let's define a `BinaryClassificationEvaluator` evaluator to evaluate the model:

```
val evaluator = new BinaryClassificationEvaluator()
    .setLabelCol("label")
    .setRawPredictionCol("prediction")
```

We use a `CrossValidator` for performing 10-fold cross-validation for best model selection:

```
val crossval = new CrossValidator()
    .setEstimator(pipeline)
    .setEvaluator(evaluator)
    .setEstimatorParamMaps(paramGrid)
    .setNumFolds(numFolds)
```

Let's now call the `fit` method so that the complete predefined pipeline, including all feature preprocessing and the LR classifier, is executed multiple times—each time with a different hyperparameter vector:

```
val cvModel = crossval.fit(Preprocessing.trainDF)
```

Now it's time to evaluate the predictive power of the SVM model on the test dataset. As a first step, we need to transform the test set with the model pipeline, which will map the features according to the same mechanism we described in the preceding feature engineering step:

```
val predictions = cvModel.transform(Preprocessing.testSet)
prediction.show(10)
>>>
```

```
+-----+--------------------+--------------------+----------+
|label|            features|       rawPrediction|prediction|
+-----+--------------------+--------------------+----------+
|  0.0|[117.0,0.0,0.0,18...|[0.08973008965728...|       0.0|
|  1.0|[65.0,0.0,0.0,129...|[-0.2242381550714...|       1.0|
|  1.0|[161.0,0.0,0.0,33...|[-1.4711802407566...|       1.0|
|  0.0|[111.0,0.0,0.0,11...|[1.32527571170096...|       0.0|
|  0.0|[49.0,0.0,0.0,119...|[0.85288284318901...|       0.0|
|  0.0|[36.0,0.0,30.0,14...|[1.62981681295705...|       0.0|
|  0.0|[65.0,0.0,0.0,211...|[-0.2107700769615...|       1.0|
|  1.0|[119.0,0.0,0.0,15...|[-0.7029272317993...|       1.0|
|  0.0|[10.0,0.0,0.0,186...|[-0.1759587872812...|       1.0|
|  0.0|[68.0,0.0,0.0,148...|[0.15925905739758...|       0.0|
+-----+--------------------+--------------------+----------+
only showing top 10 rows
```

However, seeing the previous prediction DataFrame, it is really difficult to guess the classification accuracy. In the second step, the evaluator evaluates itself using `BinaryClassificationEvaluator`, as follows:

```
val accuracy = evaluator.evaluate(predictions)
println("Classification accuracy: " + accuracy)
>>>
Classification accuracy: 0.7530180345969819
```

So we get about 75% of classification accuracy from our binary classification model. Now, using the accuracy for the binary classifier does not make enough sense.

Hence, researchers often recommend other performance metrics, such as area under the precision-recall curve and area under the ROC curve. However, for this we need to construct an RDD containing the raw scores on the test set:

```
val predictionAndLabels = predictions
    .select("prediction", "label")
    .rdd.map(x => (x(0).asInstanceOf[Double], x(1)
    .asInstanceOf[Double]))
```

Now the preceding RDD can be used to compute the two previously-mentioned performance metrics:

```
val metrics = new BinaryClassificationMetrics(predictionAndLabels)
println("Area under the precision-recall curve: " + metrics.areaUnderPR)
println("Area under the receiver operating characteristic (ROC) curve : " +
metrics.areaUnderROC)
>>>
Area under the precision-recall curve: 0.5595712265324828
Area under the receiver operating characteristic (ROC) curve:
0.7530180345969819
```

In this case, the evaluation returns 75% accuracy but only 55% precision. In the following, we again calculate some more metrics; for example, false and true positive and negative predictions are also useful to evaluate the model's performance:

```
val lp = predictions.select("label", "prediction")
val counttotal = predictions.count()

val correct = lp.filter($"label" === $"prediction").count()

val wrong = lp.filter(not($"label" === $"prediction")).count()
val ratioWrong = wrong.toDouble / counttotal.toDouble

val ratioCorrect = correct.toDouble / counttotal.toDouble

val truep = lp.filter($"prediction" === 0.0).filter($"label" ===
$"prediction").count() / counttotal.toDouble

val truen = lp.filter($"prediction" === 1.0).filter($"label" ===
$"prediction").count() / counttotal.toDouble

val falsep = lp.filter($"prediction" === 1.0).filter(not($"label" ===
$"prediction")).count() / counttotal.toDouble

val falsen = lp.filter($"prediction" === 0.0).filter(not($"label" ===
$"prediction")).count() / counttotal.toDouble
```

```
println("Total Count : " + counttotal)
println("Correct : " + correct)
println("Wrong: " + wrong)
println("Ratio wrong: " + ratioWrong)
println("Ratio correct: " + ratioCorrect)
println("Ratio true positive : " + truep)
println("Ratio false positive : " + falsep)
println("Ratio true negative : " + truen)
println("Ratio false negative : " + falsen)
>>>
```

```
Markers  Properties  Servers  Data Source Explorer  Progress  JUnit
<terminated> ChurnPredictionSVM$ [Scala Application] C:\Program Files\Java\jdk1.8.0_1
18/01/01 17:09:07 WARN NativeCodeLoader: Unable to load native-had
18/01/01 17:09:11 WARN BLAS: Failed to load implementation from: c
18/01/01 17:09:11 WARN BLAS: Failed to load implementation from: c
18/01/01 17:09:11 WARN SparkSession$Builder: Using an existing Spa
18/01/01 17:09:14 WARN Utils: Truncated the string representation
Total Count: 667
Correct: 515
Wrong: 152
Ratio wrong: 0.22788605697151423
Ratio correct: 0.7721139430284858
Ratio true positive: 0.6686656671664168
Ratio false positive: 0.1889055472263868
Ratio true negative: 0.10344827586206896
Ratio false negative: 0.038980509745127435
```

Yet, we have not received good accuracy using SVM. Moreover, there is no option to select the most suitable features, which would help us train our model with the most appropriate features. This time, we will again use a more robust classifier, such as the **decision trees (DTs)** implementation from the Apache Spark ML package.

DTs for churn prediction

DTs are commonly considered a supervised learning technique used for solving classification and regression tasks.

More technically, each branch in a DT represents a possible decision, occurrence, or reaction, in terms of statistical probability. Compared to naive Bayes, DTs are a far more robust classification technique. The reason is that at first, the DT splits the features into training and test sets. Then, it produces a good generalization to infer the predicted labels or classes. Most interestingly, a DT algorithm can handle both binary and multiclass classification problems.

For instance, in the following example figure, DTs learn from the admission data to approximate a sine curve with a set of **if...else** decision rules. The dataset contains the record of each student who applied for admission, say, to an American university. Each record contains the graduate record exam score, CGPA score, and the rank of the column. Now we will have to predict who is competent based on these three features (variables). DTs can be used to solve this kind of problem after training the DT model and pruning unwanted branches of the tree. In general, a deeper tree signifies more complex decision rules and a better-fitted model:

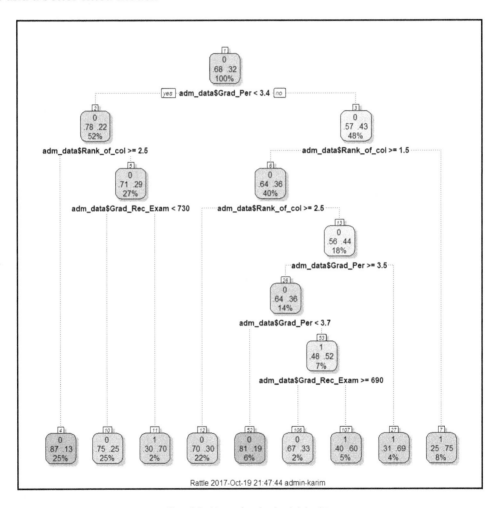

Figure 6: Decision tree for university admission data

Therefore, the deeper the tree, the more complex the decision rules and the more fitted the model is. Now let's see some pros and cons of DTs:

	Pros	Cons	Better at
Decision trees (DTs)	-Simple to implement, train, and interpret -Trees can be visualized -Requires little data preparation -Less model building and prediction time -Can handle both numeric and categorical data -Possibility of validating the model using the statistical tests -Robust against noise and missing values -High accuracy	-Interpretation is hard with large and complex trees -Duplication may occur within the same sub-tree -Possible issues with diagonal decision boundaries -Decision tree learners can create over-complex trees that do not generalize the data well -Sometimes DTs can be unstable because of small variants in the data -Learning the DT itself is an NP-complete problem -DT learners create biased trees if some classes dominate	-Targeting highly accurate classification -Medical diagnosis and prognosis -Credit risk analytics

Now, that we already know the working principle of DTs, let's start using the Spark-based implementation of DTs. Let's start by importing required packages and libraries:

```
import org.apache.spark._
import org.apache.spark.sql.SparkSession
import org.apache.spark.sql.functions._
import org.apache.spark.sql.types._
import org.apache.spark.sql._
import org.apache.spark.ml.Pipeline
import org.apache.spark.ml.classification.{DecisionTreeClassifier,
DecisionTreeClassificationModel}
import org.apache.spark.mllib.evaluation.BinaryClassificationMetrics
import org.apache.spark.ml.evaluation.BinaryClassificationEvaluator
import org.apache.spark.ml.tuning.{ParamGridBuilder, CrossValidator}
```

Now let's create a Spark session and import implicit:

```
val spark: SparkSession =
SparkSessionCreate.createSession("ChurnPredictionDecisionTrees")
import spark.implicits._
```

Now, once we have the hyperparameters defined and initialized, the next task is to instantiate a `DecisionTreeClassifier` estimator, as follows:

```
val dTree = new DecisionTreeClassifier()
                .setLabelCol("label")
                .setFeaturesCol("features")
                .setSeed(1234567L)
```

Now that we have three transformers and an estimator ready, the next task is to chain in a single pipeline—that is, each of them acts as a stage:

```
val pipeline = new Pipeline()
                .setStages(Array(PipelineConstruction.ipindexer,
                PipelineConstruction.labelindexer,
                PipelineConstruction.assembler,dTree))
```

Let's define the paramgrid to perform such a grid search over the hyperparameter space. This search is through DT's impurity, max bins, and max depth for the best model. Maximum depth of the tree: depth 0 means 1 leaf node; depth 1 means 1 internal node + 2 leaf nodes.

On the other hand, the maximum number of bins is used for separate continuous features and for choosing how to split on features at each node. More bins give higher granularity. In short, we search through decision tree's `maxDepth` and `maxBins` parameters for the best model:

```
var paramGrid = new ParamGridBuilder()
    .addGrid(dTree.impurity, "gini" :: "entropy" :: Nil)
    .addGrid(dTree.maxBins, 2 :: 5 :: 10 :: 15 :: 20 :: 25 :: 30 :: Nil)
    .addGrid(dTree.maxDepth, 5 :: 10 :: 15 :: 20 :: 25 :: 30 :: 30 :: Nil)
    .build()
```

In the preceding code segment, we're creating a progressive paramgrid through sequence format. That means we are creating the grid space with different hyperparameter combinations. This will help us provide the best model that consists of the most optimal hyperparameters.

Let's define a `BinaryClassificationEvaluator` evaluator to evaluate the model:

```
val evaluator = new BinaryClassificationEvaluator()
    .setLabelCol("label")
    .setRawPredictionCol("prediction")
```

We use a `CrossValidator` for performing 10-fold cross-validation for best model selection:

```
val crossval = new CrossValidator()
    .setEstimator(pipeline)
    .setEvaluator(evaluator)
    .setEstimatorParamMaps(paramGrid)
    .setNumFolds(numFolds)
```

Let's now call the `fit` method so that the complete predefined pipeline, including all feature preprocessing and the DT classifier, is executed multiple times—each time with a different hyperparameter vector:

```
val cvModel = crossval.fit(Preprocessing.trainDF)
```

Now it's time to evaluate the predictive power of the DT model on the test dataset. As a first step, we need to transform the test set with the model pipeline, which will map the features according to the same mechanism we described in the previous feature engineering step:

```
val predictions = cvModel.transform(Preprocessing.testSet)
prediction.show(10)
>>>
```

```
+-----+---------------+--------------------+
|label|Predicted_label|         probability|
+-----+---------------+--------------------+
|  0.0|            0.0|          [1.0,0.0]|
|  1.0|            1.0|[0.09523809523809...|
|  1.0|            1.0|          [0.0,1.0]|
|  0.0|            0.0|[0.86545454545454...|
|  0.0|            0.0|[0.86545454545454...|
|  0.0|            0.0|[0.86545454545454...|
|  0.0|            0.0|[0.80263157894736...|
|  1.0|            1.0|[0.09523809523809...|
|  0.0|            0.0|[0.86545454545454...|
|  0.0|            0.0|[0.86545454545454...|
+-----+---------------+--------------------+
```

However, seeing the preceding prediction DataFrame, it is really difficult to guess the classification accuracy. In the second step, in the evaluation is the evaluate itself using `BinaryClassificationEvaluator`, as follows:

```
val accuracy = evaluator.evaluate(predictions)
println("Classification accuracy: " + accuracy)
>>>
Accuracy: 0.870334928229665
```

So, we get about 87% of classification accuracy from our binary classification model. Now, similar to SVM and LR, we will observe the area under the precision-recall curve and the area under the ROC curve based on the following RDD containing the raw scores on the test set:

```
val predictionAndLabels = predictions
    .select("prediction", "label")
    .rdd.map(x => (x(0).asInstanceOf[Double], x(1)
    .asInstanceOf[Double]))
```

Now the preceding RDD can be used to compute the two previously-mentioned performance metrics:

```
val metrics = new BinaryClassificationMetrics(predictionAndLabels)
println("Area under the precision-recall curve: " + metrics.areaUnderPR)
println("Area under the receiver operating characteristic (ROC) curve : " +
metrics.areaUnderROC)
>>>
Area under the precision-recall curve: 0.7293101942399631
Area under the receiver operating characteristic (ROC) curve:
0.870334928229665
```

In this case, the evaluation returns 87% accuracy but only 73% precision, which is much better than that of SVM and LR. In the following, we again calculate some more metrics; for example, false and true positive and negative predictions are also useful to evaluate the model's performance:

```
val lp = predictions.select("label", "prediction")
val counttotal = predictions.count()

val correct = lp.filter($"label" === $"prediction").count()

val wrong = lp.filter(not($"label" === $"prediction")).count()

val ratioWrong = wrong.toDouble / counttotal.toDouble

val ratioCorrect = correct.toDouble / counttotal.toDouble
```

```
val truep = lp.filter($"prediction" === 0.0).filter($"label" ===
$"prediction").count() / counttotal.toDouble

val truen = lp.filter($"prediction" === 1.0).filter($"label" ===
$"prediction").count() / counttotal.toDouble

val falsep = lp.filter($"prediction" === 1.0).filter(not($"label" ===
$"prediction")).count() / counttotal.toDouble

val falsen = lp.filter($"prediction" === 0.0).filter(not($"label" ===
$"prediction")).count() / counttotal.toDouble

println("Total Count : " + counttotal)
println("Correct : " + correct)
println("Wrong: " + wrong)
println("Ratio wrong: " + ratioWrong)
println("Ratio correct: " + ratioCorrect)
println("Ratio true positive : " + truep)
println("Ratio false positive : " + falsep)
println("Ratio true negative : " + truen)
println("Ratio false negative : " + falsen)
>>>
```

```
Markers    Properties   Servers   Data Source Explorer   Prog
<terminated> ChurnPredictionDT$ [Scala Application] C:\Program Files\Jav
18/01/01 17:40:19 WARN NativeCodeLoader: Unable to load
18/01/01 17:40:22 WARN BLAS: Failed to load implementat
18/01/01 17:40:22 WARN BLAS: Failed to load implementat
18/01/01 17:40:22 WARN SparkSession$Builder: Using an e
18/01/01 17:40:25 WARN Utils: Truncated the string repr
Total Count: 667
Correct: 599
Wrong: 68
Ratio wrong: 0.10194902548725637
Ratio correct: 0.8980509745127436
Ratio true positive: 0.7796101949025487
Ratio false positive: 0.07796101949025487
Ratio true negative: 0.1184407796101949
Ratio false negative: 0.0239880059970015
```

Fantastic; we achieved 87% accuracy, but for what factors? Well, it can be debugged to get the decision tree constructed during the classification. But first, let's see at what level we achieved the best model after the cross-validation:

```
val bestModel = cvModel.bestModel
println("The Best Model and Parameters:n--------------------")
println(bestModel.asInstanceOf[org.apache.spark.ml.PipelineModel].stages(3)
)
>>>
```

The Best Model and Parameters:

```
DecisionTreeClassificationModel (uid=dtc_1fb45416b18b) of depth 5 with
53 nodes.
```

That means we achieved the best tree model at depth 5 having 53 nodes. Now let's extract those moves (that is, decisions) taken during tree construction by showing the tree. This tree helps us to find the most valuable features in our dataset:

```
bestModel.asInstanceOf[org.apache.spark.ml.PipelineModel]
    .stages(3)
    .extractParamMap

val treeModel = bestModel.asInstanceOf[org.apache.spark.ml.PipelineModel]
    .stages(3)
    .asInstanceOf[DecisionTreeClassificationModel]
println("Learned classification tree model:n" + treeModel.toDebugString)
>>>
```

Learned classification tree model:

```
If (feature 3 <= 245.2)
    If (feature 11 <= 3.0)
        If (feature 1 in {1.0})
            If (feature 10 <= 2.0)
                Predict: 1.0
            Else (feature 10 > 2.0)
            If (feature 9 <= 12.9)
                Predict: 0.0
            Else (feature 9 > 12.9)
                Predict: 1.0

        . . .
```

```
Else (feature 7 > 198.0)
    If (feature 2 <= 28.0)
        Predict: 1.0
    Else (feature 2 > 28.0)
        If (feature 0 <= 60.0)
            Predict: 0.0
        Else (feature 0 > 60.0)
            Predict: 1.0
```

In the preceding output, the `toDebugString()` function prints the tree's decision nodes and the final prediction comes out at the end leaves. It is also clearly seen that features 11 and 3 are used for decision making; they are the two most important reasons why a customer is likely to churn. But what are those two features? Let's see them:

```
println("Feature 11:" +
Preprocessing.trainDF.filter(PipelineConstruction.featureCols(11)))
println("Feature 3:" +
Preprocessing.trainDF.filter(PipelineConstruction.featureCols(3)))
>>>
Feature 11: [total_international_num_calls: double]
Feature 3: [total_day_mins: double]
```

So the customer service calls and total day minutes are selected by the decision trees, since it provides an automated mechanism for determining the most important features.

Wait! We are not finished yet. Last but not least, we will use an ensemble technique, RF, which is considered a more robust classifier than DTs. Again, let's use the Random Forest implementation from the Apache Spark ML package.

Random Forest for churn prediction

As described in `Chapter 1`, *Analyzing Insurance Severity Claim*, Random Forest is an ensemble technique that takes a subset of observations and a subset of variables to build decision trees—that is, an ensemble of DTs. More technically, it builds several decision trees and integrates them together to get a more accurate and stable prediction.

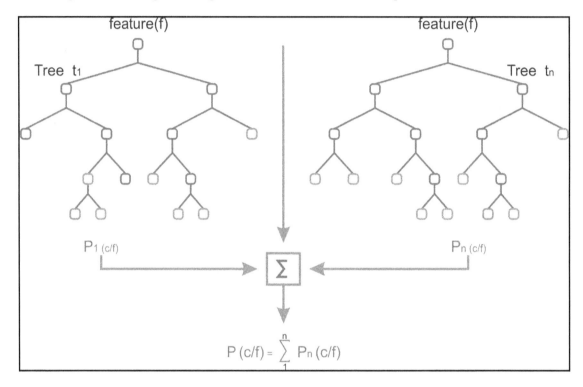

Figure 7: Random forest and its assembling technique explained

This is a direct consequence, since by maximum voting from a panel of independent juries, we get the final prediction better than the best jury (see the preceding figure). Now that we already know the working principle of RF, let's start using the Spark-based implementation of RF. Let's start by importing the required packages and libraries:

```
import org.apache.spark._
import org.apache.spark.sql.SparkSession
import org.apache.spark.sql.functions._
import org.apache.spark.sql.types._
import org.apache.spark.sql._
import org.apache.spark.ml.Pipeline
```

```
import org.apache.spark.ml.classification.{RandomForestClassifier,
RandomForestClassificationModel}
import org.apache.spark.mllib.evaluation.BinaryClassificationMetrics
import org.apache.spark.ml.evaluation.BinaryClassificationEvaluator
import org.apache.spark.ml.tuning.{ParamGridBuilder, CrossValidator}
```

Now let's create Spark session and import implicit:

```
val spark: SparkSession =
SparkSessionCreate.createSession("ChurnPredictionRandomForest")
import spark.implicits._
```

Now, once we have the hyperparameters defined and initialized, the next task is to instantiate a `DecisionTreeClassifier` estimator, as follows:

```
val rf = new RandomForestClassifier()
    .setLabelCol("label")
    .setFeaturesCol("features")
    .setSeed(1234567L)// for reproducibility
```

Now that we have three transformers and an estimator ready, the next task is to chain in a single pipeline—that is, each of them acts as a stage:

```
val pipeline = new Pipeline()
    .setStages(Array(PipelineConstruction.ipindexer,
PipelineConstruction.labelindexer,
PipelineConstruction.assembler,rf))
```

Let's define the paramgrid to perform such a grid search over the hyperparameter space:

```
val paramGrid = new ParamGridBuilder()
    .addGrid(rf.maxDepth, 3 :: 5 :: 15 :: 20 :: 50 :: Nil)
    .addGrid(rf.featureSubsetStrategy, "auto" :: "all" :: Nil)
    .addGrid(rf.impurity, "gini" :: "entropy" :: Nil)
    .addGrid(rf.maxBins, 2 :: 5 :: 10 :: Nil)
    .addGrid(rf.numTrees, 10 :: 50 :: 100 :: Nil)
    .build()
```

Let's define a `BinaryClassificationEvaluator` evaluator to evaluate the model:

```
val evaluator = new BinaryClassificationEvaluator()
    .setLabelCol("label")
    .setRawPredictionCol("prediction")
```

We use a `CrossValidator` for performing 10-fold cross-validation for best model selection:

```
val crossval = new CrossValidator()
    .setEstimator(pipeline)
    .setEvaluator(evaluator)
    .setEstimatorParamMaps(paramGrid)
    .setNumFolds(numFolds)
```

Let's now call the `fit` method so that the complete, predefined pipeline, including all feature preprocessing and the DT classifier, is executed multiple times—each time with a different hyperparameter vector:

```
val cvModel = crossval.fit(Preprocessing.trainDF)
```

Now it's time to evaluate the predictive power of the DT model on the test dataset. As a first step, we need to transform the test set to the model pipeline, which will map the features according to the same mechanism we described in the previous feature engineering step:

```
val predictions = cvModel.transform(Preprocessing.testSet)
prediction.show(10)
>>>
```

```
+-----+---------------+--------------------+
|label|Predicted_label|         probability|
+-----+---------------+--------------------+
|  0.0|            1.0|[0.47967610185334...|
|  1.0|            1.0|[0.38531389528766...|
|  1.0|            1.0|[0.06850345623033...|
|  0.0|            0.0|[0.88942965019863...|
|  0.0|            0.0|[0.79162145165495...|
|  0.0|            0.0|[0.92841581163596...|
|  0.0|            1.0|[0.41083015977062...|
|  1.0|            1.0|[0.21531047960566...|
|  0.0|            1.0|[0.49987532729656...|
|  0.0|            1.0|[0.49313495545749...|
+-----+---------------+--------------------+
only showing top 10 rows
```

However, seeing the preceding prediction DataFrame, it is really difficult to guess the classification accuracy. In the second step, in the evaluation is the evaluate itself using `BinaryClassificationEvaluator`, as follows:

```
val accuracy = evaluator.evaluate(predictions)
println("Classification accuracy: " + accuracy)
>>>
Accuracy: 0.870334928229665
```

So, we get about 87% of classification accuracy from our binary classification model. Now, similar to SVM and LR, we will observe the area under the precision-recall curve and the area under the ROC curve based on the following RDD containing the raw scores on the test set:

```
val predictionAndLabels = predictions
    .select("prediction", "label")
    .rdd.map(x => (x(0).asInstanceOf[Double], x(1)
    .asInstanceOf[Double]))
```

Now the preceding RDD can be used to compute the two previously-mentioned performance metrics:

```
val metrics = new BinaryClassificationMetrics(predictionAndLabels)

println("Area under the precision-recall curve: " + metrics.areaUnderPR)
println("Area under the receiver operating characteristic (ROC) curve : " +
metrics.areaUnderROC)
>>>
Area under the precision-recall curve: 0.7293101942399631
Area under the receiver operating characteristic (ROC) curve:
0.870334928229665
```

In this case, the evaluation returns 87% accuracy but only 73% precision, which is much better than that of SVM and LR. In the following, we again calculate some more metrics; for example, false and true positive and negative predictions are also useful to evaluate the model's performance:

```
val lp = predictions.select("label", "prediction")
val counttotal = predictions.count()

val correct = lp.filter($"label" === $"prediction").count()

val wrong = lp.filter(not($"label" === $"prediction")).count()

val ratioWrong = wrong.toDouble / counttotal.toDouble

val ratioCorrect = correct.toDouble / counttotal.toDouble

val truep = lp.filter($"prediction" === 0.0).filter($"label" ===
$"prediction").count() / counttotal.toDouble

val truen = lp.filter($"prediction" === 1.0).filter($"label" ===
$"prediction").count() / counttotal.toDouble

val falsep = lp.filter($"prediction" === 1.0).filter(not($"label" ===
$"prediction")).count() / counttotal.toDouble
```

```
val falsen = lp.filter($"prediction" === 0.0).filter(not($"label" ===
$"prediction")).count() / counttotal.toDouble

println("Total Count : " + counttotal)
println("Correct : " + correct)
println("Wrong: " + wrong)
println("Ratio wrong: " + ratioWrong)
println("Ratio correct: " + ratioCorrect)
println("Ratio true positive : " + truep)
println("Ratio false positive : " + falsep)
println("Ratio true negative : " + truen)
println("Ratio false negative : " + falsen)
>>>
```

We will get the following result:

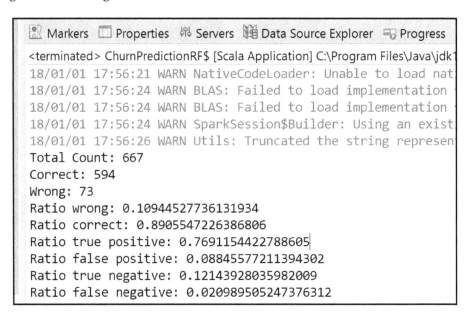

Fantastic; we achieved 91% accuracy, but for what factors? Well, similar to DT, Random Forest can be debugged to get the decision tree that was constructed during the classification. For the tree to be printed and the most important features selected, try the last few lines of code in the DT, and you're done.

Can you now guess how many different models were trained? Well, we have 10-folds on CrossValidation and five-dimensional hyperparameter space cardinalities between 2 and 7. Now let's do some simple math: 10 * 7 * 5 * 2 * 3 * 6 = 12600 models!

Note that we still make the hyperparameter space confined, with `numTrees, maxBins,` and `maxDepth` limited to 7. Also, remember that bigger trees will most likely perform better. Therefore, feel free to play around with this code and add features, and also use a bigger hyperparameter space, say, bigger trees.

Selecting the best model for deployment

From the preceding results, it can be seen that LR and SVM models have the same but higher false positive rate compared to Random Forest and DT. So we can say that DT and Random Forest have better accuracy overall in terms of true positive counts. Let's see the validity of the preceding statement with prediction distributions on pie charts for each model:

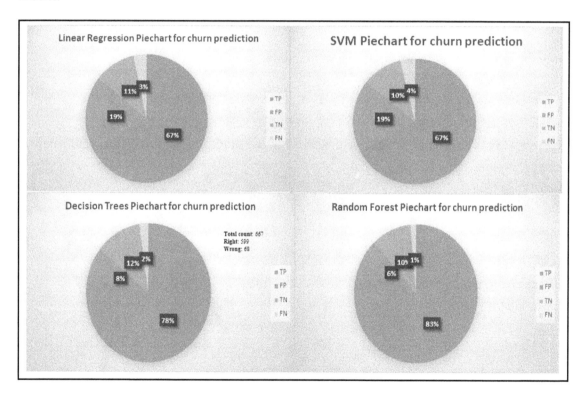

Now, it's worth mentioning that using random forest, we are actually getting high accuracy, but it's a very resource, as well as time-consuming job; the training, especially, takes a considerably longer time as compared to LR and SVM.

Therefore, if you don't have higher memory or computing power, it is recommended to increase the Java heap space prior to running this code to avoid OOM errors.

Finally, if you want to deploy the best model (that is, Random Forest in our case), it is recommended to save the cross-validated model immediately after the `fit()` method invocation:

```
// Save the workflow
cvModel.write.overwrite().save("model/RF_model_churn")
```

Your trained model will be saved to that location. The directory will include:

- The best model
- Estimator
- Evaluator
- The metadata of the training itself

Now the next task will be restoring the same model, as follows:

```
// Load the workflow back
val cvModel = CrossValidatorModel.load("model/ RF_model_churn/")
```

Finally, we need to transform the test set to the model pipeline that maps the features according to the same mechanism we described in the preceding feature engineering step:

```
val predictions = cvModel.transform(Preprocessing.testSet)
```

Finally, we evaluate the restored model:

```
val evaluator = new BinaryClassificationEvaluator()
    .setLabelCol("label")
    .setRawPredictionCol("prediction")

val accuracy = evaluator.evaluate(predictions)
    println("Accuracy: " + accuracy)
    evaluator.explainParams()

val predictionAndLabels = predictions
    .select("prediction", "label")
    .rdd.map(x => (x(0).asInstanceOf[Double], x(1)
    .asInstanceOf[Double]))

val metrics = new BinaryClassificationMetrics(predictionAndLabels)
val areaUnderPR = metrics.areaUnderPR
println("Area under the precision-recall curve: " + areaUnderPR)
```

```
val areaUnderROC = metrics.areaUnderROC
println("Area under the receiver operating characteristic (ROC) curve: " +
areaUnderROC)
>>>
```

You will receive the following output:

```
 Markers   Properties   Servers   Data Source Explorer   Progress  Ju JUnit   Console ⊠
<terminated> RandomForestModelReuse$ [Scala Application] C:\Program Files\Java\jdk1.8.0_131\bin\javaw.e
18/01/01 21:07:44 WARN NativeCodeLoader: Unable to load native-hadoop library for
18/01/01 21:07:58 WARN SparkSession$Builder: Using an existing SparkSession; some
18/01/01 21:07:59 WARN Utils: Truncated the string representation of a plan since
Accuracy: 0.8747423629002576
Area under the precision-recall curve: 0.7260962563830867
Area under the receiver operating characteristic (ROC) curve: 0.8747423629002576
Total Count: 667
Correct: 594
Wrong: 73
Ratio wrong: 0.10944527736131934
Ratio correct: 0.8905547226386806
Ratio true positive: 0.7691154422788605
Ratio false positive: 0.08845577211394302
Ratio true negative: 0.12143928035982009
Ratio false negative: 0.020989505247376312
```

Well, done! We have managed to reuse the model and do the same prediction. But, probably due to the randomness of data, we observed slightly different predictions.

Summary

In this chapter, we have seen how to develop an ML project to predict whether a customer is likely to cancel their subscription or not, and then used it to develop a real-life predictive model. We have developed predictive models using LR, SVMs, DTs, and Random Forest. We have also analyzed what types of customer data are typically used to do preliminary analysis of the data. Finally, we have seen how to choose which model to use for a production-ready environment.

In the next chapter, we will see how to develop a real-life project that collects historical and live **Bitcoin** data and predicts the price for an upcoming week, month, and so on. In addition to this, we will see how to generate a simple signal for online cryptocurrency trading.

3

High Frequency Bitcoin Price Prediction from Historical and Live Data

Bitcoin is a worldwide cryptocurrency and digital payment system considered the **first decentralized digital currency**, since the system works without a central repository or single administrator. In recent times, it has gained much popularity and attention among people around the world.

In this chapter, we will see how to develop a real-life project using Scala, Spark ML, Cryptocompare API, and Bitcoin historical (and live) data to predict the price for an upcoming week, month, and so on that help us taking automated decision for online cryptocurrency. In addition to this, we will see how to generate a simple signal for online Bitcoin trading.

Briefly, we will learn the following topics throughout this end-to-end project:

- Bitcoin, cryptocurrency, and online trading
- Historical and live-price data collection
- High-level pipeline of the prototype
- Gradient-boosted trees regression for Bitcoin price prediction
- Demo prediction and signal generation using the Scala play framework
- Future outlook—using the same technique for other datasets

Bitcoin, cryptocurrency, and online trading

Bitcoin, the first cryptocurrency by date of launch and by market cap (as of December2017) has attracted investors and traders because of its ease of starting trading, ability to stay pseudo-anonymous, and, of course, dramatic growth during its history (see *Table 1* and *Figure 1* for some statistics). This lures long-term investors; its high volatility also attracts day traders.

However, it's hard predict the value of Bitcoin in the long term, as the value behind Bitcoin is less tangible. The price mostly reflects market perception and is highly dependent on news, regulations, collaboration of governments and banks, technical issues of the platform (such as transactions fee and block size), interest of institutional investors in including Bitcoin into their portfolio, and more:

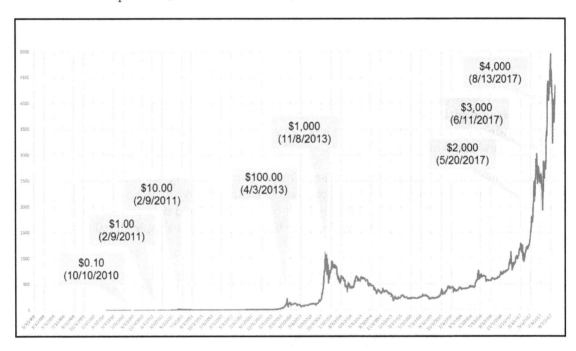

Figure 1: Bitcoin and its dramatic price increases

Nonetheless, from a short-term perspective, Bitcoin price is a by-product of market activity usually happening on a platform, called **exchange** (Bitstamp, Coinbase, Kraken, and Bitfinex among the most well-known **exchanges**). Users, after registration and after going through **KYC** (**Know Your Customer**) procedures, can trade Bitcoin in it for fiat currencies such as dollars and euros, as well as for other cryptocurrencies, called **alt-coins** or alternative coins (Ethereum, Litecoin, and Dash are well known):

Table 1 – Bitcoin historical price movement

Date	USD: 1 BTC
Jan 2009 to Mar 2010	Basically none
Mar 2010	$0.003
May 2010	Less than $0.01
Jul 2010	$0.08 ▲
Feb to Apr 2011	$1.00 ▲
8 Jul 2011	$31.00 ▲
Dec 2011	$2.00 ▼
Dec 2012	$13.00
11 Apr 2013	$266 ▲
May 2013	$130 ▼
Jun 2013	$100 ▼
Nov 2013	$350 to $1,242 ▲
Dec 2013	$600 to $1,000 ▼
Jan 2014	$750 to $1,000 ▲
Feb 2014	$550 to $750 ▲
Mar 2014	$450 to $700 ▲
Apr 2014	$340 to $530 ▼
May 2014	$440 to $630 ▲
Mar 2015	$200 to $300 ▼
Early Nov 2015	$395 to $504 ▲

May to Jun 2016	$450 to $750 ▲
Jul to Sept 2016	$600 to $630 ▼
Oct to Nov 2016	$600 to $780 ▲
Jan 2017	$800 to $1,150 ▲
5-12 Jan 2017	$750 to $920 ▼
2-3 Mar 2017	$1,290+ ▲
Apr 2017	$1,210 to $1,250 ▼
May 2017	$2,000 ▲
May to June 2017	$2,000 to $3,200+ ▲
Aug 2017	$4,400 ▲
Sept 2017	$5,000 ▲
12 Sept 2017	$2,900 ▼
13 Oct 2017	$5,600 ▲
21 Oct 2017	$6,180 ▲
6 Nov 2017	$7,300 ▲
12 Nov 2017	$5,519 to 6,295 ▼
17-20 Nov 2017	$7,600 to 8,100 ▲
15 Dec 2017	17,900 ▲

Exchanges maintain order books—lists of all buy and sell orders, with their quantities and prices—and execute when a match is found between somebody buying and somebody selling. In addition, exchanges also keep and provide statistics about the state of trading, often captured as OCHL and volume for both currencies of the trader pai. For this project, we will be using the BTC/USD cryptocurrency pair.

This data is presented as aggregated by period, from seconds to days, and even months. There are dedicated servers working on collecting Bitcoin data for professional traders and institutions. Although one cannot expect to have all orders data available free, some of it is accessible to the public and can be used.

State-of-the-art automated trading of Bitcoin

In the world of traditional securities, such as a company's stocks, it used to be humans who would do the analytics, predict the prices of stocks, and trade. Today, the development of **machine learning** (**ML**) and the growing availability of data has almost eliminated humans from high-frequency trading, as a regular person can't capture and process all data, and emotions affect one's decisions; so it's dominated by automated trading systems by investment institutions.

Currently, the volume of Bitcoin trading is relatively low compared to traditional exchanges; financial institutions, being traditionally careful and risk averse, haven't got their hands on Bitcoin trading yet (at least, it's not well-known). One of the reasons is high fees and uncertainty regarding regulations of cryptocurrencies.

So today, mostly individuals buy and sell Bitcoins, with all the consequences of irrational behavior connected to that, but some attempts to automate Bitcoin trading have been made. The most famous one was stated in a paper by MIT, and another one was by Stanford researchers, published in 2014. Many things have changed, and taking into account the massive Bitcoin price increase during these three years, anyone who just buys and holds on would be satisfied enough with the results:

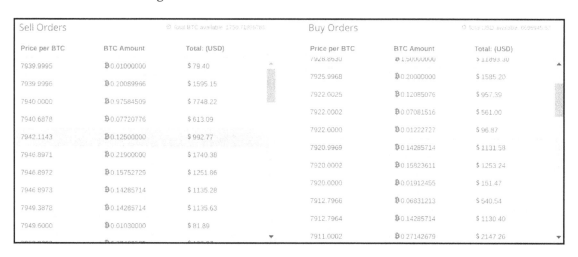

Figure 2: Bitcoin buy and sell orders (until November 2017)

Definitely, some traders use ML for trading, and such applications look promising. So far, the best possible approach that was identified from research papers is as follows.

Training

Use order book data, instead of derived OHLC + volume data. Therefore, for training and prediction, use data that looks like this:

- Split the data into a time series of a certain `size` (`size` is a parameter to tune).
- Cluster the time series data into `K` clusters (`K` is a parameter to tune). It's assumed that clusters with some natural trends would appear (sharp drop/rise in price and so on).
- For each cluster, train the regression and classifier to predict the price and price change, respectively.

Prediction

This approach considers the most recent time series with the size of a specific window and trains the model. Then it classifies the data as follows:

- Takes the most recent time series with window size used for training
- Classifies it—which of the clusters does it belong to?
- Uses the ML model for that cluster to predict the price or price change

This solution dates back to 2014, but still it gives a certain level of robustness. By having many parameters to identify, and not having the order-book historical data available easily, in this project, we use a simpler approach and dataset.

High-level data pipeline of the prototype

The goal of this chapter is to develop a prototype of a system that will predict the short-term change of Bitcoin price, using historical data to train the algorithm, and real-time data to predict and select algorithms that perform better. In the scope of this project, there is no attempt to predict the actual price in dollars, but only whether it would increase or not. This is because Bitcoin price, to some extent, is not actually about price but about market expectations. This can be seen as patterns in a trader's behavior, which, on a higher level, is represented by previous price itself.

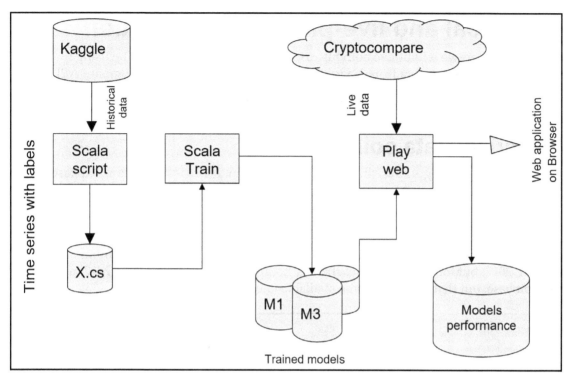

Figure 3: High-level data pipeline of the prototype

Of course, there is an objective price associated with Bitcoin; miners are willing to sell Bitcoins for profit. So the base price can be estimated by knowing all bills that all miners have to pay for the Bitcoins they mine, but that is outside the scope of this project.

From this perspective, rather than trying to predict the price in dollars, it might make sense to look for trends of the price rising, dropping, or staying the same, and act accordingly. The second goal is to build a tool for experiments that allows us to try different approaches to predicting prices and evaluate it on real-life data easily. The code has to be flexible, robust, and easily extensible.

Therefore, in summary, there are three main components of the system:

- Scala script for preprocessing of historical data into the required format
- Scala app to train the ML model
- Scala web service to predict future prices

Historical and live-price data collection

As stated earlier, we will utilize both historical as well live data. We will be using the Bitcoin historical price data from Kaggle. For the real-time data, Cryptocompare API will be used.

Historical data collection

For training the ML algorithm, there is a `Bitcoin Historical Price Data` dataset available to the public on Kaggle (version 10). The dataset can be downloaded from `https:/ /www.kaggle.com/mczielinski/bitcoin-historical-data/`. It has 1 minute OHLC data for BTC-USD pairs from several exchanges.

At the beginning of the project, for most of them, data was available from January 1, 2012 to May 31, 2017; but for the Bitstamp exchange, it's available until October 20, 2017 (as well as for Coinbase, but that dataset became available later):

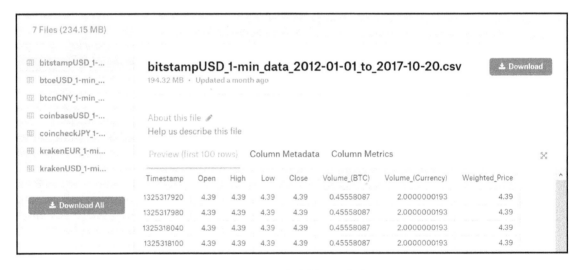

Figure 4: The Bitcoin historical dataset on Kaggle

Note that you need to be a registered user and be logged in in order to download the file. The file that we are using is `bitstampUSD_1-min_data_2012-01-01_to_2017-10-20.csv`. Now, let us get the data we have. It has eight columns:

- **Timestamp**: The time elapsed in seconds since January 1, 1970. It is 1,325,317,920 for the first row and 1,325,317,920 for the second 1. (Sanity check! The difference is 60 seconds).

- **Open**: The price at the opening of the time interval. It is 4.39 dollars. Therefore it is the price of the first trade that happened after **Timestamp** (1,325,317,920 in the first row's case).

- **Close**: The price at the closing of the time interval.

- **High**: The highest price from all orders executed during the interval.

- **Low**: The same as **High** but it is the lowest price.

- **Volume_(BTC)**: The sum of all Bitcoins that were transferred during the time interval. So, take all transactions that happened during the selected interval and sum up the BTC values of each of them.

- **Volume_(Currency)**: The sum of all dollars transferred.

- **Weighted_Price**: This is derived from the volumes of BTC and USD. By dividing all dollars traded by all bitcoins, we can get the weighted average price of BTC during this minute. So `Weighted_Price=Volume_(Currency)/Volume_(BTC)`.

One of the most important parts of the data-science pipeline after data collection (which is in a sense outsourced; we use data collected by others) is data preprocessing—clearing a dataset and transforming it to suit our needs.

Transformation of historical data into a time series

Stemming from our goal—predict the direction of price change—we might ask ourselves, *does having an actual price in dollars help to achieve this?* Historically, the price of Bitcoin was usually rising, so if we try to fit a linear regression, it will show further exponential growth (whether in the long run this will be true is yet to be seen).

Assumptions and design choices

One of the assumptions of this project is as follows: whether we are thinking about Bitcoin trading in November 2016 with a price of about $700, or trading in November 2017 with a price in the $6500-7000 range, patterns in how people trade are similar. Now, we have several other assumptions, as described in the following points:

- **Assumption one**: From what has been said previously, we can ignore the actual price and rather look at its change. As a measure of this, we can take the delta between opening and closing prices. If it is positive, it means the price grew during that minute; the price went down if it is negative and stayed the same if delta = 0.

  In the following figure, we can see that Delta was -1.25 for the first minute observed, -12.83 for the second one, and -0.23 for the third one. Sometimes, the open price can differ significantly from the close price of the previous minute (although Delta is negative during all three of the observed minutes, for the third minute the shown price was actually higher than close for a second). But such things are not very common, and usually the open price doesn't change significantly compared to the close price of the previous minute.

- **Assumption two**: The next need to consider... is predicting the price change in a **black box** environment. We do not use other sources of knowledge such as news, Twitter feeds, and others to predict how the market would react to them. This is a more advanced topic. The only data we use is price and volume. For simplicity of the prototype, we can focus on price only and construct time series data.

  Time series prediction is a prediction of a parameter based on the values of this parameter in the past. One of the most common examples is temperature prediction. Although there are many supercomputers using satellite and sensor data to predict the weather, a simple time series analysis can lead to some valuable results. We predict the price at T+60 seconds, for instance, based on the price at T, T-60s, T-120s and so on.

- **Assumption three**: Not all data in the dataset is valuable. The first 600,000 records are not informative, as price changes are rare and trading volumes are small. This can affect the model we are training and thus make end results worse. That is why the first 600,000 of rows are eliminated from the dataset.

- **Assumption four**: We need to `Label` our data so that we can use a supervised ML algorithm. This is the easiest measure, without concerns about transaction fees.

Data preprocessing

Taking into account the goals of data preparation, Scala was chosen as an easy and interactive way to manipulate data:

```scala
val priceDataFileName: String = "bitstampUSD_1-
min_data_2012-01-01_to_2017-10-20.csv"

val spark = SparkSession
    .builder()
    .master("local[*]")
    .config("spark.sql.warehouse.dir", "E:/Exp/")
    .appName("Bitcoin Preprocessing")
    .getOrCreate()

val data = spark.read.format("com.databricks.spark.csv").option("header",
"true").load(priceDataFileName)
data.show(10)
>>>
```

```
+----------+----+----+----+-----+------------+-----------------+--------------+
| Timestamp|Open|High| Low|Close|Volume_(BTC)|Volume_(Currency)|Weighted_Price|
+----------+----+----+----+-----+------------+-----------------+--------------+
|1325317920|4.39|4.39|4.39| 4.39|  0.45558087|     2.0000000193|          4.39|
|1325317980|4.39|4.39|4.39| 4.39|  0.45558087|     2.0000000193|          4.39|
|1325318040|4.39|4.39|4.39| 4.39|  0.45558087|     2.0000000193|          4.39|
|1325318100|4.39|4.39|4.39| 4.39|  0.45558087|     2.0000000193|          4.39|
|1325318160|4.39|4.39|4.39| 4.39|  0.45558087|     2.0000000193|          4.39|
|1325318220|4.39|4.39|4.39| 4.39|  0.45558087|     2.0000000193|          4.39|
|1325318280|4.39|4.39|4.39| 4.39|  0.45558087|     2.0000000193|          4.39|
|1325318340|4.39|4.39|4.39| 4.39|  0.45558087|     2.0000000193|          4.39|
|1325318400|4.39|4.39|4.39| 4.39|  0.45558087|     2.0000000193|          4.39|
|1325318460|4.39|4.39|4.39| 4.39|  0.45558087|     2.0000000193|          4.39|
+----------+----+----+----+-----+------------+-----------------+--------------+
only showing top 10 rows
```

Figure 5: A glimpse of the Bitcoin historical price dataset

```scala
println((data.count(), data.columns.size))
```

```
>>>
```

```
(3045857, 8)
```

In the preceding code, we load data from the file downloaded from Kaggle and look at what is inside. There are `3045857` rows in the dataset and `8` columns, described before. Then we create the `Delta` column, containing the difference between closing and opening prices (that is, to consider only that data where meaningful trading has started to occur):

```
val dataWithDelta = data.withColumn("Delta", data("Close") - data("Open"))
```

The following code labels our data by assigning 1 to the rows the `Delta` value of which was positive; it assigns 0 otherwise:

```
import org.apache.spark.sql.functions._
import spark.sqlContext.implicits._

val dataWithLabels = dataWithDelta.withColumn("label", when($"Close" -
$"Open" > 0, 1).otherwise(0))
rollingWindow(dataWithLabels, 22, outputDataFilePath, outputLabelFilePath)
```

This code transforms the original dataset into time series data. It takes the Delta values of `WINDOW_SIZE` rows (22 in this experiment) and makes a new row out of them. In this way, the first row has `Delta` values from `t0` to `t21`, and the second one has values from `t1` to `t22`. Then we create the corresponding array with labels (1 or 0).

Finally, we save `X` and `Y` into files where `612000` rows were cut off from the original dataset; 22 means rolling window size and 2 classes represents that labels are binary 0 and 1:

```
val dropFirstCount: Int = 612000

def rollingWindow(data: DataFrame, window: Int, xFilename: String,
yFilename: String): Unit = {
    var i = 0
    val xWriter = new BufferedWriter(new FileWriter(new File(xFilename)))
    val yWriter = new BufferedWriter(new FileWriter(new File(yFilename)))
    val zippedData = data.rdd.zipWithIndex().collect()
    System.gc()
    val dataStratified = zippedData.drop(dropFirstCount)//slice 612K

    while (i < (dataStratified.length - window)) {
        val x = dataStratified
                .slice(i, i + window)
                    .map(r => r._1.getAs[Double]("Delta")).toList
        val y = dataStratified.apply(i + window)._1.getAs[Integer]("label")
        val stringToWrite = x.mkString(",")
        xWriter.write(stringToWrite + "n")
        yWriter.write(y + "n")
        i += 1
```

```
    if (i % 10 == 0) {
        xWriter.flush()
        yWriter.flush()
        }
    }
xWriter.close()
yWriter.close()
}
```

In the preceding code segment:

```
val outputDataFilePath: String = "output/scala_test_x.csv"
val outputLabelFilePath: String = "output/scala_test_y.csv"
```

Real-time data through the Cryptocompare API

For real-time data, the Cryptocompare API is used (`https://www.cryptocompare.com/api/#`), more specifically HistoMinute (`https://www.cryptocompare.com/api/#-api-data-histominute-`), which gives us access to OHLC data for the past seven days at most. The details of the API will be discussed in a section devoted to implementation, but the API response is very similar to our historical dataset, and this data is retrieved using a regular HTTP request. For example, a simple JSON response from `https://min-api.cryptocompare.com/data/histominute?fsym=BTCtsym=USDlimit=23aggregate=1e=Bitstamp` has the following structure:

```
{
    "Response":"Success",
    "Type":100,
    "Aggregated":false,
    "Data":
    [{"time":1510774800,"close":7205,"high":7205,"low":7192.67,"open":7198,
"volumefrom":81.73,"volumeto":588726.94},
{"time":1510774860,"close":7209.05,"high":7219.91,"low":7205,"open":7205,
"volumefrom":16.39,"volumeto":118136.61},
        ... (other price data)
        ],
    "TimeTo":1510776180,
    "TimeFrom":1510774800,
    "FirstValueInArray":true,
    "ConversionType":{"type":"force_direct","conversionSymbol":""}
}
```

Through Cryptocompare HistoMinute, we can get `open`, `high`, `low`, `close`, `volumefrom`, and `volumeto` from each minute of historical data. This data is stored for 7 days only; if you need more, use the hourly or daily path. It uses BTC conversion if data is not available because the coin is not being traded in the specified currency:

Parameter	Type	Required	Default	Info
fsym	string	true		From Symbol
tsym	string	true		To Symbols
e	string	true	CCCAGG	Name of exchange
extraParams	string	false	NotAvailable	Name of your application
sign	bool	false	false	If set to true, the server will sign the requests.
tryConversion	bool	false	true	If set to false, it will try to get values without using any conversion at all
aggregate	int	false	1	
limit	int	false	1440	Max 2000
toTs	timestamp	false		

Figure 6: Open, high, low, close, and volume values through Cryptocompare HistoMinute

Now, the following method fetches the correctly formed URL of the Cryptocompare API (`https://www.cryptocompare.com/api/#-api-data-histominute-`), which is a fully formed URL with all parameters, such as currency, limit, and aggregation specified. It finally returns the future that will have a response body parsed into the data model, with the price list to be processed at an upper level:

```
import javax.inject.Inject
import play.api.libs.json.{JsResult, Json}
import scala.concurrent.Future
import play.api.mvc._
import play.api.libs.ws._
import processing.model.CryptoCompareResponse
```

```
class RestClient @Inject() (ws: WSClient) {
    def getPayload(url : String): Future[JsResult[CryptoCompareResponse]] =
{
        val request: WSRequest = ws.url(url)
        val future = request.get()
        implicit val context =
play.api.libs.concurrent.Execution.Implicits.defaultContext
        future.map {
            response => response.json.validate[CryptoCompareResponse]
            }
        }
    }
```

In the preceding code segment, the CryptoCompareResponse class is the model of API, which takes the following parameters:

- Response
- Type
- Aggregated
- Data
- FirstValueInArray
- TimeTo
- TimeFrom

Now, it has the following signature:

```
case class CryptoCompareResponse(Response : String,
    Type : Int,
    Aggregated : Boolean,
    Data : List[OHLC],
    FirstValueInArray : Boolean,
    TimeTo : Long,
    TimeFrom: Long)

object CryptoCompareResponse {
    implicit val cryptoCompareResponseReads =
Json.reads[CryptoCompareResponse]
    }
```

Again, the preceding two code segments the **open-high-low-close** (also known as **OHLC**), are a model class for mapping with CryptoAPI response `data` array internals. It takes these parameters:

- `Time`: Timestamp in seconds, `1508818680`, for instance.
- `Open`: Open price at a given minute interval.
- `High`: Highest price.
- `Low`: Lowest price.
- `Close`: Price at the closing of the interval.
- `Volumefrom`: Trading volume in the `from` currency. It's BTC in our case.
- `Volumeto`: The trading volume in the `to` currency, USD in our case.
- Dividing `Volumeto` by `Volumefrom` gives us the weighted price of BTC.

Now, it has the following signature:

```scala
case class OHLC(time: Long,
    open: Double,
    high: Double,
    low: Double,
    close: Double,
    volumefrom: Double,
    volumeto: Double)

object OHLC {
implicit val implicitOHLCReads = Json.reads[OHLC]
    }
```

Model training for prediction

Inside the project, in the package folder `prediction.training`, there is a Scala object called `TrainGBT.scala`. Before launching, you have to specify/change four things:

- In the code, you need to set up `spark.sql.warehouse.dir` in some actual place on your computer that has several gigabytes of free space: `set("spark.sql.warehouse.dir", "/home/user/spark")`
- The `RootDir` is the main folder, where all files and train models will be stored: `rootDir = "/home/user/projects/btc-prediction/"`
- Make sure that the x filename matches the one produced by the Scala script in the preceding step: `x = spark.read.format("com.databricks.spark.csv").schema(xSchema).load(rootDir + "scala_test_x.csv")`

- Make sure that the `y` filename matches the one produced by Scala
  script: `y_tmp=spark.read.format("com.databricks.spark.csv").schema`
  `(ySchema).load(rootDir + "scala_test_y.csv")`

The code for training uses the Apache Spark ML library (and libraries required for it) to train the classifier, which means they have to be present in your `class` path to be able to run it. The easiest way to do that (since the whole project uses SBT) is to run it from the project root folder by typing `sbtrun-main prediction.training.TrainGBT`, which will resolve all dependencies and launch training.

Depending on the number of iterations and depth, it can take several hours to train the model. Now let us see how training is performed on the example of the gradient-boosted trees model. First, we need to create a `SparkSession` object:

```
val spark = SparkSession
        .builder()
        .master("local[*]")
        .config("spark.sql.warehouse.dir", ""/home/user/spark/")
        .appName("Bitcoin Preprocessing")
        .getOrCreate()
```

Then, we define a schema of data for x and y. We rename the columns to `t0-t21`, to indicate that it's a time series:

```
val xSchema = StructType(Array(
    StructField("t0", DoubleType, true),
    StructField("t1", DoubleType, true),
    StructField("t2", DoubleType, true),
    StructField("t3", DoubleType, true),
    StructField("t4", DoubleType, true),
    StructField("t5", DoubleType, true),
    StructField("t6", DoubleType, true),
    StructField("t7", DoubleType, true),
    StructField("t8", DoubleType, true),
    StructField("t9", DoubleType, true),
    StructField("t10", DoubleType, true),
    StructField("t11", DoubleType, true),
    StructField("t12", DoubleType, true),
    StructField("t13", DoubleType, true),
    StructField("t14", DoubleType, true),
    StructField("t15", DoubleType, true),
    StructField("t16", DoubleType, true),
    StructField("t17", DoubleType, true),
    StructField("t18", DoubleType, true),
    StructField("t19", DoubleType, true),
    StructField("t20", DoubleType, true),
```

```
    StructField("t21", DoubleType, true))
    )
```

Then we read the files we defined for the schema. It was more convenient to generate two separate files in Scala for data and labels, so here we have to join them into a single DataFrame:

```
import spark.implicits._
val y = y_tmp.withColumn("y", 'y.cast(IntegerType))
import org.apache.spark.sql.functions._

val x_id = x.withColumn("id", monotonically_increasing_id())
val y_id = y.withColumn("id", monotonically_increasing_id())
val data = x_id.join(y_id, "id")
```

The next step is required by Spark—we need to vectorize the features:

```
val featureAssembler = new VectorAssembler()
        .setInputCols(Array("t0", "t1", "t2", "t3",
                            "t4", "t5", "t6", "t7",
                            "t8", "t9", "t10", "t11",
                            "t12", "t13", "t14", "t15",
                            "t16", "t17", "t18", "t19",
                            "t20", "t21"))
        .setOutputCol("features")
```

We split the data into train and test sets randomly in the proportion of 75% to 25%. We set the seed so that the splits would be equal among all times we run the training:

```
val Array(trainingData,testData) = dataWithLabels.randomSplit(Array(0.75,
0.25), 123)
```

We then define the model. It tells which columns are features and which are labels. It also sets parameters:

```
val gbt = new GBTClassifier()
        .setLabelCol("label")
        .setFeaturesCol("features")
        .setMaxIter(10)
        .setSeed(123)
```

Create a `pipeline` of steps—vector assembling of features and running GBT:

```
val pipeline = new Pipeline()
            .setStages(Array(featureAssembler, gbt))
```

Defining evaluator function—how the model knows whether it is doing well or not. As we have only two classes that are imbalanced, accuracy is a bad measurement; area under the ROC curve is better:

```
val rocEvaluator = new BinaryClassificationEvaluator()
        .setLabelCol("label")
        .setRawPredictionCol("rawPrediction")
        .setMetricName("areaUnderROC")
```

K-fold cross-validation is used to avoid overfitting; it takes out one-fifth of the data at each iteration, trains the model on the rest, and then tests on this one-fifth:

```
val cv = new CrossValidator()
        .setEstimator(pipeline)
        .setEvaluator(rocEvaluator)
        .setEstimatorParamMaps(paramGrid)
        .setNumFolds(numFolds)
        .setSeed(123)
val cvModel = cv.fit(trainingData)
```

After we get the trained model (which can take an hour or more depending on the number of iterations and parameters we want to iterate on, specified in `paramGrid`), we then compute the predictions on the test data:

```
val predictions = cvModel.transform(testData)
```

In addition, evaluate quality of predictions:

```
val roc = rocEvaluator.evaluate(predictions)
```

The trained model is saved for later usage by the prediction service:

```
val gbtModel = cvModel.bestModel.asInstanceOf[PipelineModel]
gbtModel.save(rootDir + "__cv__gbt_22_binary_classes_" + System.nanoTime()
/ 1000000 + ".model")
```

In summary, the code for model training is given as follows:

```
import org.apache.spark.{ SparkConf, SparkContext }
import org.apache.spark.ml.{ Pipeline, PipelineModel }

import org.apache.spark.ml.classification.{ GBTClassificationModel,
GBTClassifier, RandomForestClassificationModel, RandomForestClassifier}
import org.apache.spark.ml.evaluation.{BinaryClassificationEvaluator,
MulticlassClassificationEvaluator}
import org.apache.spark.ml.feature.{IndexToString, StringIndexer,
VectorAssembler, VectorIndexer}
```

```
import org.apache.spark.ml.tuning.{CrossValidator, ParamGridBuilder}
import org.apache.spark.sql.types.{DoubleType, IntegerType, StructField,
StructType}
import org.apache.spark.sql.SparkSession

object TrainGradientBoostedTree {
    def main(args: Array[String]): Unit = {
        val maxBins = Seq(5, 7, 9)
        val numFolds = 10
        val maxIter: Seq[Int] = Seq(10)
        val maxDepth: Seq[Int] = Seq(20)
        val rootDir = "output/"
        val spark = SparkSession
            .builder()
            .master("local[*]")
            .config("spark.sql.warehouse.dir", ""/home/user/spark/")
            .appName("Bitcoin Preprocessing")
            .getOrCreate()

        val xSchema = StructType(Array(
            StructField("t0", DoubleType, true),
            StructField("t1", DoubleType, true),
            StructField("t2", DoubleType, true),
            StructField("t3", DoubleType, true),
            StructField("t4", DoubleType, true),
            StructField("t5", DoubleType, true),
            StructField("t6", DoubleType, true),
            StructField("t7", DoubleType, true),
            StructField("t8", DoubleType, true),
            StructField("t9", DoubleType, true),
            StructField("t10", DoubleType, true),
            StructField("t11", DoubleType, true),
            StructField("t12", DoubleType, true),
            StructField("t13", DoubleType, true),
            StructField("t14", DoubleType, true),
            StructField("t15", DoubleType, true),
            StructField("t16", DoubleType, true),
            StructField("t17", DoubleType, true),
            StructField("t18", DoubleType, true),
            StructField("t19", DoubleType, true),
            StructField("t20", DoubleType, true),
            StructField("t21", DoubleType, true)))

        val ySchema = StructType(Array(StructField("y", DoubleType,
        true)))
        val x = spark.read.format("csv").schema(xSchema).load(rootDir +
        "scala_test_x.csv")
        val y_tmp =
```

```
spark.read.format("csv").schema(ySchema).load(rootDir +
"scala_test_y.csv")

import spark.implicits._
val y = y_tmp.withColumn("y", 'y.cast(IntegerType))

import org.apache.spark.sql.functions._
//joining 2 separate datasets in single Spark dataframe
val x_id = x.withColumn("id", monotonically_increasing_id())
val y_id = y.withColumn("id", monotonically_increasing_id())
val data = x_id.join(y_id, "id")
val featureAssembler = new VectorAssembler()
    .setInputCols(Array("t0", "t1", "t2", "t3", "t4", "t5",
                        "t6", "t7", "t8", "t9", "t10", "t11",
                        "t12", "t13", "t14", "t15", "t16",
                        "t17","t18", "t19", "t20", "t21"))
    .setOutputCol("features")
val encodeLabel = udf[Double, String] { case "1" => 1.0 case
                                              "0" => 0.0 }
val dataWithLabels = data.withColumn("label",
                          encodeLabel(data("y")))

//123 is seed number to get same datasplit so we can tune
params
val Array(trainingData, testData) =
dataWithLabels.randomSplit(Array(0.75, 0.25), 123)
val gbt = new GBTClassifier()
    .setLabelCol("label")
    .setFeaturesCol("features")
    .setMaxIter(10)
    .setSeed(123)
val pipeline = new Pipeline()
    .setStages(Array(featureAssembler, gbt))
// ***********************************************************
println("Preparing K-fold Cross Validation and Grid Search")
// ***********************************************************
val paramGrid = new ParamGridBuilder()
    .addGrid(gbt.maxIter, maxIter)
    .addGrid(gbt.maxDepth, maxDepth)
    .addGrid(gbt.maxBins, maxBins)
    .build()
val cv = new CrossValidator()
    .setEstimator(pipeline)
    .setEvaluator(new BinaryClassificationEvaluator())
    .setEstimatorParamMaps(paramGrid)
    .setNumFolds(numFolds)
    .setSeed(123)
// ***********************************************************
```

```
        println("Training model with GradientBoostedTrees algorithm")
        // ***************************************************************
        // Train model. This also runs the indexers.
        val cvModel = cv.fit(trainingData)
        cvModel.save(rootDir + "cvGBT_22_binary_classes_" +
        System.nanoTime() / 1000000 + ".model")
        println("Evaluating model on train and test data and
        calculating RMSE")
        //
********************************************************************
        // Make a sample prediction
        val predictions = cvModel.transform(testData)

        // Select (prediction, true label) and compute test error.
        val rocEvaluator = new BinaryClassificationEvaluator()
            .setLabelCol("label")
            .setRawPredictionCol("rawPrediction")
            .setMetricName("areaUnderROC")
        val roc = rocEvaluator.evaluate(predictions)
        val prEvaluator = new BinaryClassificationEvaluator()
            .setLabelCol("label")
            .setRawPredictionCol("rawPrediction")
            .setMetricName("areaUnderPR")
        val pr = prEvaluator.evaluate(predictions)
        val gbtModel = cvModel.bestModel.asInstanceOf[PipelineModel]
        gbtModel.save(rootDir + "__cv__gbt_22_binary_classes_" +
        System.nanoTime()/1000000 +".model")

        println("Area under ROC curve = " + roc)
        println("Area under PR curve= " + pr)
        println(predictions.select().show(1))
        spark.stop()
    }
}
```

Now let us see how the training went:

```
>>>
Area under ROC curve = 0.6045355104779828
Area under PR curve= 0.3823834607704922
```

Therefore, we have not received very high accuracy, as the ROC is only 60.50% out of the best GBT model. Nevertheless, if we tune the hyperparameters, we will get better accuracy.

However, as I did not have enough time, I did not iterate the training for long, but you should definitely try.

Scala Play web service

As an application framework, Play2 was chosen as an easy-to-configure and robust framework. Compared to Spring (another popular framework), it takes less time to make a small app from scratch. The Play comes with Guice for dependency injection and SBT as the package manager:

- **Spark ML**: The Spark ML library was chosen as it is one of the best-maintained libraries in the Java world. Many algorithms not available in the library itself are implemented by third-party developers and can be trained on top of Spark. A drawback of Spark is that it is quite slow, as by design it is supposed to be distributed; so it uses Hadoop and writes a lot into the filesystem.

- **Akka**: This allows implementing the actor's pattern—having several instances of independent objects and passing messages to each other concurrently, which increases robustness.

- **Anorm**: The library to work with SQL on top of JDBC. Slick is another option and it is more powerful, but compatibility issues between libraries required for Akka and Slick made it worth choosing another library.

- **H2**: A database that is the default for Play and Ruby-on-Rails as an easy-to-start database, with the possibility to store data in a local database file without the need to install a DB server. This gives portability and increases the speed of development. In later stages, it can be replaced with another, as Scala code isn't tied to any particular database; all of it is done on the configuration level.

Concurrency through Akka actors

Concurrency is achieved through utilization of the `actor` model using the Akka Scala library. Actors act as independent entities and can pass async messages to other actors. In this project, there are three actors: `SchedulerActor`, `PredictionActor`, and `TraderActor`:

- `SchedulerActor`: Requests price data, stores them into DB, sends a message with prices to `PredictionActor`, receives an answer, and passes it to `TraderActor`.

- `PredictionActor`: After receiving a message with prices, it predicts the next price using the best model available (this has to be chosen in `application.conf`; we will see the details later on). It passes a message with the prediction back to `SchedulerActor`, uses the rest of the modes from the `model` folder to make predictions on previous data, and uses the latest price to evaluate predictions. The results of such predictions are stored in the DB.
- `TraderActor`: After receiving a message about prediction, using `rules` (which at this moment are as simple as *buy if the price is predicted to grow and do nothing otherwise*), this writes its decision into logs. It can send an HTTP request to a URL to trigger this decision.

Web service workflow

Now let's take a deeper look into how code works to perform predictions. As shown earlier, every 60 seconds, the app is triggered to fetch data from Cryptocompare, store prices into the database, and run predictions, saving backtrack test results about quality prediction.

In this section, we'll look deeper into which Scala classes play an important role in this project and how they communicate.

JobModule

When the application is launched, everything starts with `JobModule`. It configures the creation of `Scheduler`, which sends messages to `SchedulerActor` as given in the `application.conf` rate:

```scala
class JobModule extends AbstractModule with AkkaGuiceSupport {
    def configure(): Unit = {
        //configuring launch of price-fetching Actor
        bindActor[SchedulerActor]("scheduler-actor")
        bind(classOf[Scheduler]).asEagerSingleton()
    }
}
```

To enable this module, inside `application.conf`, the following line is required:

```scala
play.modules.enabled += "modules.jobs.JobModule"
```

Scheduler

Scheduler takes the frequency constant from the `application.conf` and uses the `Actor` system to send an `update` message (the content does not matter; `SchedulerActor` reacts to any message) to `SchedulerActor` every X seconds:

```
class Scheduler @Inject()
    (val system: ActorSystem, @Named("scheduler-actor") val schedulerActor:
ActorRef, configuration:    Configuration)(implicit ec: ExecutionContext)
{
    //constants.frequency is set in conf/application.conf file
    val frequency = configuration.getInt("constants.frequency").get
    var actor = system.scheduler.schedule(
    0.microseconds, //initial delay: whether execution starts immediately
after app launch
    frequency.seconds, //every X seconds, specified above
    schedulerActor,
    "update")
}
```

SchedulerActor

The relevant parts of the code are displayed and explained. Now let us see how to obtain price data:

```
def constructUrl(exchange: String): String =
{
"https://min-api.cryptocompare.com/data/histominute?fsym=BTC&tsym=USD&limit
=23&aggregate=1&e=" + exchange
 }
```

`ConstructUrl` returns a completely formed URL for the request to the Cryptocompare API. More details are given in section related to the API:

```
final val predictionActor = system.actorOf(Props(new
PredictionActor(configuration, db)))
final val traderActor = system.actorOf(Props(new TraderActor(ws)))
```

Creates instances of `PredictionActor` and `TraderActor`:

```
override def receive: Receive = {
```

The `Receive` method is defined in the `actor` trait and has to be implemented. It is triggered when someone passes a message to this `actor` (`Scheduler` in our case):

```
case _ =>
    val futureResponse=restClient.getPayload(constructUrl(exchange))
```

In the preceding code, `case _ =>` means that we react to any message of any type and content. The first thing that is done is an async call to the Cryptocompare API by the URL specified before. This is done with the help of `RestClient`, which returns `Future` with the response JSON. After receiving the response (inside `futureResponse` on complete callback), `.json` is mapped into the custom case class `CryptoCompareResponse`:

```
case class CryptoCompareResponse(Response: String, Type: Int, Aggregated:
Boolean, Data: List[OHLC],       FirstValueInArray: Boolean, TimeTo:
Long,TimeFrom: Long)
```

The case class is similar to **POJO (Plain Old Java Object)** without the need to write constructors and getters/setters:

```
object CryptoCompareResponse {
        implicit val cryptoCompareResponseReads =
Json.reads[CryptoCompareResponse]
            }
```

This companion object is required for mapping JSON into this class. The `CryptocompareResponse` object stores the output of the API—a list of OHLC data, time range of data and others which that are not relevant to us. The `OHLC` class corresponds to actual price data:

```
case class OHLC(time: Long, open: Double,
                high: Double,
                low: Double,
                close: Double,
                volumefrom: Double,
                volumeto: Double)
```

After the data is ready, prices are stored in the DB by calling `storePriceData(cryptoCompareResponse)`. At first, it does a batch insert (using Anorm's **BatchSQL**) into the `PRICE_STAGING` table and re-inserts into `PRICE` with deduplication with respect to timestamp, as we are receiving overlapping price data:

```
val batch = BatchSql(
        """|INSERT INTO
PRICE_STAGING(TIMESTAMP,EXCHANGE,PRICE_OPEN,PRICE_CLOSED,VOLUME_BTC,
            VOLUME_USD)| VALUES({timestamp}, {exchange}, {priceOpen},
{priceClosed}, {volumeBTC},
```

```
{volumeUSD})""".stripMargin,transformedPriceDta.head,transformedPriceDta.ta
il:_*)
val res: Array[Int] = batch.execute() // array of update count
val reInsert = SQL(
        """
        |INSERT INTO PRICE(TIMESTAMP, EXCHANGE, PRICE_OPEN, PRICE_CLOSED,
VOLUME_BTC, VOLUME_USD)
        |SELECT  TIMESTAMP, EXCHANGE, PRICE_OPEN, PRICE_CLOSED,
VOLUME_BTC, VOLUME_USD
        |FROM PRICE_STAGING AS s
        |WHERE NOT EXISTS (
        |SELECT *
        |FROM PRICE As t
        |WHERE t.TIMESTAMP = s.TIMESTAMP
        |)
      """.stripMargin).execute()
    Logger.debug("reinsert " + reInsert)
```

After storing into the DB, `SchedulerActor` transforms OHLC data into (timestamp, delta) tuples, where delta is (`closePrice-openPrice`). So the format is suitable for the ML model. The transformed data is passed as a message to `PredictionActor` with explicit waiting for a response. This is done by using the ? operator. We ask the prediction `actor`:

```
(predictionActor ?
CryptoCompareDTOToPredictionModelTransformer.tranform(cryptoCompareResponse
)).mapTo[CurrentDataWithShortTermPrediction].map {
```

Its response is mapped to the `CurrentDataWithShortTermPrediction` class and passed to `TraderActor` using the ! operator. Unlike ?, the ! operator does not require a response:

```
predictedWithCurrent =>
traderActor ! predictedWithCurrent}
```

This was basic a walkthrough of `SchedulerActor`. We read data from the Cryptocompare API, store it into the database, send to `PredictionActor` and wait for its response. Then we forward its response to `TraderActor`.

Now let's see what happens inside `PredictionActor`.

PredictionActor and the prediction step

The Scala web application, which takes the most recent Bitcoin price data on the Bitstamp exchange every minute from the Cryptocompare API, uses a trained ML classifier to predict the direction of price change for the next minute. It notifies the user about the decision.

Now, to launch it, from a directory with project type sbt run (or $ sudo sbt run when required). Now let us see the contents of the application.conf file:

```
# This is the main configuration file for the application.
# Secret key
# The secret key is used to secure cryptographics functions.
# If you deploy your application to several instances be sure to use the
same key!
application.secret="%APPLICATION_SECRET%"
# The application languages
application.langs="en"
# Global object class
# Define the Global object class for this application.
# Default to Global in the root package.sb
# application.global=Global
# Router
# Define the Router object to use for this application.
# This router will be looked up first when the application is starting up,
# so make sure this is the entry point.
# Furthermore, it's assumed your route file is named properly.
# So for an application router like `my.application.Router`,
# you may need to define a router file `conf/my.application.routes`.
# Default to Routes in the root package (and conf/routes)
# application.router=my.application.Routes
# Database configuration
# You can declare as many datasources as you want.
# By convention, the default datasource is named `default`
rootDir = "<path>/Bitcoin_price_prediction/"
db.default.driver = org.h2.Driver
db.default.url = "jdbc:h2: "<path>/Bitcoin_price_prediction/DataBase"
db.default.user = user
db.default.password = ""
play.evolutions.db.default.autoApply = true
# Evolutions
# You can disable evolutions if needed
# evolutionplugin=disabled
# Logger
# You can also configure logback (http://logback.qos.ch/),
# by providing an application-logger.xml file in the conf directory.
# Root logger:
logger.root=ERROR
# Logger used by the framework:
logger.play=INFO
# Logger provided to your application:
logger.application=DEBUG
#Enable JobModule to run scheduler
play.modules.enabled += "modules.jobs.JobModule"
```

```
#Frequency in seconds to run job. Might make sense to put 30 seconds, for
recent data
constants.frequency = 30
ml.model_version = "gbt_22_binary_classes_32660767.model"
```

Now you can understand that there are also several variables to configure/change based on your platform and choice:

- Change the `rootDir` directory to the one you have used in `TrainGBT`:

    ```
    rootDir = "<path>/ Bitcoin_price_prediction"
    ```

- Specify the name for the database file:

    ```
    db.default.url = "jdbc:h2:
    "<path>/Bitcoin_price_prediction/DataBase"
    ```

- Specify the version of the model that is used for the actual prediction:

    ```
    ml.model_version = "gbt_22_binary_classes_32660767.model"
    ```

 Note that the folder with such a name has to be inside `rootDir`. So inside `rootDir`, create a folder named `models` and copy all the folders of trained models there.

This class also implements the `actor` trait and overrides the receive method. The best practice for it is to define types that can be received by the `actor` inside the companion object, thus establishing an interface for other classes:

```
object PredictionActor {
    def props = Props[PredictionActor]
    case class PriceData(timeFrom: Long,
                         timeTo: Long,
                         priceDelta: (Long, Double)*)
    }
```

At first, `PredictionActor` loads a list of models from the `models` folder and loads the `etalon` model:

```
val models: List[(Transformer, String)] =
            SubDirectoryRetriever.getListOfSubDirectories(modelFolder)
            .map(modelMap =>
(PipelineModel.load(modelMap("path")),modelMap("modelName")))
        .toList
```

First, we extract a list of subdirectories inside the `models` folder, and from each of them, we load the trained `PipeLine` model. In a similar way, the `etalon` model is loaded, but we already know its directory. Here's how a message of the `PriceData` type is handled inside the `receive` method:

```
override def receive: Receive = {
    case data: PriceData =>
        val priceData = shrinkData(data, 1, 22)
        val (predictedLabelForUnknownTimestamp, details) =
predictionService.predictPriceDeltaLabel(priceData,productionModel)
```

The predicted label (string) and classification details are logged, so is it possible to see the probability distribution for each class? If the `actor` receives a message of another type, an error is shown and nothing more is done. Then the results are sent back to `SchedulerActor` and sent in the variable `predictedWithCurrent`, as was shown in the preceding code:

```
sender() !
CurrentDataWithShortTermPrediction(predictedLabelForUnknownTimestamp, data)
```

The `sender` is an `ActorRef` reference to an object that has sent the message we are processing at the moment, so we can pass the message back with the `!` operator. Then, for each model we have loaded in the beginning, we predict the label for 1-minute-old data (rows 0-21 out of 23 in total) and get the actual price delta for the latest minute we know:

```
models.foreach { mlModel =>
    val (predictedLabel, details)
=predictionService.predictPriceDeltaLabel(shrinkData(data, 0, 21),
mlModel._1)
    val actualDeltaPoint = data.priceDelta.toList(22)
```

For each model, we store the following in the DB name of the model: the timestamp for each test prediction made, the label that was predicted by the model, and the actual delta. This information is used later to generate reports on the model's performance:

```
storeShortTermBinaryPredictionIntoDB( mlModel._2, actualDeltaPoint._1,
predictedLabel, actualDeltaPoint._2)
```

TraderActor

`TraderActor` receives the prediction and, based on the label, writes a log message. It can trigger an HTTP request to the specified endpoint:

```
override def receive: Receive = {
```

```
case data: CurrentDataWithShortTermPrediction =>
    Logger.debug("received short-term prediction" + data)
    data.prediction match {
        case "0" => notifySellShortTerm()
        case "1" => notifyHoldShortTerm()
}
```

Predicting prices and evaluating the model

ShortTermPredictionServiceImpl is the class that actually performs the prediction with the given model and data. At first, it transforms PriceData into a Spark DataFrame with the scheme corresponding to the one used for training by calling transformPriceData(priceData: PriceData). Then, the model.transform(dataframe) method is called; we extract the variables we need, write into the debugger log and return to the caller:

```
override def predictPriceDeltaLabel(priceData: PriceData, mlModel:
org.apache.spark.ml.Transformer): (String, Row) = {
        val df = transformPriceData(priceData)
        val prediction = mlModel.transform(df)
        val predictionData = prediction.select("probability", "prediction",
"rawPrediction").head()
        (predictionData.get(1).asInstanceOf[Double].toInt.toString,
predictionData)
        }
```

While running, the application collects data about the prediction output: predicted label and actual price delta. This information is used to build the root web page, displaying statistics such as **TPR (true positive rate)**, **FPR (false positive rate)**, **TNR (true negative rate)**, and **FNR (false negative rate)**, which were described earlier.

These statistics are counted on the fly from the SHORT_TERM_PREDICTION_BINARY table. Basically, by using the CASE-WHEN construction, we add new columns: TPR, FPR, TNR, and FNR. They are defined as follows:

- TPR with value 1 if the predicted label was 1 and price delta was > 0, and value 0 otherwise
- FPR with value 1 if the predicted label was 1 and price delta was <= 0, and value 0 otherwise
- TNR with value 1 if the predicted label was 0 and price delta was <= 0, and value 0 otherwise

- FNR with value 1 if the predicted label was 0 and price delta was > 0, and value 0 otherwise

Then, all records are grouped by model name, and TPR, FPR, TNR, and FNR are summed up, giving us the total numbers for each model. Here is the SQL code responsible for this:

```
SELECT MODEL, SUM(TPR) as TPR, SUM(FPR) as FPR, SUM(TNR) as TNR,
    SUM(FNR) as FNR, COUNT(*) as TOTAL FROM (SELECT *,
    case when PREDICTED_LABEL='1' and ACTUAL_PRICE_DELTA > 0
        then 1 else 0 end as TPR,
    case when PREDICTED_LABEL='1' and ACTUAL_PRICE_DELTA <=0
        then 1 else 0 end as FPR,
    case when PREDICTED_LABEL='0' and ACTUAL_PRICE_DELTA <=0
        then 1 else 0 end as TNR,
    case when PREDICTED_LABEL='0' and ACTUAL_PRICE_DELTA > 0
        then 1 else 0 end as FNR
FROM SHORT_TERM_PREDICTION_BINARY)
GROUP BY MODEL
```

Demo prediction using Scala Play framework

Now that we have seen all the steps for this project, it's time to see a live demo. We will wrap up the whole application as a Scala Play web app. Well, before seeing the demo, let's get our project up and running. However knowing some basic of RESTful architecture using Scala Play would be helpful.

Why RESTful architecture?

Well, Play's architecture is RESTful by default. At its core, Play is based on the Model-View-Controller pattern. Each entry point, paired with an HTTP verb, maps to a Controller function. The controller enables views to be web pages, JSON, XML, or just about anything else.

Play's stateless architecture enables horizontal scaling, ideal for serving many incoming requests without having to share resources (such as a session) between them. It is at the forefront of the Reactive programming trend, in which servers are event-based and parallel processing is used to cater to the ever-increasing demands of modern websites.

In certain configurations, Play enables fully asynchronous and non-blocking I/O throughout the entire application. The purpose is to reach new heights in terms of scalability on the web through efficient thread management and parallel processing, while avoiding the **callback hell** that JavaScript-based solutions tend to engender.

AngularJs is a JavaScript-based open-source front-end web application framework mainly maintained by Google and by a community of individuals and corporations to address many of the challenges encountered in developing single-page applications.

Now question would be why AngularJS? Well, HTML is great for declaring static documents, but it falters when we try to use it for declaring dynamic views in web-applications. AngularJS lets you extend HTML vocabulary for your application. The resulting environment is extraordinarily expressive, readable, and quick to develop.

Another question would be, are not there any alternatives? Well, other frameworks deal with HTML's shortcomings by either abstracting away HTML, CSS, and/or JavaScript or by providing an imperative way for manipulating the DOM. Neither of these address the root problem that HTML was not designed for dynamic views.

Finally, what is about the extensibility? Well, AngularJS is a toolset for building the framework most suited to your application development. It is fully extensible and works well with other libraries. Every feature can be modified or replaced to suit your unique development workflow and feature needs. Read on to find out how.

Project structure

The wrapped up Scala web ML app has the following directory structure:

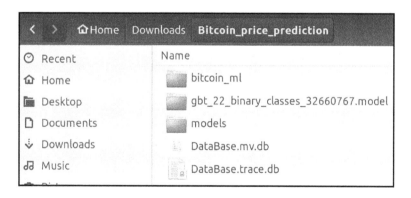

Figure 7: Scala ML web app directory structure

In the preceding structure, `bitcoin_ml` folder has all the backend and frontend codes. The `models` folder has all the trained models. An example-trained model is given in the `gbt_22_binary_classes_32660767` folder. Finally, database files and traces are there in the `DataBase.mv.db` and `DataBase.trace.db` files respectively.

Then let us see the sub-folder structure of the `bitcoin_ml` folder that contains the actual codes:

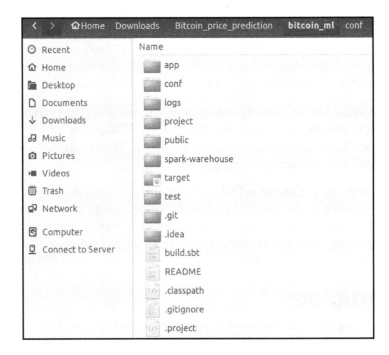

Figure 8: The bitcoin_ml directory structure

In the preceding figure, the `conf` folder has the Scala web app configuration file, `application.conf` containing necessary configurations (as shown already). All the dependencies are defined in the `build.sbt` file shown as follows:

```
libraryDependencies ++= Seq(jdbc, evolutions,
 "com.typesafe.play" %% "anorm" % "2.5.1",
 cache, ws, specs2 % Test, ws)

unmanagedResourceDirectories in Test <+= baseDirectory(_ /
"target/web/public/test")
resolvers += "scalaz-bintray" at "https://dl.bintray.com/scalaz/releases"

resolvers ++= Seq(
    "apache-snapshots" at "http://repository.apache.org/snapshots/")
    routesGenerator := InjectedRoutesGenerator
    val sparkVersion = "2.2.0"
    libraryDependencies += "org.apache.spark" %% "spark-mllib" %
sparkVersion
    libraryDependencies += "org.apache.hadoop" % "hadoop-mapreduce-client-
core" % "2.7.2"
    libraryDependencies += "org.apache.hadoop" % "hadoop-common" % "2.7.2"
    libraryDependencies += "commons-io" % "commons-io" % "2.4"
    libraryDependencies += "org.codehaus.janino" % "janino" % "3.0.7"
//fixing       "java.lang.ClassNotFoundException:
de.unkrig.jdisasm.Disassembler" exception

    libraryDependencies ++= Seq(
     "com.typesafe.slick" %% "slick" % "3.1.1",
     "org.slf4j" % "slf4j-nop" % "1.6.4"
)
```

To be frank, at the beginning of writing, I did not think of wrapping up this application as a Scala Play web app. Therefore, things went a bit unstructured. However, do not worry to know more about backend as well frontend, refer to the options trading application in `Chapter 7`, *Options Trading Using Q-Learning and Scala Play Framework*.

Running the Scala Play web app

To run the application, just follow these steps:

1. Download the historical Bitcoin data from `https://www.kaggle.com/ mczielinski/bitcoin-historical-data`. Then unzip and extract the `.csv` file.
2. Open your preferred IDE (for example, Eclipse/IntelliJ) and create the Maven or SBT project.

3. Run the `Preprocess.scala` script to convert the historical data into a time series. This script should generate two `.csv` files (that is, `scala_test_x.csv` and `scala_test_y.csv`).

4. Then train the `GradientBoostedTree` model (use `TrainGBT.scala` script) using the previously generated files.

5. Save the best (i.e. cross-validated) `Pipeline` model containing all the pipelines' steps.

6. Then download the Scala Play app and all the files (that is, `Bitcoin_price_prediction`) from the Packt repository or GitHub (see in the book).

7. Then copy the trained model to `Bitcoin_price_prediction/models/`.

8. Then: `$ cd Bitcoin_price_prediction/bitcoin_ml/conf/` and update the parameter values in the `application.conf` as shown earlier.

9. Finally, run the project using the `$ sudo sbt run` command.

After launching with `$ sudo sbt run`, the application will read all models from the `models` folder, the `etalon` model being specified by `ml.model_version`. Every 30 seconds (specified in `constants.frequency = 30` in `application.conf`), the latest price data is retrieved from the Cryptocompare API. A prediction using the `etalon` model is made and the results are shown to the user in the form of a log message in the console, with the possibility to trigger an HTTP request to the specified endpoint.

After that, all models from the `models` folder are used to make a prediction on the previous 22-minute data and use the latest price data for a current minute as a way to check the quality of predictions. All predictions made by each model are stored in a database file. When a user visits `http://localhost:9000`, a table with a summary of predictions is shown to the user:

- Model name
- TPR, (not rate actually, in this case, just raw count) - how many times model predicted that price would increase and how many times that was true
- FPR, how many times model has predicted price increase, but price dropped or stayed the same
- TNR, how many times model predicted non-increase of price and was correct
- FNR, how many times model predicted non-increase of price and was wrong
- Total count of predictions made by the model

Alright, here we go, after launching the app using $ sudo sbt `run` (on a terminal):

```
abel for timestamp: 1516836240Details: probability distribution: [0.6036457093603714,0.39635429063962857]
 label: 0.0 rawPrediction: [0.21033948366056338,-0.21033948366056338]
[info] application - we should not buy -> price will not increase ====> Signal
[info] application - SchedulerActor job runs at 1516836380451
[info] application - __cv__gbt_22_binary_classes_95522293.model has predicted 1 label, actual price delta
 was 0.1999999999989086
[info] application - __cv__gbt_22_binary_classes_94940481.model has predicted 1 label, actual price delta
 was 0.1999999999989086
[info] application - gbt_22_binary_classes_32660767.model has predicted 0 label, actual price delta was 0
.1999999999989086
[info] application - Predicting next price change: gbt_22_binary_classes_32660767.model has predicted 1 l
abel for timestamp: 1516836300Details: probability distribution: [0.46438621191794804,0.535613788082052]
Label: 1.0 rawPrediction: [-0.07134839872345475,0.07134839872345475] ====> Raw prediction
[info] application - we should buy -> price will go up
[info] application - SchedulerActor job runs at 1516836410452
[info] application - __cv__gbt_22_binary_classes_95522293.model has predicted 1 label, actual price delta
 was 0.1999999999989086
[info] application - __cv__gbt_22_binary_classes_94940481.model has predicted 1 label, actual price delta
 was 0.1999999999989086
[info] application - gbt_22_binary_classes_32660767.model has predicted 0 label, actual price delta was 0
.1999999999989086
[info] application - Predicting next price change: gbt_22_binary_classes_32660767.model has predicted 1 l
abel for timestamp: 1516836300Details: probability distribution: [0.46438621191794804,0.535613788082052]
label: 1.0 rawPrediction: [-0.07134839872345475,0.07134839872345475]
```

Figure 9: Sample signals generated by the model based on historical prices and live data

The preceding figure shows some sample signals generated by our model based on historical prices and live data. Additionally, we can see the raw prediction by the model. When you try to access the app from your browser at `http://localhost:9000`, you should see this (the count will increase with time, though):

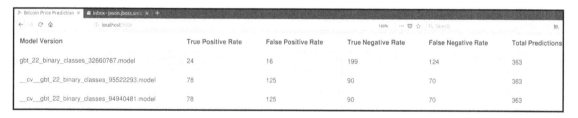

Model Version	True Positive Rate	False Positive Rate	True Negative Rate	False Negative Rate	Total Predictions
gbt_22_binary_classes_32660767.model	24	16	199	124	363
__cv__gbt_22_binary_classes_95522293.model	78	125	90	70	363
__cv__gbt_22_binary_classes_94940481.model	78	125	90	70	363

Figure 10: Model performance using the Scala Play2 framework

In the preceding figure, the performance is not satisfactory, but I would suggest that you train the model with the most suitable hyperparameters and for more iterations, for example, 10,000 times. Additionally, in the next section, I tried to provide some more insights and improvement guidelines.

Finally, if you plan to deploy this application after making some extension (if any), then I would suggest to take a quick look at the last section in `Chapter 7`, *Options Trading Using Q-Learning and Scala Play Framework*, where you will find deployment guideline on server to be exposed as web app.

Summary

In this chapter, a complete ML pipeline was implemented, from collecting historical data, to transforming it into a format suitable for testing hypotheses, training ML models, and running a prediction on `Live` data, and with the possibility to evaluate many different models and select the best one.

The test results showed that, as in the original dataset, about 600,000 minutes out of 2.4 million can be classified as **increasing price** (close price was higher than open price); the dataset can be considered imbalanced. Although random forests are usually performed well on an imbalanced dataset, the area under the ROC curve of 0.74 isn't best. As we need to have fewer false positives (fewer times when we trigger **purchase** and the price drops), we might consider a punishing model for such errors in a stricter way.

Although the results achieved by classifiers can't be used for profitable trading, there is a foundation on top of which new approaches can be tested in a relatively rapid way. Here, some possible directions for further development are listed:

- Implementation of the pipeline discussed in the beginning: Convert your time series data into several clusters and train the regression model/classifier for each of them; then classify recent data into one of the clusters and use the prediction model trained for that cluster. As by definition, ML is **deriving patterns from data**, there might not be only one pattern that fits all of the history of Bitcoin; that's why we need to understand that a market can be in different phases, and each phase has its own pattern.
- One of the major challenges with Bitcoin price prediction might be that the training data (historical) doesn't belong to the same distribution as test data during random splits into train-test sets. As the patterns in price changed during 2013 and 2016, they might belong to completely different distributions. It might require a manual inspection of data and some infographics. Probably, someone has already done this research.

- One of the main things to try would be to train two **one-versus-all** classifiers: one is trained to predict when the price grows higher than 20$, for example. Another predicts when the price drop by 20$; so it makes sense to take long/short positions, respectively.

- Maybe, predicting the delta of the next minute isn't what we need; we'd rather predict the average price. As the Open price can be much higher than last minute's Close price, and the Close price of the next minute can be slightly less than open but still higher than current, it would make it profitable trade. So how to exactly label data is also an open question.

- Try with different time-series window size (even 50 minutes might suit) using ARIMA time series prediction model, as it is one of the most widely used algorithms. Then try to predict price change, not for the next minute but for 2-3 following minutes. Additionally, try by incorporating trading volume as well.

- Label the data as **price increased** if the price was higher by 20$ during at least one of three following minutes so that we can make a profit from trade.

- Currently, `Scheduler` isn't synchronized with Cryptocompare minutes. This means we can get data about the minute interval 12:00:00 - 12:00:59 at any point of the following minute - 12:01:00 or 12:01:59. In the latter case, it doesn't make sense to make trade, as we made a prediction based on already **old** data.

- Instead of making a prediction every minute on **older** data to accumulate prediction results for `actor`, it's better to take maximum available HistoMinute data (seven days), split it into time series data using a Scala script that was used for historical data, and predict for seven days' worth of data. Run this as a scheduled job once a day; it should reduce the load on the DB and `PredictionActor`.

- Compared to usual datasets, where the order of rows doesn't matter much, in Bitcoin, historical data rows are sorted by ascending order of date, which means that:
  - Latest data might be more relevant to today's price, and less can be more; taking a smaller subset of data might give better performance
  - The ways of subsampling data can matter (splitting into train-test sets)
  - Finally try with LSTM network for even better predictive accuracy (see chapter 10 for some clue)

The understanding of variations in genome sequences assists us in identifying people who are predisposed to common diseases, solving rare diseases, and finding the corresponding population group of individuals from a larger population group. Although classical ML techniques allow researchers to identify groups (clusters) of related variables, the accuracy and effectiveness of these methods diminish for large and high-dimensional datasets such as the whole human genome. On the other hand, deep neural network architectures (the core of deep learning) can better exploit large-scale datasets to build complex models.

In the next chapter, we will see how to apply the K-means algorithm on large-scale genomic data from the 1,000 Genomes Project aiming at clustering genotypic variants at the population scale. Then we'll train an H2O-based deep learning model for predicting geographic ethnicity. Finally, Spark-based Random Forest will be used to enhance the predictive accuracy.

4
Population-Scale Clustering and Ethnicity Prediction

Understanding variations in genome sequences assists us in identifying people who are predisposed to common diseases, curing rare diseases, and finding the corresponding population group of individuals from a larger population group. Although classical machine learning techniques allow researchers to identify groups (that is, clusters) of related variables, the accuracy and effectiveness of these methods diminish for large and high-dimensional datasets such as the whole human genome.

On the other hand, **Deep Neural Networks (DNNs)** form the core of **deep learning (DL)** and provide algorithms to model complex, high-level abstractions in data. They can better exploit large-scale datasets to build complex models.

In this chapter, we apply the K-means algorithm to large-scale genomic data from the 1000 Genomes project analysis aimed at clustering genotypic variants at the population scale. Finally, we train an H2O-based DNN model and a Spark-based random forest model for predicting geographic ethnicity. The theme of this chapter is *give me your genetic variants data and I will tell your ethnicity*.

Nevertheless, we will configure H2O so that the same setting can be used in upcoming chapters too. Concisely, we will learn the following topics throughout this end-to-end project:

- Population-scale clustering and geographic ethnicity prediction
- The 1000 Genomes project, a deep catalog of human genetic variants
- Algorithms and tools

- Using K-means for population-scale clustering
- Using H2O for ethnicity prediction
- Using random forest for ethnicity prediction

Population scale clustering and geographic ethnicity

Next-generation genome sequencing (NGS) reduces overhead and time for genomic sequencing, leading to big data production in an unprecedented way. In contrast, analyzing this large-scale data is computationally expensive and increasingly becomes the key bottleneck. This increase in NGS data in terms of number of samples overall and features per sample demands solutions for massively parallel data processing, which imposes extraordinary challenges on machine learning solutions and bioinformatics approaches. The use of genomic information in medical practice requires efficient analytical methodologies to cope with data from thousands of individuals and millions of their variants.

One of the most important tasks is the analysis of genomic profiles to attribute individuals to specific ethnic populations, or the analysis of nucleotide haplotypes for disease susceptibility. The data from the 1000 Genomes project serves as the prime source to analyze genome-wide **single nucleotide polymorphisms** (SNPs) at scale for the prediction of the individual's ancestry with regards to continental and regional origins.

Machine learning for genetic variants

Research has revealed that population groups from Asia, Europe, Africa, and America can be separated based on their genomic data. However, it is more challenging to accurately predict the haplogroup and the continent of origin, that is, geography, ethnicity, and language. Other research shows that the Y chromosome lineage can be geographically localized, forming the evidence for (geographically) clustering the human alleles of the human genotypes.

Thus, the clustering of individuals is correlated with geographic origin and ancestry. Since race depends on ancestry as well, the clusters are also correlated with the more traditional concepts of race, but the correlation is not perfect since genetic variation occurs according to probabilistic principles. Therefore, it does not follow a continuous distribution in different races and rather overlaps across or spills into different populations.

As a result, the identification of ancestry, or even race, may prove to be useful for biomedical reasons, but any direct assessment of disease-related genetic variation will ultimately yield more accurate and beneficial information.

The datasets provided by various genomics projects, such as **The Cancer Genome Atlas (TCGA)**, **International Cancer Genome Consortium (ICGC)**, **1000 Genomes Projects**, and **Personal Genome Project (PGP)**, dispose of large-scale data. For fast processing of such data, ADAM and Spark-based solutions have been proposed and are now widely used in genomics data analytics research.

Spark forms the most efficient data-processing framework and, in addition, provides primitives for in-memory cluster computing, for example, for querying the user data repeatedly. This makes Spark an excellent candidate for machine learning algorithms that outperform the Hadoop-based MapReduce framework. By using the genetic variants dataset from the 1000 Genomes project, we will try to answer the following questions:

- How is human genetic variation distributed geographically among different population groups?
- Can we use the genomic profile of individuals to attribute them to specific populations or derive disease susceptibility from their nucleotide haplotype?
- Is the individual's genomic data suitable to predict geographic origin (that is, the population group for an individual)?

In this project, we addressed the preceding questions in a scalable and more efficient way. Particularly, we examined how we applied Spark and ADAM for large-scale data processing, H2O for K-means clustering of the whole population to determine inter- and intra-population groups, and MLP-based supervised learning by tuning more hyperparameters to more accurately predict the population group for an individual according to the individual's genomic data. Do not worry at this point; we will provide the technical details on working with these technologies in a later section.

However, before getting started, let's take a brief journey to the 1000 Genomes Project dataset to provide you with some justification on why interoperating these technologies is really important.

1000 Genomes Projects dataset description

The data from the 1000 Genomes project is a very large catalog of human genetic variants. The project aims to determine genetic variants with frequencies higher than 1% in the populations studied. The data has been made openly available and freely accessible through public data repositories to scientists worldwide. Also, the data from the 1000 Genomes project is widely used to screen variants discovered in exome data from individuals with genetic disorders and in cancer genome projects.

The genotype dataset in **Variant Call Format** (**VCF**) provides the data of human individuals (that is, samples) and their genetic variants, and in addition, the global allele frequencies as well as the ones for the super populations. The data denotes the population's region for each sample which is used for the predicted category in our approach. Specific chromosomal data (in VCF format) may have additional information denoting the super-population of the sample or the sequencing platform used. For multiallelic variants, each alternative **allele frequency** (**AF**) is presented in a comma-separated list, shown as follows:

```
1 15211 rs78601809 T G 100 PASS AC=3050;
 AF=0.609026;
 AN=5008;
 NS=2504;
 DP=32245;
 EAS_AF=0.504;
 AMR_AF=0.6772;
 AFR_AF=0.5371;
 EUR_AF=0.7316;
 SAS_AF=0.6401;
 AA=t|||;
 VT=SNP
```

The AF is calculated as the quotient of **Allele Count** (**AC**) and **Allele Number** (**AN**) and NS is the total number of samples with data, whereas _AF denotes the AF for a specific region.

The 1000 Genomes Project started in 2008; the consortium consisted of more than 400 life scientists and phase 3 finished in September 2014 covering 2,504 individuals from 26 populations (that is, ethnic backgrounds) in total. In total, over 88 million variants (84.7 million **single nucleotide polymorphisms** (**SNPs**), 3.6 million short insertions/deletions (indels), and 60,000 structural variants) have been identified as high-quality haplotypes.

In short, 99.9% of the variants consist of SNPs and short indels. Less important variants—including SNPs, indels, deletions, complex short substitutions, and other structural variant classes—have been removed for quality control. As a result, the third phase release leaves 84.4 million variants.

Each of the 26 populations has about 60-100 individuals from Europe, Africa, America (South and North), and Asia (South and East). The population samples are grouped into super-population groups according to their predominant ancestry: East Asian (**CHB**, **JPT**, **CHS**, **CDX**, and **KHV**), European (**CEU**, **TSI**, **FIN**, **GBR**, and **IBS**), African (**YRI**, **LWK**, **GWD**, **MSL**, **ESN**, **ASW**, and **ACB**), American (**MXL**, **PUR**, **CLM**, and **PEL**), and South Asian (**GIH**, **PJL**, **BEB**, **STU**, and **ITU**). For details, refer to *Figure 1*:

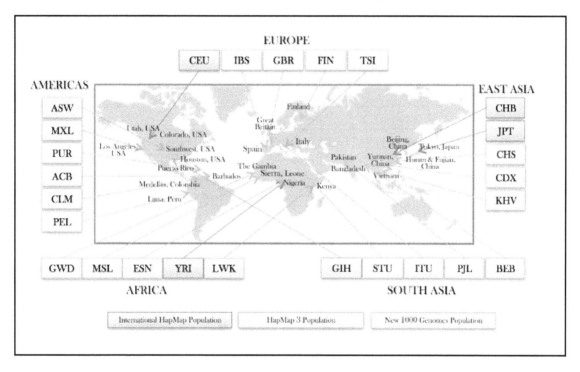

Figure 1: Geographic ethnic groups from 1000 Genomes project's release 3 (source http://www.internationalgenome.org/)

The released datasets provide the data for 2,504 healthy adults (18 years and older, third project phase); only reads with at least 70 **base pairs** (**bp**) have been used until more advanced solutions are available. All genomic data from all samples were combined to attribute all variants to a region. However, note that specific haplotypes may not occur in the genomes of a particular region; that is, the multi-sample approach allows attributing variants to an individual's genotype even if the variants are not covered by sequencing reads from that sample.

In other words, overlapping reads are provided and the single sample genomes have not necessarily been consolidated. All individuals were sequenced using both of these:

- Whole-genome sequencings (*mean depth = 7.4x*, where x is the number of reads, on average, that are likely to be aligned at a given reference *bp*)
- Targeted exome sequencing (*mean depth = 65.7x*)

In addition, individuals and their first-degree relatives such as an adult offspring were genotyped using high-density SNP microarrays. Each genotype comprises all 23 chromosomes and a separate panel file denotes the sample and population information. *Table 1* gives an overview of the different releases of the 1000 Genomes project:

Table 1 – Statistics of the 1000 Genomes project's genotype dataset (source: `http://www.internationalgenome.org/data`)

1000 genome release	Variants	Individual	Populations	File format
Phase 3	Phase 3	2,504	26	VCF
Phase 1	37.9 million	1,092	14	VCF
Pilot	14.8 million	179	4	VCF

The AF in the five super-population groups, **EAS=East Asian**, **EUR=European**, **AFR=African**, **AMR=American**, **SAS=South Asian** populations are calculated from allele numbers (AN, range= [0, 1]).

See the details of the panel file at `ftp://ftp.1000genomes.ebi.ac.uk/vol1/ftp/release/20130502/integrated_call_samples_v3.20130502.ALL.panel`.

Algorithms, tools, and techniques

Large-scale data from release 3 of the 1000 Genomes project contributes to 820 GB of data. Therefore, ADAM and Spark are used to pre-process and prepare the data (that is, training, testing, and validation sets) for the MLP and K-means models in a scalable way. Sparkling water transforms the data between H2O and Spark.

Then, K-means clustering, the MLP (using H2O) are trained. For the clustering and classification analysis, the genotypic information from each sample is required using the sample ID, variation ID, and the count of the alternate alleles where the majority of variants that we used were SNPs and indels.

Now, we should know the minimum info about each tool used such as ADAM, H2O, and some background information on the algorithms such as K-means, MLP for clustering, and classifying the population groups.

H2O and Sparkling water

H2O is an AI platform for machine learning. It offers a rich set of machine learning algorithms and a web-based data processing UI that comes as both open sources as well as commercial. Using H2O, it's possible to develop machine learning and DL applications with a wide range of languages, such as Java, Scala, Python, and R:

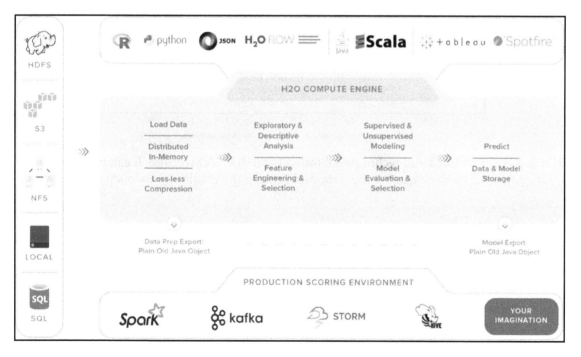

Figure 2: The H2O compute engine and available features (source: https://h2o.ai/)

It also has the ability to interface with Spark, HDFS, SQL, and NoSQL databases. In short, H2O works with R, Python, and Scala on Hadoop/Yarn, Spark, or laptop. On the other hand, Sparkling water combines the fast, scalable ML algorithms of H2O with the capabilities of Spark. It drives the computation from Scala/R/Python and utilizes the H2O flow UI. In short, Sparkling *water = H2O + Spark*.

Throughout the next few chapters, we will explore and the wide rich features of H2O and Sparkling water; however, I believe it would be useful to provide a diagram of all of the functional areas that it covers:

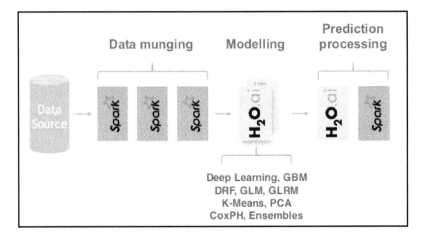

Figure 3: A glimpse of available algorithms and the supported ETL techniques (source: https://h20.ai/)

This is a list of features and techniques curated from the H2O website. It can be used for wrangling data, modeling using the data, and scoring the resulting models:

- Process
- Model
- The scoring tool
- Data profiling
- **Generalized linear models (GLM)**
- Predict
- Summary statistics
- Decision trees
- Confusion matrix
- Aggregate, filter, bin, and derive columns
- **Gradient boosting machine (GBM)**

- AUC
- Slice, log transform, and anonymize
- K-means
- Hit ratio
- Variable creation
- Anomaly detection
- PCA/PCA score
- DL
- Multimodel scoring
- Training and validation sampling plan
- Naive Bayes
- Grid search

The following figure shows how to provide a clear method of describing the way in which H2O Sparkling water can be used to extend the functionality of Apache Spark. Both H2O and Spark are open source systems. Spark MLlib contains a great deal of functionality, while H2O extends this with a wide range of extra functionalities, including DL. It offers tools to transform, model, and score the data, as we can find in Spark ML. It also offers a web-based user interface to interact with:

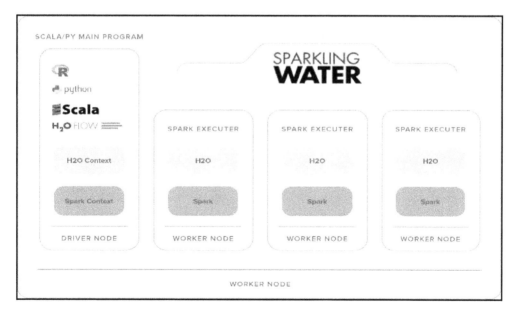

Figure 4: Sparkling water extends H2O and interoperates with Spark (source: https://h2o.ai/)

The following figure shows how H2O integrates with Spark. As we already know, Spark has master and worker servers; the workers create executors to do the actual work. The following steps occur to run a Sparkling water-based application:

- Spark's submit command sends the Sparkling water JAR to the Spark master
- The Spark master starts the workers and distributes the JAR file
- The Spark workers start the executor JVMs to carry out the work
- The Spark executor starts an H2O instance

The H2O instance is embedded with the Executor JVM, and so it shares the JVM heap space with Spark. When all of the H2O instances have started, H2O forms a cluster, and then the H2O flow web interface is made available:

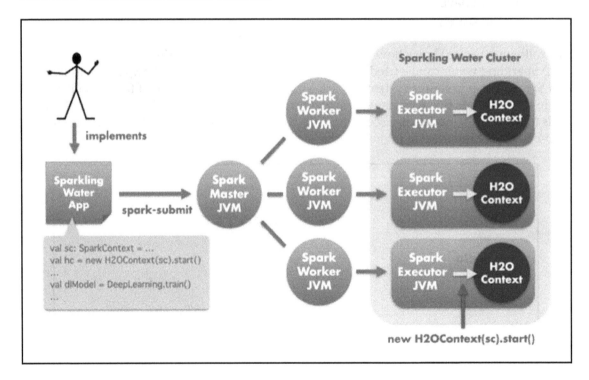

Figure 5: How Sparkling water fits into the Spark architecture (source:
http://blog.cloudera.com/blog/2015/10/how-to-build-a-machine-learning-app-using-sparkling-water-and-apache-spark/)

The preceding figure explains how H2O fits into the Spark architecture and how it starts, but what about data sharing? Now the question would be: how does data pass between Spark and H2O? The following diagram explains this:

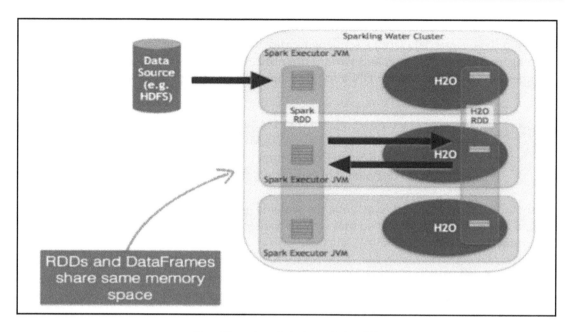

Figure 6: Data passing mechanism between Spark and H2O

To get a clearer view of the preceding figure, a new H2O RDD data structure has been created for H2O and Sparkling water. It is a layer based at the top of an H2O frame, each column of which represents a data item and is independently compressed to provide the best compression ratio.

ADAM for large-scale genomics data processing

Analyzing DNA and RNA sequencing data requires large-scale data processing to interpret the data according to its context. Excellent tools and solutions have been developed at academic labs, but often fall short on scalability and interoperability. By this means, ADAM is a genomics analysis platform with specialized file formats built using Apache Avro, Apache Spark and Parquet.

However, large-scale data processing solutions such as ADAM-Spark can be applied directly to the output data from a sequencing pipeline, that is, after quality control, mapping, read preprocessing, and variant quantification using single sample data. Some examples are DNA variants for DNA sequencing, read counts for RNA sequencing, and so on.

 See more at `http://bdgenomics.org/` and the related publication: Massie, Matt and Nothaft, Frank et al., ADAM: Genomics Formats and Processing Patterns for Cloud Scale Computing, UCB/EECS-2013-207, EECS Department, University of California, Berkeley.

In our study, ADAM is used to achieve the scalable genomics data analytics platform with support for the VCF file format so that we can transform genotype-based RDD into a Spark DataFrame.

Unsupervised machine learning

Unsupervised learning is a type of machine learning algorithm used for grouping related data objects and finding hidden patterns by inferencing from unlabeled datasets—that is, training sets consisting of input data without labels.

Let's see a real-life example. Suppose you have a large collection of non-pirated and totally legal MP3 files in a crowded and massive folder on your hard drive. Now, what if you could build a predictive model that helps you automatically group together similar songs and organize them into your favorite categories, such as country, rap, and rock?

This is an act of assigning an item to a group so that an MP3 is added to the respective playlist in an unsupervised way. For classification, we assume that you are given a training dataset of correctly labeled data. Unfortunately, we do not always have that luxury when we collect data in the real world.

For example, suppose we would like to divide a huge collection of music into interesting playlists. How can we possibly group together songs if we do not have direct access to their metadata? One possible approach is a mixture of various ML techniques, but clustering is often at the heart of the solution:

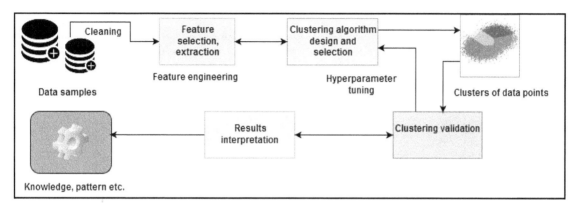

Figure 7: Clustering data samples at a glance

In other words, the main objective of unsupervised learning algorithms is to explore unknown/hidden patterns in input data that is unlabeled. Unsupervised learning, however, also comprehends other techniques to explain the key features of the data in an exploratory way to find the hidden patterns. To overcome this challenge, clustering techniques are used widely to group unlabeled data points based on certain similarity measures in an unsupervised way.

Population genomics and clustering

Clustering analysis is about dividing data samples or data points and putting them into corresponding homogeneous classes or clusters. Thus, a simple definition of clustering can be thought of as the process of organizing objects into groups whose members are similar in some way, as shown in.

This way, a cluster is a collection of objects that have some similarity between them and are dissimilar to the objects belonging to other clusters. If collections of genetic variants are given, clustering algorithms put these objects into a group based on similarity—that is, population groups or super-population groups.

How does K-means work?

A clustering algorithm, such as K-means, locates the centroid of the group of data points. However, to make clustering accurate and effective, the algorithm evaluates the distance between each point from the centroid of the cluster.

Eventually, the goal of clustering is to determine intrinsic grouping in a set of unlabeled data. For example, the K-means algorithm tries to cluster related data points within the predefined **three** (that is, $k = 3$) clusters as shown in *Figure 8*:

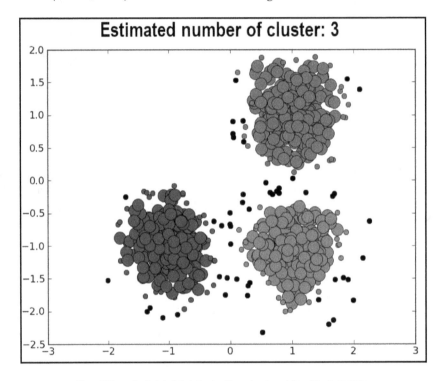

Figure 8: The results of a typical clustering algorithm and a representation of the cluster centers

In our case, using a combined approach of Spark, ADAM and H2O are capable of processing large amounts of variant data points. Suppose, we have n data points (x_i, i=1, 2... n, example, genetic variants) that need to be partitioned into *k* clusters. Then K-means assigns a cluster to each data point and aiming to find the positions μ_i, i=1...k of the clusters that minimize the distance from the data points to the cluster. Mathematically, K-means tries to achieve the goal by solving an equation—that is, an optimization problem:

$$arg\ \min_c \sum_{i=1}^{k} \sum_{X \in c_i} d(X, \mu_i) = arg\ \min_c \sum_{i=1}^{k} \sum_{X \in c_i} ||X - \mu_i||_2^2$$

In the preceding equation, c_i is the set of data points that assigned to cluster *i* and $d(x, \mu_i) = ||x - \mu_i||_2^2$ is the Euclidean distance to be calculated. The algorithm computes this distance between data points and the center of the k clusters by minimizing the **Within-Cluster Sum of Squares** (that is, **WCSS**), where c_i is the set of points belonging to cluster *i*.

Therefore, we can understand that the overall clustering operation using K-means is not a trivial one but an NP-hard optimization problem. Which also means that K-means algorithm not only tries to find the global minima but also often is stuck in different solutions. The K-means algorithm proceeds by alternating between two steps:

- **Cluster assignment step**: Assign each observation to the cluster whose mean yields the least **WCSS**. The sum of squares is the squared Euclidean distance.
- **Centroid update step**: Calculate the new means to be the centroids of the observations in the new clusters.

In a nutshell, the overall approach of K-means training can be described in following figure:

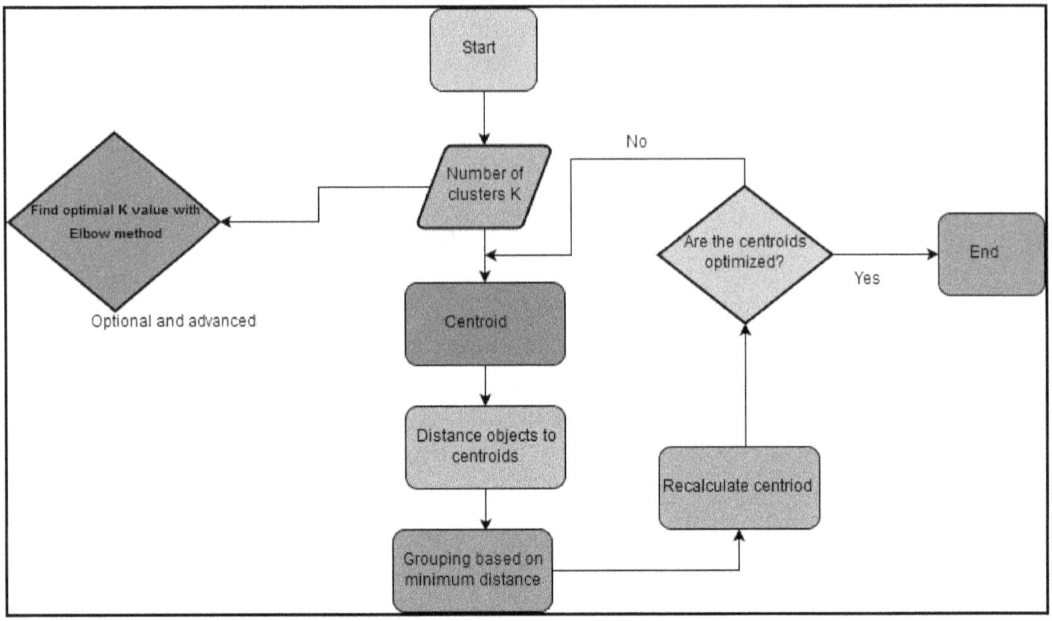

Figure 9: Overall approach of the K-means algorithm process

DNNs for geographic ethnicity prediction

Multilayer Perceptron (**MLP**) is an example of a DNN that is a feed-forward neural network; that is, there are only connections between the neurons from different layers. There is one (pass through) input layer, one or more layers of **linear threshold units** (**LTUs**) (called **hidden layers**), and one final layer of LTUs (called the **output layer**).

Each layer, excluding the output layer, involves a bias neuron and is fully connected to the next layer, forming a fully connected bipartite graph. The signal flows exclusively from the input to the output, that is, one-directional (**feed-forward**).

Until recently, an MLP was trained using the back-propagation training algorithm, but now the optimized version (that is, Gradient Descent) uses a reverse-mode auto diff; that is, the neural networks are trained with SGD using back-propagation as a gradient computing technique. Two layers of abstraction are used in DNN training for solving classification problems:

- **Gradient computation**: Using back-propagation
- **Optimization level**: Using SGD, ADAM, RMSPro, and Momentum optimizers to compute the gradient computed earlier

In each training cycle, the algorithm feeds the data into the network and computes the state and output for every neuron in the consecutive layers. The approach then measures the output error over the network, that is, the gap between the expected output and the current output, and the contribution from each neuron in the last hidden layer towards the neuron's output error.

Iteratively, the output error is propagated back to the input layer through all hidden layers and the error gradient is calculated across all connection weights during backward propagation:

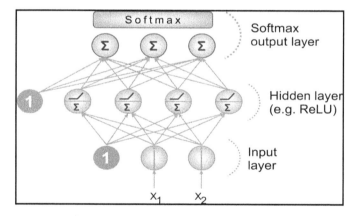

Figure 10: A modern MLP consisting of input layer, ReLU, and softmax

For a multiclass classification task, the output layer is typically determined by a shared softmax function (see *Figure 2* for more) in contrast to individual activation functions, and each output neuron provides the estimated probability for the corresponding class.

Additionally, we will be using tree ensembles such as random forest for the classification. At this moment, I believe we can skip the basic introduction of RF since we have covered it in detail in Chapter 1, *Analyzing Insurance Severity Claims*, Chapter 2, *Analyzing and Predicting Telecommunication Churn*, and Chapter 3, *High-Frequency Bitcoin Price Prediction from Historical Data*. Well, it is time for the being stared. Nonetheless, it is always good to have your programming environment ready before getting your hands dirty.

Configuring programming environment

In this section, we describe how to configure our programming environment so that we can interoperate with Spark, H2O, and Adam. Note that using H2O on a laptop or desktop is quite resource intensive. Therefore, make sure that your laptop has at least 16 GB of RAM and enough storage.

Anyway, I am going to make this project a Maven project on Eclipse. However, you can try to define the same dependencies in SBT too. Let us define the properties tag on a `pom.xml` file for a Maven-friendly project:

```
<properties>
    <spark.version>2.2.1</spark.version>
    <scala.version>2.11.12</scala.version>
    <h2o.version>3.16.0.2</h2o.version>
    <sparklingwater.version>2.2.6</sparklingwater.version>
    <adam.version>0.23.0</adam.version>
</properties>
```

Then we can the latest version of the Spark 2.2.1 version (any 2.x version or even higher should work fine):

```
<dependency>
    <groupId>org.apache.spark</groupId>
    <artifactId>spark-core_2.11</artifactId>
    <version>${spark.version}</version>
</dependency>
```

Then we need to declare the dependencies for H2O and Sparkling water that match the version specified in the properties tag. Later versions might also work, and you can try:

```
<dependency>
    <groupId>ai.h2o</groupId>
    <artifactId>sparkling-water-core_2.11</artifactId>
    <version>2.2.6</version>
</dependency>
<dependency>
```

```
    <groupId>ai.h2o</groupId>
    <artifactId>sparkling-water-examples_2.11</artifactId>
    <version>2.2.6</version>
</dependency>
<dependency>
    <groupId>ai.h2o</groupId>
    <artifactId>h2o-core</artifactId>
    <version>${h2o.version}</version>
</dependency>
<dependency>
    <groupId>ai.h2o</groupId>
    <artifactId>h2o-scala_2.11</artifactId>
    <version>${h2o.version}</version>
</dependency>
<dependency>
    <groupId>ai.h2o</groupId>
    <artifactId>h2o-algos</artifactId>
    <version>${h2o.version}</version>
</dependency>
<dependency>
    <groupId>ai.h2o</groupId>
    <artifactId>h2o-app</artifactId>
    <version>${h2o.version}</version>
</dependency>
<dependency>
    <groupId>ai.h2o</groupId>
    <artifactId>h2o-persist-hdfs</artifactId>
    <version>${h2o.version}</version>
</dependency>
<dependency>
    <groupId>ai.h2o</groupId>
    <artifactId>google-analytics-java</artifactId>
    <version>1.1.2-H2O-CUSTOM</version>
</dependency>
```

Finally, let's define ADAM and its dependencies:

```
<dependency>
    <groupId>org.bdgenomics.adam</groupId>
    <artifactId>adam-core_2.11</artifactId>
    <version>0.23.0</version>
</dependency>
```

When I tried this on a Windows machine, additionally I had to install `joda-time` dependencies. Let us do it (but depending your platform, it might not be needed):

```
<dependency>
    <groupId>joda-time</groupId>
```

```
      <artifactId>joda-time</artifactId>
      <version>2.9.9</version>
</dependency>
```

Once you create a Maven project in Eclipse (manually from the IDE or using $ mvn install), all the required dependencies will be downloaded! We are ready to code now!

Wait! How about seeing the UI of H2O on the browser? For this, we have to manually download the H2O JAR somewhere in our computer and run it as a regular .jar file. In short, it's a three-way process:

- Download the **Latest Stable Release** H$_2$O from https://www.h2o.ai/download/. Then unzip it; it contains everything you need to get started.
- From your terminal/command prompt, run the .jar using java -jar h2o.jar.
- Point your browser to http://localhost:54321:

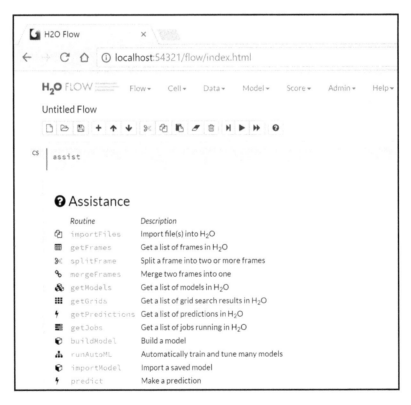

Figure 11: The UI of H2O FLOW

This shows the available features of the latest version (that is, h2o-3.16.0.4 as of 19 January 2018) of H2O. However, I am not going to explain everything here, so let's stop exploring because I believe for the time being this much knowledge about H2O and Sparking water will be enough.

Data pre-processing and feature engineering

I already stated that all the 24 VCF files contribute 820 GB of data. Therefore, I decided to use the genetic variant of chromosome Y only one two make the demonstration clearer. The size is around 160 MB, which is not meant to pose huge computational challenges. You can download all the VCF files as well as the panel file from `ftp://ftp.1000genomes.ebi.ac.uk/vol1/ftp/release/20130502/`.

Let us get started. We start by creating `SparkSession`, the gateway for the Spark application:

```
val spark:SparkSession = SparkSession
    .builder()
    .appName("PopStrat")
    .master("local[*]")
    .config("spark.sql.warehouse.dir", "C:/Exp/")
    .getOrCreate()
```

Then let's show Spark the path of both VCF and the panel file:

```
val genotypeFile =
"<path>/ALL.chrY.phase3_integrated_v2a.20130502.genotypes.vcf"
val panelFile = "<path>/integrated_call_samples_v3.20130502.ALL.panel "
```

We process the panel file using Spark to access the target population data and identify the population groups. We first create a set of the populations that we want to predict:

```
val populations = Set("FIN", "GBR", "ASW", "CHB", "CLM")
```

Then we need to create a map of sample ID → population so that we can filter out the samples we are not interested in:

```
def extract(file: String,
filter: (String, String) => Boolean): Map[String, String] = {
Source
    .fromFile(file)
    .getLines()
    .map(line => {
val tokens = line.split(Array('t', ' ')).toList
```

```
tokens(0) -> tokens(1)
}).toMap.filter(tuple => filter(tuple._1, tuple._2))
}

val panel: Map[String, String] = extract(
panelFile,
(sampleID: String, pop: String) => populations.contains(pop))
```

Note that the panel file produces the sample ID of all individuals, population groups, ethnicities, super population groups, and the genders shown as follows:

Sample ID	Pop Group	Ethnicity	Super pop. group	Gender
HG00096	GBR	British in England and Scotland	EUR	male
HG00171	FIN	Finnish in Finland	EUR	female
HG00472	CHS	Southern Han Chinese	EAS	male
HG00551	PUR	Puerto Ricans from Puerto Rico	AMR	female

Figure 12: Contents of a sample panel file

Then load the ADAM genotypes and filter the genotypes so that we're left with only those in the populations we're interested in:

```
val allGenotypes: RDD[Genotype] = sc.loadGenotypes(genotypeFile).rdd
val genotypes: RDD[Genotype] = allGenotypes.filter(genotype => {
    panel.contains(genotype.getSampleId)
    })
```

The next job would be converting the `Genotype` objects into our own `SampleVariant` objects to try to conserve memory. Then, the `genotype` object is converted into a `SampleVariant` object that contains only the data we need for further processing: the sample ID, which uniquely identifies a particular sample; a variant ID, which uniquely identifies a particular genetic variant; and a count of alternate alleles (only when the sample differs from the reference genome).

The signature that prepares a sample variant is given here; it takes `sampleID`, `variationId`, and the `alternateCount`:

```
case class SampleVariant(sampleId: String,
        variantId: Int,
        alternateCount: Int)
```

Alright! Let us find `variantID` from the `genotype` file. A `varitantId` is a `String` type consisting of the name, start, and the end position in the chromosome:

```
def variantId(genotype: Genotype): String = {
    val name = genotype.getVariant.getContigName
    val start = genotype.getVariant.getStart
    val end = genotype.getVariant.getEnd
  s"$name:$start:$end"
}
```

Once we have the `variantID`, we should hunt for the alternate count. In the `genotype` file, the objects that do not have an allele reference are roughly genetic alternates:

```
def alternateCount(genotype: Genotype): Int = {
    genotype.getAlleles.asScala.count(_ != GenotypeAllele.REF)
  }
```

Lastly, we construct a simple variant object. For this, we need to intern sample IDs as they will be repeated a lot in a VCF file:

```
def toVariant(genotype: Genotype): SampleVariant = {
    new SampleVariant(genotype.getSampleId.intern(),
            variantId(genotype).hashCode(),
            alternateCount(genotype))
      }
```

Excellent! We have been able to construct simple variants. Now, the next challenging task is to prepare `variantsRDD` before we are able to create the `variantsBySampleId` RDD:

```
val variantsRDD: RDD[SampleVariant] = genotypes.map(toVariant)
```

Then we have to group the variants by sample ID so that we can process the variants sample by sample. After that, we can get the total number of samples to be used to find variants that are missing for some samples. Lastly, we have to group the variants by variant ID and filter out those variants that are missing from some samples:

```
val variantsBySampleId: RDD[(String, Iterable[SampleVariant])] =
variantsRDD.groupBy(_.sampleId)

val sampleCount: Long = variantsBySampleId.count()
println("Found " + sampleCount + " samples")

val variantsByVariantId: RDD[(Int, Iterable[SampleVariant])] =
variantsRDD.groupBy(_.variantId).filter {
        case (_, sampleVariants) => sampleVariants.size == sampleCount
    }
```

Now let's make a map of variant ID → count of samples with an alternate count of greater than zero. Then we filter out those variants that are not in our desired frequency range. The objective here is simply to reduce the number of dimensions in the dataset to make it easier to train the model:

```
val variantFrequencies: collection.Map[Int, Int] = variantsByVariantId
.map {
    case (variantId, sampleVariants) =>
        (variantId, sampleVariants.count(_.alternateCount > 0))
        }.collectAsMap()
```

The total number of samples (or individuals) has been determined before grouping them based on their variant IDs and filtering out variants without support by the samples to simplify the data pre-processing and to better cope with the very large number of variants (in total 84.4 million).

Figure 13 shows a conceptual view of a genotype variants collection in the 1000 Genomes project and exposes the feature extraction process from the same data to train our K-means and MLP models:

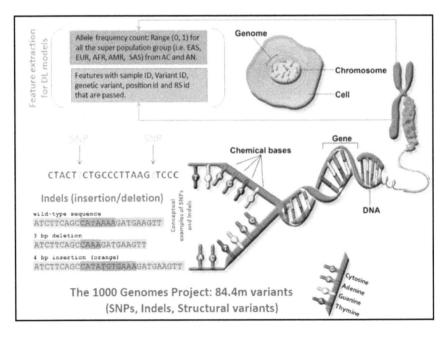

Figure 13: Conceptual view of the genotype variants collection in the 1000 Genomes project

The specified range is arbitrary and was chosen because it includes a reasonable number of variants, but not too many. To be more specific, for each variant, the frequency for alternate alleles have been calculated, and variants with less than 12 alternate alleles have been excluded, leaving about 3 million variants in the analysis (for 23 chromosome files):

```
val permittedRange = inclusive(11, 11)
val filteredVariantsBySampleId: RDD[(String, Iterable[SampleVariant])] =
    variantsBySampleId.map {
        case (sampleId, sampleVariants) =>
        val filteredSampleVariants = sampleVariants.filter(
        variant =>
        permittedRange.contains(
        variantFrequencies.getOrElse(variant.variantId, -1)))
    (sampleId, filteredSampleVariants)
    }
```

Once we has `filteredVariantsBySampleId`, the next task is to sort the variants for each sample ID. Each sample should now have the same number of sorted variants:

```
val sortedVariantsBySampleId: RDD[(String, Array[SampleVariant])] =
    filteredVariantsBySampleId.map {
        case (sampleId, variants) =>
        (sampleId, variants.toArray.sortBy(_.variantId))
        }
    println(s"Sorted by Sample ID RDD: " +
sortedVariantsBySampleId.first())
```

All items in the RDD should now have the same variants in the same order. The final task is to use `sortedVariantsBySampleId` to construct an RDD of `Row` containing the region and the alternate count:

```
val rowRDD: RDD[Row] = sortedVariantsBySampleId.map {
    case (sampleId, sortedVariants) =>
        val region: Array[String] = Array(panel.getOrElse(sampleId,
"Unknown"))
        val alternateCounts: Array[Int] =
sortedVariants.map(_.alternateCount)
        Row.fromSeq(region ++ alternateCounts)
        }
```

Therefore, we can just use the first one to construct our header for the training data frame:

```
val header = StructType(
        Seq(StructField("Region", StringType)) ++
        sortedVariantsBySampleId
            .first()
            ._2
```

```
        .map(variant => {
            StructField(variant.variantId.toString, IntegerType)
}))
```

Well done! Up to this point, we have our RDD and the header `StructType`. So now, we can play with both H2O and the Spark deep/machine learning algorithm with minimal adjustment/conversion. The overall flow of this end-to-end project can be seen in the following figure:

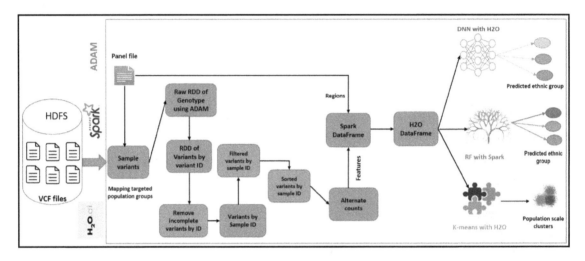

Figure 14: The pipeline of the overall approach

Model training and hyperparameter tuning

Once we have `rowRDD` and the header, the next task is to construct the rows of our Schema DataFrame from the variants using the header and `rowRDD`:

```
val sqlContext = spark.sqlContext
val schemaDF = sqlContext.createDataFrame(rowRDD, header)
schemaDF.printSchema()
schemaDF.show(10)
>>>
```

```
+------+-----------+-----------+-----------+-----------+-----------+-----------+
|Region|-2099651974|-2086354790|-2051555302|-2033308294|-2031516326|-1948345126|
+------+-----------+-----------+-----------+-----------+-----------+-----------+
|   GBR|          1|          1|          0|          0|          0|          0|
|   CHB|          0|          0|          0|          0|          0|          0|
|   CHB|          0|          0|          0|          0|          0|          0|
|   ASW|          0|          0|          0|          0|          0|          0|
|   ASW|          0|          0|          0|          0|          0|          0|
|   CHB|          0|          0|          0|          0|          0|          0|
|   ASW|          0|          0|          0|          0|          0|          1|
|   GBR|          0|          0|          0|          0|          0|          0|
|   ASW|          0|          0|          0|          0|          0|          0|
|   ASW|          0|          0|          0|          0|          0|          1|
+------+-----------+-----------+-----------+-----------+-----------+-----------+
only showing top 10 rows
```

Figure 15: A snapshot of the training dataset containing features and the label (that is, Region) columns

In the preceding DataFrame, only a few columns, including the label, are shown so that it fits on the page.

Spark-based K-means for population-scale clustering

In a previous section, we have seen how the K-means work. So we can directly dive into the implementation. Since the training will be unsupervised, we need to drop the label column (that is, `Region`):

```
val sqlContext = sparkSession.sqlContext
val schemaDF = sqlContext.createDataFrame(rowRDD, header).drop("Region")
schemaDF.printSchema()
schemaDF.show(10)
>>>
```

```
+-----------+-----------+-----------+-----------+-----------+-----------+-----------+-----------+
|-2099651974|-2086354790|-2051555302|-2033308294|-2031516326|-1948345126|-1933334022|-1900872614|
+-----------+-----------+-----------+-----------+-----------+-----------+-----------+-----------+
|          1|          1|          0|          0|          0|          0|          0|          0|
|          0|          0|          0|          0|          0|          0|          0|          0|
|          0|          0|          0|          0|          0|          0|          0|          0|
|          0|          0|          0|          0|          0|          0|          0|          0|
|          0|          0|          0|          0|          0|          0|          0|          0|
|          0|          0|          0|          0|          0|          0|          0|          0|
|          0|          0|          0|          0|          0|          1|          0|          0|
|          0|          0|          0|          0|          0|          0|          0|          0|
|          0|          0|          0|          0|          0|          0|          1|          0|
|          0|          0|          0|          0|          0|          1|          1|          0|
+-----------+-----------+-----------+-----------+-----------+-----------+-----------+-----------+
```

Figure 16: A snapshot of the training dataset for K-means without the label (that is, Region)

Now, we have seen in Chapters 1, *Analyzing Insurance Severity Claims* and Chapter 2, *Analyzing and Predicting Telecommunication Churn* that Spark expects two columns (that is, features and label) for supervised training, and for unsupervised training, it expects only a single column containing the features. Since we dropped the label column, we now need to amalgamate the entire variable column into a single features column. So for this, we will again use the VectorAssembler() transformer. At first, let's select the columns to be embedded into a vector space:

```
val featureCols = schemaDF.columns
```

Then we instantiate the VectorAssembler() transformer, specifying the input columns and the output column:

```
val assembler =
new VectorAssembler()
    .setInputCols(featureCols)
    .setOutputCol("features")
val assembleDF = assembler.transform(schemaDF).select("features")
```

Now let's see how it looks:

```
assembleDF.show()
>>>
```

```
+--------------------+
|            features|
+--------------------+
|(59,[0,1],[1.0,1.0])|
|(59,[35,51],[1.0,...|
|(59,[39,42],[1.0,...|
|(59,[11,16,18,28,...|
|(59,[9,16],[1.0,1...|
|(59,[28,35],[1.0,...|
|(59,[5,9,10,16,28...|
|    (59,[17],[1.0])|
|(59,[6,9,13,21,44...|
|(59,[5,6,18,19,21...|
|    (59,[31],[1.0])|
|(59,[6,11,51],[1....|
|(59,[13,38,39],[1...|
|(59,[11,17,28,35,...|
|    (59,[35],[1.0])|
|    (59,[12],[1.0])|
|     (59,[2],[1.0])|
|(59,[6,10,38,43,4...|
|(59,[0,1,29,34,51...|
|(59,[21,26],[1.0,...|
+--------------------+
only showing top 20 rows
```

Figure 17: A snapshot of the feature vectors for the K-means

Since our dataset is very highly dimensional, we can use some dimensionality algorithms such as PCA. So let's do it by instantiating a PCA() transformer as follows:

```
val pca =
new PCA()
    .setInputCol("features")
    .setOutputCol("pcaFeatures")
    .setK(50)
    .fit(assembleDF)
```

Then we transform the assembled DataFrame (that is, assembled) and the top 50 principle components. You can adjust the number though. Finally, to avoid the ambiguity, we renamed the pcaFeatures column to features:

```
val pcaDF = pca.transform(assembleDF)
            .select("pcaFeatures")
            .withColumnRenamed("pcaFeatures", "features")
pcaDF.show()
>>>
```

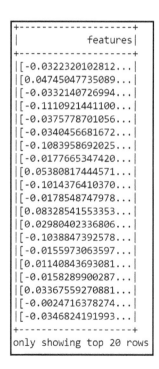

```
+--------------------+
|            features|
+--------------------+
|[-0.0322320102812...|
|[0.04745047735089...|
|[-0.0332140726994...|
|[-0.1110921441100...|
|[-0.0375778701056...|
|[-0.0340456681672...|
|[-0.1083958692025...|
|[-0.0177665347420...|
|[0.05380817444571...|
|[-0.1014376410370...|
|[-0.0178548747978...|
|[0.08328541553353...|
|[0.02980402336806...|
|[-0.1038847392578...|
|[-0.0155973063597...|
|[0.01140843693081...|
|[-0.0158289900287...|
|[0.03367559270881...|
|[-0.0024716378274...|
|[-0.0346824191993...|
+--------------------+
only showing top 20 rows
```

Figure 18: A snapshot of the top 50 principal components as the most important features

Excellent! Everything went smoothly. Finally, we are ready to train the K-means algorithm:

```
val kmeans =
new KMeans().setK(5).setSeed(12345L)
val model = kmeans.fit(pcaDF)
```

So let's evaluate clustering by computing the **Within-Set Sum of Squared Errors (WSSSE)**:

```
val WSSSE = model.computeCost(pcaDF)
println("Within-Cluster Sum of Squares for k = 5 is" + WSSSE)
>>>
```

Determining the number of optimal clusters

The beauty of clustering algorithms such as K-means is that they do the clustering on the data with an unlimited number of features. They are great tools to use when you have raw data and would like to know the patterns in that data. However, deciding on the number of clusters prior doing the experiment might not be successful and may sometimes lead to an overfitting or underfitting problem.

On the other hand, one common thing to all three algorithms (that is, K-means, bisecting K-means, and Gaussian mixture) is that the number of clusters must be determined in advance and supplied to the algorithm as a parameter. Hence, informally, determining the number of clusters is a separate optimization problem to be solved.

Now we will use a heuristic approach based on the Elbow method. We start from K = 2 clusters, then we run the K-means algorithm for the same dataset by increasing K and observing the value of the cost function WCSS:

```
val iterations = 20
for (i <- 2 to iterations) {
        val kmeans = new KMeans().setK(i).setSeed(12345L)
        val model = kmeans.fit(pcaDF)
        val WSSSE = model.computeCost(pcaDF)
        println("Within-Cluster Sum of Squares for k = " + i + " is " +
                WSSSE)
    }
```

At some point, a big drop in cost function can be observed, but then the improvement became marginal with the increasing value of k. As suggested in cluster analysis literature, we can pick the k after the last big drop of WCSS as an optimal one. Now, let's see the WCSS values for a different number of clusters between 2 and 20 for example:

```
Within-Cluster Sum of Squares for k = 2 is 453.161838161838
Within-Cluster Sum of Squares for k = 3 is 438.2392344497606
Within-Cluster Sum of Squares for k = 4 is 390.2278787878787
Within-Cluster Sum of Squares for k = 5 is 397.72112098427874
Within-Cluster Sum of Squares for k = 6 is 367.8890909090908
Within-Cluster Sum of Squares for k = 7 is 362.3360347662672
Within-Cluster Sum of Squares for k = 8 is 347.49306362861336
Within-Cluster Sum of Squares for k = 9 is 327.5002901103624
Within-Cluster Sum of Squares for k = 10 is 327.29376873556436
Within-Cluster Sum of Squares for k = 11 is 315.2954156954155
Within-Cluster Sum of Squares for k = 12 is 320.2478696814693
Within-Cluster Sum of Squares for k = 13 is 308.7674242424241
Within-Cluster Sum of Squares for k = 14 is 314.64784054938576
Within-Cluster Sum of Squares for k = 15 is 297.38523698523704
Within-Cluster Sum of Squares for k = 16 is 294.26114718614707
Within-Cluster Sum of Squares for k = 17 is 284.34890572390555
Within-Cluster Sum of Squares for k = 18 is 280.35662525879917
Within-Cluster Sum of Squares for k = 19 is 272.765762015762
Within-Cluster Sum of Squares for k = 20 is 272.05702362771336
```

Now let us discuss how to take advantage of the Elbow method for determining the number of clusters. As shown next, we calculated the cost function, WCSS, as a function of a number of clusters for the K-means algorithm applied to Y chromosome genetic variants from the selected population groups.

It can be observed that a somewhat **big drop** occurs when k = 9 (which is not a drastic drop though). Therefore, we choose the number of clusters to be 10, as shown in *Figure 10*:

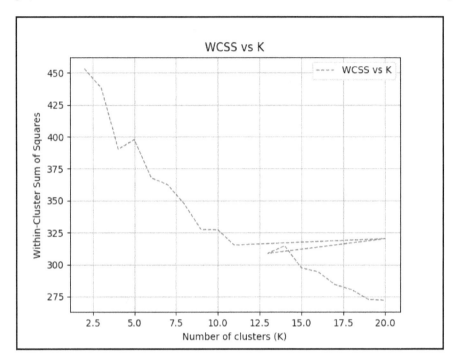

Figure 19: Number of clusters as a function of WCSS

Using H2O for ethnicity prediction

Up to this point, we have seen how to cluster genetic variants. We have also used the Elbow method and found the number of optimal k, the tentative number cluster. Now we should explore another task that we planned at the beginning—that is, ethnicity prediction.

In the previous K-means section, we prepared a Spark DataFrame named schemaDF. That one cannot be used with H2O. However, an additional conversion is necessary. We use the asH2OFrame() method to convert the Spark DataFrame into an H2O frame:

```
val dataFrame = h2oContext.asH2OFrame(schemaDF)
```

Now, one important thing you should remember while using H2O is that if you do not convert the label column into categorical, it will treat the classification task as regression. To get rid of this, we can use the `toCategoricalVec()` method from H2O. Since H2O frames are resilient, we can further update the same frame:

```
dataFrame.replace(dataFrame.find("Region"),
dataFrame.vec("Region").toCategoricalVec()).remove()
dataFrame.update()
```

Now our H2O frame is ready to train an H2O-based DL model (which is DNN, or to be more specific, a deep MLP). However, before we start the training, let's randomly split the DataFrame into 60% training, 20% test, and 20% validation data using the H2O built-in `FrameSplitter()` method:

```scala
val frameSplitter = new FrameSplitter(
        dataFrame, Array(.8, .1), Array("training", "test", "validation")
        .map(Key.make[Frame]),null)

water.H2O.submitTask(frameSplitter)
val splits = frameSplitter.getResult
val training = splits(0)
val test = splits(1)
val validation = splits(2)
```

Fantastic! Our train, test, and validation sets are ready, so let us set the parameters for our DL model:

```scala
// Set the parameters for our deep learning model.
val deepLearningParameters = new DeepLearningParameters()
        deepLearningParameters._train = training
        deepLearningParameters._valid = validation
        deepLearningParameters._response_column = "Region"
        deepLearningParameters._epochs = 200
        deepLearningParameters._l1 = 0.01
        deepLearningParameters._seed = 1234567
        deepLearningParameters._activation =
Activation.RectifierWithDropout
        deepLearningParameters._hidden = Array[Int](128, 256, 512)
```

In the preceding setting, we have specified an MLP having three hidden layers with 128, 256 and 512 neurons respectively. So altogether, there are five layers including the input and the output layer. The training will iterate up to 200 epoch. Since we have used too many neurons in the hidden layer, we should use the dropout to avoid overfitting. To avoid achieve a better regularization, we used the l1 regularization.

The preceding setting also states that we will train the model using the training set, and additionally the validation set will be used to validate the training. Finally, the response column is `Region`. On the other hand, the seed is used to ensure reproducibility.

So all set! Now let's train the DL model:

```
val deepLearning = new DeepLearning(deepLearningParameters)
val deepLearningTrained = deepLearning.trainModel
val trainedModel = deepLearningTrained.get
```

Depending on your hardware configuration, it might take a while. Therefore, it is time to rest and get some coffee maybe! Once we have the trained model, we can see the training error:

```
val error = trainedModel.classification_error()
println("Training Error: " + error)
>>>
Training Error: 0.5238095238095238
```

Unfortunately, the training was not that great! Nevertheless, we should try with different combination of hyperparameters. The error turns out to be high though, but let us not worry too much and evaluate the model, compute some model metrics, and evaluate model quality:

```
val trainMetrics =
ModelMetricsSupport.modelMetrics[ModelMetricsMultinomial](trainedModel,
test)
val met = trainMetrics.cm()

println("Accuracy: "+ met.accuracy())
println("MSE: "+ trainMetrics.mse)
println("RMSE: "+ trainMetrics.rmse)
println("R2: " + trainMetrics.r2)
>>>
Accuracy: 0.42105263157894735
MSE: 0.49369297490740655
RMSE: 0.7026328877211816
R2: 0.6091597281983032
```

Not so high accuracy! However, you should try with other VCF files and by tuning the hyperparameters too. For example, after reducing the neurons in the hidden layers and with l2 regularization and 100 epochs, I had about 20% improvement:

```
val deepLearningParameters = new DeepLearningParameters()
        deepLearningParameters._train = training
        deepLearningParameters._valid = validation
```

```
        deepLearningParameters._response_column = "Region"
        deepLearningParameters._epochs = 100
        deepLearningParameters._l2 = 0.01
        deepLearningParameters._seed = 1234567
        deepLearningParameters._activation =
Activation.RectifierWithDropout
        deepLearningParameters._hidden = Array[Int](32, 64, 128)
>>>
Training Error: 0.47619047619047616
Accuracy: 0.5263157894736843
MSE: 0.39112548936806274
RMSE: 0.6254002633258662
R2: 0.690358987583617
```

Another improvement clue is here. Apart from these hyperparameters, another advantage of using H2O-based DL algorithms is that we can take the relative variable/feature importance. In previous chapters, we have seen that when using a Random Forest algorithm in Spark, it is also possible to compute the variable importance.

Therefore, the idea is that if your model does not perform well, it would be worth dropping less important features and doing the training again. Now, it is possible to find the feature importance during supervised training. I have observed this feature importance:

			Variable	Relative Importance	Scaled Importance	Percentage
14436	FJ-1-13	INFO:	1158554348	1.000000	1.000000	0.048158
14436	FJ-1-13	INFO:	382875466	0.875208	0.875208	0.042148
14436	FJ-1-13	INFO:	-2090607845	0.731845	0.731845	0.035244
14436	FJ-1-13	INFO:	-819576211	0.672748	0.672748	0.032398
14436	FJ-1-13	INFO:	-1260378822	0.638622	0.638622	0.030755
14436	FJ-1-13	INFO:	2007209848	0.610795	0.610795	0.029414
14436	FJ-1-13	INFO:	-1335940486	0.599973	0.599973	0.028893
14436	FJ-1-13	INFO:	-1322225030	0.594180	0.594180	0.028614
14436	FJ-1-13	INFO:	450084336	0.586172	0.586172	0.028229
14436	FJ-1-13	INFO:	-255958118	0.578301	0.578301	0.027850
14436	FJ-1-13	INFO:	---			
14436	FJ-1-13	INFO:	-1900872614	0.211800	0.211800	0.010200
14436	FJ-1-13	INFO:	-1867424774	0.201258	0.201258	0.009692
14436	FJ-1-13	INFO:	1354464014	0.195077	0.195077	0.009394
14436	FJ-1-13	INFO:	-41485958	0.194468	0.194468	0.009365
14436	FJ-1-13	INFO:	-626609286	0.185900	0.185900	0.008952
14436	FJ-1-13	INFO:	-512787196	0.175550	0.175550	0.008454
14436	FJ-1-13	INFO:	-1042530870	0.171109	0.171109	0.008240
14436	FJ-1-13	INFO:	82236026	0.168544	0.168544	0.008117
14436	FJ-1-13	INFO:	1956396058	0.156438	0.156438	0.007534
14436	FJ-1-13	INFO:	1607716763	0.146275	0.146275	0.007044

Figure 20: Relative feature importance using H2O

Now the question would be why don't you drop them and try training again and observe if the accuracy has increased or not? Well, I leave it up to the readers.

Using random forest for ethnicity prediction

In the previous section, we have seen how to use H2O for ethnicity prediction. However, we could not achieve better prediction accuracy. Therefore, H2O is not mature enough to compute all the necessary performance metrics.

So why don't we try Spark-based tree ensemble techniques such as Random Forest or GBTs? Because we have seen that in most cases, RF shows better predictive accuracy, so let us try with that one.

In the K-means section, we've already prepared the Spark DataFrame named `schemaDF`. Therefore, we can simply transform the variables into feature vectors that we described before. Nevertheless, for this, we need to exclude the label column. We can do it using the `drop()` method as follows:

```
val featureCols = schemaDF.columns.drop(1)
val assembler =
new VectorAssembler()
    .setInputCols(featureCols)
    .setOutputCol("features")
val assembleDF = assembler.transform(schemaDF).select("features", "Region")
assembleDF.show()
```

At this point, you can further reduce the dimensionality and extract the most principal components using PCA or any other feature selector algorithm. However, I will leave it up to you. Since Spark expects the label column to be numeric, we have to convert the ethnic group name into numeric. We can use `StringIndexer()` for this. It is straightforward:

```
val indexer =
new StringIndexer()
    .setInputCol("Region")
    .setOutputCol("label")

val indexedDF =  indexer.fit(assembleDF)
                .transform(assembleDF)
                .select("features", "label")
```

Then we randomly split the dataset for training and testing. In our case, let's use 75% for the training and the rest for the testing:

```
val seed = 12345L
val splits = indexedDF.randomSplit(Array(0.75, 0.25), seed)
val (trainDF, testDF) = (splits(0), splits(1))
```

Since this this a small dataset, considering this fact, we can cache both the train and test set for faster access:

```
trainDF.cache
testDF.cache
val rf = new RandomForestClassifier()
    .setLabelCol("label")
    .setFeaturesCol("features")
    .setSeed(1234567L)
```

Now let's create a paramGrid for searching through decision tree's maxDepth parameter for the best model:

```
val paramGrid =
new ParamGridBuilder()
    .addGrid(rf.maxDepth, 3 :: 5 :: 15 :: 20 :: 25 :: 30 :: Nil)
    .addGrid(rf.featureSubsetStrategy, "auto" :: "all" :: Nil)
    .addGrid(rf.impurity, "gini" :: "entropy" :: Nil)
    .addGrid(rf.maxBins, 3 :: 5 :: 10 :: 15 :: 25 :: 35 :: 45 :: Nil)
    .addGrid(rf.numTrees, 5 :: 10 :: 15 :: 20 :: 30 :: Nil)
    .build()

val evaluator = new MulticlassClassificationEvaluator()
    .setLabelCol("label")
    .setPredictionCol("prediction")
```

Then we set up the 10-fold cross validation for an optimized and stable model. This will reduce the chances of overfitting:

```
val numFolds = 10
val crossval =
new CrossValidator()
    .setEstimator(rf)
    .setEvaluator(evaluator)
    .setEstimatorParamMaps(paramGrid)
    .setNumFolds(numFolds)
```

Well, now we are ready for the training. So let's train the random forest model with the best hyperparameters setting:

```
val cvModel = crossval.fit(trainDF)
```

Now that we have the cross-validated and the best model, why don't we evaluate the model using the test set. Why not? First, we compute the prediction DataFrame for each instance. Then we use the `MulticlassClassificationEvaluator()` to evaluate the performance since this is a multiclass classification problem.

Additionally, we compute performance metrics such as `accuracy`, `precision`, `recall`, and `f1` measure. Note that using RF classifier, we can get `weightedPrecision` and the `weightedRecall`:

```
val predictions = cvModel.transform(testDF)
predictions.show(10)
>>>
```

```
+--------------------+-----+--------------------+--------------------+----------+
|            features|label|       rawPrediction|         probability|prediction|
+--------------------+-----+--------------------+--------------------+----------+
|(53,[1,3,4,14,21,...|  1.0|[0.38297872340425...|[0.02553191489361...|       2.0|
|(53,[2,8,25,26,27...|  4.0|[0.36666666666666...|[0.02444444444444...|       4.0|
|(53,[3,14,44],[1....|  1.0|[3.90762287854543...|[0.26050819190302...|       2.0|
|(53,[13,34,41],[1...|  4.0|[1.68452289397281...|[0.11230152626485...|       4.0|
|     (53,[15],[1.0])|  0.0|[5.12742506561441...|[0.34182833770762...|       0.0|
|(53,[15,31],[1.0,...|  0.0|[9.67183173350930...|[0.64478878223395...|       0.0|
|         (53,[],[])|  1.0|[5.51940674120168...|[0.36796044941344...|       0.0|
|         (53,[],[])|  2.0|[5.51940674120168...|[0.36796044941344...|       0.0|
|(53,[2,3,14,21,35...|  2.0|[3.92063117699910...|[0.26137541179994...|       2.0|
|(53,[3,17,18,39,4...|  1.0|[0.8,11.333333333...|[0.05333333333333...|       1.0|
+--------------------+-----+--------------------+--------------------+----------+
only showing top 10 rows
```

Figure 21: Raw prediction probability, true label, and the predicted label using random forest

```
val metric =
new MulticlassClassificationEvaluator()
    .setLabelCol("label")
    .setPredictionCol("prediction")

val evaluator1 = metric.setMetricName("accuracy")
val evaluator2 = metric.setMetricName("weightedPrecision")
val evaluator3 = metric.setMetricName("weightedRecall")
val evaluator4 = metric.setMetricName("f1")
```

Now let's compute the classification `accuracy`, `precision`, `recall`, `f1` measure and error on test data:

```
val accuracy = evaluator1.evaluate(predictions)
val precision = evaluator2.evaluate(predictions)
val recall = evaluator3.evaluate(predictions)
val f1 = evaluator4.evaluate(predictions)
```

Finally, we print the performance metrics:

```
println("Accuracy = " + accuracy);
println("Precision = " + precision)
println("Recall = " + recall)
println("F1 = " + f1)
println(s"Test Error = ${1 - accuracy}")
>>>
Accuracy = 0.7196470196470195
Precision = 0.7196470196470195
Recall = 0.7196470196470195
F1 = 0.7196470196470195
Test Error = 0.28035298035298046
```

Yes, it turns out to be a better performer. This is bit unexpected since we hoped to have better predictive accuracy from a DL model, but we did not. As I already stated, we can still try with other parameters of H2O. Anyway, we can now see around 25% improvement using random forest. However, probably, it can still be improved.

Summary

In this chapter, we saw how to interoperate with a few big data tools such as Spark, H2O, and ADAM for handling a large-scale genomics dataset. We applied the Spark-based K-means algorithm to genetic variants data from the 1000 Genomes project analysis, aiming to cluster genotypic variants at the population scale.

Then we applied an H2O-based DL algorithm and Spark-based Random Forest models to predict geographic ethnicity. Additionally, we learned how to install and configure H2O for DL. This knowledge will be used in later chapters. Finally and importantly, we learned how to use H2O to compute variable importance in order to select the most important features in a training set.

In the next chapter, we will see how effectively we can use the **Latent Dirichlet Allocation (LDA)** algorithm for finding useful patterns in data. We will compare other topic modeling algorithms and the scalability power of LDA. In addition, we will utilize **Natural Language Processing (NLP)** libraries such as Stanford NLP.

5
Topic Modeling - A Better Insight into Large-Scale Texts

Topic modeling (**TM**) is a technique widely used in mining text from a large collection of documents. These topics can then be used to summarize and organize documents that include the topic terms and their relative weights. The dataset that will be used for this project is just in plain unstructured text format.

We will see how effectively we can use the **Latent Dirichlet Allocation** (**LDA**) algorithm for finding useful patterns in the data. We will compare other TM algorithms and the scalability power of LDA. In addition, we will utilize **Natural Language Processing** (**NLP**) libraries, such as Stanford NLP.

In a nutshell, we will learn the following topics throughout this end-to-end project:

- Topic modelling and text clustering
- How does LDA algorithm work?
- Topic modeling with LDA, Spark MLlib, and Standard NLP
- Other topic models and the scalability testing of LDA
- Model deployment

Topic modeling and text clustering

In TM, a topic is defined by a cluster of words, with each word in the cluster having a probability of occurrence for the given topic, and different topics having their respective clusters of words along with corresponding probabilities. Different topics may share some words, and a document can have more than one topic associated with it. So in short, we have a collection of text datasets—that is, a set of text files. Now the challenging part is finding useful patterns about the data using LDA.

There is a popular TM approach, based on LDA, where each document is considered a mixture of topics and each word in a document is considered randomly drawn from a document's topics. The topics are considered hidden and must be uncovered via analyzing joint distributions to compute the conditional distribution of hidden variables (topics), given the observed variables and words in documents. The TM technique is widely used in the task of mining text from a large collection of documents. These topics can then be used to summarize and organize documents that include the topic terms and their relative weights (see *Figure 1*):

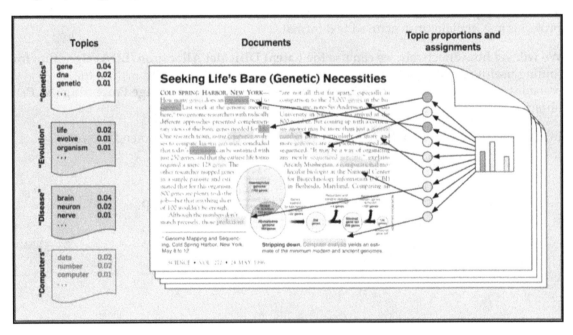

Figure 1: TM in a nutshell (source: Blei, D.M. et al., Probabilistic topic models, ACM communication, 55(4(, 77-84, 2012)))

As the number of topics that can be seen in the preceding figure is a lot smaller than the vocabulary associated with the document collection, the topic-space representation can be viewed as a dimensionality-reduction process as well:

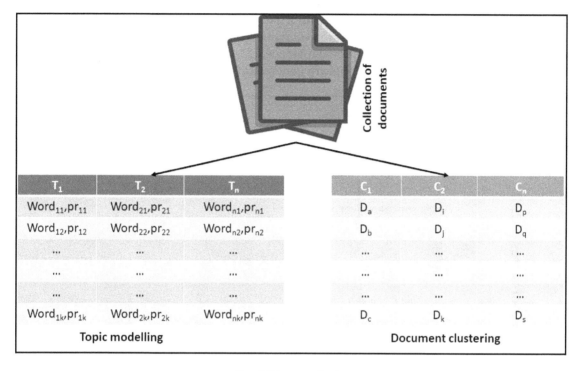

Figure 2: TM versus text clustering

In contrast to TM, in document clustering, the basic idea is to group documents into different groups based on a well-known similarity measure. To perform grouping, each document is represented by a vector representing the weights assigned to words in the document.

It is common to perform weighting using the term frequency-inverse document frequency (also known also the **TF-IDF** scheme). The end result of clustering is a list of clusters with every document showing up in one of the clusters. The basic difference between TM and text clustering can be illustrated by the following figure:

How does LDA algorithm work?

LDA is a topic model that infers topics from a collection of text documents. LDA can be thought of as a clustering algorithm where topics correspond to cluster centers, and documents correspond to examples (rows) in a dataset. Topics and documents both exist in a feature space, where feature vectors are vectors of word counts (bags of words). Instead of estimating a clustering using a traditional distance, LDA uses a function based on a statistical model of how text documents are generated (see in *Figure 3*):

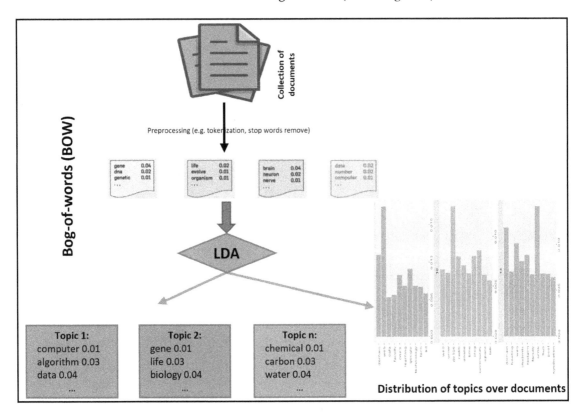

Figure 3: Working principle of LDA algorithms on a collection of documents

Particularly, we would like to discuss which topics people talk about most from the large collection of text. Since the release of Spark 1.3, MLlib supports the LDA, which is one of the most successfully used TM techniques in the area of text mining and NLP.

Moreover, LDA is also the first MLlib algorithm to adopt Spark GraphX. The following terminologies are worth knowing before we formally start our TM application:

- "word" = "term": an element of the vocabulary
- "token": instance of a term appearing in a document
- "topic": multinomial distribution over words representing some concept

The RDD-based LDA algorithm developed in Spark is a topic model designed for text documents. It is based on the original LDA paper (journal version): Blei, Ng, and Jordan, *Latent Dirichlet Allocation*, JMLR, 2003.

This implementation supports different inference algorithms via the setOptimizer function. The EMLDAOptimizer learns clustering using **expectation-maximization** (**EM**) on the likelihood function and yields comprehensive results, while OnlineLDAOptimizer uses iterative mini-batch sampling for online variational inference and is generally memory-friendly.

 EM is an iterative way to approximate the maximum likelihood function. In practice, when the input data is incomplete, has missing data points, or has hidden latent variables, ML estimation can find the best fit model.

LDA takes in a collection of documents as vectors of word counts and the following parameters (set using the builder pattern):

- K: Number of topics (that is, cluster centers) (default is 10).
- ldaOptimizer: Optimizer to use for learning the LDA model, either EMLDAOptimizer or OnlineLDAOptimizer (default is EMLDAOptimizer).
- Seed: Random seed for the reproducibility (optional though).
- docConcentration: Drichilet parameter for prior over documents distributions over topics. Larger values encourage smoother inferred distributions (default is -Vectors.dense(-1)).
- topicConcentration: Drichilet parameter for prior over topics' distributions over terms (words). Larger values ensure smoother inferred distributions (default is -1).
- maxIterations: Limit on the number of iterations (default is 20).

- `checkpointInterval`: If using checkpointing (set in the Spark configuration), this parameter specifies the frequency with which checkpoints will be created. If `maxIterations` is large, using check pointing can help reduce shuffle file sizes on disk and help with failure recovery (default is 10).

```
        Topic: 0                              Topic: 1
Terms | Index | Weight                 Terms | Index | Weight
---------------------                  ---------------------
space    10665    0.046582             smile    10668    0.129227
just     10667    0.034397             just     10667    0.024922
posted   10637    0.016093             good     10663    0.022404
love     10661    0.015652             hope     10645    0.017981
photo    10639    0.013296             going    10655    0.015764
cosmic   10635    0.013212             thanks   10648    0.014945
angry    10656    0.012860             time     10662    0.014941
like     10666    0.012629             like     10666    0.014827
life     10640    0.012107             think    10659    0.014438
time     10662    0.011634             work     10649    0.012702
---------------------                  ---------------------
Sum:= 0.188459750219041                Sum:= 0.28215004471848354

        Topic: 2                              Topic: 3
Terms | Index | Weight                 Terms | Index | Weight
---------------------                  ---------------------
grin     10664    0.078958             like     10666    0.030890
yang     10628    0.029173             just     10667    0.020093
kita     10574    0.017318             know     10660    0.016473
disgust           10618    0.016325    good     10663    0.013343
udah     10544    0.014584             that     10651    0.012687
science           10590    0.012792    people   10658    0.012137
space    10665    0.011765             right    10654    0.012097
nggak    10501    0.011290             think    10659    0.011395
kalo     10476    0.010203             love     10661    0.010943
angry    10656    0.009313             does     10646    0.009002
---------------------                  ---------------------
Sum:= 0.21172148557919923              Sum:= 0.14905966677477597
```

Figure 4: The topic distribution and how it looks

Let's see an example. Assume there are n balls in a basket having w different colors. Now also assume each term in a vocabulary has one of w colors. Now also assume that the vocabulary terms are distributed in m topics. Now the frequency of occurrence of each color in the basket is proportional to the corresponding term's weight in topic, φ.

Then the LDA algorithm incorporates a term weighting scheme by making the size of each ball proportional to the weight of its corresponding term. In *Figure 4*, n terms have the total weights in a topic, for example, topic 0 to 3. *Figure 4* shows topic distribution from randomly generated Tweet text.

Now that we have seen that by using TM, we find the structure within an unstructured collection of documents. Once the structure is **discovered**, as shown in *Figure 4*, we can answer several questions as follows:

- What is document X about?
- How similar are documents X and Y?
- If I am interested in topic Z, which documents should I read first?

In the next section, we will see an example of TM using a Spark MLlib-based LDA algorithm to answer the preceding questions.

Topic modeling with Spark MLlib and Stanford NLP

In this subsection, we represent a semi-automated technique of TM using Spark. Using other options as defaults, we train LDA on the dataset downloaded from GitHub at `https:/ /github.com/minghui/Twitter-LDA/tree/master/data/Data4Model/test`. However, we will use more well-known text datasets in the model reuse and deployment phase later in this chapter.

Implementation

The following steps show TM from data reading to printing the topics, along with their term weights. Here's the short workflow of the TM pipeline:

```
object topicmodelingwithLDA {
    def main(args: Array[String]): Unit = {
        val lda =
        new LDAforTM()
// actual computations are done here
        val defaultParams = Params().copy(input = "data/docs/") //Loading
parameters for training
            lda.run(defaultParams)
// Training the LDA model with the default parameters.
        }
}
```

We also need to import some related packages and libraries:

```
import edu.stanford.nlp.process.Morphology
import edu.stanford.nlp.simple.Document
import org.apache.log4j.{Level, Logger}
import scala.collection.JavaConversions._
import org.apache.spark.{SparkConf, SparkContext}
import org.apache.spark.ml.Pipeline
import org.apache.spark.ml.feature._
import org.apache.spark.ml.linalg.{Vector => MLVector}
import org.apache.spark.mllib.clustering.{DistributedLDAModel,
EMLDAOptimizer, LDA, OnlineLDAOptimizer, LDAModel}
import org.apache.spark.mllib.linalg.{ Vector, Vectors }
import org.apache.spark.rdd.RDD
import org.apache.spark.sql.{Row, SparkSession}
```

The actual computation on TM is done in the `LDAforTM` class. The `Params` is a case class, which is used for loading the parameters to train the LDA model. Finally, we train the LDA model using the parameters setting via the `Params` class. Now we will explain each step broadly with step-by-step source code:

Step 1 - Creating a Spark session

Let's create a Spark session by defining the number of computing cores, the SQL warehouse, and the application name as follows:

```
val spark = SparkSession
    .builder
    .master("local[*]")
    .config("spark.sql.warehouse.dir", "C:/data/")
    .appName(s"LDA")
    .getOrCreate()
```

Step 2 - Creating vocabulary and tokens count to train the LDA after text pre-processing

The `run()` method takes `params` such as input text, predefined vocabulary size, and stop word file:

```
def run(params: Params)
```

Then, it starts text pre-processing for the LDA model as follows (that is, inside the `run` method):

```
// Load documents, and prepare them for LDA.
val preprocessStart = System.nanoTime()
val (corpus, vocabArray, actualNumTokens) = preprocess(params.input,
params.vocabSize, params.stopwordFile)
```

The `Params` case class is used to define the parameters to train the LDA model. This goes as follows:

```
//Setting the parameters before training the LDA model
case class Params(var input: String = "", var ldaModel: LDAModel = null,
    k: Int = 5,
    maxIterations: Int = 100,
    docConcentration: Double = 5,
    topicConcentration: Double = 5,
    vocabSize: Int = 2900000,
    stopwordFile: String = "data/docs/stopWords.txt",
    algorithm: String = "em",
    checkpointDir: Option[String] = None,
    checkpointInterval: Int = 100)
```

For better result, you set these parameters in try and error basis. Alternatively, you should go with the cross-validation for even better performance. Now that if you want to checkpoint the current parameters, uses the following line of code:

```
if (params.checkpointDir.nonEmpty) {
    spark.sparkContext.setCheckpointDir(params.checkpointDir.get)
    }
```

The `preprocess` method is used to process the raw text. First, let's read the whole text using the `wholeTextFiles()` method as follows:

```
val initialrdd = spark.sparkContext.wholeTextFiles(paths).map(_._2)
initialrdd.cache()
```

In the preceding code, `paths` are the path of the text files. Then, we need to prepare the morphological RDD from the raw text after, based on the `lemma` texts, as follows:

```
val rdd = initialrdd.mapPartitions { partition =>
    val morphology = new Morphology()
    partition.map { value => helperForLDA.getLemmaText(value, morphology) }
}.map(helperForLDA.filterSpecialCharacters)
```

Here, the `getLemmaText()` method from the `helperForLDA` class supplies the `lemma` texts after filtering the special characters, such as (`"""[! @ # $ % ^ & * ( ) _ + - - , "`
`' ; : . ` ? --]`), as regular expressions, using the `filterSpaecialChatacters()` method. The method goes as follows:

```
def getLemmaText(document: String, morphology: Morphology) = {
    val string =
    new StringBuilder()
    val value =
    new Document(document).sentences().toList.flatMap {
        a =>
        val words = a.words().toList
        val tags = a.posTags().toList
        (words zip tags).toMap.map {
        a =>
        val newWord = morphology.lemma(a._1, a._2)
        val addedWoed =
    if (newWord.length > 3) {
        newWord
            }
    else { "" }
        string.append(addedWoed + " ")
        }
        }
    string.toString()
}
```

It is to be noted that the `Morphology()` class computes the base form of English words by removing only inflections (not derivational morphology). That is, it only does noun plurals, pronoun case, and verb endings, and not things such as comparative adjectives or derived nominal. The `getLemmaText()` method takes the document and the corresponding morphology and finally returns the lemmatized texts.

This comes from the Stanford NLP group. To use this, you should have the following import in the main class file: `edu.stanford.nlp.process.Morphology`. In the `pom.xml` file, you will have to include the following entries as dependencies:

```
<dependency>
    <groupId>edu.stanford.nlp</groupId>
    <artifactId>stanford-corenlp</artifactId>
    <version>3.6.0</version>
</dependency>
<dependency>
    <groupId>edu.stanford.nlp</groupId>
    <artifactId>stanford-corenlp</artifactId>
    <version>3.6.0</version>
```

```
    <classifier>models</classifier>
</dependency>
```

The `filterSpecialCharacters()` goes as follows:

```
def filterSpecialCharacters(document: String) = document.replaceAll("""[! @
# $ % ^ & * ( ) _ + - - , " ' ; : . ` ? --]""", " ")
```

Once we have the RDD with special characters removed, we can create a DataFrame for building the text analytics pipeline:

```
rdd.cache()
initialrdd.unpersist()
val df = rdd.toDF("docs")
df.show()
```

The DataFrame contains only document tags. A snapshot of the DataFrame is as follows:

Figure 5: Raw texts from the input dataset

Now if you look at the preceding DataFrame carefully, you will see that we still need to tokenize them. Moreover, there are stop words in the DataFrame, such as this, with, and so on, so we need to remove them as well. First, let's tokenize them using the RegexTokenizer API as follows:

```
val tokenizer = new RegexTokenizer()
                .setInputCol("docs")
                .setOutputCol("rawTokens")
```

Now let's remove all the stop words as follows:

```
val stopWordsRemover = new StopWordsRemover()
                .setInputCol("rawTokens")
                .setOutputCol("tokens")
stopWordsRemover.setStopWords(stopWordsRemover.getStopWords ++
customizedStopWords)
```

Furthermore, we also need to apply count vectors to find only the important features from the tokens. This will help make the pipeline chained as the pipeline stage. Let's do it as follows:

```
val countVectorizer = new CountVectorizer()
                .setVocabSize(vocabSize)
                .setInputCol("tokens")
                .setOutputCol("features")
```

> When an a-priori dictionary is not available, CountVectorizer can be used as an Estimator to extract the vocabulary and generate a CountVectorizerModel. In other words, CountVectorizer is used to convert a collection of text documents to vectors of token (that is, term) counts. The CountVectorizerModel produces sparse representations for the documents over the vocabulary, which can then be fed to LDA. More technically, when the fit() method is invoked for the fitting process, CountVectorizer will select the top vocabSize words ordered by term frequency across the corpus.

Now, create the pipeline by chaining the transformers (tokenizer, stopWordsRemover, and countVectorizer) as follows:

```
val pipeline = new Pipeline().setStages(Array(tokenizer, stopWordsRemover,
countVectorizer))
```

Now, let's fit and transform the pipeline toward the vocabulary and number of tokens:

```
val model = pipeline.fit(df)
val documents = model.transform(df).select("features").rdd.map {
    case Row(features: MLVector) => Vectors.fromML(features)
}.zipWithIndex().map(_.swap)
```

Finally, return the vocabulary and token count pairs as follows:

```
(documents, model.stages(2).asInstanceOf[CountVectorizerModel].vocabulary,
documents.map(_._2.numActives).sum().toLong) Now let's see the statistics
of the training data:

println() println("Training corpus summary:")
println("------------------------------")
println("Training set size: " + actualCorpusSize + " documents")
println("Vocabulary size: " + actualVocabSize + " terms")
println("Number of tockens: " + actualNumTokens + " tokens")
println("Preprocessing time: " + preprocessElapsed + " sec")
println("------------------------------")
println()
>>>
Training corpus summary:
------------------------------
Training set size: 19 documents
Vocabulary size: 21611 terms
Number of tockens: 75784 tokens
Preprocessing time: 46.684682086 sec
```

Step 3 - Instantiate the LDA model before training

Let us instantiate the LDA model before we begin training it with the following code:

```
val lda = new LDA()
```

Step 4 - Set the NLP optimizer

For better and optimized results from the LDA model, we need to set the optimizer that contains an algorithm for LDA, and performs the actual computation that stores the internal data structure (for example, graph or matrix) and other parameters for the algorithm.

Here we use the `EMLDAOPtimizer` optimizer. You can also use the `OnlineLDAOptimizer()` optimizer. The `EMLDAOPtimizer` stores a *data + parameter* graph, plus algorithm parameters. The underlying implementation uses EM.

First, let's instantiate the `EMLDAOptimizer` by adding `(1.0 / actualCorpusSize)` along with a very low learning rate (that is, 0.05) to `MiniBatchFraction` to converge the training on a tiny dataset like ours as follows:

```
val optimizer = params.algorithm.toLowerCase
    match {
        case "em" =>
            new EMLDAOptimizer
// add (1.0 / actualCorpusSize) to MiniBatchFraction be more robust on tiny
datasets.
        case "online" =>
            new OnlineLDAOptimizer().setMiniBatchFraction(0.05 + 1.0 /
actualCorpusSize)
        case _ =>
            thrownew IllegalArgumentException("Only em, online are
supported but got
            ${params.algorithm}.")
    }
```

Now, set the optimizer using the `setOptimizer()` method from the LDA API as follows:

```
lda.setOptimizer(optimizer)
    .setK(params.k)
    .setMaxIterations(params.maxIterations)
    .setDocConcentration(params.docConcentration)
    .setTopicConcentration(params.topicConcentration)
    .setCheckpointInterval(params.checkpointInterval)
```

Step 5 - Training the LDA model

Let's start training the LDA model using the training corpus and keep track of the training time as follows:

```
val startTime = System.nanoTime()
ldaModel = lda.run(corpus)

val elapsed = (System.nanoTime() - startTime) / 1e9
println("Finished training LDA model. Summary:")
println("Training time: " + elapsed + " sec")
```

Now additionally, we can save the trained model for future reuse that can goes as follows:

```
//Saving the model for future use
params.ldaModel.save(spark.sparkContext, "model/LDATrainedModel")
```

 Note that once you have finished the training and got the most optimal training, uncomment the preceding line before you deploy the model. Otherwise, it will get stopped by throwing an exception in the model reuse phase.

For the text we have, the LDA model took 6.309715286 seconds to train. Note these timing codes are optional. Here we provide them for reference purposes only to get an idea of the training time:

Step 6 - Prepare the topics of interest

Prepare the top 5 topics with each topic having 10 terms. Include the terms and their corresponding weights:

```
val topicIndices = ldaModel.describeTopics(maxTermsPerTopic = 10)
println(topicIndices.length)
val topics = topicIndices.map {
    case (terms, termWeights) => terms.zip(termWeights).map {
    case (term, weight) => (vocabArray(term.toInt), weight)
    }
}
```

Step 7 - Topic modelling

Print the top 10 topics, showing the top-weighted terms for each topic. Also, include the total weight in each topic as follows:

```
var sum = 0.0
println(s"${params.k} topics:")
topics.zipWithIndex.foreach {
    case (topic, i) =>
        println(s"TOPIC $i")
        println("-------------------------------")
        topic.foreach {
    case (term, weight) =>
        term.replaceAll("\s", "")
        println(s"$termt$weight")
        sum = sum + weight
    }
```

```
println("----------------------------")
println("weight: " + sum)
println()
```

Now let's see the output of our LDA model towards topics modeling:

```
5 topics:
TOPIC 0
----------------------------
come 0.00701833594262213635
make 0.006893251344696077
look 0.006629265338364568
know 0.006592594912464674
take 0.006074234442310174
little 0.005876330712306203
think 0.005153843469004155
time 0.0050685675513282525
hand 0.004524837827665401
well 0.004224698942533204
----------------------------
weight: 0.05805596048329406
TOPIC 1
----------------------------
thus 0.008447268016707914
ring 0.00750959344769264
fate 0.006802070476284118
trojan 0.006310545607626158
bear 0.006244268350438889
heav 0.005479939900136969
thro 0.005185211621694439
shore 0.004618008184651363
fight 0.004161178536600401
turnus 0.003899151842042464
----------------------------
weight: 0.11671319646716942
TOPIC 2
----------------------------
aladdin 7.077183389325728E-4
sultan 6.774311890861097E-4
magician 6.127791175835228E-4
genie 6.06094509479989E-4
vizier 6.051618911188781E-4
princess 5.654756758514474E-4
fatima 4.050749957608771E-4
flatland 3.47788388834721E-4
want 3.4263963705536023E-4
spaceland 3.371784715458026E-4
----------------------------
```

```
weight: 0.1219205386824187
TOPIC 3
-------------------------------
aladdin 7.325869707607238E-4
sultan 7.012354862373387E-4
magician 6.343184784726607E-4
genie 6.273921840260785E-4
vizier 6.264266945018852E-4
princess 5.849046214967484E-4
fatima 4.193089052802858E-4
flatland 3.601371993827707E-4
want 3.5398019331108816E-4
spaceland 3.491505202713831E-4
--------------------------
weight: 0.12730997993615964
TOPIC 4
-----------------------------
captain 0.02931475169407467
fogg 0.02743105575940755
nautilus 0.022748371008515483
passepartout 0.01802140608022664
nemo 0.016678258146358142
conseil 0.012129894049747918
phileas 0.010441664411654412
canadian 0.006217638883315841
vessel 0.00618937301246955
land 0.00615311666365297
----------------------------
weight: 0.28263550964558276
```

From the preceding output, we can see that topic five of the input documents has the most weight, at `0.28263550964558276`. This topic discusses terms such as `captain`, `fogg`, `nemo`, `vessel`, and `land`.

Step 8 - Measuring the likelihood of two documents

Now to get some more statistics, such as maximum likelihood or log likelihood on the document, we can use the following code:

```
if (ldaModel.isInstanceOf[DistributedLDAModel]) {
    val distLDAModel = ldaModel.asInstanceOf[DistributedLDAModel]
    val avgLogLikelihood = distLDAModel.logLikelihood /
actualCorpusSize.toDouble
    println("The average log likelihood of the training data: " +
```

```
avgLogLikelihood)
    println()
}
```

The preceding code calculates the average log likelihood of the LDA model as an instance of the distributed version of the LDA model:

```
The average log likelihood of the training data: -209692.79314860413
```

 For more information on the likelihood measurement, interested readers should refer to `https://en.wikipedia.org/wiki/Likelihood_function`.

Now imagine that we've computed the preceding metric for document X and Y. Then we can answer the following question:

- How similar are documents X and Y?

The thing is, we should try to get the lowest likelihood from all the training documents and use it as a threshold for the previous comparison. Finally, to answer the third and final question:

- If I am interested in topic Z, which documents should I read first?

A minimal answer: taking a close look at the topic distributions and the relative term weights, we can decide which document we should read first.

Other topic models versus the scalability of LDA

Throughout this end-to-end project, we have used LDA, which is one of the most popular TM algorithms used for text mining. We could use more robust TM algorithms, such as **Probabilistic Latent Sentiment Analysis (pLSA)**, **Pachinko Allocation Model (PAM)**, and **Hierarchical Drichilet Process (HDP)** algorithms.

However, pLSA has the overfitting problem. On the other hand, both HDP and PAM are more complex TM algorithms used for complex text mining, such as mining topics from high-dimensional text data or documents of unstructured text. Finally, non-negative matrix factorization is another way to find topics in a collection of documents. Irrespective of the approach, the output of all the TM algorithms is a list of topics with associated clusters of words.

The previous example shows how to perform TM using the LDA algorithm as a standalone application. The parallelization of LDA is not straightforward, and there have been many research papers proposing different strategies. The key obstacle in this regard is that all methods involve a large amount of communication.

According to the blog on the Databricks website (`https://databricks.com/blog/2015/03/25/topic-modeling-with-lda-mllib-meets-graphx.html`), here are the statistics of the dataset and related training and test sets that were used during the experimentation:

- **Training set size**: 4.6 million documents
- **Vocabulary size**: 1.1 million terms
- **Training set size**: 1.1 billion tokens (~239 words/document)
- 100 topics
- 16-worker EC2 cluster, for example, M4.large or M3.medium depending upon budget and requirements

For the preceding setting, the timing result was 176 seconds/iteration on average over 10 iterations. From these statistics, it is clear that LDA is quite scalable for a very large number of the corpus as well.

Deploying the trained LDA model

For this mini deployment, let's use a real-life dataset: PubMed. A sample dataset containing PubMed terms can be downloaded from: `https://nlp.stanford.edu/software/tmt/tmt-0.4/examples/pubmed-oa-subset.csv`. This link actually contains a dataset in CSV format but has a strange name, `4UK1UkTX.csv`.

To be more specific, the dataset contains some abstracts of some biological articles, their publication year, and the serial number. A glimpse is given in the following figure:

ID	Year	Short abstract
1	1978	1H NMR of valine tRNA modified bases. Evidence for multiple conformations.
2	1978	ABBREVIATIONS IN MEDICINE
3	1978	3'End labelling of RNA with 32P suitable for rapid gel sequencing.
4	1978	ABBREVIATIONS IN MEDICINE
5	1978	Absence of plant uptake and translocation of polybrominated biphenyls (PBBs).
6	1978	Abstracts/Sommaires/Zusammenfassungen

Figure 6: A snapshot of the sample dataset

In the following code, we have already saved the trained LDA model for future use as follows:

```
params.ldaModel.save(spark.sparkContext, "model/LDATrainedModel")
```

The trained model will be saved to the previously mentioned location. The directory will include data and metadata about the model and the training itself as shown in the following figure:

```
∨ 🗁 LDATrainedModel
  ∨ 🗁 data
    ∨ 🗁 globalTopicTotals
        📄 _SUCCESS
        📄 part-00000-380112d7-bb79-43c4-bb98-4d822a6bbb0e-c000.snappy.parquet
    ∨ 🗁 tokenCounts
        📄 _SUCCESS
        📄 part-00000-7ad3ac19-0ea3-4ad3-b006-f8144eb541ee-c000.snappy.parquet
        📄 part-00001-7ad3ac19-0ea3-4ad3-b006-f8144eb541ee-c000.snappy.parquet
    ∨ 🗁 topicCounts
        📄 _SUCCESS
        📄 part-00000-94cc28de-a16a-40e2-82f9-0d5ece5744f4-c000.snappy.parquet
        📄 part-00001-94cc28de-a16a-40e2-82f9-0d5ece5744f4-c000.snappy.parquet
  ∨ 🗁 metadata
      📄 _SUCCESS
      📄 part-00000
```

Figure 7: The directory structure of the trained and saved LDA model

As expected, the data folder has some parquet files containing global topics, their counts, tokens and their counts, and the topics with their respective counts. Now the next task will be restoring the same model as follows:

```
//Restoring the model for reuse
val savedLDAModel = DistributedLDAModel.load(spark.sparkContext,
"model/LDATrainedModel/")

//Then we execute the following workflow:
val lda = new LDAforTM()
// actual computations are done here

 // Loading the parameters to train the LDA model
val defaultParams = Params().copy(input = "data/4UK1UkTX.csv",
savedLDAModel)
lda.run(defaultParams)
// Training the LDA model with the default parameters.
spark.stop()

>>>
 Training corpus summary:
 ------------------------------
 Training set size: 1 documents
 Vocabulary size: 14670 terms
 Number of tockens: 14670 tokens
 Preprocessing time: 12.921435786 sec
 ------------------------------
 Finished training LDA model.
 Summary:
 Training time: 23.243336895 sec
 The average log likelihood of the training data: -1008739.37857908
 5 topics:
 TOPIC 0
 ------------------------------
 rrb 0.015234818404037585
 lrb 0.015154125349208018
 sequence 0.008924621534990771
 gene 0.007391453509409655
 cell 0.007020265462594214
 protein 0.006479622004524878
 study 0.004954523307983932
 show 0.0040023453035193685
 site 0.0038006126784248945
 result 0.0036634344941610534
 ------------------------------
 weight: 0.07662582204885438
 TOPIC 1
```

```
------------------------------
rrb 1.745030693927338E-4
lrb 1.7450110447001028E-4
sequence 1.7424254444446083E-4
gene 1.7411236867642102E-4
cell 1.7407234230511066E-4
protein 1.7400587965300172E-4
study 1.737407317498879E-4
show 1.7347354627656383E-4
site 1.7339989737227756E-4
result 1.7334522348574853E-4
-------------------------
weight: 0.07836521875668061
TOPIC 2
------------------------------
rrb 1.745030693927338E-4
lrb 1.7450110447001028E-4
sequence 1.7424254444446083E-4
gene 1.7411236867642102E-4
cell 1.7407234230511066E-4
protein 1.7400587965300172E-4
study 1.737407317498879E-4
show 1.7347354627656383E-4
site 1.7339989737227756E-4
result 1.7334522348574853E-4
-------------------------
weight: 0.08010461546450684
TOPIC 3
------------------------------
rrb 1.745030693927338E-4
lrb 1.7450110447001028E-4
sequence 1.7424254444446083E-4
gene 1.7411236867642102E-4
cell 1.7407234230511066E-4
protein 1.7400587965300172E-4
study 1.737407317498879E-4
show 1.7347354627656383E-4
site 1.7339989737227756E-4
result 1.7334522348574853E-4
-------------------------
weight: 0.08184401217233307
TOPIC 4
------------------------------
rrb 1.745030693927338E-4
lrb 1.7450110447001028E-4
sequence 1.7424254444446083E-4
gene 1.7411236867642102E-4
cell 1.7407234230511066E-4
```

```
protein 1.7400587965300172E-4
study 1.737407317498879E-4
show 1.7347354627656383E-4
site 1.7339989737227756E-4
result 1.7334522348574853E-4
---------------------------
weight: 0.0835834088801593
```

Well done! We have managed to reuse the model and do the same prediction. But, probably due to the randomness of data, we observed a slightly different prediction. Let's see the complete code to get a clearer view:

```scala
package com.packt.ScalaML.Topicmodeling
import org.apache.spark.sql.SparkSession
import org.apache.spark.mllib.clustering.{DistributedLDAModel, LDA}

object LDAModelReuse {
    def main(args: Array[String]): Unit = {
        val spark = SparkSession
                    .builder
                    .master("local[*]")
                    .config("spark.sql.warehouse.dir", "data/")
                    .appName(s"LDA_TopicModelling")
                    .getOrCreate()

//Restoring the model for reuse
    val savedLDAModel = DistributedLDAModel.load(spark.sparkContext,
"model/LDATrainedModel/")
    val lda = new LDAforTM()
// actual computations are done here
    val defaultParams = Params().copy(input = "data/4UK1UkTX.csv",
savedLDAModel)
//Loading params
    lda.run(defaultParams)
// Training the LDA model with the default parameters.
    spark.stop()
        }
    }
```

Summary

In this chapter, we have seen how effectively we can use and combine the LDA algorithm and NLP libraries, such as Stanford NLP, for finding useful patterns from large-scale text. We have seen a comparative analysis between TM algorithms and the scalability power of LDA.

Finally, for a real-life example and use case, interested readers can refer to the blog article at `https://blog.codecentric.de/en/2017/01/topic-modeling-codecentric-blog-articles/`.

Netflix is an American entertainment company founded by Reed Hastings and Marc Randolph on August 29, 1997, in Scotts Valley, California. It specializes in, providing, streaming media and video-on-demand, online and DVD by mail. In 2013, Netflix expanded into film and television production, as well as online distribution. Netflix uses a model-based collaborative filtering approach for real-time movie recommendations for its subscribers.

In the next chapter, we will see two end-to-end projects: an item-based **collaborative filtering** for movie-similarity measurements, and a model-based movie-recommendation engine with Spark to recommend movies to new users. We will see how to interoperate between **ALS** and **Matrix Factorization** for these two scalable movie recommendation engines.

6
Developing Model-based Movie Recommendation Engines

Netflix is an American entertainment company founded by Reed Hastings and Marc Randolph on August 29, 1997, in Scotts Valley, California. It specializes in and provides streaming media, video-on-demand online, and DVD by mail. In 2013, Netflix expanded into film and television production, as well as online distribution. Netflix uses a model-based collaborative filtering approach for real-time movie recommendation for its subscribers.

In this chapter, we will see two end-to-end projects and develop a model for item-based collaborative filtering for movie similarity measurement and a model-based movie recommendation engine with Spark that recommends movies for new users. We will see how to interoperate between ALS and **matrix factorization** (**MF**) for these two scalable movie recommendation engines. We will use the movie lens dataset for the project. Finally, we will see how to deploy the best model in production.

In a nutshell, we will learn the following topics through two end-to-end projects:

- Recommendation system—how and why?
- Item-based collaborative filtering for movie similarity
- Model-based movie recommendation with Spark
- Model deployment

Recommendation system

A **recommendation system** (that is, **recommendation engine or RE**) is a subclass of information filtering systems that helps predict the **rating** or **preference** based on the ratings given by users to an item. In recent years, recommendation systems have become increasingly popular. In short, a recommender system tries to predict potential items a user might be interested in based on history for other users.

Consequently, they're being used in many areas such as movies, music, news, books, research articles, search queries, social tags, products, collaborations, comedy, restaurants, fashion, financial services, life insurance, and online dating. There are a couple of ways to develop recommendation engines that typically produce a list of recommendations, for example, collaborative and content-based filtering or the personality-based approach.

Collaborative filtering approaches

Using collaborative filtering approaches, an RE can be built based on a user's past behavior where numerical ratings are given on purchased items. Sometimes, it can be developed on similar decisions made by other users who also have purchased the same items. From the following figure, you can get some idea of different recommender systems:

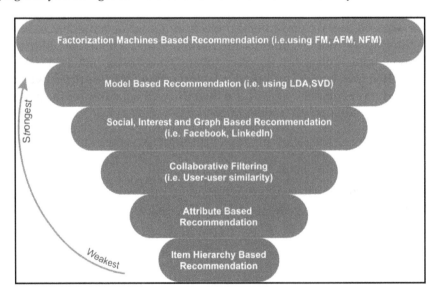

Figure 1: A comparative view of different recommendation systems

Collaborative filtering-based approaches often suffer from three problems—cold start, scalability, and sparsity:

- **Cold start**: Sometimes gets stuck when a large amount of data about users is required for making a more accurate recommendation system.
- **Scalability**: A large amount of computation power is often necessary to calculate recommendations out of a dataset with millions of users and products.
- **Sparsity**: This often happens with a crowd-sourced dataset when a huge number of items are sold on major e-commerce sites. In such a case, active users may rate only a small subset of the items sold—that is, even the most popular items have very few ratings. Accordingly, the user versus items matrix becomes very sparse. In other words, a large-scale sparse matrix cannot be handled.

To overcome these issues, a particular type of collaborative filtering algorithm uses MF, a low-rank matrix approximation technique. We will see an example later in this chapter.

Content-based filtering approaches

Using content-based filtering approaches, a series of discrete characteristics of an item is utilized to recommend additional items with similar properties. Sometimes it is based on a description of the item and a profile of the user's preferences. These approaches try to recommend items that are similar to those that a user liked in the past or is using currently.

A key issue with content-based filtering is whether the system is able to learn user preferences from users' actions regarding one content source and use them across other content types. When this type of RE is deployed, it can be used to predict items or ratings for items that the user is interested in.

Hybrid recommender systems

As you have seen, there are several pros and cons of using collaborative filtering and content-based filtering. Therefore, to overcome the limitations of these two approaches, recent trends have shown that a hybrid approach can be more effective and accurate by combining collaborative filtering and content-based filtering. Sometimes, factorization approaches such as MF and **Singular Value Decomposition (SVD)** are used to make them robust. Hybrid approaches can be implemented in several ways:

- At first, content-based and collaborative-based predictions are computed separately, and later on we combine them, that is, unification of these two into one model. In this approach, FM and SVD are used extensively.

- Adding content-based capabilities to a collaborative-based approach or vice versa. Again, FM and SVD are used for better prediction.

Netflix is a good example that uses this hybrid approach to make a recommendation to its subscribers. This site makes recommendations in two ways:

- **Collaborative filtering**: By comparing the watching and searching habits of similar users
- **Content-based filtering**: By offering movies that share characteristics with films that a user has rated highly

Model-based collaborative filtering

AS shown in *Figure 1*, I really planned to implement a systematic project using factorization machines it turns out to be time constraint. Therefore, decided to develop a movie recommendation using a collaborative filtering approach. Collaborative filtering based methods are classified as:

- Memory-based, that is, a user-based algorithm
- Model-based collaborative filtering, that is, kernel-mapping

In the model-based collaborative filtering technique, users and products are described by a small set of factors, also called **latent factors** (**LFs**). The LFs are then used to predict the missing entries. The **Alternating Least Squares** (**ALS**) algorithm is used to learn these LFs. From a computational perspective, model-based collaborative filtering is commonly used in many companies such as Netflix for real-time movie recommendations.

The utility matrix

In a hybrid recommendation system, there are two classes of entities: users and items (examples are movies, products, and so on). Now, as a user, you might have preferences for certain items. Therefore, these preferences must be extracted from data about items, users, or ratings. Often this data is represented as a utility matrix, such as a user-item pair. This type of value can represent what is known about the degree of preference of that user for a particular item. The entry in the matrix, that is, a table, can come from an ordered set. For example, integers 1-5 can be used to represent the number of stars that the user gave as a rating for items.

We have argued that often users might not have rated items; that is, most entries are **unknown**. This also means that the matrix might be sparse. An unknown rating implies that we have no explicit information about the user's preference for the item. *Table 1* shows an example utility matrix. The matrix represents the ratings of users about movies on a 1-5 scale, 5 being the highest rating. A blank entry means no users have provided any rating about those movies.

Here **HP1**, **HP2**, and **HP3** are acronyms for the movies **Harry Potter I**, **II**, and **III**, respectively; **TW** is for **Twilight**; and **SW1**, **SW2**, and **SW3** represent **Star Wars** episodes **1**, **2**, and **3**, respectively. The users are represented by capital letters **A**, **B**, **C**, and **D**:

	HP1	HP2	HP3	TW	SW1	SW2	SW3
A	4			5	1		
B	5	5	4				
C				2	4	5	
D		3					3

Figure 2: Utility matrix (user versus movies matrix)

There are many blank entries for the user-movie pairs. This means that users have not rated those movies. In a real-life scenario, the matrix might be even sparser, with the typical user rating only a tiny fraction of all available movies. Now, using this matrix, the goal is to predict the blanks in the utility matrix. Let's see an example. Suppose we are curious to know whether user **A** likes **SW2**. However, this is really difficult to determine since there is little evidence in the matrix in *Table 1*.

Thus, in practice, we might develop a movie recommendation engine to consider the uncommon properties of movies, such as producer name, director name, lead stars, or even the similarity of their names. This way, we can compute the similarity of movies **SW1** and **SW2**. This similarity would drive us to conclude that since A did not like **SW1**, they are not likely to enjoy **SW2** either.

However, this might not work for the larger dataset. Therefore, with much more data, we might observe that the people who rated both **SW1** and **SW2** were inclined to give them similar ratings. Finally, we can conclude that **A** would also give **SW2** a low rating, similar to **A**'s rating of **SW1**.

Spark-based movie recommendation systems

The implementation in Spark MLlib supports model-based collaborative filtering. In the model-based collaborative filtering technique, users and products are described by a small set of factors, also called LFs. In this section, we will see two complete examples of how it works toward recommending movies for new users.

Item-based collaborative filtering for movie similarity

Firstly, we read the ratings from a file. For this project, we can use the MovieLens 100k rating dataset from `http://www.grouplens.org/node/73`. The training set ratings are in a file called `ua.base`, while the movie item data is in `u.item`. On the other hand, `ua.test` contains the test set to evaluate our model. Since we will be using this dataset, we should acknowledge the GroupLens Research Project team at the University of Minnesota who wrote the following text:

F. Maxwell Harper and Joseph A. Konstan. 2015. The MovieLens Datasets: *History and Context*. ACM Transactions on **Interactive Intelligent Systems (TiiS)** 5, 4, Article 19 (December 2015), 19 pages. DOI: `http://dx.doi.org/10.1145/2827872`.

This dataset consists of 100,000 ratings of 1 to 5 from 943 users on 1,682 movies. Each user has rated at least 20 movies. It also contains simple demographic info about the users (age, gender, occupation, and zip code).

Step 1 - Importing necessary libraries and creating a Spark session

We need to import a Spark session so that we can create the Spark session, the gateway of our Spark app:

```
import org.apache.spark.sql.SparkSession
val spark: SparkSession = SparkSession
    .builder()
    .appName("MovieSimilarityApp")
    .master("local[*]")
    .config("spark.sql.warehouse.dir", "E:/Exp/")
    .getOrCreate()
```

Step 2 - Reading and parsing the dataset

Let's use Spark's `textFile` method to read a text file from your preferred storage such as HDFS or the local filesystem. However, it's up to us to specify how to split the fields. While reading the input dataset, we do `groupBy` first and transform after the join with a `flatMap` operation to get the required fields:

```scala
val TRAIN_FILENAME = "data/ua.base"
val TEST_FIELNAME = "data/ua.test"
val MOVIES_FILENAME = "data/u.item"

  // get movie names keyed on id
val movies = spark.sparkContext.textFile(MOVIES_FILENAME)
    .map(line => {
      val fields = line.split("\|")
      (fields(0).toInt, fields(1))
    })
val movieNames = movies.collectAsMap()
  // extract (userid, movieid, rating) from ratings data
val ratings = spark.sparkContext.textFile(TRAIN_FILENAME)
    .map(line => {
      val fields = line.split("t")
      (fields(0).toInt, fields(1).toInt, fields(2).toInt)
    })
```

Step 3 - Computing similarity

Using item-based collaborative filtering, we can compute how similar two movies are to each other. We follow these steps:

1. For every pair of movies (**A**, **B**), we find all the users who rated both **A** and **B**
2. Now, using the preceding ratings, we compute a Movie **A** vector, say **X**, and a Movie **B** vector, say **Y**
3. Then we calculate the correlation between **X** and **Y**
4. If a user watches movie **C**, we can then recommend the most correlated movies with it

We then compute the various vector metrics for each ratings vector **X** and **Y**, such as size, dot product, norm, and so on. We will use these metrics to compute the various similarity metrics between pairs of movies, that is, (**A**, **B**). For each movie pair (**A**, **B**), we then compute several measures such as cosine similarity, Jaccard similarity correlation, and regularized correlation. Let's get started. The first two steps are as follows:

```
// get num raters per movie, keyed on movie id
val numRatersPerMovie = ratings
    .groupBy(tup => tup._2)
    .map(grouped => (grouped._1, grouped._2.size))

// join ratings with num raters on movie id
val ratingsWithSize = ratings
    .groupBy(tup => tup._2)
    .join(numRatersPerMovie)
    .flatMap(joined => {
        joined._2._1.map(f => (f._1, f._2, f._3, joined._2._2))
    })
```

The `ratingsWithSize` variable now contains the following fields: user, movie, rating, and numRaters. The next step is to make a dummy copy of ratings for self-join. Technically, we join to userid and filter movie pairs so that we do not double-count and exclude self-pairs:

```
val ratings2 = ratingsWithSize.keyBy(tup => tup._1)
val ratingPairs =
    ratingsWithSize
        .keyBy(tup => tup._1)
        .join(ratings2)
        .filter(f => f._2._1._2 < f._2._2._2)
```

Now let's compute the raw inputs to similarity metrics for each movie pair:

```
val vectorCalcs = ratingPairs
    .map(data => {
        val key = (data._2._1._2, data._2._2._2)
        val stats =
            (data._2._1._3 * data._2._2._3, // rating 1 * rating 2
                data._2._1._3, // rating movie 1
                data._2._2._3, // rating movie 2
                math.pow(data._2._1._3, 2), // square of rating movie 1
                math.pow(data._2._2._3, 2), // square of rating movie 2
                data._2._1._4, // number of raters movie 1
                data._2._2._4) // number of raters movie 2
        (key, stats)
    })
    .groupByKey()
```

```
.map(data => {
    val key = data._1
    val vals = data._2
    val size = vals.size
    val dotProduct = vals.map(f => f._1).sum
    val ratingSum = vals.map(f => f._2).sum
    val rating2Sum = vals.map(f => f._3).sum
    val ratingSq = vals.map(f => f._4).sum
    val rating2Sq = vals.map(f => f._5).sum
    val numRaters = vals.map(f => f._6).max
    val numRaters2 = vals.map(f => f._7).max
        (key, (size, dotProduct, ratingSum, rating2Sum, ratingSq,
rating2Sq, numRaters, numRaters2))})
```

Here are the third and the fourth steps for computing the similarity. We compute similarity metrics for each movie pair:

```
val similarities =
    vectorCalcs
        .map(fields => {
            val key = fields._1
            val (size, dotProduct, ratingSum, rating2Sum, ratingNormSq,
rating2NormSq, numRaters, numRaters2) = fields._2
            val corr = correlation(size, dotProduct, ratingSum, rating2Sum,
ratingNormSq, rating2NormSq)
            val regCorr = regularizedCorrelation(size, dotProduct, ratingSum,
rating2Sum, ratingNormSq, rating2NormSq, PRIOR_COUNT, PRIOR_CORRELATION)
            val cosSim = cosineSimilarity(dotProduct,
scala.math.sqrt(ratingNormSq), scala.math.sqrt(rating2NormSq))
            val jaccard = jaccardSimilarity(size, numRaters, numRaters2)
            (key, (corr, regCorr, cosSim, jaccard))})
```

Next is the implementation of the methods we just used. We start with the `correlation()` method for computing the correlation between the two vectors (*A*, *B*) as *cov(A, B)/(stdDev(A) * stdDev(B))*:

```
def correlation(size: Double, dotProduct: Double, ratingSum: Double,
    rating2Sum: Double, ratingNormSq: Double, rating2NormSq: Double) = {
    val numerator = size * dotProduct - ratingSum * rating2Sum
    val denominator = scala.math.sqrt(size * ratingNormSq - ratingSum *
ratingSum)
                        scala.math.sqrt(size * rating2NormSq - rating2Sum *
rating2Sum)
    numerator / denominator}
```

Now, the correlation is regularized by adding virtual pseudocounts over a prior, *RegularizedCorrelation = w * ActualCorrelation + (1 - w) * PriorCorrelation where w = # actualPairs / (# actualPairs + # virtualPairs)*:

```
def regularizedCorrelation(size: Double, dotProduct: Double, ratingSum:
Double,
    rating2Sum: Double, ratingNormSq: Double, rating2NormSq: Double,
    virtualCount: Double, priorCorrelation: Double) = {
    val unregularizedCorrelation = correlation(size, dotProduct, ratingSum,
rating2Sum, ratingNormSq, rating2NormSq)
    val w = size / (size + virtualCount)
    w * unregularizedCorrelation + (1 - w) * priorCorrelation
  }
```

The cosine similarity between the two vectors A, B is dotProduct(A, B) / (norm(A) * norm(B)):

```
def cosineSimilarity(dotProduct: Double, ratingNorm: Double, rating2Norm:
Double) = {
    dotProduct / (ratingNorm * rating2Norm)
  }
```

Finally, the Jaccard Similarity between the two sets *A, B* is |*Intersection (A, B)*| / |*Union (A, B)*|:

```
def jaccardSimilarity(usersInCommon: Double, totalUsers1: Double,
totalUsers2: Double) = {
    val union = totalUsers1 + totalUsers2 - usersInCommon
    usersInCommon / union
  }
```

Step 4 - Testing the model

Let's see the 10 movies most similar to `Die Hard (1998)`, ranked by regularized correlation:

```
evaluateModel("Die Hard (1988)")
>>>
```

```
Die Hard (1988) | Fearless (1993) | -0.7674 | -0.4338 | 0.8622 | 0.0549
Die Hard (1988) | How to Make an American Quilt (1995) | -0.5106 | -0.3919 | 0.9056 | 0.1284
Die Hard (1988) | Rich Man's Wife, The (1996) | -0.8807 | -0.3626 | 0.9109 | 0.0303
Die Hard (1988) | Flubber (1997) | -0.5881 | -0.3619 | 0.8630 | 0.0632
Die Hard (1988) | His Girl Friday (1940) | -0.5411 | -0.3608 | 0.9478 | 0.0778
Die Hard (1988) | Believers, The (1987) | -0.8416 | -0.3466 | 0.8789 | 0.0302
Die Hard (1988) | Crow: City of Angels, The (1996) | -0.4753 | -0.3268 | 0.8096 | 0.0913
Die Hard (1988) | Barb Wire (1996) | -0.4983 | -0.3265 | 0.8632 | 0.0805
Die Hard (1988) | Ninotchka (1939) | -0.6143 | -0.3218 | 0.8956 | 0.0464
Die Hard (1988) | Goofy Movie, A (1995) | -0.8528 | -0.3198 | 0.8540 | 0.0253
```

In the preceding figure, the columns are Movie 1, Movie 2, Correlation, Reg-Correlation, Cosine Similarity, and Jaccard Similarity. Now let's see the 10 movies most similar to *Postino, Il* (1994), ranked by regularized correlation:

```
evaluateModel("Postino, Il (1994)")
>>>
```

```
Postino, Il (1994) | Volcano (1997) | -0.4861 | -0.3926 | 0.8369 | 0.1419
Postino, Il (1994) | Inventing the Abbotts (1997) | -0.7423 | -0.3888 | 0.9075 | 0.0636
Postino, Il (1994) | Safe (1995) | -0.7462 | -0.3535 | 0.9568 | 0.0549
Postino, Il (1994) | Until the End of the World (Bis ans Ende der Welt) (1991) | -0.8343 | -0.3435 | 0.8963 | 0.0400
Postino, Il (1994) | Cinderella (1950) | -0.4649 | -0.3392 | 0.9236 | 0.1071
Postino, Il (1994) | Man Without a Face, The (1993) | -0.6124 | -0.3340 | 0.8783 | 0.0571
Postino, Il (1994) | Mad City (1997) | -0.7482 | -0.3325 | 0.9370 | 0.0419
Postino, Il (1994) | First Knight (1995) | -0.5258 | -0.3236 | 0.8544 | 0.0714
Postino, Il (1994) | Santa Clause, The (1994) | -0.6433 | -0.3217 | 0.8539 | 0.0433
Postino, Il (1994) | Breakdown (1997) | -0.4763 | -0.3175 | 0.9216 | 0.0948
```

Finally, let's see the 10 movies most similar to Star Wars (1977), ranked by regularized correlation:

```
evaluateModel("Star Wars (1977)")
>>>
```

```
Star Wars (1977) | Fathers' Day (1997) | -0.6625 | -0.4417 | 0.9074 | 0.0397
Star Wars (1977) | Jason's Lyric (1994) | -0.9661 | -0.3978 | 0.8110 | 0.0141
Star Wars (1977) | Lightning Jack (1994) | -0.7906 | -0.3953 | 0.9361 | 0.0202
Star Wars (1977) | Marked for Death (1990) | -0.5922 | -0.3807 | 0.8729 | 0.0361
Star Wars (1977) | Mixed Nuts (1994) | -0.6219 | -0.3731 | 0.8806 | 0.0303
Star Wars (1977) | Poison Ivy II (1995) | -0.7443 | -0.3722 | 0.7169 | 0.0201
Star Wars (1977) | In the Realm of the Senses (Ai no corrida) (1976) | -0.8090 | -0.3596 | 0.8108 | 0.0162
Star Wars (1977) | What Happened Was... (1994) | -0.9045 | -0.3392 | 0.8781 | 0.0121
Star Wars (1977) | Female Perversions (1996) | -0.8039 | -0.3310 | 0.8670 | 0.0141
Star Wars (1977) | Celtic Pride (1996) | -0.6062 | -0.3175 | 0.8998 | 0.0220
```

Now, from the outputs, we can see that some movie pairs have very few common raters; it can be seen that using raw correlation resulted in suboptimal similarities. Using cosine similarity did not perform well, though it is a standard similarity metric for collaborative filtering approaches.

The reason is that there are many movies having a cosine similarity of 1.0. By the way, the preceding `evaluateModel()` method, which tests a few movies (substituting the contains call with the relevant movie name), goes as follows:

```
def evaluateModel(movieName: String): Unit = {
    val sample = similarities.filter(m => {
    val movies = m._1
    (movieNames(movies._1).contains(movieName))
    })
// collect results, excluding NaNs if applicable
val result = sample.map(v => {
val m1 = v._1._1
val m2 = v._1._2
val corr = v._2._1
val rcorr = v._2._2
val cos = v._2._3
val j = v._2._4
(movieNames(m1), movieNames(m2), corr, rcorr, cos, j)
}).collect().filter(e => !(e._4 equals Double.NaN)) // test for NaNs must
use equals rather than ==
    .sortBy(elem => elem._4).take(10)
    // print the top 10 out
result.foreach(r => println(r._1 + " | " + r._2 + " | " +
r._3.formatted("%2.4f") + " | " + r._4.formatted("%2.4f")
    + " | " + r._5.formatted("%2.4f") + " | " + r._6.formatted("%2.4f")))
}
```

You can understand the limitations of these types of collaborative filtering-based approaches. Of course there are computational complexities, but you're partially right. The most important aspects are that these does not have the ability to predict missing entries in real-life use cases. They also have some already-mentioned problems such as cold start, scalability, and sparsity. Therefore, we will see how we can improve these limitations using model-based recommendation systems in Spark MLlib.

Model-based recommendation with Spark

To make a preference prediction for any user, collaborative filtering uses a preference by other users of similar interests and predicts movies of your interests, that are unknown to you. Spark MLlib uses **Alternate Least Squares** (**ALS**) to make a recommendation. Here is a glimpse of a collaborative filtering method used in the ALS algorithm:

Table 1 – User-movie matrix

Users	M1	M2	M3	M4
U1	2	4	3	1
U2	0	0	4	4
U3	3	2	2	3
U4	2	?	3	?

In the preceding table, user ratings on movies are represented as a matrix (that is, a user-item matrix), where a cell represents ratings for a particular movie by a user. The cell with **?** represents the movies user **U4** is not aware of or hasn't seen. Based on the current preference of **U4**, the cell with **?** can be filled in with an approximate rating of users who have similar interests as **U4**. So at this point, ALS cannot do it alone, but the LFs are then used to predict the missing entries.

The Spark API provides the implementation of the ALS algorithm, which is used to learn these LFs based on the following six parameters:

- `numBlocks`: This is the number of blocks used to parallelize computation (set to -1 to auto-configure).
- `rank`: This is the number of LFs in the model.
- `iterations`: This is the number of iterations of ALS to run. ALS typically converges to a reasonable solution in 20 iterations or less.
- `lambda`: This specifies the regularization parameter in ALS.
- `implicitPrefs`: This specifies whether to use the explicit feedback from the ALS variant (or one user defined) for implicit feedback data.
- `alpha`: This is a parameter applicable to the implicit feedback variant of ALS that governs the baseline confidence in preference observations.

Note that to construct an ALS instance with default parameters, you can set the value based on your requirements. The default values are as follows: numBlocks: -1, rank: 10, iterations: 10, lambda: 0.01, implicitPrefs: false, and alpha: 1.0.

Data exploration

The movie and the corresponding rating dataset were downloaded from the MovieLens website (https://movielens.org). According to the data description on the MovieLens website, all the ratings are described in the ratings.csv file. Each row of this file, followed by the header, represents one rating of one movie by one user.

The CSV dataset has the following columns: userId, movieId, rating, and timestamp. These are shown in *Figure 14*. The rows are ordered first by userId and within the user by movieId. Ratings are made on a five-star scale, with half-star increments (0.5 stars up to a total of 5.0 stars). The timestamps represent the seconds since midnight in **Coordinated Universal Time (UTC)** on January 1, 1970. We have 105,339 ratings from 668 users on 10,325 movies:

```
+------+-------+------+----------+
|userId|movieId|rating|timestamp |
+------+-------+------+----------+
|1     |16     |4.0   |1217897793|
|1     |24     |1.5   |1217895807|
|1     |32     |4.0   |1217896246|
|1     |47     |4.0   |1217896556|
|1     |50     |4.0   |1217896523|
|1     |110    |4.0   |1217896150|
|1     |150    |3.0   |1217895940|
|1     |161    |4.0   |1217897864|
|1     |165    |3.0   |1217897135|
|1     |204    |0.5   |1217895786|
|1     |223    |4.0   |1217897795|
|1     |256    |0.5   |1217895764|
|1     |260    |4.5   |1217895864|
|1     |261    |1.5   |1217895750|
|1     |277    |0.5   |1217895772|
|1     |296    |4.0   |1217896125|
|1     |318    |4.0   |1217895860|
|1     |349    |4.5   |1217897058|
|1     |356    |3.0   |1217896231|
|1     |377    |2.5   |1217896373|
+------+-------+------+----------+
only showing top 20 rows
```

Figure 2: A snap of the rating dataset

On the other hand, movie information is contained in the `movies.csv` file. Each row, apart from the header information, represents one movie containing these columns: `movieId`, `title`, and `genres` (see *Figure 2*). Movie titles are either created or inserted manually or imported from the website of the movie database at `https://www.themoviedb.org/`. The release year, however, is shown in brackets.

Since movie titles are inserted manually, some errors or inconsistencies may exist in these titles. Readers are, therefore, recommended to check the IMDb database (`https://www.imdb.com/`) to make sure that there are no inconsistencies or incorrect titles with the corresponding release year:

```
+--------+----------------------------------+------------------------------------------------+
|movieId|title                             |genres                                          |
+--------+----------------------------------+------------------------------------------------+
|1      |Toy Story (1995)                  |Adventure|Animation|Children|Comedy|Fantasy|
|2      |Jumanji (1995)                    |Adventure|Children|Fantasy                      |
|3      |Grumpier Old Men (1995)           |Comedy|Romance                                  |
|4      |Waiting to Exhale (1995)          |Comedy|Drama|Romance                            |
|5      |Father of the Bride Part II (1995)|Comedy                                          |
|6      |Heat (1995)                       |Action|Crime|Thriller                           |
|7      |Sabrina (1995)                    |Comedy|Romance                                  |
|8      |Tom and Huck (1995)               |Adventure|Children                              |
|9      |Sudden Death (1995)               |Action                                          |
|10     |GoldenEye (1995)                  |Action|Adventure|Thriller                       |
|11     |American President, The (1995)    |Comedy|Drama|Romance                            |
|12     |Dracula: Dead and Loving It (1995)|Comedy|Horror                                   |
|13     |Balto (1995)                      |Adventure|Animation|Children                    |
|14     |Nixon (1995)                      |Drama                                           |
|15     |Cutthroat Island (1995)           |Action|Adventure|Romance                        |
|16     |Casino (1995)                     |Crime|Drama                                     |
|17     |Sense and Sensibility (1995)      |Drama|Romance                                   |
|18     |Four Rooms (1995)                 |Comedy                                          |
|19     |Ace Ventura: When Nature Calls (1995)|Comedy                                       |
|20     |Money Train (1995)                |Action|Comedy|Crime|Drama|Thriller              |
+--------+----------------------------------+------------------------------------------------+
only showing top 20 rows
```

Figure 3: Title and genres for top 20 movies

Genres are in a separated list and are selected from the following genre categories:

- Action, Adventure, Animation, Children's, Comedy, and Crime
- Documentary, Drama, Fantasy, Film-Noir, Horror, and Musical
- Mystery, Romance, Sci-Fi, Thriller, Western, and War

Movie recommendation using ALS

In this subsection, we will show you how to recommend movies to other users through a systematic example, from data collection to movie recommendation.

Step 1 - Import packages, load, parse, and explore the movie and rating dataset

We will load, parse, and do some exploratory analysis. However, before that, let's import the necessary packages and libraries:

```
package com.packt.ScalaML.MovieRecommendation
import org.apache.spark.sql.SparkSession
import org.apache.spark.mllib.recommendation.ALS
import org.apache.spark.mllib.recommendation.MatrixFactorizationModel
import org.apache.spark.mllib.recommendation.Rating
import scala.Tuple2
import org.apache.spark.rdd.RDD
```

This code segment should return you the DataFrame of the ratings:

```
val ratigsFile = "data/ratings.csv"
val df1 = spark.read.format("com.databricks.spark.csv").option("header",
true).load(ratigsFile)
val ratingsDF = df1.select(df1.col("userId"), df1.col("movieId"),
df1.col("rating"), df1.col("timestamp"))
ratingsDF.show(false)
```

The following code segment shows you the DataFrame of the movies:

```
val moviesFile = "data/movies.csv"
val df2 = spark.read.format("com.databricks.spark.csv").option("header",
"true").load(moviesFile)
val moviesDF = df2.select(df2.col("movieId"), df2.col("title"),
df2.col("genres"))
```

Step 2 - Register both DataFrames as temp tables to make querying easier

To register both datasets, we can use the following code:

```
ratingsDF.createOrReplaceTempView("ratings")
moviesDF.createOrReplaceTempView("movies")
```

This will help to make in-memory querying faster by creating a temporary view as a table in the memory. The lifetime of the temporary table using the `createOrReplaceTempView` () method is tied to `[[SparkSession]]`, which was used to create this DataFrame.

Step 3 - Explore and query for related statistics

Let's check the ratings-related statistics. Just use the following code lines:

```
val numRatings = ratingsDF.count()
val numUsers = ratingsDF.select(ratingsDF.col("userId")).distinct().count()
val numMovies =
ratingsDF.select(ratingsDF.col("movieId")).distinct().count()
println("Got " + numRatings + " ratings from " + numUsers + " users on " +
numMovies + " movies.")
>>>
Got 105339 ratings from 668 users on 10325 movies.
```

You should find $105,339$ ratings from 668 users on $10,325$ movies. Now, let's get the maximum and minimum ratings along with the count of users who have rated a movie. However, you need to perform an SQL query on the rating table we just created in memory in the previous step. Making a query here is simple, and it is similar to making a query from a MySQL database or RDBMS.

However, if you are not familiar with SQL-based queries, you are advised to look at the SQL query specification to find out how to perform a selection using SELECT from a particular table, how to perform ordering using ORDER, and how to perform a joining operation using the JOIN keyword. Well, if you know the SQL query, you should get a new dataset using a complex SQL query, as follows:

```
// Get the max, min ratings along with the count of users who have rated a
movie.
val results = spark.sql("select movies.title, movierates.maxr,
movierates.minr, movierates.cntu "
        + "from(SELECT ratings.movieId,max(ratings.rating) as maxr,"
        + "min(ratings.rating) as minr,count(distinct userId) as cntu "
        + "FROM ratings group by ratings.movieId) movierates "
        + "join movies on movierates.movieId=movies.movieId " + "order by
movierates.cntu desc")
results.show(false)
```

Output:

```
+-----------------------------------------------------------------------+----+----+----+
|title                                                                  |maxr|minr|cntu|
+-----------------------------------------------------------------------+----+----+----+
|Pulp Fiction (1994)                                                    |5.0 |0.5 |325 |
|Forrest Gump (1994)                                                    |5.0 |0.5 |311 |
|Shawshank Redemption, The (1994)                                       |5.0 |0.5 |308 |
|Jurassic Park (1993)                                                   |5.0 |1.0 |294 |
|Silence of the Lambs, The (1991)                                       |5.0 |0.5 |290 |
|Star Wars: Episode IV - A New Hope (1977)                              |5.0 |0.5 |273 |
|Matrix, The (1999)                                                     |5.0 |0.5 |261 |
|Terminator 2: Judgment Day (1991)                                      |5.0 |0.5 |253 |
|Schindler's List (1993)                                                |5.0 |0.5 |248 |
|Braveheart (1995)                                                      |5.0 |0.5 |248 |
|Fugitive, The (1993)                                                   |5.0 |1.0 |244 |
|Toy Story (1995)                                                       |5.0 |1.0 |232 |
|Usual Suspects, The (1995)                                             |5.0 |1.0 |228 |
|Star Wars: Episode V - The Empire Strikes Back (1980)                  |5.0 |0.5 |228 |
|Raiders of the Lost Ark (Indiana Jones and the Raiders of the Lost Ark) (1981)|5.0 |1.0 |224 |
|Star Wars: Episode VI - Return of the Jedi (1983)                      |5.0 |0.5 |222 |
|Batman (1989)                                                          |5.0 |0.5 |217 |
|American Beauty (1999)                                                 |5.0 |1.0 |216 |
|Back to the Future (1985)                                              |5.0 |1.5 |213 |
|Godfather, The (1972)                                                  |5.0 |1.0 |210 |
+-----------------------------------------------------------------------+----+----+----+
only showing top 20 rows
```

Figure 4: Max and min ratings along with the count of users who have rated a movie

To get some insight, we need to know more about the users and their ratings. Now let's find the 10 most active users and how many times they rated a movie:

```
val mostActiveUsersSchemaRDD = spark.sql("SELECT ratings.userId, count(*)
as ct from ratings "+ "group by ratings.userId order by ct desc limit 10")
mostActiveUsersSchemaRDD.show(false)
>>>
```

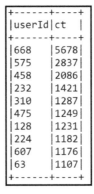

Figure 5: Top 10 active users and how many times they rated a movie

Let's have a look at a particular user and find the movies that, say user, 668 rated higher than 4:

```
val results2 = spark.sql(
                "SELECT ratings.userId, ratings.movieId,"
              + "ratings.rating, movies.title FROM ratings JOIN movies"
              + "ON movies.movieId=ratings.movieId"
              + "where ratings.userId=668 and ratings.rating > 4")
results2.show(false)
>>>
```

```
+------+-------+------+----------------------------+
|userId|movieId|rating|title                       |
+------+-------+------+----------------------------+
|668   |6      |5.0   |Heat (1995)                 |
|668   |858    |5.0   |Godfather, The (1972)       |
|668   |898    |5.0   |Philadelphia Story, The (1940)|
|668   |908    |5.0   |North by Northwest (1959)   |
|668   |910    |5.0   |Some Like It Hot (1959)     |
|668   |912    |5.0   |Casablanca (1942)           |
|668   |913    |5.0   |Maltese Falcon, The (1941)  |
|668   |914    |5.0   |My Fair Lady (1964)         |
|668   |919    |5.0   |Wizard of Oz, The (1939)    |
|668   |1183   |5.0   |English Patient, The (1996) |
|668   |1204   |5.0   |Lawrence of Arabia (1962)   |
|668   |1217   |5.0   |Ran (1985)                  |
|668   |1219   |5.0   |Psycho (1960)               |
|668   |1256   |5.0   |Duck Soup (1933)            |
|668   |1283   |5.0   |High Noon (1952)            |
|668   |1938   |5.0   |Lost Weekend, The (1945)    |
|668   |1945   |5.0   |On the Waterfront (1954)    |
|668   |1947   |5.0   |West Side Story (1961)      |
|668   |2644   |5.0   |Dracula (1931)              |
|668   |2728   |5.0   |Spartacus (1960)            |
+------+-------+------+----------------------------+
only showing top 20 rows
```

Figure 6: Movies that user 668 rated higher than 4

Step 4 - Prepare training and test rating data and check the counts

The following code splits the ratings RDD into training data RDD (75%) and test data RDD (25%). Seed here is optional but is required for reproducibility purposes:

```
// Split ratings RDD into training RDD (75%) & test RDD (25%)
val splits = ratingsDF.randomSplit(Array(0.75, 0.25), seed = 12345L)
val (trainingData, testData) = (splits(0), splits(1))
val numTraining = trainingData.count()
val numTest = testData.count()
println("Training: " + numTraining + " test: " + numTest)
```

You should notice that there are 78,792 ratings in training and 26,547 ratings in the test DataFrame.

Step 5 - Prepare the data for building the recommendation model using ALS

The ALS algorithm takes the RDD of ratings for training. To do so, the following code illustrates for building the recommendation model using APIs:

```
val ratingsRDD = trainingData.rdd.map(row => {
                    val userId = row.getString(0)
                    val movieId = row.getString(1)
                    val ratings = row.getString(2)
                    Rating(userId.toInt, movieId.toInt, ratings.toDouble)
})
```

The `ratingsRDD` is an RDD of ratings that contains `userId`, `movieId`, and the corresponding ratings from the training dataset we prepared in the previous step. On the other hand, a test RDD is also required for evaluating the model. The following `testRDD` also contains the same information coming from the test DataFrame we prepared in the previous step:

```
val testRDD = testData.rdd.map(row => {
    val userId = row.getString(0)
    val movieId = row.getString(1)
    val ratings = row.getString(2)
    Rating(userId.toInt, movieId.toInt, ratings.toDouble)
})
```

Step 6 - Build an ALS user product matrix

Build an ALS user matrix model based on `ratingsRDD` by specifying the maximal iteration, a number of blocks, alpha, rank, lambda, seed, and `implicitPrefs`. Essentially, this technique predicts missing ratings for specific users and specific movies based on ratings for those movies from other users who gave similar ratings for other movies:

```
val rank = 20
val numIterations = 15
val lambda = 0.10
val alpha = 1.00 val block = -1
val seed = 12345L
val implicitPrefs = false

val model = new ALS().setIterations(numIterations)
        .setBlocks(block).setAlpha(alpha)
        .setLambda(lambda)
```

```
.setRank(rank) .setSeed(seed)
.setImplicitPrefs(implicitPrefs)
.run(ratingsRDD)
```

Finally, we iterated the model for learning 15 times. With this setting, we got good prediction accuracy. Readers are advised to apply hyperparameter tuning to get to know the most optimum values for these parameters. Furthermore, set the number of blocks for both user blocks and product blocks to parallelize the computation into a pass -1 for an auto-configured number of blocks. The value is -1.

Step 7 - Making predictions

Let's get the top six movie predictions for user 668. The following source code can be used to make the predictions:

```
// Making Predictions. Get the top 6 movie predictions for user 668
println("Rating:(UserID, MovieID, Rating)") println("---------------------
------------")
val topRecsForUser = model.recommendProducts(668, 6) for (rating <-
topRecsForUser) { println(rating.toString()) } println("-------------------
---------------")
>>>
```

```
Rating:(UserID, MovieID, Rating)
---------------------------------
Rating(668,5304,4.8525842164777435)
Rating(668,25961,4.8525842164777435)
Rating(668,101862,4.8525842164777435)
Rating(668,80969,4.779325934293423)
Rating(668,93040,4.7528736838886)
Rating(668,25795,4.676957397667861)
---------------------------------
```

Figure 7: Top six movie predictions for user 668

Step 8 - Evaluating the model

In order to verify the quality of the model, **Root Mean Squared Error** (**RMSE**) is used to measure the difference between values predicted by a model and the values actually observed. By default, the smaller the calculated error, the better the model. In order to test the quality of the model, the test data is used (which was split in *step 4*).

According to many machine learning practitioners, RMSE is a good measure of accuracy, but only for comparing forecasting errors of different models for a particular variable. They say it is not fit for comparing between variables as it is scale dependent. The following line of code calculates the RMSE value for the model that was trained using the training set:

```
val rmseTest = computeRmse(model, testRDD, true)
println("Test RMSE: = " + rmseTest) //Less is better
```

For this setting, we get this output:

```
Test RMSE: = 0.9019872589764073
```

This method computes the RMSE to evaluate the model. The lesser the RMSE, the better the model and its prediction capability. It is to be noted that `computeRmse()` is a UDF that goes as follows:

```
def computeRmse(model: MatrixFactorizationModel, data: RDD[Rating],
implicitPrefs: Boolean): Double = {                val predictions: RDD[Rating] =
model.predict(data.map(x => (x.user, x.product)))
    val predictionsAndRatings = predictions.map { x => ((x.user,
x.product), x.rating) }
        .join(data.map(x => ((x.user, x.product), x.rating))).values
    if (implicitPrefs) { println("(Prediction, Rating)")
        println(predictionsAndRatings.take(5).mkString("n")) }
        math.sqrt(predictionsAndRatings.map(x => (x._1 - x._2) * (x._1 -
x._2)).mean())
    }
>>>
```

```
(Prediction, Rating)
(3.848087516442212,3.5)
(4.647813269020743,5.0)
(3.578002886107389,4.0)
(3.681217214985231,3.0)
(2.844685318141285,3.0)
```

Finally, let's provide some movie recommendation for a specific user. Let's get the top six movie predictions for user `668`:

```
println("Recommendations: (MovieId => Rating)")
println("-------------------------------------")
val recommendationsUser = model.recommendProducts(668, 6)
recommendationsUser.map(rating => (rating.product,
rating.rating)).foreach(println) println("--------------------------------
-")
>>>
```

```
Recommendations: (MovieId => Rating)
----------------------------------
(5304,4.8525842164777435)
(25961,4.8525842164777435)
(101862,4.8525842164777435)
(80969,4.779325934293423)
(93040,4.7528736838886)
(25795,4.676957397667861)
----------------------------------
```

The performance of the preceding model could be increased more, we believe. However, so far, there's no model tuning facility of our knowledge available for the MLlib-based ALS algorithm.

 Interested readers should refer to this URL for more on tuning ML-based ALS models: `https://spark.apache.org/docs/preview/ml-collaborative-filtering.html`.

Selecting and deploying the best model

It is worth mentioning that the first model developed in the first project cannot be persisted since it is just a few lines of code for computing movie similarity. It also has another limitation that we did not cover earlier. It can compute the similarity between two movies, but what about more than two movies? Frankly speaking, a model like the first one would rarely be deployed for a real-life movie. So let's focus on the model-based recommendation engine instead.

Although ratings from users will keep coming, still it might be worth it to store the current one. Therefore, we also want to persist our current base model for later use in order to save time when starting up the server. The idea is to use the current model for real-time movie recommendations.

Nevertheless, we might also save time if we persist some of the RDDs we have generated, especially those that took longer to process. The following line saves our trained ALS model (see the `MovieRecommendation.scala` script for details):

```
//Saving the model for future use
val savedALSModel = model.save(spark.sparkContext, "model/MovieRecomModel")
```

Unlike another Spark model, the ALS model that we saved will contain only data and some metadata in parquet format from the training, as shown in the following screenshot:

```
∨ ⌂ MovieRecomModel
  ∨ ⌂ data
    ∨ ⌂ product
        ▤ _SUCCESS
        ▤ part-00000-07fe32cf-be2c-4431-873c-bd4d5d8408d1-c000.snappy.parquet
        ▤ part-00001-07fe32cf-be2c-4431-873c-bd4d5d8408d1-c000.snappy.parquet
        ▤ part-00002-07fe32cf-be2c-4431-873c-bd4d5d8408d1-c000.snappy.parquet
        ▤ part-00003-07fe32cf-be2c-4431-873c-bd4d5d8408d1-c000.snappy.parquet
        ▤ part-00004-07fe32cf-be2c-4431-873c-bd4d5d8408d1-c000.snappy.parquet
        ▤ part-00005-07fe32cf-be2c-4431-873c-bd4d5d8408d1-c000.snappy.parquet
        ▤ part-00006-07fe32cf-be2c-4431-873c-bd4d5d8408d1-c000.snappy.parquet
        ▤ part-00007-07fe32cf-be2c-4431-873c-bd4d5d8408d1-c000.snappy.parquet
    ∨ ⌂ user
        ▤ _SUCCESS
        ▤ part-00000-9a2d7b64-9052-470d-833c-1bf1b33dda83-c000.snappy.parquet
        ▤ part-00001-9a2d7b64-9052-470d-833c-1bf1b33dda83-c000.snappy.parquet
        ▤ part-00002-9a2d7b64-9052-470d-833c-1bf1b33dda83-c000.snappy.parquet
        ▤ part-00003-9a2d7b64-9052-470d-833c-1bf1b33dda83-c000.snappy.parquet
        ▤ part-00004-9a2d7b64-9052-470d-833c-1bf1b33dda83-c000.snappy.parquet
        ▤ part-00005-9a2d7b64-9052-470d-833c-1bf1b33dda83-c000.snappy.parquet
        ▤ part-00006-9a2d7b64-9052-470d-833c-1bf1b33dda83-c000.snappy.parquet
        ▤ part-00007-9a2d7b64-9052-470d-833c-1bf1b33dda83-c000.snappy.parquet
  ∨ ⌂ metadata
      ▤ _SUCCESS
      ▤ part-00000
```

Now, the next task would be to restore the same model and provide a similar workflow as shown in the preceding steps:

```scala
val same_model = MatrixFactorizationModel.load(spark.sparkContext,
"model/MovieRecomModel/")
```

Nevertheless I won't confuse you, especially if you're new to Spark and Scala. Here's the complete code that predicts the ratings of user 558:

```scala
package com.packt.ScalaML.MovieRecommendation

import org.apache.spark.sql.SparkSession
import org.apache.spark.mllib.recommendation.ALS
import org.apache.spark.mllib.recommendation.MatrixFactorizationModel
import org.apache.spark.mllib.recommendation.Rating
```

```scala
import scala.Tuple2
import org.apache.spark.rdd.RDD

object RecommendationModelReuse {
    def main(args: Array[String]): Unit = {
        val spark: SparkSession = SparkSession.builder()
                                  .appName("JavaLDAExample")
                                  .master("local[*]")
                                  .config("spark.sql.warehouse.dir",
"E:/Exp/")
                                  .getOrCreate()

        val ratigsFile = "data/ratings.csv"
        val ratingDF =  spark.read
                        .format("com.databricks.spark.csv")
                        .option("header", true)
                        .load(ratigsFile)

        val selectedRatingsDF = ratingDF.select(ratingDF.col("userId"),
ratingDF.col("movieId"),
ratingDF.col("rating"), ratingDF.col("timestamp"))

        // Randomly split ratings RDD into training data RDD (75%) and test
data RDD (25%)
        val splits = selectedRatingsDF.randomSplit(Array(0.75, 0.25), seed
= 12345L)
        val testData = splits(1)
        val testRDD = testData.rdd.map(row => {
        val userId = row.getString(0)
        val movieId = row.getString(1)
        val ratings = row.getString(2)
        Rating(userId.toInt, movieId.toInt, ratings.toDouble) })

        //Load the workflow back
        val same_model = MatrixFactorizationModel.load(spark.sparkContext,
"model/MovieRecomModel/")

        // Making Predictions. Get the top 6 movie predictions for user 668
        println("Rating:(UserID, MovieID, Rating)")
        println("----------------------------------")
        val topRecsForUser = same_model.recommendProducts(458, 10)

        for (rating <- topRecsForUser) {
            println(rating.toString()) }

        println("----------------------------------")
        val rmseTest = MovieRecommendation.computeRmse(same_model, testRDD,
true)
```

```
        println("Test RMSE: = " + rmseTest) //Less is better

        //Movie recommendation for a specific user. Get the top 6 movie
predictions for user 668
        println("Recommendations: (MovieId => Rating)")
        println("---------------------------------")
        val recommendationsUser = same_model.recommendProducts(458, 10)

        recommendationsUser.map(rating =>
        (rating.product, rating.rating)).foreach(println)
        println("---------------------------------")
        spark.stop()
    }
}
```

If the preceding script is executed successfully, you should see the following output:

```
Rating:(UserID, MovieID, Rating)
---------------------------------
Rating(458,670,4.687132475422945)
Rating(458,214,4.62504244476065)
Rating(458,3467,4.603944438428056)
Rating(458,858,4.590518214337291)
Rating(458,2745,4.57253593653456)
Rating(458,7158,4.5580179461102235)
Rating(458,1546,4.5526318073335865)
Rating(458,1797,4.551033119658062)
Rating(458,6301,4.550922059713256)
Rating(458,1361,4.522913373522734)
---------------------------------
(Prediction, Rating)
(3.848087516442212,3.5)
(4.647813269020743,5.0)
(3.578002886107389,4.0)
(3.681217214985231,3.0)
(2.844685318141285,3.0)

Test RMSE: = 0.9019872589764074

Recommendations: (MovieId => Rating)
---------------------------------
(670,4.687132475422945)
(214,4.62504244476065)
(3467,4.603944438428056)
(858,4.590518214337291)
(2745,4.57253593653456)
(7158,4.5580179461102235)
(1546,4.5526318073335865)
(1797,4.551033119658062)
(6301,4.550922059713256)
(1361,4.522913373522734)
---------------------------------
```

Well done! We have managed to reuse the model and do the same prediction but for a different user, that is, 558. However, probably due to the randomness of the data, we observed a slightly different RMSE.

Summary

In this chapter, we implemented two end-to-end projects to develop item-based collaborative filtering for movie similarity measurement and model-based recommendation with Spark. We also saw how to interoperate between ALS and MF and develop scalable movie recommendations engines. Finally, we saw how to deploy this model in production.

As human beings, we learn from past experiences. We haven't gotten so charming by accident. Years of positive compliments as well as criticism have all helped shape us into what we are today. You learn what makes people happy by interacting with friends, family, and even strangers, and you figure out how to ride a bike by trying out different muscle movements until it just clicks. When you perform actions, you're sometimes rewarded immediately. This is all about **Reinforcement Learning (RL)**.

The next chapter is all about designing a machine learning project driven by criticisms and rewards. We will see how to apply RL algorithms for developing options trading applications using real-life IBM stock and option price datasets.

7
Options Trading Using Q-learning and Scala Play Framework

As human beings, we learn from experiences. We have not become so charming by accident. Years of positive compliments as well as negative criticism, have all helped shape us into who we are today. We learn how to ride a bike by trying out different muscle movements until it just clicks. When you perform actions, you are sometimes rewarded immediately. This is all about **Reinforcement learning** (RL).

This chapter is all about designing a machine learning system driven by criticisms and rewards. We will see how to apply RL algorithms for a predictive model on real-life datasets.

From the trading point of view, an option is a contract that gives its owner the right to buy (call option) or sell (put option) a financial asset (underlying) at a fixed price (the strike price) at or before a fixed date (the expiry date).

We will see how to develop a real-life application for such options trading using an RL algorithm called **QLearning**. To be more precise, we will solve the problem of computing the best strategy in options trading, and we want to trade certain types of options given some market conditions and trading data.

The IBM stock datasets will be used to design a machine learning system driven by criticisms and rewards. We will start from RL and its theoretical background so that the concept is easier to grasp. Finally, we will wrap up the whole application as a web app using Scala Play Framework.

Concisely, we will learn the following topics throughout this end-to-end project:

- Using Q-learning—an RL algorithm
- Options trading—what is it all about?
- Overview of technologies
- Implementing Q-learning for options trading
- Wrapping up the application as a web app using Scala Play Framework
- Model deployment

Reinforcement versus supervised and unsupervised learning

Whereas supervised and unsupervised learning appear at opposite ends of the spectrum, RL exists somewhere in the middle. It is not supervised learning because the training data comes from the algorithm deciding between exploration and exploitation. In addition, it is not unsupervised because the algorithm receives feedback from the environment. As long as you are in a situation where performing an action in a state produces a reward, you can use RL to discover a good sequence of actions to take the maximum expected rewards.

The goal of an RL agent will be to maximize the total reward that it receives in the end. The third main subelement is the `value` function. While rewards determine an immediate desirability of the states, values indicate the long-term desirability of states, taking into account the states that may follow and the available rewards in these states. The `value` function is specified with respect to the chosen policy. During the learning phase, an agent tries actions that determine the states with the highest value, because these actions will get the best number of rewards in the end.

Using RL

Figure 1 shows a person making decisions to arrive at their destination. Moreover, suppose that on your drive from home to work, you always choose the same route. However, one day your curiosity takes over and you decide to try a different path, hoping for a shorter commute. This dilemma of trying out new routes or sticking to the best-known route is an example of exploration versus exploitation:

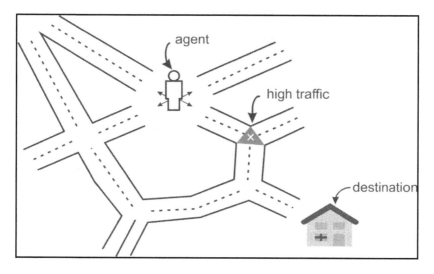

Figure 1: An agent always tries to reach the destination by passing through the route

RL techniques are being used in many areas. A general idea that is being pursued right now is creating an algorithm that does not need anything apart from a description of its task. When this kind of performance is achieved, it will be applied virtually everywhere.

Notation, policy, and utility in RL

You may notice that RL jargon involves incarnating the algorithm into taking actions in situations to receive rewards. In fact, the algorithm is often referred to as an agent that acts with the environment. You can just think of it is an intelligent hardware agent that is sensing with sensors and interacting with the environment using its actuators. Therefore, it should not be a surprise that much of RL theory is applied in robotics. Now, to extend our discussion further, we need to know a few terminologies:

- **Environment**: An environment is any system having states and mechanisms to transition between different states. For example, the environment for a robot is the landscape or facility it operates in.
- **Agent**: An agent is an automated system that interacts with the environment.
- **State**: The state of the environment or system is the set of variables or features that fully describe the environment.

- **Goal**: A goal is a state that provides a higher discounted cumulative reward than any other state. A high cumulative reward prevents the best policy from being dependent on the initial state during training.
- **Action**: An action defines the transition between states, where an agent is responsible for performing, or at least recommending, an action. Upon execution of an action, the agent collects a reward (or punishment) from the environment.
- **Policy**: The policy defines the action to be performed and executed for any state of the environment.
- **Reward**: A reward quantifies the positive or negative interaction of the agent with the environment. Rewards are essentially the training set for the learning engine.
- **Episode** (also known as **trials**): This defines the number of steps necessary to reach the goal state from an initial state.

We will discuss more on policy and utility later in this section. *Figure 2* demonstrates the interplay between **states**, **actions**, and **rewards**. If you start at state s_1, you can perform action a_1 to obtain a reward $r(s_1, a_1)$. Arrows represent **actions**, and **states** are represented by circles:

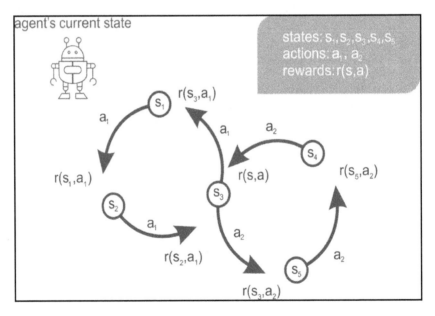

Figure 2: An agent performing an action on a state produces a reward

A robot performs actions to change between different states. But how does it decide which action to take? Well, it is all about using a different or concrete policy.

Policy

In RL lingo, we call a strategy **policy**. The goal of RL is to discover a good strategy. One of the most common ways to solve it is by observing the long-term consequences of actions in each state. The short-term consequence is easy to calculate: it's just the reward. Although performing an action yields an immediate reward, it is not always a good idea to greedily choose the action with the best reward. That is a lesson in life too, because the most immediate best thing to do may not always be the most satisfying in the long run. The best possible policy is called the optimal policy, and it is often the holy grail of RL, as shown in *Figure 3*, which shows the optimal action, given any state:

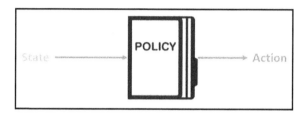

Figure 3: A policy defines an action to be taken in a given state

We have seen one type of policy where the agent always chooses the action with the greatest immediate reward, called **greedy policy**. Another simple example of a policy is arbitrarily choosing an action, called **random policy**. If you come up with a policy to solve a, RL problem, it is often a good idea to double-check that your learned policy performs better than both the random and the greedy policies.

In addition, we will see how to develop another robust policy called **policy gradients**, where a neural network learns a policy for picking actions by adjusting its weights through gradient descent using feedback from the environment. We will see that, although both the approaches are used, policy gradient is more direct and optimistic.

Utility

The long-term reward is called a **utility**. It turns out that if we know the utility of performing an action upon a state, then it is easy to solve RL. For example, to decide which action to take, we simply select the action that produces the highest utility. However, uncovering these utility values is difficult. The utility of performing an action a at a state s is written as a function, $Q(s, a)$, called the **utility function**. This predicts the expected immediate reward, and rewards following an optimal policy given the state-action input, as shown in *Figure 4*:

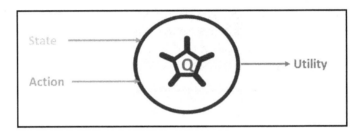

Figure 4: Using a utility function

Most RL algorithms boil down to just three main steps: infer, do, and learn. During the first step, the algorithm selects the best action (a) given a state (s) using the knowledge it has so far. Next, it perform the action to find out the reward (r) as well as the next state (s'). Then it improves its understanding of the world using the newly acquired knowledge (s, r, a, s'). However, as I think you will agree, this is just a naive way to calculate the utility.

Now, the question is: what could be a more robust way to compute it? We can calculate the utility of a particular state-action pair (s, a) by recursively considering the utilities of future actions. The utility of your current action is influenced not only by the immediate reward but also the next best action, as shown in the following formula:

$$Q(s, a) = r(s, a) + \gamma \max Q(s', a')$$

s' denotes the next state, and a' denotes the next action. The reward of taking action a in state s is denoted by $r(s, a)$. Here, γ is a hyperparameter that you get to choose, called the discount factor. If γ is 0, then the agent chooses the action that maximizes the immediate reward. Higher values of γ will make the agent give more importance to considering long-term consequences. In practice, we have more such hyperparameter to be considered. For example, if a vacuum cleaner robot is expected to learn to solve tasks quickly, but not necessarily optimally, we may want to set a faster learning rate.

Alternatively, if a robot is allowed more time to explore and exploit, we may tune down the learning rate. Let us call the learning rate α and change our utility function as follows (note that when $\alpha = 1$, both the equations are identical):

$$Q(s,a) \rightarrow Q(s,a) + \alpha(r(s,a) + \gamma \, max \, Q(s^{'},a^{'}) - Q(s,a))$$

In summary, an RL problem can be solved if we know this $Q(s, a)$ function. Here comes an algorithm called Q-learning.

A simple Q-learning implementation

Q-learning is an algorithm that can be used in financial and market trading applications, such as options trading. One reason is that the best policy is generated through training. that is, RL defines the model in Q-learning over time and is constantly updated with any new episode. Q-learning is a method for optimizing (cumulated) discounted reward, making far-future rewards less prioritized than near-term rewards; Q-learning is a form of model-free RL. It can also be viewed as a method of asynchronous **dynamic programming (DP)**.

It provides agents with the capability of learning to act optimally in Markovian domains by experiencing the consequences of actions, without requiring them to build maps of the domains. In short, Q-learning qualifies as an RL technique because it does not strictly require labeled data and training. Moreover, the Q-value does not have to be a continuous, differentiable function.

On the other hand, Markov decision processes provide a mathematical framework for modeling decision-making in situations where outcomes are partly random and partly under the control of a decision-maker. Therein, the probability of the random variables at a future point of time depends only on the information at the current point in time and not on any of the historical values. In other words, the probability is independent of historical states.

Components of the Q-learning algorithm

This implementation is highly inspired by the Q-learning implementation from a book, written by Patrick R. Nicolas, *Scala for Machine Learning - Second Edition*, Packt Publishing Ltd., September 2017. Thanks to the author and Packt Publishing Ltd. The source code is available at `https://github.com/PacktPublishing/Scala-for-Machine-Learning-Second-Edition/tree/master/src/main/scala/org/scalaml/reinforcement`.

Interested readers can take a look at the the original implementation at the extended version of course can be downloaded from Packt repository or GitHub repo of this book. The key components of implementation of the Q-learning algorithm are a few classes—`QLearning`, `QLSpace`, `QLConfig`, `QLAction`, `QLState`, `QLIndexedState`, and `QLModel`—as described in the following points:

- `QLearning`: Implements training and prediction methods. It defines a data transformation of type `ETransform` using a configuration of type `QLConfig`.
- `QLConfig`: This parameterized class defines the configuration parameters for the Q-learning. To be more specific, it is used to hold an explicit configuration from the user.
- `QLAction`: This is a class that defines actions between on source state and multiple destination states.
- `QLPolicy`: This is an enumerator used to define the type of parameters used to update the policy during the training of the Q-learning model.
- `QLSpace`: This has two components: a sequence of states of type `QLState` and the identifier, `id`, of one or more goal states within the sequence.
- `QLState`: Contains a sequence of `QLAction` instances that help in the transition from one state to another. It is also used as a reference for the object or instance for which the state is to be evaluated and predicted.
- `QLIndexedState`: This class returns an indexed state that indexes a state in the search toward the goal state.
- `QLModel`: This is used to generate a model through the training process. Eventually, it contains the best policy and the accuracy of a model.

Note that, apart from the preceding components, an optional constraint function limits the scope of the search for the next most rewarding action from the current state. The following diagram shows the key components of the Q-learning algorithm and their interaction:

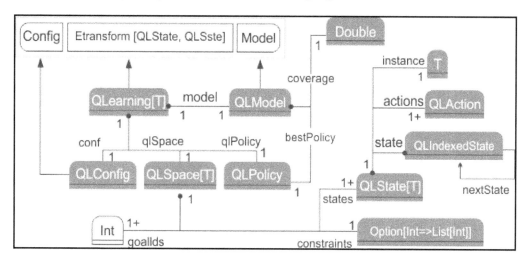

Figure 5: Components of the QLearning algorithm and their interaction

States and actions in QLearning

The QLAction class specifies the transition from one state to another state. It takes two parameters—that is, from and to. Both of them have their own integer identifiers that need to be greater than 0:

- from: A source of the action
- to: Target of the action

The signature is given as follows:

```
case class QLAction(from: Int, to: Int) {
    require(from >= 0, s"QLAction found from:
    $from required: >=0")require(to >= 0, s"QLAction found to:
    $to required: >=0")

    override def toString: String = s"n
    Action: state
    $from => state $to"
}
```

The QLState class defines the state in the Q-learning. It takes three parameters:

- id: An identifier that uniquely identifies a state
- actions: A list of actions for the transition from this state to other states,
- instance: A state may have properties of type T, independent from the state transition

Here is the signature of the class:

```
case class QLState[T](id: Int, actions: Seq[QLAction] = List.empty,
instance: T) {
    import QLState._check(id)
    final def isGoal: Boolean = actions.nonEmpty
    override def toString: String =s"state: $id ${actions.mkString(" ")
        }
    nInstance: ${instance.toString}"
}
```

In the preceding code, the toString() method is used for textual representation of a state in Q-learning. The state is defined by its ID and the list of actions it may potentially trigger.

 The state might not have any actions. This is usually the case with the goal or absorbing state. In this case, the list is empty. The parameterized instance is a reference to the object for which the state is computed.

Now we know the state and action to perform. However, the QLearning agent needs to know the search space of the form (States x Actions). The next step consists of creating the graph or search space.

The search space

The search space is the container responsible for any sequence of states. The QLSpace class defines the search space (States x Actions) for the Q-learning algorithm, as shown in the following figure:

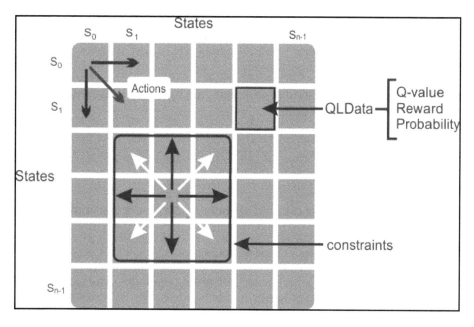

Figure 6: State transition matrix with QLData (Q-value, reward, probability)

The search space can be provided by the end user with a list of states and actions, or automatically created by providing the number of states by taking the following parameters:

- `States`: The sequence of all possible states defined in the Q-learning search space
- `goalIds`: A list of identifiers of states that are goals

Now let us see the implementation of the class. It is rather a large code block. So let us start from the constructor that generates a map named `statesMap`. It retrieves the state using its id and the array of goals, `goalStates`:

```
private[scalaml] class QLSpace[T] protected (states: Seq[QLState[T]],
goalIds: Array[Int]) {
    import QLSpace._check(states, goalIds)
```

Then it creates a map of the states as an immutable Map of state ID and state instance:

```scala
private[this] val statesMap: immutable.Map[Int, QLState[T]] = states.map(st
=> (st.id, st)).toMap
```

Now that we have a policy and a state of an action, the next task is to compute the maximum value given a state and policy:

```scala
final def maxQ(state: QLState[T], policy: QLPolicy): Double = {
    val best=states.filter(_ != state).maxBy(st=>policy.EQ(state.id,
st.id))policy.EQ(state.id, best.id)
    }
```

Additionally, we need to know the number of states by accessing the number of states in the search space:

```scala
final def getNumStates: Int = states.size
```

Then the `init` method selects an initial state for training episodes. The state is randomly selected if the `state0` argument is invalid:

```scala
def init(state0: Int): QLState[T] =
    if (state0 < 0) {
        val r = new Random(System.currentTimeMillis
            + Random.nextLong) states(r.nextInt(states.size - 1))
        }
    else states(state0)
```

Finally, the `nextStates` method retrieves the list of states resulting from the execution of all the actions associated with that state. The search space `QLSpace` is created by the factory method `apply` defined in the `QLSpace` companion object, as shown here:

```scala
final def nextStates(st: QLState[T]): Seq[QLState[T]] =
            if (st.actions.isEmpty) Seq.empty[QLState[T]]
            else st.actions.flatMap(ac => statesMap.get(ac.to))
```

Additionally, how do you know whether the current state is a goal state? Well, the `isGoal()` method does the trick.

It accepts a parameter called `state`, which is *a* state that is tested against the goal and returns `Boolean`: `true` if this state is a goal state; otherwise, it returns false:

```scala
final def isGoal(state: QLState[T]): Boolean =
goalStates.contains(state.id)
```

The apply method creates a list of states using the instances set, the goals, and the constraining function `constraints` as input. Each state creates its list of actions. The actions are generated from this state to any other states:

```
def apply[T](goal: Int,instances: Seq[T],constraints: Option[Int =>
List[Int]]): QLSpace[T] =
    apply(Array[Int](goal), instances, constraints)
```

The function constraints limit the scope of the actions that can be triggered from any given state, as shown in figure X.

The policy and action-value

The `QLData` class encapsulates the attributes of the policy in the Q-learning algorithm by creating a `QLData` record or instance with a given reward, probability, and Q-value that is computed and updated during training. The probability variable is used to model the intervention condition for an action to be executed.

If the action does not have any external constraint, the probability is 1 (that is, the highest), and it is zero otherwise (that is, the action is not allowed anyhow). The signature is given as follows:

```
final private[scalaml] class QLData(
    val reward: Double,
    val probability: Double = 1.0) {

    import QLDataVar._
    var value: Double = 0.0
    @inline final def estimate: Double = value * probability

    final def value(varType: QLDataVar): Double = varType
            match {
                case REWARD => reward
                case PROB => probability
                case VALUE => value
        }
override def toString: String = s"nValue= $value Reward= $reward
Probability= $probability"}
```

In the preceding code block, the Q-Value updated during training using the Q-learning formula, but the overall value is computed for an action by using its reward, adjusted by its probability, and then returning the adjusted value. Then the `value()` method selects the attribute of an element of the Q-learning policy using its type. It takes the `varType` of the attribute (that is, REWARD, PROBABILITY, and VALUE) and returns the value of this attribute.

Finally, the toString() method helps to represent the value, reward, and the probability. Now that we know how the data will be manipulated, the next task is to create a simple schema that initializes the reward and probability associated with each action. The following Scala case is a class named QLInput; it inputs to the Q-learning search space (QLSpace) and policy (QLPolicy):

```
case class QLInput(from: Int, to: Int, reward: Double = 1.0, prob: Double = 1.0)
```

In the preceding signature, the constructor creates an action input to Q-learning. It takes four parameters:

- from, the identifier for the source state
- to, the identifier for the target or destination state
- reward, which is the credit or penalty to transition from the state with id from to the state with id to
- prob, the probability of transition from the state from to the state to

TIP

In the preceding class, the from and to arguments are used for a specific action, but the last two arguments are the reward collected at the completion of the action and its probability, respectively. Both the actions have a reward and a probability of 1 by default. In short, we only need to create an input for actions that have either a higher reward or a lower probability.

The number of states and the sequence of input define the policy of type QLPolicy, which is a data container. An action has a Q-value (also known as **action-value**), a reward, and a probability. The implementation defines these three values in three separate matrices—*Q* for the action values, *R* for rewards, and *P* for probabilities—in order to stay consistent with the mathematical formulation. Here is the workflow for this class:

1. Initialize the policy using the input probabilities and rewards (see the qlData variable).

2. Compute the number of states from the input size (see the numStates variable).

3. Set the Q value for an action from state from to state to (see the setQ method) and get the Q-value using the get() method.

4. Retrieve the Q-value for a state transition action from state from to state to (see the Q method).

5. Retrieve the estimate for a state transition action from state `from` to state `to` (see the `EQ` method), and return the value in a `double`.

6. Retrieve the reward for a state transition action from state `from` to state `to` (see the R method).

7. Retrieve the probability for a state transition action from state `from` to state `to` (see the P method).

8. Compute the minimum and maximum value for `Q` (see the `minMaxQ` method).

9. Retrieve the pair (index source state, index destination state) whose transition is a positive value. The index of the state is converted to a Double (see the `EQ: Vector[DblPair]` method).

10. Get the textual description of the reward matrix for this policy using the first `toString()` method.

11. Textual representation of any one of the following: Q-value, reward, or probability matrix using the second `toString()` method.

12. Validate the `from` and `to` value using the `check()` method.

Now let us see the class definition consisting of the preceding workflow:

```
final private[scalaml] class QLPolicy(val input: Seq[QLInput]) {
    import QLDataVar._QLPolicy.check(input)
    private[this] val qlData = input.map(qlIn => new QLData(qlIn.reward,
qlIn.prob))
    private[this] val numStates = Math.sqrt(input.size).toInt

    def setQ(from: Int, to: Int, value: Double): Unit =
        {check(from, to, "setQ")qlData(from * numStates + to).value =
value}

    final def get(from: Int, to: Int, varType: QLDataVar): String
    {f"${qlData(from * numStates + to).value(varType)}%2.2f"}

    final def Q(from: Int, to: Int): Double = {check(from, to, "Q")
qlData(from * numStates + to).value}
    final def EQ(from: Int, to: Int): Double = {check(from, to, "EQ")
qlData(from * numStates + to).estimate}
    final def R(from: Int, to: Int): Double = {check(from, to, "R")
qlData(from * numStates + to).reward}
    final def P(from: Int, to: Int): Double = {check(from, to, "P")
qlData(from * numStates + to).probability}

    final def minMaxQ: DblPair = {
        val r = Range(0, numStates)
        val _min = r.minBy(from => r.minBy(Q(from, _)))
```

```
        val _max = r.maxBy(from => r.maxBy(Q(from, _)))(_min, _max) }

    final def EQ: Vector[DblPair] = {
        import scala.collection.mutable.ArrayBuffer
        val r = Range(0, numStates)r.flatMap(from =>r.map(to => (from, to,
Q(from, to)))).map {
        case (i, j, q) =>
            if (q > 0.0) (i.toDouble, j.toDouble)
            else (0.0, 0.0) }.toVector}

override def toString: String = s"Rewardn${toString(REWARD)}"

def toString(varType: QLDataVar): String = {
    val r = Range(1, numStates)r.map(i => r.map(get(i, _,
varType)).mkString(",")).mkString("n") }
    private def check(from: Int, to: Int, meth: String): Unit =
{require(from >= 0 && from <                    numStates,s"QLPolicy.
        $meth Found from:
        $from required >= 0 and <
        $numStates")require(to >= 0 && to < numStates,s"QLPolicy.
        $meth Found to: $to required >= 0 and < $numStates")
}
```

QLearning model creation and training

The `QLearning` class encapsulates the Q-learning algorithm, more specifically the action-value updating equation. It is a data transformation of type `ETransform` (we will see this later on) with an explicit configuration of type `QLConfig`. This class is a generic parameterized class that implements the `QLearning` algorithm. The Q-learning model is initialized and trained during the instantiation of the class so it can be in the correct state for runtime prediction.

Therefore, the class instances have only two states: successfully trained and failed training (we'll see this later).

The implementation does not assume that every episode (or training cycle) will be successful. At the completion of training, the ratio of labels over the initial training set is computed. The client code is responsible for evaluating the quality of the model by testing the ratio (see the model evaluation section).

The constructor takes the configuration of the algorithm (that is, `config`), the search space (that is, `qlSpace`), and the policy (that is, `qlPolicy`) parameters and creates a Q-learning algorithm:

```
final class QLearning[T](conf: QLConfig,qlSpace: QLSpace[T],qlPolicy:
QLPolicy)
    extends ETransform[QLState[T], QLState[T]](conf) with Monitor[Double]
```

The model is automatically created effectively if the minimum coverage is reached (or trained) during instantiation of the class, which is essentially a Q-learning model.

The following `train()` method is applied to each episode with randomly generated initial states. Then it computes the coverage (based on the `minCoverage` configuration value supplied by the `conf` object) as the number of episodes for each the goal state was reached:

```
private def train: Option[QLModel] = Try {
    val completions = Range(0, conf.numEpisodes).map(epoch =>
        if (heavyLiftingTrain (-1)) 1 else 0)
        .sum
        completions.toDouble / conf.numEpisodes
        }
    .filter(_ > conf.minCoverage).map(new QLModel(qlPolicy, _)).toOption;
```

In the preceding code block, the `heavyLiftingTrain(state0: Int)` method does the heavy lifting at each episode (or epoch). It triggers the search by selecting either the initial state state 0 or a random generator *r* with a new seed, if `state0` is < 0.

At first, it gets all the states adjacent to the current state, and then it selects the most rewarding of the list of adjacent states. If the next most rewarding state is a goal state, we are done. Otherwise, it recomputes the policy value for the state transition using the reward matrix (that is, `QLPolicy.R`).

For the recomputation, it applies the Q-learning updating formula by updating the Q-Value for the policy; then it invokes the search method with the new state and incremented iterator. Let's see the body of this method:

```
private def heavyLiftingTrain(state0: Int): Boolean = {
    @scala.annotation.tailrec
    def search(iSt: QLIndexedState[T]): QLIndexedState[T] = {
        val states = qlSpace.nextStates(iSt.state)
        if (states.isEmpty || iSt.iter >= conf.episodeLength)
            QLIndexedState(iSt.state, -1)
        else {
            val state = states.maxBy(s => qlPolicy.EQ(iSt.state.id, s.id))
            if (qlSpace.isGoal(state))
```

```
                        QLIndexedState(state, iSt.iter)

                else {
                    val fromId = iSt.state.id
                    val r = qlPolicy.R(fromId, state.id)
                    val q = qlPolicy.Q(fromId, state.id)
                    val nq = q + conf.alpha * (r + conf.gamma *
qlSpace.maxQ(state, qlPolicy) - q)
                        count(QVALUE_COUNTER, nq)
                        qlPolicy.setQ(fromId, state.id, nq)
                        search(QLIndexedState(state, iSt.iter + 1))
                        }
                }
            }

    val finalState = search(QLIndexedState(qlSpace.init(state0), 0))
    if (finalState.iter == -1)
        false
    else
        qlSpace.isGoal(finalState.state)
        }
    }
```

As a list of policies and training coverage is given, let us get the trained model:

```
    private[this] val model: Option[QLModel] = train
```

Note that the preceding model is trained using the input data (see the class `QLPolicy`) used for training the Q-learning algorithm using the inline `getInput()` method:

```
    def getInput: Seq[QLInput] = qlPolicy.input
```

Now we need to do one of the most important steps that will be used in our options trading application. Therefore, we need to retrieve the model for Q-learning as an option:

```
    @inline
    finaldef getModel: Option[QLModel] = model
```

The overall application fails if the model is not defined (see the `validateConstraints()` method for validation):

```
    @inline
    finaldef isModel: Boolean = model.isDefined
    override def toString: String = qlPolicy.toString + qlSpace.toString
```

Then, a recursive computation of the next most rewarding state is performed using Scala tail recursion. The idea is to search among all states and recursively select the state with the most awards given for the best policy.

```scala
@scala.annotation.tailrec
private def nextState(iSt: QLIndexedState[T]): QLIndexedState[T] = {
        val states = qlSpace.nextStates(iSt.state)
        if (states.isEmpty || iSt.iter >= conf.episodeLength)
            iSt
        else {
            val fromId = iSt.state.id
            val qState = states.maxBy(s =>
model.map(_.bestPolicy.EQ(fromId, s.id)).getOrElse(-1.0))
                nextState(QLIndexedState[T](qState, iSt.iter + 1))
        }
}
```

In the preceding code block, the `nextState()` method retrieves the eligible states that can be transitioned to from the current state. Then it extracts the state, `qState`, with the most rewarding policy by incrementing the iteration counter. Finally, it returns the states if there are no more states or if the method does not converge within the maximum number of allowed iterations supplied by the `config.episodeLength` parameter.

 Tip recursion: In Scala, tail recursion is a very effective construct used to apply an operation to every item of a collection. It optimizes the management of the function stack frame during recursion. The annotation triggers a validation of the condition necessary for the compiler to optimize function calls.

Finally, the configuration of the Q-learning algorithm, `QLConfig`, specifies:

- The learning rate, `alpha`
- The discount rate, `gamma`
- The maximum number of states (or length) of an episode, `episodeLength`
- The number of episodes (or epochs) used in training, `numEpisodes`
- The minimum coverage required to select the best policy, `minCoverage`

These are shown as follows:

```scala
case class QLConfig(alpha: Double,gamma: Double,episodeLength:
Int,numEpisodes: Int,minCoverage: Double)
extends Config {
import QLConfig._check(alpha, gamma, episodeLength, numEpisodes,
minCoverage) }
```

Now we are almost done, except that the validation is not completed. However, let us first see the companion object for the configuration of the Q-learning algorithm. This singleton defines the constructor for the `QLConfig` class and validates its parameters:

```
private[scalaml] object QLConfig {
        private val NO_MIN_COVERAGE = 0.0
        private val MAX_EPISODES = 1000

        private def check(alpha: Double,gamma: Double,
                    episodeLength: Int,numEpisodes: Int,
                    minCoverage: Double): Unit = {
                require(alpha > 0.0 && alpha < 1.0,s"QLConfig found
    alpha: $alpha required
                            > 0.0 and < 1.0")
                require(gamma > 0.0 && gamma < 1.0,s"QLConfig found
    gamma $gamma required
                            > 0.0 and < 1.0")
                require(numEpisodes > 2 && numEpisodes <
    MAX_EPISODES,s"QLConfig found
                            $numEpisodes $numEpisodes required > 2 and <
    $MAX_EPISODES")
                require(minCoverage >= 0.0 && minCoverage <=
    1.0,s"QLConfig found $minCoverage
                            $minCoverage required > 0 and <= 1.0")
        }
```

Excellent! We have seen how to implement the `QLearning` algorithm in Scala. However, as I said, the implementation is based on openly available sources, and the training may not always converge. One important consideration for such an online model is validation. A commercial application (or even a fancy Scala web app, which we will be covering in the next section) may require multiple types of validation mechanisms regarding the states transition, reward, probability, and Q-value matrices.

QLearning model validation

One critical validation is to verify that the user-defined constraints function does not create a dead-end in the search or training of Q-learning. The function constraints establish the list of states that can be accessed from a given state through actions. If the constraints are too tight, some of the possible search paths may not reach the goal state. Here is a simple validation of the constraints function:

```
def validateConstraints(numStates: Int, constraint: Int => List[Int]):
Boolean = {require(numStates > 1,        s"QLearning validateConstraints
found $numStates states should be >1")!Range(0,
```

```
    numStates).exists(constraint(_).isEmpty)
}
```

Making predictions using the trained model

Now that we can select the state with the most awards given for the best policy recursively (see the `nextState` method in the following code), an online training method for the Q-learning algorithm can be performed for options trading, for example.

So, once the Q-learning model is trained using the supplied data, the next state can be predicted using the Q-learning model by overriding the data transformation method (`PipeOperator`, that is, `|`) with a transformation of a state to a predicted goal state:

```
override def |> : PartialFunction[QLState[T], Try[QLState[T]]] = {
    case st: QLState[T]
        if isModel =>
            Try(
            if (st.isGoal) st
        else nextState(QLIndexedState[T](st, 0)).state)
    }
```

I guess that's enough of a mouthful, though it would have been good to evaluate the model. But evaluating on a real-life dataset, it would be even better, because running and evaluating a model's performance on fake data is like buying a new car and never driving it. Therefore, I would like to wrap up the implementation part and move on to the options trading application using this Q-learning implementation.

Developing an options trading web app using Q-learning

The trading algorithm is the process of using computers programmed to follow a defined set of instructions for placing a trade in order to generate profits at a speed and frequency that is impossible for a human trader. The defined sets of rules are based on timing, price, quantity, or any mathematical model.

Problem description

Through this project, we will predict the price of an option on a security for N days in the future according to the current set of observed features derived from the time of expiration, the price of the security, and volatility. The question would be: what model should we use for such an option pricing model? The answer is that there are actually many; Black-Scholes stochastic **partial differential equations (PDE)** is one of the most recognized.

In mathematical finance, the Black-Scholes equation is necessarily a PDE overriding the price evolution of a European call or a European put under the Black-Scholes model. For a European call or put on an underlying stock paying no dividends, the equation is:

$$\frac{\partial V}{\partial t} + \frac{1}{2}\sigma^2 S^2 \frac{\partial^2 V}{\partial S^2} + rS\frac{\partial V}{\partial S} - rV = 0$$

Where V is the price of the option as a function of stock price S and time t, r is the risk-free interest rate, and σ σ (displaystyle sigma) is the volatility of the stock. One of the key financial insights behind the equation is that anyone can perfectly hedge the option by buying and selling the underlying asset in just the right way without any risk. This hedge implies that there is only one right price for the option, as returned by the Black-Scholes formula.

Consider a January maturity call option on an IBM with an exercise price of $95. You write a January IBM put option with an exercise price of $85. Let us consider and focus on the call options of a given security, IBM. The following chart plots the daily price of the IBM stock and its derivative call option for May 2014, with a strike price of $190:

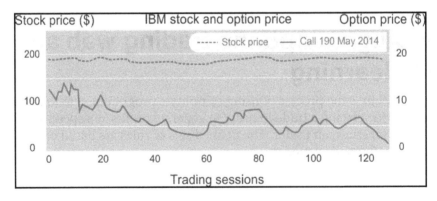

Figure 7: IBM stock and call $190 May 2014 pricing in May-Oct 2013

Now, what will be the profit and loss be for this position if IBM is selling at $87 on the option maturity date? Alternatively, what if IBM is selling at $100? Well, it is not easy to compute or predict the answer. However, in options trading, the price of an option depends on a few parameters, such as time decay, price, and volatility:

- Time to expiration of the option (time decay)
- The price of the underlying security
- The volatility of returns of the underlying asset

A pricing model usually does not consider the variation in trading volume in terms of the underlying security. Therefore, some researchers have included it in the option trading model. As we have described, any RL-based algorithm should have an explicit state (or states), so let us define the state of an option using the following four normalized features:

- **Time decay** (timeToExp): This is the time to expiration once normalized in the range of (0, 1).
- **Relative volatility** (volatility): within a trading session, this is the relative variation of the price of the underlying security. It is different than the more complex volatility of returns defined in the Black-Scholes model, for example.
- **Volatility relative to volume** (vltyByVol): This is the relative volatility of the price of the security adjusted for its trading volume.
- **Relative difference between the current price and the strike price** (priceToStrike): This measures the ratio of the difference between the price and the strike price to the strike price.

The following graph shows the four normalized features that can be used for the IBM option strategy:

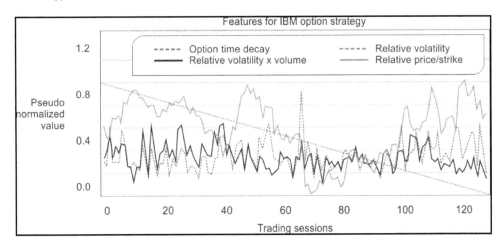

Figure 8: Normalized relative stock price volatility, volatility relative to trading volume, and price relative to strike price for the IBM stock

Now let us look at the stock and the option price dataset. There are two files IBM.csv and IBM_O.csv contain the IBM stock prices and option prices, respectively. The stock price dataset has the date, the opening price, the high and low price, the closing price, the trade volume, and the adjusted closing price. A shot of the dataset is given in the following diagram:

Date	Open	High	Low	Close	Volume	Adj Close
2014-10-03	188.11	189.37	187.56	188.67	3071500	188.67
2014-10-02	187.66	187.78	186.24	186.91	2283100	186.91
2014-10-01	189.91	190.40	186.79	187.17	3705400	187.17
2014-09-30	189.64	190.85	189.15	189.83	2870300	189.83
2014-09-29	188.51	189.96	188.12	189.64	2336300	189.64
2014-09-26	188.93	190.33	188.61	190.06	2493900	190.06
2014-09-25	192.05	192.50	188.97	189.01	4151400	189.01
2014-09-24	191.00	192.45	189.88	192.31	3082600	192.31
2014-09-23	192.75	193.07	191.52	191.62	3301800	191.62

Figure 9: IBM stock data

On the other hand, `IBM_O.csv` has 127 option prices for IBM Call 190 Oct 18, 2014. A few values are 1.41, 2.24, 2.42, 2.78, 3.46, 4.11, 4.51, 4.92, 5.41, 6.01, and so on. Up to this point, can we develop a predictive model using a `QLearning`, algorithm that can help us answer the previously mentioned question: Can it tell us the how IBM can make maximum profit by utilizing all the available features?

Well, we know how to implement the `QLearning`, and we know what option trading is. Another good thing is that the technologies that will be used for this project such as Scala, Akka, Scala Play Framework, and RESTful services are already discussed in `Chapter 3`, *High-Frequency Bitcoin Price Prediction from Historical Data*. Therefore, it may be possible. Then we try it to develop a Scala web project that helps us maximize the profit.

Implementating an options trading web application

The goal of this project is to create an options trading web application that creates a QLearning model from the IBM stock data. Then the app will extract the output from the model as a JSON object and show the result to the user. *Figure 10*, shows the overall workflow:

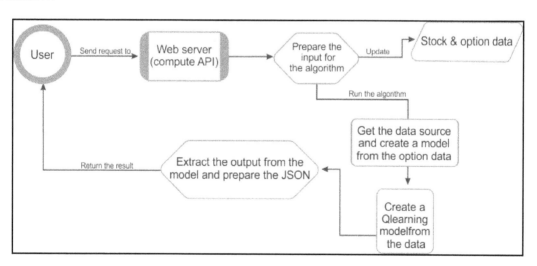

Figure 10: Workflow of the options trading Scala web

The compute API prepares the input for the Q-learning algorithm, and the algorithm starts by extracting the data from the files to build the option model. Then it performs operations on the data such as normalization and discretization. It passes all of this to the Q-learning algorithm to train the model. After that, the compute API gets the model from the algorithm, extracts the best policy data, and puts it onto JSON to be returned to the web browser. Well, the implementation of the options trading strategy using Q-learning consists of the following steps:

- Describing the property of an option
- Defining the function approximation
- Specifying the constraints on the state transition

Creating an option property

Considering the market volatility, we need to be a bit more realistic, because any longer-term prediction is quite unreliable. The reason is that it would fall outside the constraint of the discrete Markov model. So, suppose we want to predict the price for next two days—that is, $N = 2$. That means the price of the option two days in the future is the value of the reward profit or loss. So, let us encapsulate the following four parameters:

- `timeToExp`: Time left until expiration as a percentage of the overall duration of the option
- Volatility normalized Relative volatility of the underlying security for a given trading session
- `vltyByVol`: Volatility of the underlying security for a given trading session relative to a trading volume for the session
- `priceToStrike`: Price of the underlying security relative to the Strike price for a given trading session

The `OptionProperty` class defines the property of a traded option on a security. The constructor creates the property for an option:

```scala
class OptionProperty(timeToExp: Double,volatility: Double,vltyByVol:
Double,priceToStrike: Double) {
        val toArray = Array[Double](timeToExp, volatility, vltyByVol,
priceToStrike)
        require(timeToExp > 0.01, s"OptionProperty time to expiration found
$timeToExp required 0.01")
    }
```

Creating an option model

Now we need to create an OptionModel to act as the container and the factory for the properties of the option. It takes the following parameters and creates a list of option properties, propsList, by accessing the data source of the four features described earlier:

- The symbol of the security.
- The strike price for option, strikePrice.
- The source of the data, src.
- The minimum time decay or time to expiration, minTDecay. Out-of-the-money options expire worthlessly, and in-the-money options have a very different price behavior as they get closer to the expiration. Therefore, the last minTDecay trading sessions prior to the expiration date are not used in the training process.
- The number of steps (or buckets), nSteps, is used in approximating the values of each feature. For instance, an approximation of four steps creates four buckets: (0, 25), (25, 50), (50, 75), and (75, 100).

Then it assembles OptionProperties and computes the normalized minimum time to the expiration of the option. Then it computes an approximation of the value of options by discretization of the actual value in multiple levels from an array of options prices; finally it returns a map of an array of levels for the option price and accuracy. Here is the constructor of the class:

```
class OptionModel(
    symbol: String,
    strikePrice: Double,
    src: DataSource,
    minExpT: Int,
    nSteps: Int
    )
```

Inside this class implementation, at first, a validation is done using the check() method, by checking the following:

- strikePrice: A positive price is required
- minExpT: This has to be between 2 and 16
- nSteps: Requires a minimum of two steps

Here's the invocation of this method:

```
check(strikePrice, minExpT, nSteps)
```

The signature of the preceding method is shown in the following code:

```
def check(strikePrice: Double, minExpT: Int, nSteps: Int): Unit = {
    require(strikePrice > 0.0, s"OptionModel.check price found $strikePrice
required > 0")
    require(minExpT > 2 && minExpT < 16, s"OptionModel.check Minimum
expiration time found $minExpT                    required ]2, 16[")
    require(nSteps > 1, s"OptionModel.check, number of steps found $nSteps
required > 1")
    }
```

Once the preceding constraint is satisfied, the list of option properties, named `propsList`, is created as follows:

```
val propsList = (for {
    price <- src.get(adjClose)
    volatility <- src.get(volatility)
    nVolatility <- normalize[Double](volatility)
    vltyByVol <- src.get(volatilityByVol)
    nVltyByVol <- normalize[Double](vltyByVol)
    priceToStrike <- normalize[Double](price.map(p => 1.0 - strikePrice /
p))
    }
    yield {
        nVolatility.zipWithIndex./:(List[OptionProperty]()) {
            case (xs, (v, n)) =>
            val normDecay = (n + minExpT).toDouble / (price.size + minExpT)
            new OptionProperty(normDecay, v, nVltyByVol(n),
priceToStrike(n))  :: xs
            }
        .drop(2).reverse
    }).get
```

In the preceding code block, the factory uses the `zipWithIndex` Scala method to represent the index of the trading sessions. All feature values are normalized over the interval (0, 1), including the time decay (or time to expiration) of the `normDecay` option.

The `quantize()` method of the `OptionModel` class converts the normalized value of each option property of features into an array of bucket indices. It returns a map of profit and loss for each bucket keyed on the array of bucket indices:

```
def quantize(o: Array[Double]): Map[Array[Int], Double] = {
    val mapper = new mutable.HashMap[Int, Array[Int]]
    val acc: NumericAccumulator[Int] = propsList.view.map(_.toArray)
    map(toArrayInt(_)).map(ar => {
        val enc = encode(ar)
        mapper.put(enc, ar)
```

```
        enc
            })
    .zip(o)./:(
    new NumericAccumulator[Int]) {
        case (_acc, (t, y)) => _acc += (t, y); _acc
            }
        acc.map {
        case (k, (v, w)) => (k, v / w) }
            .map {
        case (k, v) => (mapper(k), v) }.toMap
    }
```

The method also creates a mapper instance to index the array of buckets. An accumulator, acc, of type NumericAccumulator extends the Map[Int, (Int, Double)] and computes this tuple *(number of occurrences of features on each bucket, sum of the increase or decrease of the option price).*

The toArrayInt method converts the value of each option property (timeToExp, volatility, and so on) into the index of the appropriate bucket. The array of indices is then encoded to generate the id or index of a state. The method updates the accumulator with the number of occurrences and the total profit and loss for a trading session for the option. It finally computes the reward on each action by averaging the profit and loss on each bucket. The signature of the encode(), toArrayInt() is given in the following code:

```
private def encode(arr: Array[Int]): Int = arr./:((1, 0)) {
    case ((s, t), n) => (s * nSteps, t + s * n) }._2
        private def toArrayInt(feature: Array[Double]): Array[Int] =
feature.map(x => (nSteps *
            x).floor.toInt)

final class NumericAccumulator[T]
    extends mutable.HashMap[T, (Int, Double)] {
    def +=(key: T, x: Double): Option[(Int, Double)] = {
        val newValue =
    if (contains(key)) (get(key).get._1 + 1, get(key).get._2 + x)
    else (1, x)
    super.put(key, newValue)
    }
}
```

Finally, and most importantly, if the preceding constraints are satisfied (you can modify these constraints though) and once the instantiation of the `OptionModel` class generates a list of `OptionProperty` elements if the constructor succeeds; otherwise, it generates an empty list.

Putting it altogether

Because we have implemented the Q-learning algorithm, we can now develop the options trading application using Q-learning. However, at first, we need to load the data using the `DataSource` class (we will see its implementation later on). Then we can create an option model from the data for a given stock with default strike and minimum expiration time parameters, using `OptionModel`, which defines the model for a traded option, on a security. Then we have to create the model for the profit and loss on an option given the underlying security.

The profit and loss are adjusted to produce positive values. It instantiates an instance of the Q-learning class, that is, a generic parameterized class that implements the Q-learning algorithm. The Q-learning model is initialized and trained during the instantiation of the class, so it can be in the correct state for the runtime prediction.

Therefore, the class instances have only two states: successfully trained and failed training Q-learning value action. Then the model is returned to get processed and visualized.

So, let us create a Scala object and name it `QLearningMain`. Then, inside the `QLearningMain` object, define and initialize the following parameters:

- `Name`: Used to indicate the reinforcement algorithm's name (for our case, it's Q-learning)
- `STOCK_PRICES`: File that contains the stock data
- `OPTION_PRICES`: File that contains the available option data
- `STRIKE_PRICE`: Option strike price
- `MIN_TIME_EXPIRATION`: Minimum expiration time for the option recorded
- `QUANTIZATION_STEP`: Steps used in discretization or approximation of the value of the security
- `ALPHA`: Learning rate for the Q-learning algorithm
- `DISCOUNT` (gamma): Discount rate for the Q-learning algorithm
- `MAX_EPISODE_LEN`: Maximum number of states visited per episode
- `NUM_EPISODES`: Number of episodes used during training

- `MIN_COVERAGE`: Minimum coverage allowed during the training of the Q-learning model
- `NUM_NEIGHBOR_STATES`: Number of states accessible from any other state
- `REWARD_TYPE`: Maximum reward or Random

Tentative initializations for each parameter are given in the following code:

```
val name: String = "Q-learning"// Files containing the historical prices
for the stock and option
val STOCK_PRICES = "/static/IBM.csv"
val OPTION_PRICES = "/static/IBM_O.csv"// Run configuration parameters
val STRIKE_PRICE = 190.0 // Option strike price
val MIN_TIME_EXPIRATION = 6 // Min expiration time for option recorded
val QUANTIZATION_STEP = 32 // Quantization step (Double => Int)
val ALPHA = 0.2 // Learning rate
val DISCOUNT = 0.6 // Discount rate used in Q-Value update equation
val MAX_EPISODE_LEN = 128 // Max number of iteration for an episode
val NUM_EPISODES = 20 // Number of episodes used for training.
val NUM_NEIGHBHBOR_STATES = 3 // No. of states from any other state
```

Now the `run()` method accepts as input the reward type (`Maximum reward` in our case), quantized step (in our case, `QUANTIZATION_STEP`), alpha (the learning rate, `ALPHA` in our case) and gamma (in our case, it's `DISCOUNT`, the discount rate for the Q-learning algorithm). It displays the distribution of values in the model. Additionally, it displays the estimated Q-value for the best policy on a Scatter plot (we will see this later). Here is the workflow of the preceding method:

1. First, it extracts the stock price from the `IBM.csv` file
2. Then it creates an option model `createOptionModel` using the stock prices and quantization, `quantizeR` (see the `quantize` method for more and the main method invocation later)
3. The option prices are extracted from the `IBM_o.csv` file
4. After that, another model, `model`, is created using the option model to evaluate it on the option prices, `oPrices`
5. Finally, the estimated Q-Value (that is, *Q-value = value * probability*) is displayed On a Scatter plot using the `display` method

By amalgamating the preceding steps, here's the signature of the `run()` method:

```
private def run(rewardType: String,quantizeR: Int,alpha: Double,gamma:
Double): Int = {
    val sPath = getClass.getResource(STOCK_PRICES).getPath
    val src = DataSource(sPath, false, false, 1).get
    val option = createOptionModel(src, quantizeR)

    val oPricesSrc = DataSource(OPTION_PRICES, false, false, 1).get
    val oPrices = oPricesSrc.extract.get

    val model = createModel(option, oPrices, alpha, gamma)model.map(m =>
{if (rewardType != "Random")
    display(m.bestPolicy.EQ,m.toString,s"$rewardType with quantization
order
        $quantizeR")1}).getOrElse(-1)
}
```

Now here is the signature of the `createOptionModel()` method that creates an option model using (see the `OptionModel` class):

```
private def createOptionModel(src: DataSource, quantizeR: Int): OptionModel
=
    new OptionModel("IBM", STRIKE_PRICE, src, MIN_TIME_EXPIRATION,
quantizeR)
```

Then the `createModel()` method creates a model for the profit and loss on an option given the underlying security. Note that the option prices are quantized using the `quantize()` method defined earlier. Then the constraining method is used to limit the number of actions available to any given state. This simple implementation computes the list of all the states within a radius of this state. Then it identifies the neighboring states within a predefined radius.

Finally, it uses the input data to train the Q-learning model to compute the minimum value for the profit, a loss so the maximum loss is converted to a null profit. Note that the profit and loss are adjusted to produce positive values. Now let us see the signature of this method:

```
def createModel(ibmOption: OptionModel,oPrice: Seq[Double],alpha:
Double,gamma: Double): Try[QLModel] = {
    val qPriceMap = ibmOption.quantize(oPrice.toArray)
    val numStates = qPriceMap.size
    val neighbors = (n: Int) => {
def getProximity(idx: Int, radius: Int): List[Int] = {
    val idx_max =
        if (idx + radius >= numStates) numStates - 1
```

```
    else idx + radius
    val idx_min =
        if (idx < radius) 0
        else idx - radiusRange(idx_min, idx_max + 1).filter(_ !=
idx)./:(List[Int]())((xs, n) => n :: xs)}getProximity(n,
NUM_NEIGHBHBOR_STATES)
        }
    val qPrice: DblVec = qPriceMap.values.toVector
    val profit: DblVec = normalize(zipWithShift(qPrice, 1).map {
        case (x, y) => y - x}).get
    val maxProfitIndex = profit.zipWithIndex.maxBy(_._1)._2
    val reward = (x: Double, y: Double) => Math.exp(30.0 * (y - x))
    val probabilities = (x: Double, y: Double) =>
        if (y < 0.3 * x) 0.0
        else 1.0println(s"$name Goal state index: $maxProfitIndex")
        if (!QLearning.validateConstraints(profit.size, neighbors))
            thrownew IllegalStateException("QLearningEval Incorrect states
transition constraint")
    val instances = qPriceMap.keySet.toSeq.drop(1)
    val config = QLConfig(alpha, gamma, MAX_EPISODE_LEN, NUM_EPISODES, 0.1)
    val qLearning =
QLearning[Array[Int]](config,Array[Int](maxProfitIndex),profit,reward,proba
bilities,instances,Some(neighbors))    val model0 = qLearning.getModel
        if (model0.isDefined) {
    val numTransitions = numStates * (numStates - 1)println(s"$name
Coverage ${model0.get.coverage} for $numStates states and $numTransitions
transitions")
    val profile = qLearning.dumpprintln(s"$name Execution
profilen$profile")display(qLearning)Success(model0.get) }
        else Failure(new IllegalStateException(s"$name model undefined"))
}
```

Note that if the preceding invocation cannot create an option model, the code fails to show a message that the model creation failed. Nonetheless, remember that the minCoverage used in the following line is important, considering the small dataset we used (because the algorithm will converge very quickly):

```
val config = QLConfig(alpha, gamma, MAX_EPISODE_LEN, NUM_EPISODES, 0.0)
```

Although we've already stated that it is not assured that the model creation and training will be successful, a Naïve clue would be using a very small `minCoverage` value between `0.0` and `0.22`. Now, if the preceding invocation is successful, then the model is trained and ready for making prediction. If so, then the display method is used to display the estimated *Q-value = value * probability* in a Scatter plot. Here is the signature of the method:

```
private def display(eq: Vector[DblPair],results: String,params: String):
Unit = {
    import org.scalaml.plots.{ScatterPlot, BlackPlotTheme, Legend}
    val labels = Legend(name, s"Q-learning config: $params", "States",
"States")ScatterPlot.display(eq,
        labels, new BlackPlotTheme)
}
```

Hang on and do not lose patience! We are finally ready to see a simple rn and inspect the result. So let us do it:

```
def main(args: Array[String]): Unit = {
 run("Maximum reward",QUANTIZATION_STEP, ALPHA, DISCOUNT)
 }
>>>
Action: state 71 => state 74
Action: state 71 => state 73
Action: state 71 => state 72
Action: state 71 => state 70
Action: state 71 => state 69
Action: state 71 => state 68...Instance: [I@1f021e6c - state: 124
Action: state 124 => state 125
Action: state 124 => state 123
Action: state 124 => state 122
Action: state 124 => state 121Q-learning Coverage 0.1 for 126 states and
15750 transitions
Q-learning Execution profile
Q-Value -> 5.572310105096295, 0.013869013819834967, 4.5746487300071825,
0.4037703812585325, 0.17606260549479869, 0.09205272504875522,
0.023205692430068765, 0.06363082458984902, 50.405283888218435...
6.5530411130514015
Model: Success(Optimal policy: Reward -
1.00,204.28,115.57,6.05,637.58,71.99,12.34,0.10,4939.71,521.30,402.73, with
coverage: 0.1)
```

Evaluating the model

The preceding output shows the transition from one state to another, and for the **0.1** coverage, the QLearning model had 15,750 transitions for 126 states to reach goal state 37 with optimal rewards. Therefore, the training set is quite small and only a few buckets have actual values. So we can understand that the size of the training set has an impact on the number of states. QLearning will converge too fast for a small training set (like what we have for this example).

However, for a larger training set, QLearning will take time to converge; it will provide at least one value for each bucket created by the approximation. Also, by seeing those values, it is difficult to understand the relation between Q-values and states.

So what if we can see the Q-values per state? Why not! We can see them on a scatter plot:

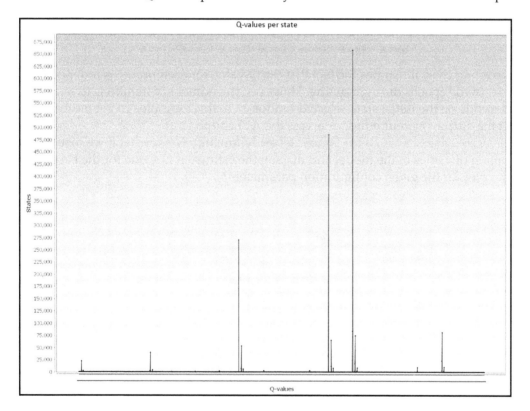

Figure 11: Q-value per state

Now let us display the profile of the log of the Q-value (`QLData.value`) as the recursive search (or training) progress for different episodes or epochs. The test uses a learning rate α = 0.1 and a discount rate γ = 0.9 (see more in the deployment section):

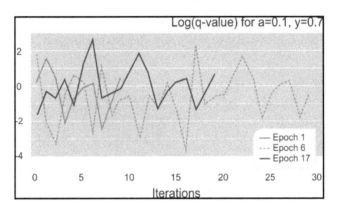

Figure 12: Profile of the logarithmic Q-Value for different epochs during Q-learning training

The preceding chart illustrates the fact that the Q-value for each profile is independent of the order of the epochs during training. However, the number of iterations to reach the goal state depends on the initial state selected randomly in this example. To get more insights, inspect the output on your editor or access the API endpoint at `http://localhost:9000/api/compute` (see following). Now, what if we display the distribution of values in the model and display the estimated Q-value for the best policy on a Scatter plot for the given configuration parameters?

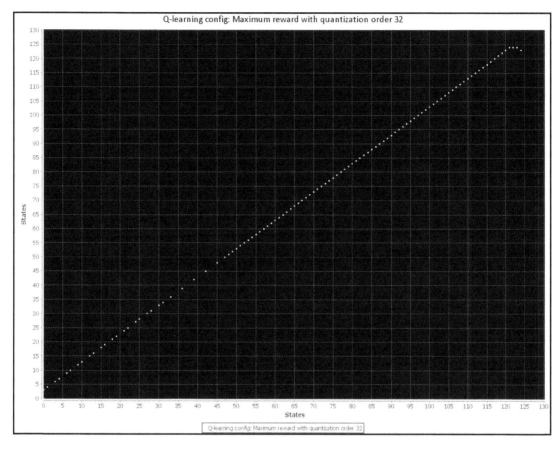

Figure 13: Maximum reward with quantization 32 with the QLearning

The final evaluation consists of evaluating the impact of the learning rate and discount rate on the coverage of the training:

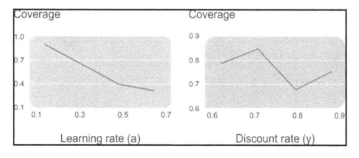

Figure 14: Impact of the learning rate and discount rate on the coverage of the training

The coverage decreases as the learning rate increases. This result confirms the general rule of using *learning rate < 0.2*. A similar test to evaluate the impact of the discount rate on the coverage is inconclusive. We could have thousands of such configuration parameters with different choices and combinations. So, what if we can wrap the whole application as a Scala web app similar to what we did in `Chapter 3`, *High-Frequency Bitcoin Price Prediction from Historical Data*? I guess it would not be that bad an idea. So let us dive into it.

Wrapping up the options trading app as a Scala web app

The idea is to get the trained model and construct the best policy JSON output for the maximum reward case. `PlayML` is a web app that uses the options trading Q-learning algorithm to provide a compute API endpoint that takes the input dataset and some options to calculate the q-values and returns them in JSON format to be modeled in the frontend.

The wrapped up Scala web ML app has the following directory structure:

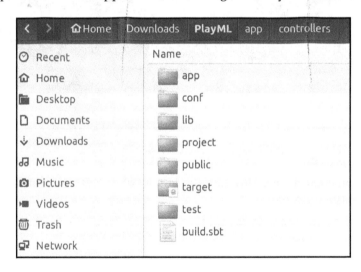

Figure 15: Scala ML web app directory structure

In the preceding structure, the app folder has both the original QLearning implementation (see the `ml` folder) and some additional backend code. The `controller` subfolder has a Scala class named `API.scala`, used as the Scala controller for controlling the model behavior from the frontend. Finally, `Filters.scala` acts as the `DefaultHttpFilters`:

Figure 16: The ml directory structure

The `conf` folder has the Scala web app configuration file, `application.conf`, containing the necessary configurations. All the dependencies are defined in the `build.sbt` file, as shown in the following code:

```
name := "PlayML"version := "1.0"
lazy val `playml` = (project in file(".")).enablePlugins(PlayScala)
resolvers += "scalaz-bintray"
scalaVersion := "2.11.11"
libraryDependencies ++= Seq(filters, cache, ws, "org.apache.commons" %
"commons-math3" %
        "3.6","com.typesafe.play" %% "play-json" % "2.5",
        "org.jfree" % "jfreechart" % "1.0.17",
        "com.typesafe.akka" %% "akka-actor" % "2.3.8",
        "org.apache.spark" %% "spark-core" % "2.1.0",
        "org.apache.spark" %% "spark-mllib" % "2.1.0",
        "org.apache.spark" %% "spark-streaming" % "2.1.0")
```

The `lib` folder has some `.jar` files used as external dependencies defined in the `build.sbt` file. The `public` folder has the static pages used in the UI. Additionally, the data files `IBM.csv` and `IBM_0.csv` are also there. Finally, the target folder holds the application as a packaged (if any).

The backend

In the backend, I encapsulated the preceding Q-learning implementation and additionally created a Scala controller that controls the model behavior from the frontend. The structure is given here:

```scala
import java.nio.file.Paths
import org.codehaus.janino.Java
import ml.stats.TSeries.{normalize, zipWithShift}
import ml.workflow.data.DataSource
import ml.trading.OptionModel
import ml.Predef.{DblPair, DblVec}
import ml.reinforcement.qlearning.{QLConfig, QLModel, QLearning}
import scala.util.{Failure, Success, Try}
import play.api._
import play.api.data.Form
import play.api.libs.json._
import play.api.mvc._
import scala.util.{Failure, Success, Try}

class API extends Controller {
    protected val name: String = "Q-learning"
    private var sPath =
Paths.get((s"${"public/data/IBM.csv"}")).toAbsolutePath.toString
    private var oPath =
Paths.get((s"${"public/data/IBM_O.csv"}")).toAbsolutePath.toString

    // Run configuration parameters
    private var STRIKE_PRICE = 190.0 // Option strike price
    private var MIN_TIME_EXPIRATION = 6 // Minimum expiration time for the
option recorded
    private var QUANTIZATION_STEP = 32 // Quantization step (Double => Int)
    private var ALPHA = 0.2 // Learning rate
    private var DISCOUNT = 0.6 // Discount rate used in the Q-Value update
equation
    private var MAX_EPISODE_LEN = 128 // Maximum number of iteration for an
episode
    private var NUM_EPISODES = 20 // Number of episodes used for training.
    private var MIN_COVERAGE = 0.1
    private var NUM_NEIGHBOR_STATES = 3 // Number of states accessible from
any other state
    private var REWARD_TYPE = "Maximum reward"
    private var ret = JsObject(Seq())
    private var retry = 0

    private def run(REWARD_TYPE: String,quantizeR: Int,alpha: Double,gamma:
Double) = {
```

```
        val maybeModel = createModel(createOptionModel(DataSource(sPath,
false, false, 1).get, quantizeR),              DataSource(oPath, false,
false, 1).get.extract.get, alpha, gamma)
        if (maybeModel != None) {
            val model = maybeModel.get
            if (REWARD_TYPE != "Random") {
                var value = JsArray(Seq())
                var x = model.bestPolicy.EQ.distinct.map(x => {value =
value.append(JsObject(Seq("x" ->              JsNumber(x._1), "y" ->
JsNumber(x._2))))})ret = ret.+("OPTIMAL", value)
                }
            }
        }
/** Create an option model for a given stock with default strike and
minimum expiration time parameters.
*/
    privatedef createOptionModel(src: DataSource, quantizeR: Int):
OptionModel =
        new OptionModel("IBM", STRIKE_PRICE, src, MIN_TIME_EXPIRATION,
quantizeR)
/** Create a model for the profit and loss on an option given
* the underlying security. The profit and loss is adjusted to
* produce positive values.
*/
    privatedef createModel(ibmOption: OptionModel,oPrice:
Seq[Double],alpha: Double,gamma: Double): Option[QLModel] = {
        val qPriceMap = ibmOption.quantize(oPrice.toArray)
        val numStates = qPriceMap.size
        val neighbors = (n: Int) => {
            def getProximity(idx: Int, radius: Int): List[Int] = {
            val idx_max = if (idx + radius >= numStates) numStates - 1
            else idx + radius
            val idx_min = if (idx < radius) 0
                    else idx -
radiusscala.collection.immutable.Range(idx_min, idx_max + 1)
                        .filter(_ != idx)./:(List[Int]())((xs, n) => n
:: xs)
                }
            getProximity(n, NUM_NEIGHBOR_STATES)
        }
    // Compute the minimum value for the profit, loss so the maximum
loss is converted to a null profit
        val qPrice: DblVec = qPriceMap.values.toVector
        val profit: DblVec = normalize(zipWithShift(qPrice, 1).map {
        case (x, y) => y - x }).get
        val maxProfitIndex = profit.zipWithIndex.maxBy(_._1)._2
        val reward = (x: Double, y: Double) => Math.exp(30.0 * (y - x))
```

```scala
      val probabilities = (x: Double, y: Double) =>
          if (y < 0.3 * x) 0.0 else 1.0ret = ret.+("GOAL_STATE_INDEX",
JsNumber(maxProfitIndex))
          if (!QLearning.validateConstraints(profit.size, neighbors))
{ret = ret.+("error",                      JsString("QLearningEval
Incorrect states transition constraint"))

          thrownew IllegalStateException("QLearningEval Incorrect states
transition constraint")}

          val instances = qPriceMap.keySet.toSeq.drop(1)
          val config = QLConfig(alpha, gamma, MAX_EPISODE_LEN,
NUM_EPISODES, MIN_COVERAGE)
          val qLearning = QLearning[Array[Int]](config,Array[Int]
(maxProfitIndex),profit,reward,probabilities,instances,Some(neighbors))
          val model0 = qLearning.getModel

          if (model0.isDefined) {
              val numTransitions = numStates * (numStates - 1)ret =
ret.+("COVERAGE",
              JsNumber(model0.get.coverage))ret =
ret.+("COVERAGE_STATES", JsNumber(numStates))
              ret = ret.+("COVERAGE_TRANSITIONS",
JsNumber(numTransitions))
              var value = JsArray()
              var x = qLearning._counters.last._2.distinct.map(x =>
{value = value.append(JsNumber(x))
              })
              ret = ret.+("Q_VALUE", value)model0
              }
          else {
              if (retry > 5) {ret = ret.+("error", JsString(s"$name model
undefined"))
                  return None
               }
              retry += 1Thread.sleep(500)
              return createModel(ibmOption,oPrice,alpha,gamma)
              }
          }
      }
def compute = Action(parse.anyContent) { request =>
    try {
        if (request.body.asMultipartFormData != None) {
            val formData = request.body.asMultipartFormData.get
            if (formData.file("STOCK_PRICES").nonEmpty &&
formData.file("STOCK_PRICES").get.filename.nonEmpty)sPath =
formData.file("STOCK_PRICES").get.ref.file.toString
            if (formData.file("OPTION_PRICES").nonEmpty &&
formData.file("OPTION_PRICES").get.filename.nonEmpty)oPath =
```

```
formData.file("OPTION_PRICES").get.ref.file.toString
            val parts = formData.dataParts
            if (parts.get("STRIKE_PRICE") != None)STRIKE_PRICE =
parts.get("STRIKE_PRICE").get.mkString("").toDouble
            if (parts.get("MIN_TIME_EXPIRATION") !=
None)MIN_TIME_EXPIRATION =
parts.get("MIN_TIME_EXPIRATION").get.mkString("").toInt
            if (parts.get("QUANTIZATION_STEP") != None)QUANTIZATION_STEP =
parts.get("QUANTIZATION_STEP").get.mkString("").toInt
            if (parts.get("ALPHA") != None)ALPHA =
parts.get("ALPHA").get.mkString("").toDouble
            if (parts.get("DISCOUNT") != None)DISCOUNT =
parts.get("DISCOUNT").get.mkString("").toDouble
            if (parts.get("MAX_EPISODE_LEN") != None)MAX_EPISODE_LEN =
parts.get("MAX_EPISODE_LEN").get.mkString("").toInt
            if (parts.get("NUM_EPISODES") != None)NUM_EPISODES =
parts.get("NUM_EPISODES").get.mkString("").toInt
            if (parts.get("MIN_COVERAGE") != None)MIN_COVERAGE =
parts.get("MIN_COVERAGE").get.mkString("").toDouble
            if (parts.get("NUM_NEIGHBOR_STATES") !=
None)NUM_NEIGHBOR_STATES =
parts.get("NUM_NEIGHBOR_STATES").get.mkString("").toInt
            if (parts.get("REWARD_TYPE") != None)REWARD_TYPE =
parts.get("REWARD_TYPE").get.mkString("")
            }
        ret = JsObject(Seq("STRIKE_PRICE" ->
        JsNumber(STRIKE_PRICE),"MIN_TIME_EXPIRATION" ->
JsNumber(MIN_TIME_EXPIRATION),
        "QUANTIZATION_STEP" ->
JsNumber(QUANTIZATION_STEP),
        "ALPHA" -> JsNumber(ALPHA),
        "DISCOUNT" -> JsNumber(DISCOUNT),
        "MAX_EPISODE_LEN" ->
JsNumber(MAX_EPISODE_LEN),
        "NUM_EPISODES" -> JsNumber(NUM_EPISODES),
        "MIN_COVERAGE" -> JsNumber(MIN_COVERAGE),
        "NUM_NEIGHBOR_STATES" ->
JsNumber(NUM_NEIGHBOR_STATES),
        "REWARD_TYPE" -> JsString(REWARD_TYPE)))
        run(REWARD_TYPE, QUANTIZATION_STEP, ALPHA, DISCOUNT)
    }
    catch {
        case e: Exception => {
            ret = ret.+("exception", JsString(e.toString))
                }
            }
```

```
        Ok(ret)
    }
}
```

Look at the preceding code carefully; it has more or less the same structure as the QLearningMain.scala file. There are only two important things here, as follows:

- Compute is done as an Action that takes the input from the UI and computes the value
- Then the result is returned as a JSON object using the JsObject() method to be shown on the UI (see the following)

The frontend

The app consists of two main parts: the API endpoint, built with the play framework, and the frontend single-page application, built with Angular.js. The frontend app sends the data to the API to get computed and then shows the results using chart.js. Here are the steps that we need for this:

- Initialize the form
- Communicate with the API
- Populate the view with coverage data and charts

The algorithm's JSON output should be as follows:

- All the config parameters are returned
- GOAL_STATE_INDEX, the maximum Profit Index
- COVERAGE, the ratio of training trials or epochs that reach a predefined goal state
- COVERAGE_STATES, the size of the quantized option values
- COVERAGE_TRANSITIONS, the number of states squared
- Q_VALUE, the q-value of all the states
- OPTIMAL, the states with the most reward returned if the reward type isn't random

The frontend code initiates the Angular.js app with the chart.js module as follows (see in the PlayML/public/assets/js/main.js file):

```
angular.module("App", ['chart.js']).controller("Ctrl", ['$scope', '$http',
function ($scope, $http) {
// First we initialize the form:
$scope.form = {REWARD_TYPE: "Maximum reward",NUM_NEIGHBOR_STATES:
3,STRIKE_PRICE: 190.0,MIN_TIME_EXPIRATION: 6,QUANTIZATION_STEP: 32,ALPHA:
0.2,DISCOUNT: 0.6,MAX_EPISODE_LEN: 128,NUM_EPISODES: 20,MIN_COVERAGE: 0.1
};
```

Then the run button action prepares the form data to be sent to the API and sends the data to the backend. Next, it passes the returned data to the result variable to be used in the frontend. Then, it clears the charts and recreates them; if an optimal is found, it initializes the optimal chart. Finally, if the Q-value is found initialize, the q-value chart is getting initialized:

```
$scope.run = function () {
    var formData = new FormData(document.getElementById('form'));
    $http.post('/api/compute', formData, {
    headers: {'Content-Type': undefined}}).then(function
successCallback(response) {
    $scope.result = response.data;
    $('#canvasContainer').html('');

    if (response.data.OPTIMAL) {
        $('#canvasContainer').append('<canvas
id="optimalCanvas"></canvas>')
Chart.Scatter(document.getElementById("optimalCanvas").getContext("2d"),
{data: { datasets:                [{data: response.data.OPTIMAL}] }, options:
{...}});}if (response.data.Q_VALUE) {
        $('#canvasContainer').append('<canvas id="valuesCanvas"></canvas>')
Chart.Line(document.getElementById("valuesCanvas").getContext("2d"), {
        data: { labels: new Array(response.data.Q_VALUE.length), datasets:
[{
        data: response.data.Q_VALUE }] }, options: {...}});}})};}]
    );
```

The preceding frontend code is then embedded in the HTML (see PlayML/public/index.html) to get the UI to be accessed on the Web as a fancy app at http://localhost:9000/. Feel free to edit the content according to your requirement. We will see the details soon.

Running and Deployment Instructions

As was already stated in `Chapter 3`, *High-Frequency Bitcoin Price Prediction from Historical Data*, you need Java 1.8+ and SBT as the dependencies. Then follow these instructions:

- Download the app. I named the code `PlayML.zip`.
- Unzip the file and you will get the folder `ScalaML`.
- Go to the PlayML project folder.
- Run `$ sudo sbt run` to download all the dependencies and run the app.

Then the application can be accessed at `http://localhost:9000/`, where we can upload the IBM stock and option prices and, of course, provide other config parameters:

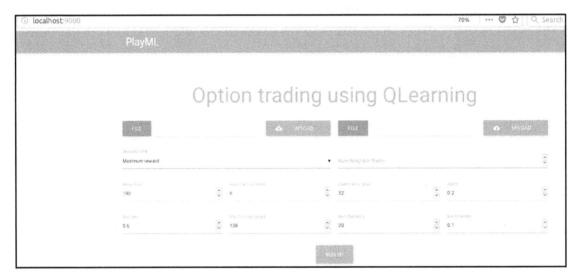

Figure 17: The UI of options trading using QLearning

Now, if you upload the stock price and option price data and click on the run button, a graph will be generated as follows:

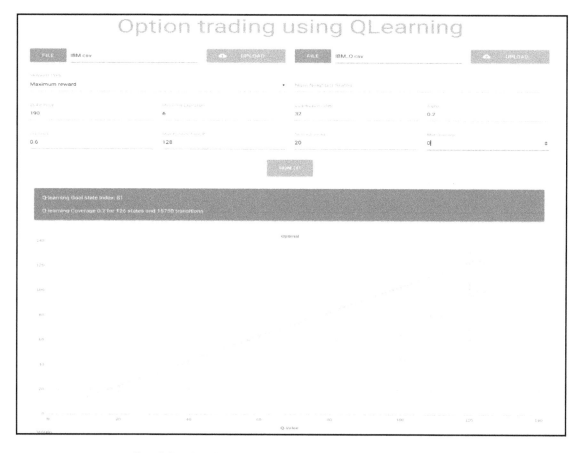

Figure 18: QLearning reaches goal state 81 with a coverage of 0.2 for 126 states and 15,750 transitions

On the other hand, the API endpoint can be accessed at `http://localhost:9000/api/compute`.

Figure 19: The API endpoint (abridged)

Model deployment

You can easily deploy your application as a standalone server by setting the application HTTP port to 9000, for example:

```
$ /path/to/bin/<project-name> -Dhttp.port=9000
```

Note that you probably need root permissions to bind a process to this port. Here is a short workflow:

- Run `$ sudo sbt dist` to build application binary. The output can be found at `PlayML /target/universal/APP-NAME-SNAPSHOT.zip`. In our case, it's `playml-1.0.zip`.
- Now, to run the application, unzip the file and then run the script in the `bin` directory:

```
$ unzip APP-NAME-SNAPSHOT.zip$ APP-NAME-SNAPSHOT /bin/ APP-NAME -Dhttp.port=9000
```

Then you need to configure your web server to map to the app port configuration. Nevertheless, you can easily deploy your application as a standalone server by setting the application HTTP port to `9000`:

```
$ /path/to/bin/<project-name> -Dhttp.port=9000
```

However, if you plan to host several applications on the same server or load-balance several instances of your application for scalability or fault tolerance, you can use a frontend HTTP server. Note that using a frontend HTTP server will rarely give you better performance than using a Play server directly.

However, HTTP servers are very good at handling HTTPS, conditional GET requests, and static assets, and many services assume that a frontend HTTP server is part of your architecture. Additional information can be found at `https://www.playframework.com/documentation/2.6.x/HTTPServer`.

Summary

In this chapter, we learned how to develop a real-life application called options trading using a RL algorithm called Q-learning. The IBM stock datasets were used to design a machine learning system driven by criticisms and rewards. Additionally, we learned some theoretical background. Finally, we learned how to wrap up a Scala desktop application as a web app using Scala Play Framework and deploy it in production.

In the next chapter, we will see two examples of building very robust and accurate predictive models for predictive analytics using H2O on a bank marketing dataset. For this example, we will be using bank marketing datasets. The data is related to direct marketing campaigns of a Portuguese banking institution. The marketing campaigns were based on phone calls. The goal of this end-to-end project will be to predict that the client will subscribe a term deposit.

8
Clients Subscription Assessment for Bank Telemarketing using Deep Neural Networks

In this chapter, we will see two examples of how to build very robust and accurate predictive models for predictive analytics using H2O on a bank marketing dataset. The data is related to the direct marketing campaigns of a Portuguese banking institution. The marketing campaigns were based on phone calls. The goal of this end-to-end project is to predict that the client will subscribe to a term deposit.

Throughout this project, the following topics will be covered in this chapter:

- Client subscription assessment
- Dataset description
- Exploratory analysis of the dataset
- Client subscription assessment using H2O
- Tuning hyperparameters

Client subscription assessment through telemarketing

Some time ago, due to the global financial crisis, getting credit in international markets became more restricted for banks. This turned attention to internal customers and their deposits to gather funds. This led to a demand for information about a client's behavior for their deposits and their response to telemarketing campaigns conducted by the banks periodically. Often, more than one contact to the same client is required in order to assess whether the product (bank term deposit) will be (**yes**) or will be (**no**) subscribed.

The aim of this project is to implement an ML model that predicts that the client will subscribe to a term deposit (variable y). In short, this is a binary classification problem. Now, before we start implementing our application, we need to know about the dataset. Then we will see an explanatory analysis of the dataset.

Dataset description

There are two sources that I would like to acknowledge. This dataset was used in a research paper published by Moro et al, *A Data-Driven Approach to Predict the Success of Bank Telemarketing*, Decision Support Systems, Elsevier, June 2014. Later on, it was donated to the UCI Machine Learning repository and can be downloaded from `https://archive.ics.uci.edu/ml/datasets/bank+marketing`. According to the dataset description, there are four datasets:

- `bank-additional-full.csv`: This includes all examples (41,188) and 20 inputs, ordered by date (from May 2008 to November 2010), very close to the data analyzed by Moro et al, 2014
- `bank-additional.csv`: This includes 10% of the examples (4,119), randomly selected from 1 and 20 inputs
- `bank-full.csv`: This includes all the examples and 17 inputs, ordered by date (an older version of this dataset with fewer inputs)
- `bank.csv`: This includes 10% of the examples and 17 inputs randomly selected from three (an older version of this dataset with fewer inputs)

There are 21 attributes in the dataset. The independent variables, that is, features, can be further categorized as bank-client-related data (attributes 1 to 7), related to the last contact with the current campaign (attributes 8 to 11), other attributes (attributes 12 to 15), and social and economic context attributes (attributes 16 to 20). The dependent variable is specified by `y`, the last attribute (21):

ID	Attribute	Explanation
1	age	Age in numbers.
2	job	This is the type of job in a categorical format, with these possible values: `admin`, `blue-collar`, `entrepreneur`, `housemaid`, `management`, `retired`, `self-employed`, `services`, `student`, `technician`, `unemployed`, and `unknown`.
3	marital	This is the marital status in a categorical format, with these possible values: `divorced`, `married`, `single`, and `unknown`. Here, `divorced` means divorced or widowed.
4	education	This is the educational background in categorical format, with possible values as follows: `basic.4y`, `basic.6y`, `basic.9y`, `high.school`, `illiterate`, `professional.course`, `university.degree`, and `unknown`.
5	default	This is a categorical format with possible values in credit in default as `no`, `yes`, and `unknown`.
6	housing	Does the customer have a housing loan?
7	loan	The personal loan in a categorical format, with possible values as `no`, `yes`, and `unknown`.
8	contact	This is the contact communication type in a categorical format. The possible values are `cellular` and `telephone`.
9	month	This is the last contact month of the year in a categorical format with possible values `jan`, `feb`, `mar`, ..., `nov`, and `dec`.
10	day_of_week	This is the last contact day of the week in a categorical format with possible values `mon`, `tue`, `wed`, `thu`, and `fri`.
11	duration	This is the last contact duration, in seconds (numerical value). This attribute highly affects the output target (for example, if `duration=0`, then `y=no`). Yet, the duration is not known before a call is performed. Also, after the end of the call, `y` is obviously known. Thus, this input should only be included for benchmark purposes and should be discarded if the intention is to have a realistic predictive model.
12	campaign	This is the number of contacts performed during this campaign and for this client.
13	pdays	This is the number of days that passed by after the client was last contacted by a previous campaign (numeric; 999 means client was not previously contacted).
14	previous	This is the number of contacts performed before this campaign and for this client (numeric).
15	poutcome	The outcome of the previous marketing campaign (categorical: `failure`, `nonexistent`, and `success`).
16	emp.var.rate	Employment variation rate—quarterly indicator (numeric).
17	cons.price.idx	Consumer price index—monthly indicator (numeric).
18	cons.conf.idx	Consumer confidence index—monthly indicator (numeric).
19	euribor3m	Euribor 3 month rate—daily indicator (numeric).
20	nr.employed	Number of employees—quarterly indicator (numeric).
21	y	Signifies whether the client has subscribed a term deposit. It has possible binary (`yes` and `no`) values.

Table 1: Description of the bank marketing dataset

For the exploratory analysis of the dataset, we will be using Apache Zeppelin and Spark. We'll start by visualizing the distributions of the categorical features, and then the numeric features. At the end, we'll compute some statistics that describe numeric features. But before that, let's configure Zeppelin.

Installing and getting started with Apache Zeppelin

Apache Zeppelin is a web-based notebook that enables you to do data analytics in an interactive way. Using Zeppelin, you can make beautiful, data-driven, interactive, and collaborative documents with SQL, Scala, and more. The Apache Zeppelin interpreter concept allows any language/data processing backend to be plugged into Zeppelin. Currently, Apache Zeppelin supports many interpreters such as Apache Spark, Python, JDBC, Markdown, and Shell.

Apache Zeppelin is a relatively newer technology from Apache Software Foundation that enables the data scientist, engineer, and practitioner to do data exploration, visualization, sharing, and collaboration with multiple programming language backends (such as Python, Scala, Hive, SparkSQL, Shell, Markdown, and more). Since using other interpreters is not the goal of this book, we'll be using Spark on Zeppelin, and all the codes will be written using Scala. In this section, therefore, we will show you how to configure Zeppelin using a binary package that contains only the Spark interpreter. Apache Zeppelin officially supports, and is tested in, the following environments:

Requirements	Value/Version
Oracle JDK	1.7+ (set `JAVA_HOME`)
OS	Mac OS X Ubuntu 14.X+ CentOS 6.X+ Windows 7 Pro SP1+

As shown in the preceding table, Java is required to execute Spark code on Zeppelin. Therefore, if it is not set up, install and set up java on any of the platforms mentioned earlier. The latest release of Apache Zeppelin can be downloaded from `https://zeppelin.apache.org/download.html`. Each release has three options:

- **Binary package with all interpreters**: Contains all the support for many interpreters. For example, Spark, JDBC, Pig, Beam, Scio, BigQuery, Python, Livy, HDFS, Alluxio, Hbase, Scalding, Elasticsearch, Angular, Markdown, Shell, Flink, Hive, Tajo, Cassandra, Geode, Ignite, Kylin, Lens, Phoenix, and PostgreSQL are currently supported in Zeppelin.
- **Binary package with Spark interpreter**: Usually, this contains only the Spark interpreter. It also contains an interpreter net-install script.
- **Source**: You can also build Zeppelin with all the latest changes from the GitHub repository (more on this later). To show you how to install and configure Zeppelin, we have downloaded the binary package from this site's mirror. Once you have downloaded it, unzip it somewhere on your machine. Suppose the path where you have unzipped the file is `/home/Zeppelin/`.

Building from the source

You can also build Zeppelin with all the latest changes from the GitHub repository. If you want to build from the source, you must first install the following dependencies:

- **Git**: Any version
- **Maven**: 3.1.x or higher
- **JDK**: 1.7 or higher

If you haven't installed Git and Maven yet, check out the Build requirements at `http://zeppelin.apache.org/docs/latest/install/build.html#build-requirements`. Due to page limitations, we have not discussed all the steps in detail. Interested readers should refer to this URL more details on Apache Zeppelin website at `http://zeppelin.apache.org/`.

Starting and stopping Apache Zeppelin

On all UNIX-like platforms (such as Ubuntu, Mac, and so on), use the following command:

```
$ bin/zeppelin-daemon.sh start
```

If the preceding command is successfully executed, you should observe the following logs on the terminal:

```
asif@ubuntu:~/Zeppelin$ bin/zeppelin-daemon.sh start
Log dir doesn't exist, create /home/asif/Zeppelin/logs
Pid dir doesn't exist, create /home/asif/Zeppelin/run
Zeppelin start                                      [  OK  ]
asif@ubuntu:~/Zeppelin$
```

Figure 1: Starting Zeppelin from the Ubuntu terminal

If you are on Windows, use the following command:

```
$ binzeppelin.cmd
```

After Zeppelin has started successfully, go to `http://localhost:8080` with your web browser and you will see that Zeppelin is running. More specifically, you'll see this on your browser:

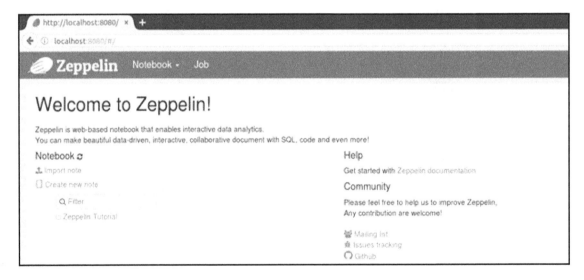

Figure 2: Zeppelin is running on http://localhost:8080

Congratulations! You have successfully installed Apache Zeppelin! Now let's access Zeppelin on the browser at `http://localhost:8080/` and get started on our data analytics once we have configured the preferred interpreter. Now, to stop Zeppelin from the command line, issue this command:

```
$ bin/zeppelin-daemon.sh stop
```

Creating notebooks

Once you are on `http://localhost:8080/`, you can explore different options and menus that help you understand how to get familiar with Zeppelin. For more information on Zeppelin and its user-friendly UI, interested readers can refer to `http://zeppelin.apache.org/docs/latest/`. Now let's first create a sample notebook and get started. As shown in the following figure, you can create a new notebook by clicking on the **Create new note** option in *Figure 2*:

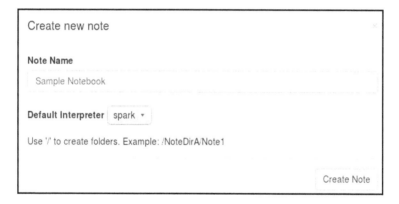

Figure 3: Creating a sample Zeppelin notebook

As shown in *Figure 3*, the default interpreter is selected as Spark. In the drop-down list, you will see only Spark since you have downloaded the Spark-only binary package for Zeppelin.

Exploratory analysis of the dataset

Well done! We have been able to install, configure, and get started with Zeppelin. Now let's get going. We will see how the variables are correlated with the label. We start by loading the dataset in Apache, as follows:

```
val trainDF = spark.read.option("inferSchema", "true")
            .format("com.databricks.spark.csv")
            .option("delimiter", ";")
            .option("header", "true")
            .load("data/bank-additional-full.csv")
trainDF.registerTempTable("trainData")
```

Label distribution

Let's see the class distribution. We will use the SQL interpreter for this. Just execute the following SQL query on the Zeppelin notebook:

```
%sql select y, count(1) from trainData group by y order by y
>>>
```

Job distribution

Now let's see whether the job titles have any correlation with the subscription decision:

```
%sql select job,y, count(1) from trainData group by job, y order by job, y
```

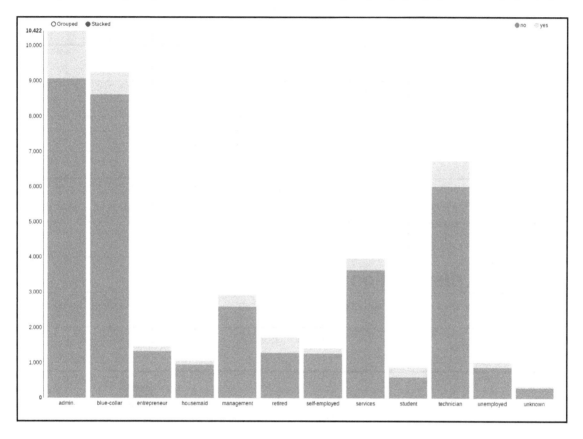

From the chart we can see that most of the clients have jobs as admin, blue-collar, or technician, while students and retired clients have the biggest *count(y)* / *count (n)* ratio.

Marital distribution

Does marital status have a correlation with the subscription decision? Let's see:

```
%sql select marital,y, count(1) from trainData group by marital,y order by
marital,y
>>>
```

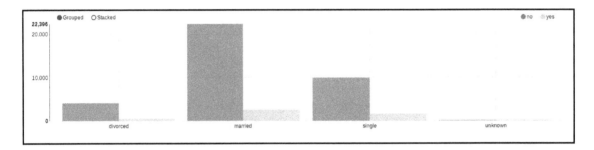

The distribution shows that the subscriptions are proportional to the number of instances regardless of the marital status of the client.

Education distribution

Now let's see whether educational status has a correlation with the subscription decision:

```
%sql select education,y, count(1) from trainData group by education,y order
by education,y
```

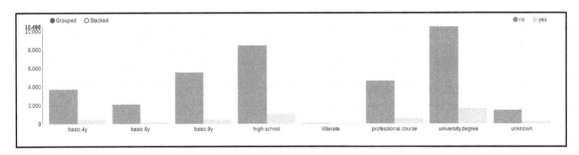

Thus, similar to marital status, the education level gives no clue about the subscriptions. Now let's keep exploring other variables.

Default distribution

Let's check whether default credit has a correlation with the subscription decision:

```
%sql select default,y, count(1) from trainData group by default,y order by
default,y
```

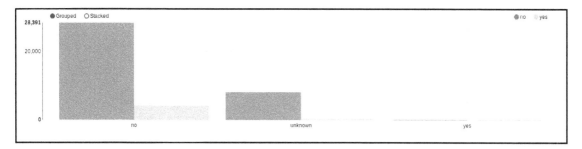

This chart shows there are almost no clients with default credit and clients with no default credit have a slight subscription ratio.

Housing distribution

Now let's see whether having a house has an interesting correlation with the subscription decision:

```
%sql select housing,y, count(1) from trainData group by housing,y order by
housing,y
```

The preceding figures say that housing also gives no clue about subscription.

Loan distribution

Now let's look at loan distribution:

```
%sql select loan,y, count(1) from trainData group by loan,y order by loan,y
```

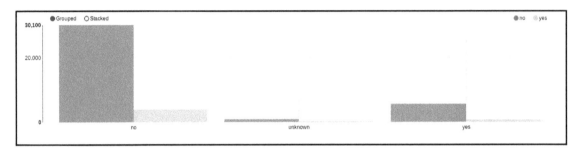

The chart shows that most of the clients have no personal loan and loans have no effect on the subscription ratio.

Contact distribution

Now let's check whether the medium of contact has a significant correlation with the subscription decision:

```
%sql select contact,y, count(1) from trainData group by contact,y order by contact,y
```

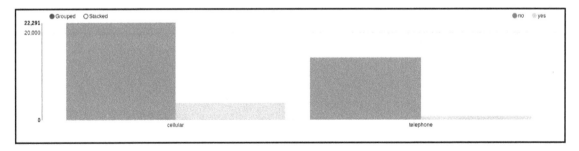

Month distribution

It might sound funny, but the month of telemarketing can have a significant correlation with the subscription decision:

```
%sql select month,y, count(1) from trainData group by month,y order by
month,y
```

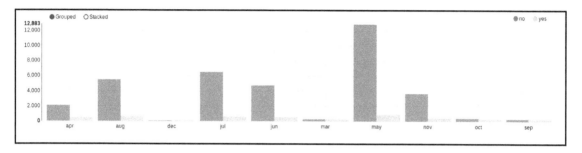

So, the preceding chart shows that the highest subscription ratios are obtained for months that have fewer instances (for example, December, March, October, and September).

Day distribution

Now, what about the day of the week and its correlation with the subscription decision:

```
%sql select day_of_week,y, count(1) from trainData group by day_of_week,y
order by day_of_week,y
```

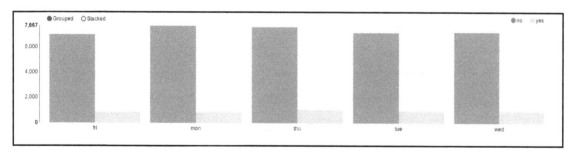

The day feature has a uniform distribution, so it's not that significant.

Previous outcome distribution

What about the previous outcome and its correlation with the subscription decision:

```
%sql select poutcome,y, count(1) from trainData group by poutcome,y order
by poutcome,y
```

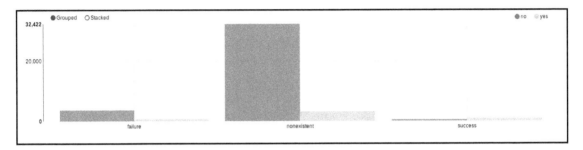

The distribution shows that clients with a successful outcome from the previous marketing campaign will most likely subscribe. At the same time, those clients represent the minority of the dataset.

Age feature

Let us see how age correlates with the subscription decision:

```
%sql select age,y, count(1) from trainData group by age,y order by age,y
```

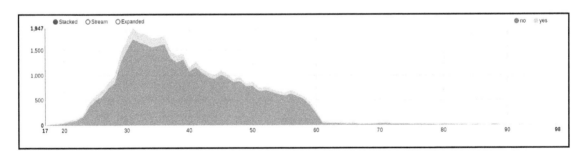

The normalized chart shows that most of the clients are aged between **25** and **60**.

The following chart shows that the bank gets a high subscription ratio with clients in the age interval *(25, 60)*.

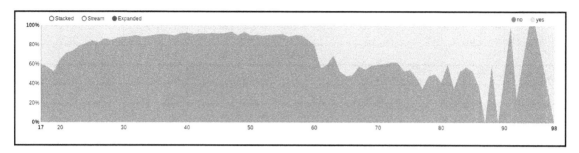

Duration distribution

Let us now take a look at how the duration of calls is related to subscription:

```
%sql select duration,y, count(1) from trainData group by duration,y order
by duration,y
```

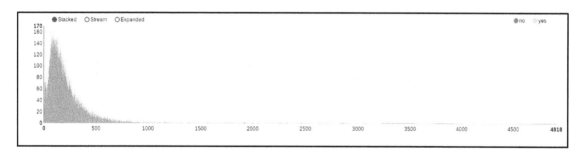

The charts show that most of the calls are short and the subscription ratio is proportional to the call duration. The expanded version provides better insight:

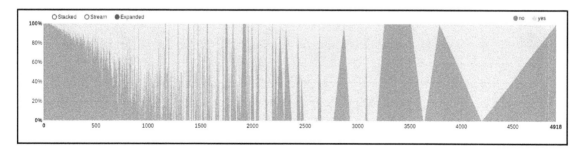

Campaign distribution

Now we will see how campaign distribution is correlated to subscription:

```
%sql select campaign, count(1), y from trainData group by campaign,y order
by campaign,y
```

The charts show that most of the clients are contacted less than five times and the more a client is contacted, the less he/she is likely to subscribe. Now the expanded version provides better insight:

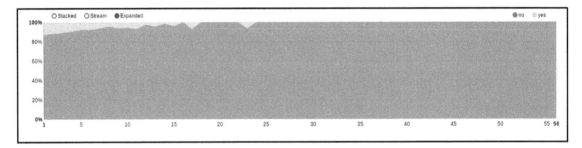

Pdays distribution

Lets us now take a look at how the `pdays` distribution is correlated to subscription:

```
%sql select pdays, count(1), y from trainData group by pdays,y order by
pdays,y
```

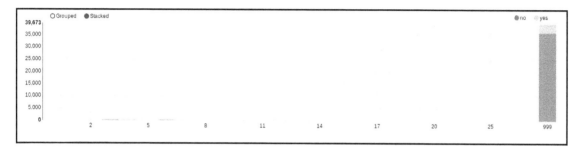

The chart shows that most of the clients were not previously contacted.

Previous distribution

In the following command, we can see how the previous distribution affects the subscription:

```
%sql select previous, count(1), y from trainData group by previous,y order
by previous,y
```

Like the previous chart, this one confirms that most of the clients were not previously contacted for this campaign.

emp_var_rate distributions

The following command shows how `emp_var_rate` distributions correlate with the subscription:

```
%sql select emp_var_rate, count(1), y from trainData group by
emp_var_rate,y order by emp_var_rate,y
```

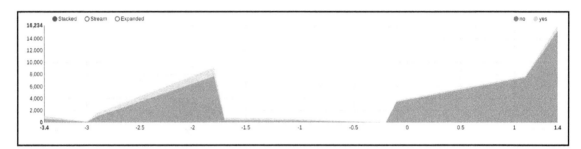

The charts show that clients with a less common employment variation rate will be more likely to subscribe than other clients. Now the expanded version provides a better insight:

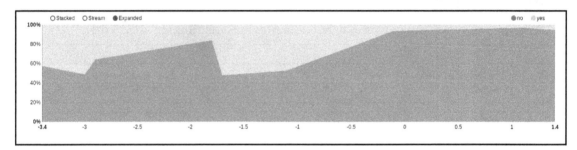

cons_price_idx features

The correlation between `con_price_idx` features and subscription can be computed by the following command:

```
%sql select cons_price_idx, count(1), y from trainData group by
cons_price_idx,y order by cons_price_idx,y
```

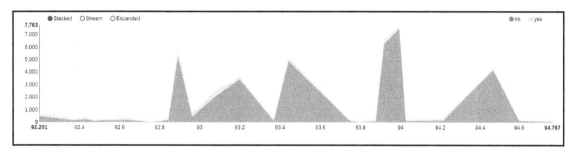

The charts show that clients with a less common consumer price index are more likely to subscribe compared to other clients. Now, the expanded version provides better insight:

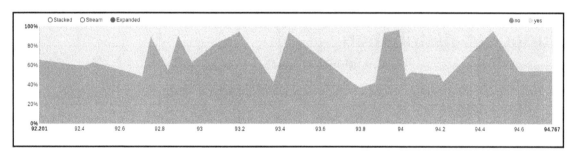

cons_conf_idx distribution

The correlation between `cons_conf_idx` distribution and subscription can be computed by the following command:

```
%sql select cons_conf_idx, count(1), y from trainData group by
cons_conf_idx,y order by cons_conf_idx,y
```

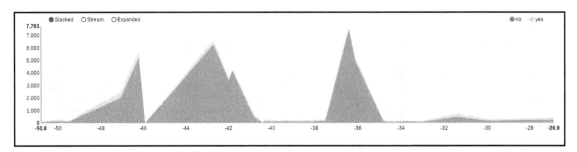

Clients with less common consumer confidence index are more likely to subscribe compared to other clients.

Euribor3m distribution

Let us see how `euribor3m` distribution is correlated to subscription:

```
%sql select euribor3m, count(1), y from trainData group by euribor3m,y
order by euribor3m,y
```

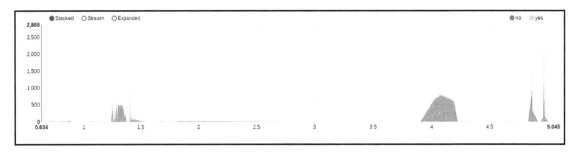

This chart shows that the euribor 3-month rate has a large range and most of the clients cluster around four or five values of that feature.

nr_employed distribution

The correlation between `nr_employed` distribution and subscription can be seen with the help of the following command:

```
%sql select nr_employed, count(1), y from trainData group by nr_employed,y
order by nr_employed,y
```

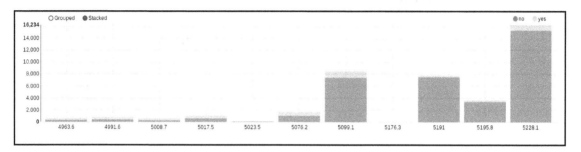

The chart shows that the subscription rate is inversely proportional to the number of employees.

Statistics of numeric features

We will now take a look at the statistics of numeric features:

```
import org.apache.spark.sql.types._

val numericFeatures = trainDF.schema.filter(_.dataType != StringType)
val description = trainDF.describe(numericFeatures.map(_.name): _*)

val quantils = numericFeatures
                .map(f=>trainDF.stat.approxQuantile(f.name,
                  Array(.25,.5,.75),0)).transposeval

rowSeq = Seq(Seq("q1"+:quantils(0): _*),
            Seq("median"+:quantils(1): _*),
            Seq("q3"+:quantils(2): _*))

val rows = rowSeq.map(s=> s match{
    case Seq(a:String,b:Double,c:Double,d:Double,
             e:Double,f:Double,g:Double,
             h:Double,i:Double,j:Double,k:Double)=>
(a,b,c,d,e,f,g,h,i,j,k)})
        val allStats = description.unionAll(sc.parallelize(rows).toDF)
        allStats.registerTempTable("allStats")
```

```
%sql select * from allStats
>>>
```

summary	age	duration	campaign	pdays	previous
count	41188.00	41188.00	41188.00	41188.00	41188.00
mean	40.02	258.29	2.57	962.48	0.17
stddev	10.42	259.28	2.77	186.91	0.49
min	17.00	0.00	1.00	0.00	0.00
max	98.00	4918.00	56.00	999.00	7.00
q1	32.00	102.00	1.00	999.00	0.00
median	38.00	180.00	2.00	999.00	0.00
q3	47.00	319.00	3.00	999.00	0.00

summary	emp_var_rate	cons_price_idx	cons_conf_idx	euribor3m	nr_employed
count	41188.00	41188.00	41188.00	41188.00	41188.00
mean	0.08	93.58	-40.50	3.62	5167.04
stddev	1.57	0.58	4.63	1.73	72.25
min	-3.40	92.20	-50.80	0.63	4963.60
max	1.40	94.77	-26.90	5.05	5228.10
q1	-1.80	93.08	-42.70	1.34	5099.10
median	1.10	93.75	-41.80	4.86	5191.00
q3	1.40	93.99	-36.40	4.96	5228.10

Implementing a client subscription assessment model

To predict a client subscription assessment, we use the deep learning classifier implementation from H2O. First, we set up and create a Spark session:

```
val spark = SparkSession.builder
        .master("local[*]")
        .config("spark.sql.warehouse.dir", "E:/Exp/") // change accordingly
        .appName(s"OneVsRestExample")
        .getOrCreate()
```

Then we load the dataset as a data frame:

```
spark.sqlContext.setConf("spark.sql.caseSensitive", "false");
val trainDF = spark.read.option("inferSchema","true")
            .format("com.databricks.spark.csv")
            .option("delimiter", ";")
            .option("header", "true")
            .load("data/bank-additional-full.csv")
```

Although there are categorical features in this dataset, there is no need to use a `StringIndexer` since the categorical features have small domains. By indexing them, an order relationship that does not exist is introduced. Thus, a better solution is to use One Hot Encodng, and it turns out that H2O, by default, uses this encoding strategy for enumerations.

In the dataset description, I have already stated that the `duration` feature is only available after the label is known. So it can't be used for prediction. Therefore, we should drop it as unavailable before calling the client:

```
val withoutDuration = trainDF.drop("duration")
```

So far, we have used Sparks built-in methods for loading the dataset and dropping unwanted features, but now we need to set up `h2o` and import its implicits:

```
implicit val h2oContext = H2OContext.getOrCreate(spark.sparkContext)
import h2oContext.implicits._implicit

val sqlContext = SparkSession.builder().getOrCreate().sqlContext
import sqlContext.implicits._
```

We then shuffle the training dataset and transform it into an H2O frame:

```
val H2ODF: H2OFrame = withoutDuration.orderBy(rand())
```

String features are then converted into categorical (type "2 Byte" stands for the String type of H2O):

```
H2ODF.types.zipWithIndex.foreach(c=> if(c._1.toInt== 2)
toCategorical(H2ODF,c._2))
```

In the preceding line of code, `toCategorical()` is a user-defined function used to transform a string feature into a categorical feature. Here's the signature of the method:

```
def toCategorical(f: Frame, i: Int): Unit =
{f.replace(i,f.vec(i).toCategoricalVec)f.update()}
```

Now it's time to split the dataset into 60% training, 20% validation, and 20% test datasets:

```
val sf = new FrameSplitter(H2ODF, Array(0.6, 0.2),
                        Array("train.hex", "valid.hex", "test.hex")
                        .map(Key.make[Frame](_)), null)

water.H2O.submitTask(sf)
val splits = sf.getResultval (train, valid, test) = (splits(0), splits(1),
splits(2))
```

Then we train the deep learning model using the training set and validate the training using the validation set, as follows:

```
val dlModel = buildDLModel(train, valid)
```

In the preceding line, `buildDLModel()` is a user-defined function that sets up a deep learning model and trains it using the train and validation data frames:

```
def buildDLModel(train: Frame, valid: Frame,epochs: Int = 10,
            l1: Double = 0.001,l2: Double = 0.0,
            hidden: Array[Int] = Array[Int](256, 256, 256)
            )(implicit h2oContext: H2OContext):
    DeepLearningModel = {import h2oContext.implicits._
            // Build a model
    val dlParams = new DeepLearningParameters()
        dlParams._train = traindlParams._valid = valid
        dlParams._response_column = "y"
        dlParams._epochs = epochsdlParams._l1 = l2
        dlParams._hidden = hidden

    val dl = new DeepLearning(dlParams, water.Key.make("dlModel.hex"))
    dl.trainModel.get
    }
```

In this code, we have instantiated a deep learning (that is, MLP) network of three hidden layers, L1 regularization and that intended to iterate the training for only 10 times. Note that these are hyperparameters and nothing is tuned. So feel free to change this and see the performance to get a set of the most optimized parameters. Once the training phase is completed, we print the training metrics (that is, AUC):

```
val auc = dlModel.auc()println("Train AUC: "+auc)
println("Train classification error" + dlModel.classification_error())
>>>
Train AUC: 0.8071186909427446
Train classification error: 0.13293674881631662
```

About 81% accuracy does not seem good. We now evaluate the model on the test set. We predict the labels of the testing dataset:

```
val result = dlModel.score(test)('predict)
```

Then we add the original labels to the result:

```
result.add("actual",test.vec("y"))
```

Transform the result into a Spark DataFrame and print the confusion matrix:

```
val predict_actualDF =
h2oContext.asDataFrame(result)predict_actualDF.groupBy("actual","predict").
count.show
>>>
```

```
+------+-------+-----+
|actual|predict|count|
+------+-------+-----+
|    no|     no| 6654|
|    no|    yes|  678|
|   yes|    yes|  509|
|   yes|     no|  398|
+------+-------+-----+
```

Now, the preceding confusion matrix can be represented by the following plot using Vegas:

```
Vegas().withDataFrame(predict_actualDF)
    .mark(Bar)
     .encodeY(field="*", dataType=Quantitative, AggOps.Count,
axis=Axis(title="",format=".2f"),hideAxis=true)
    .encodeX("actual", Ord)
    .encodeColor("predict", Nominal,
scale=Scale(rangeNominals=List("#FF2800", "#1C39BB")))
    .configMark(stacked=StackOffset.Normalize)
    .show()
>>>
```

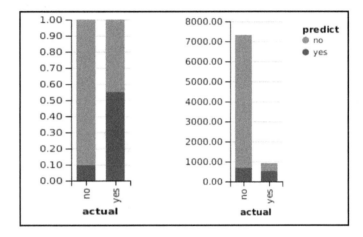

Figure 4: Graphical representation of the confusion matrix—normalized (left) versus un-normalized (right)

Now let's see the overall performance summary on the test set—that is, test AUC:

```
val trainMetrics =
ModelMetricsSupport.modelMetrics[ModelMetricsBinomial](dlModel,
test)println(trainMetrics)
>>>
```

```
Model Metrics Type: Binomial
 Description: N/A
 model id: dlModel.hex
 frame id: test.hex
 MSE: 0.08054043
 RMSE: 0.28379646
 AUC: 0.7632699
 logloss: 0.28570446
 mean_per_class_error: 0.27243903
 default threshold: 0.22040662169456482
 CM: Confusion Matrix (Row labels: Actual class; Column labels: Predicted class):
            no    yes   Error         Rate
     no   6621    669  0.0918     669 / 7,290
    yes    430    519  0.4531     430 / 949
 Totals  7051   1188  0.1334   1,099 / 8,239
```

So the test accuracy in terms of AUC is 76%, which is not that great. But why don't we iterate the training an additional number of times (say, 1,000 times)? Well, I leave it up to you. But still, we can visually inspect the precision-recall curve to see how the evaluation phase went:

```
val auc = trainMetrics._auc//tp,fp,tn,fn
val metrics = auc._tps.zip(auc._fps).zipWithIndex.map(x => x match {
    case ((a, b), c) => (a, b, c) })

val fullmetrics = metrics.map(_ match {
    case (a, b, c) => (a, b, auc.tn(c), auc.fn(c)) })

val precisions = fullmetrics.map(_ match {
    case (tp, fp, tn, fn) => tp / (tp + fp) })

val recalls = fullmetrics.map(_ match {
    case (tp, fp, tn, fn) => tp / (tp + fn) })

val rows = for (i <- 0 until recalls.length)
    yield r(precisions(i), recalls(i))

val precision_recall = rows.toDF()

//precision vs recall
Vegas("ROC", width = 800, height = 600)
```

```
        .withDataFrame(precision_recall).mark(Line)
        .encodeX("re-call", Quantitative)
        .encodeY("precision", Quantitative)
        .show()
>>>
```

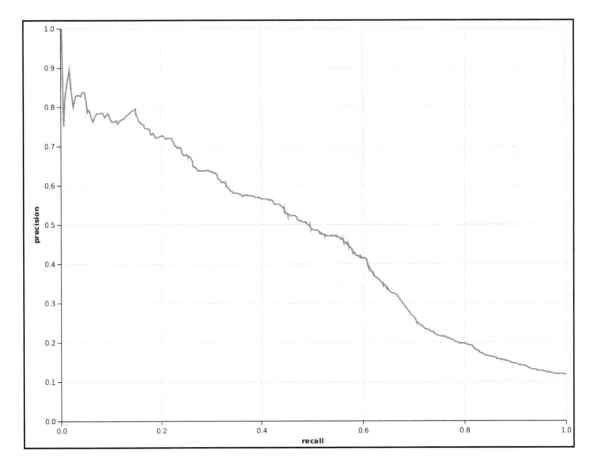

Figure 5: Precision-recall curve

We then compute and draw the sensitivity specificity curve:

```
val sensitivity = fullmetrics.map(_ match {
    case (tp, fp, tn, fn) => tp / (tp + fn) })

val specificity = fullmetrics.map(_ match {
    case (tp, fp, tn, fn) => tn / (tn + fp) })
val rows2 = for (i <- 0 until specificity.length)
    yield r2(sensitivity(i), specificity(i))
```

```
val sensitivity_specificity = rows2.toDF

Vegas("sensitivity_specificity", width = 800, height = 600)
    .withDataFrame(sensitivity_specificity).mark(Line)
    .encodeX("specificity", Quantitative)
    .encodeY("sensitivity", Quantitative).show()
>>>
```

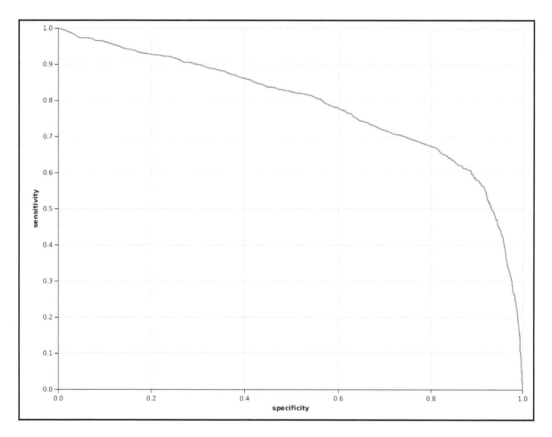

Figure 6: Sensitivity specificity curve

Now the sensitivity specificity curve tells us the relationship between correctly predicted classes from both labels. For example, if we have 100% correctly predicted fraud cases, there will be no correctly classified non-fraud cases and vice versa. Finally, it would be great to take a closer look at this a little differently, by manually going through different prediction thresholds and calculating how many cases were correctly classified in the two classes.

More specifically, we can visually inspect true positives, false positives, true negatives, and false negatives over different prediction thresholds, say **0.0** to **1.0**:

```
val withTh = auc._tps.zip(auc._fps).zipWithIndex.map(x => x match {
    case ((a, b), c) => (a, b, auc.tn(c), auc.fn(c), auc._ths(c)) })

val rows3 = for (i <- 0 until withTh.length)
    yield r3(withTh(i)._1, withTh(i)._2, withTh(i)._3, withTh(i)._4,
withTh(i)._5)
```

First, let's draw the true positive one:

```
Vegas("tp", width = 800, height = 600).withDataFrame(rows3.toDF)
    .mark(Line).encodeX("th", Quantitative)
    .encodeY("tp", Quantitative)
    .show
>>>
```

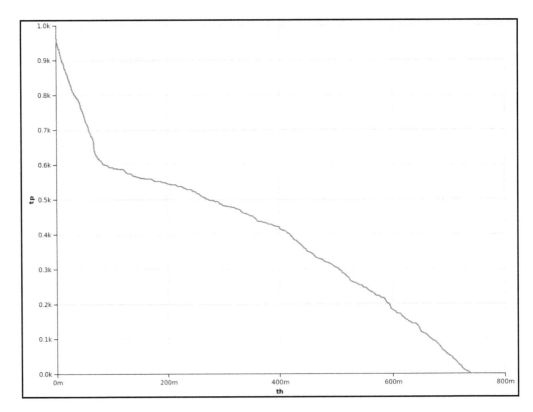

Figure 7: True positives across different prediction thresholds in [0.0, 1.0]

Secondly, let's draw the false positive one:

```
Vegas("fp", width = 800, height = 600)
    .withDataFrame(rows3.toDF).mark(Line)
    .encodeX("th", Quantitative)
    .encodeY("fp", Quantitative)
    .show
>>>
```

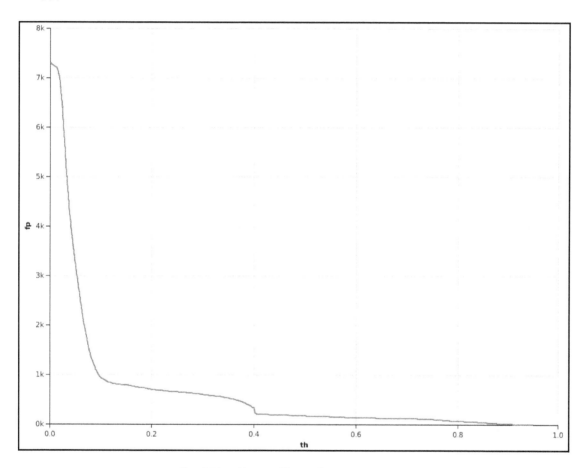

Figure 8: False positives across different prediction thresholds in [0.0, 1.0]

Then, it's the turn of the true negative ones:

```
Vegas("tn", width = 800, height = 600)
    .withDataFrame(rows3.toDF).mark(Line)
    .encodeX("th", Quantitative)
    .encodeY("tn", Quantitative)
    .show
>>>
```

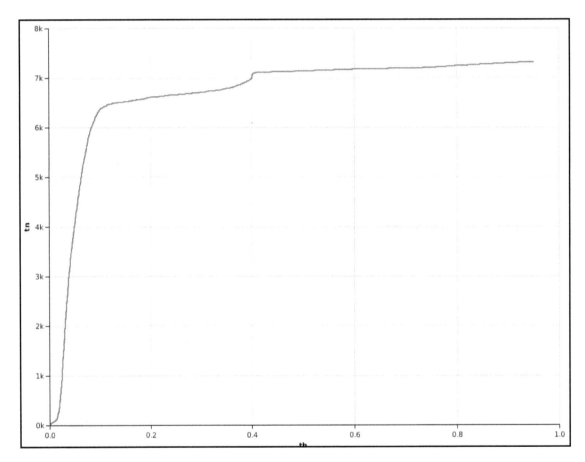

Figure 9: False positives across different prediction thresholds in [0.0, 1.0]

Finally, let's draw the false negative ones as follows:

```
Vegas("fn", width = 800, height = 600)
    .withDataFrame(rows3.toDF).mark(Line)
    .encodeX("th", Quantitative)
    .encodeY("fn", Quantitative)
    .show
>>>
```

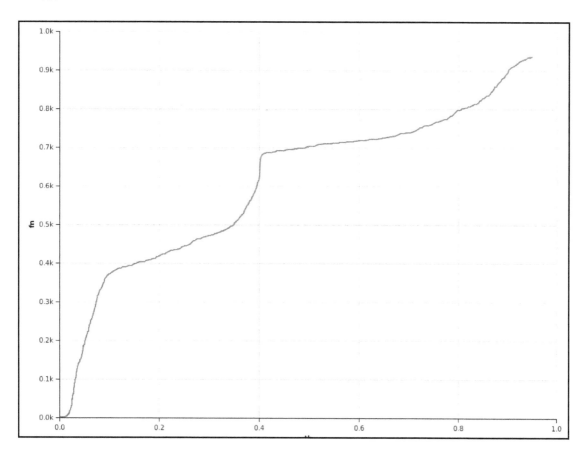

Figure 10: False positives across different prediction thresholds in [0.0, 1.0]

Therefore, the preceding plots tell us that we can increase the number of correctly classified non-fraud cases without losing correctly classified fraud cases when we increase the prediction threshold from the default **0.5** to **0.6**.

Apart from these two auxiliary methods, I have defined three Scala case classes for computing `precision`, `recall`, `sensitivity`, `specificity`, true positives (`tp`), true negatives (`tn`), false positives (`fp`), false negatives (`fn`), and so on. The signature is as follows:

```
case class r(precision: Double, recall: Double)
case class r2(sensitivity: Double, specificity: Double)
case class r3(tp: Double, fp: Double, tn: Double, fn: Double, th: Double)
```

Finally, stop the Spark session and H2O context. The `stop()` method invocation will shut down the H2O context and Spark cluster respectively:

```
h2oContext.stop(stopSparkContext = true)
spark.stop()
```

The first one especially is more important; otherwise, it sometimes does not stop the H2O flow but still holds the computing resources.

Hyperparameter tuning and feature selection

The flexibility of neural networks is also one of their main drawbacks: there are many hyperparameters to tweak. Even in a simple MLP, you can change the number of layers, the number of neurons per layer, the type of activation function to use in each layer, the number of epochs, the learning rate, weight initialization logic, drop-out keep probability, and so on. How do you know what combination of hyperparameters is best for your task?

Of course, you can use grid search with cross-validation to find the right hyperparameters for linear machine learning models, but for deep learning models, there are many hyperparameters to tune. And since training a neural network on a large dataset takes a lot of time, you will only be able to explore a tiny part of the hyperparameter space in a reasonable amount of time. Here are some useful insights.

Number of hidden layers

For many problems, you can start with one or two hidden layers and it will work just fine using two hidden layers with the same total amount of neurons, in roughly the same amount of training time. For more complex problems, you can gradually ramp up the number of hidden layers until you start overfitting the training set. Very complex tasks, such as large image classification or speech recognition, typically require networks with dozens of layers and they need a large amount of training data.

Number of neurons per hidden layer

Obviously, the number of neurons in the input and output layers is determined by the type of input and output your task requires. For example, if your dataset has a shape of 28 x 28, it should expect to have input neurons of size 784, and the output neurons should be equal to the number of classes to be predicted.

We have seen in this project how it works in practice in the next example using MLP, where we set 256 neurons, four each for the hidden layers; that's just one hyperparameter to tune instead of one per layer. Just like the number of layers, you can try increasing the number of neurons gradually until the network starts overfitting.

Activation functions

In most cases, you can use the ReLU activation function in the hidden layers. It is a bit faster to compute than other activation functions, and gradient descent does not get stuck as much on plateaus compared to the logistic function or the hyperbolic tangent function, which usually saturated at one.

For the output layer, the softmax activation function is generally a good choice for classification tasks. For regression tasks, you can simply use no activation function. Other activation functions include Sigmoid and Tanh. The current implementation of the H2O-based deep learning model supports the following activation functions:

- ExpRectifier
- ExpRectifierWithDropout
- Maxout
- MaxoutWithDropout
- Rectifier
- RectifierWthDropout

- Tanh
- TanhWithDropout

Apart from Tanh (the default one in H2O), I have not tried any other activation functions for this project. However, you should definitely try.

Weight and bias initialization

Initializing the weight and biases for the hidden layers is an important hyperparameter to be taken care of:

- **Do not do all-zero initialization**: A reasonable-sounding idea might be to set all the initial weights to zero, but it does not work in practice because if every neuron in the network computes the same output, there will be no source of asymmetry between neurons as their weights are initialized to be the same.
- **Small random numbers**: It is also possible to initialize the weights of the neurons to small numbers but not identically zero. Alternatively, it is also possible to use small numbers drawn from a uniform distribution.
- **Initializing the biases**: It is possible, and common, to initialize the biases to zero since the asymmetry breaking is provided by small random numbers in the weights. Setting the biases to a small constant value, such as 0.01 for all biases, ensures that all ReLU units can propagate a gradient. However, it neither performs well nor does consistent improvement. Therefore, sticking to zero is recommended.

Regularization

There are several ways of controlling the training of neural networks to prevent overfitting in the training phase, for example, L2/L1 regularization, max-norm constraints, and dropout:

- **L2 regularization**: This is probably the most common form of regularization. Using the gradient descent parameter update, L2 regularization signifies that every weight will be decayed linearly towards zero.
- **L1 regularization**: For each weight w, we add the term $\lambda|w|$ to the objective. However, it is also possible to combine L1 and L2 regularization *to achieve* elastic net regularization.

- **Max-norm constraints**: Used to enforce an absolute upper bound on the magnitude of the weight vector for each hidden layer neuron. Projected gradient descent can then be used further to enforce the constraint.

- **Dropout**: When working with a neural network, we need another placeholder for dropout, which is a hyperparameter to be tuned and the training time but not the test time. It is implemented by only keeping a neuron active with some probability, say *p<1.0*, or setting it to zero otherwise. The idea is to use a single neural net at test time without dropout. The weights of this network are scaled-down versions of the trained weights. If a unit is retained with `dropout_keep_prob` < *1.0* during training, the outgoing weights of that unit are multiplied by *p* at test time (*Figure 17*).

Apart from these hyperparameters, another advantage of using H2O-based deep learning algorithms is that we can take the relative variable/feature importance. In previous chapters, we saw that by using the random forest algorithm in Spark, it is also possible to compute the variable importance.

So, the idea is that if your model does not perform well, it would be worth dropping the less important features and doing the training again. Now, it is possible to find the feature importance during supervised training. I have observed this feature importance:

```
INFO: Variable Importances:
INFO:                  Variable Relative Importance Scaled Importance Percentage
INFO:                 month.mar           1.000000           1.000000   0.057811
INFO:                 month.dec           0.742578           0.742578   0.042930
INFO:        education.illiterate         0.727627           0.727627   0.042065
INFO:               default.yes           0.711488           0.711488   0.041132
INFO:            marital.unknown          0.681409           0.681409   0.039393
INFO:                 month.sep           0.642754           0.642754   0.037159
INFO:               job.unknown           0.637595           0.637595   0.036860
INFO:                 month.oct           0.619677           0.619677   0.035824
INFO:               job.student           0.536696           0.536696   0.031027
INFO:              job.housemaid          0.520993           0.520993   0.030119
INFO: ---
INFO:           job.missing(NA)           0.000000           0.000000   0.000000
INFO:         month.missing(NA)           0.000000           0.000000   0.000000
INFO:     education.missing(NA)           0.000000           0.000000   0.000000
INFO: day_of_week.missing(NA)             0.000000           0.000000   0.000000
INFO:       marital.missing(NA)           0.000000           0.000000   0.000000
INFO:          loan.missing(NA)           0.000000           0.000000   0.000000
INFO:       default.missing(NA)           0.000000           0.000000   0.000000
INFO:       housing.missing(NA)           0.000000           0.000000   0.000000
INFO:      poutcome.missing(NA)           0.000000           0.000000   0.000000
INFO:       contact.missing(NA)           0.000000           0.000000   0.000000
```

Figure 25: Relative variable importance

Now the question would be: why don't you drop them and try training again to see if the accuracy has increased or not? Well, I leave it up to the readers.

Summary

In this chapter, we saw how to develop a **machine learning** (**ML**) project using H2O on a bank marketing dataset for predictive analytics. We were able to predict that the client would subscribe to a term deposit with an accuracy of 80%. Furthermore, we saw how to tune typical neural network hyperparameters. Considering the fact that this small-scale dataset, final improvement suggestion would be using Spark based Random Forest, Decision trees or gradient boosted trees for better accuracy.

In the next chapter, we will use a dataset having more than 284,807 instances of credit card use, where only 0.172% of transactions are fraudulent—that is, highly unbalanced data. So it would make sense to use autoencoders to pretrain a classification model and apply anomaly detection to predict possible fraud transaction—that is, we expect our fraud cases to be anomalies within the whole dataset.

9
Fraud Analytics Using Autoencoders and Anomaly Detection

Detecting and preventing fraud in financial companies, such as banks, insurance companies, and credit unions, is an important task in order to see a business grow. So far, in the previous chapter, we have seen how to use classical supervised machine learning models; now it's time to use other, unsupervised learning algorithms, such as autoencoders.

In this chapter, we will use a dataset having more than 284,807 instances of credit card use and for each transaction, where only 0.172% transactions are fraudulent. So, this is highly imbalanced data. And hence it would make sense to use autoencoders to pre-train a classification model and apply an anomaly detection technique to predict possible fraudulent transactions; that is, we expect our fraud cases to be anomalies within the whole dataset.

In summary, we will learn the following topics through this end-to-end project:

- Outlier and anomaly detection using outliers
- Using autoencoders in unsupervised learning
- Developing a fraud analytics predictive model
- Hyperparameters tuning, and most importantly, feature selection

Outlier and anomaly detection

Anomalies are the unusual and unexpected patterns in an observed world. Thus analyzing, identifying, understanding, and predicting anomalies from seen and unseen data is one of the most important task in data mining. Therefore, detecting anomalies allows extracting critical information from data which then can be used for numerous applications.

While anomaly is a generally accepted term, other synonyms, such as outliers, discordant observations, exceptions, aberrations, surprises, peculiarities or contaminants, are often used in different application domains. In particular, anomalies and outliers are often used interchangeably. Anomaly detection finds extensive use in fraud detection for credit cards, insurance or health care, intrusion detection for cyber-security, fault detection in safety critical systems, and military surveillance for enemy activities.

The importance of anomaly detection stems from the fact that for a variety of application domains anomalies in data often translate to significant actionable insights. When we start exploring a highly unbalanced dataset, there are three possible interpretation of your dataset using kurtosis. Consequently, the following questions need to be answered and known by means of data exploration before applying the feature engineering:

- What is the percentage of the total data being present or not having null or missing values for all the available fields? Then try to handle those missing values and interpret them well without losing the data semantics.
- What is the correlation between the fields? What is the correlation of each field with the predicted variable? What values do they take (that is, categorical or on categorical, numerical or alpha-numerical, and so on)?

Then find out if the data distribution is skewed or not. You can identify the skewness by seeing the outliers or long tail (slightly skewed to the right or positively skewed, slightly skewed to the left or negatively skewed, as shown in Figure 1). Now identify if the outliers contribute towards making the prediction or not. More statistically, your data has one of the 3 possible kurtosis as follows:

- Mesokurtic if the measure of kurtosis is less than but almost equal to 3
- Leptokurtic if the measure of kurtosis is more than 3
- Platykurtic if the measure of kurtosis is less than 3

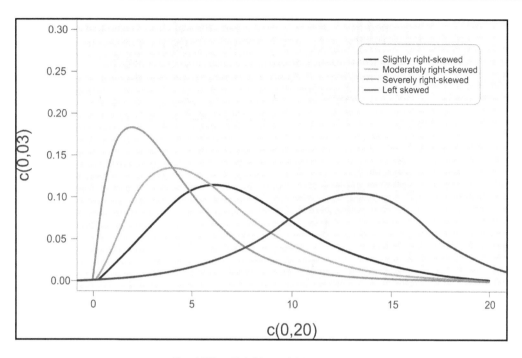

Figure 1: Different kind of skewness in imbalance dataset

Let's give an example. Suppose you are interested in fitness walking and you walked on a sports ground or countryside in the last four weeks (excluding the weekends). You spent the following time (in minutes to finish a 4 KM walking track):15, 16, 18, 17.16, 16.5, 18.6, 19.0, 20.4, 20.6, 25.15, 27.27, 25.24, 21.05, 21.65, 20.92, 22.61, 23.71, 35, 39, and 50. Compute and interpret the skewness and kurtosis of these values using R would produce a density plot as follows.

The interpretation presented in *Figure 2* of the distribution of data (workout times) shows the density plot is skewed to the right so is leptokurtic. So the data points to the right-most position can be thought as the unusual or suspicious for our use case. So we can potentially identify or remove them to make our dataset balanced. However, this is not the purpose of this project but only the identification is.

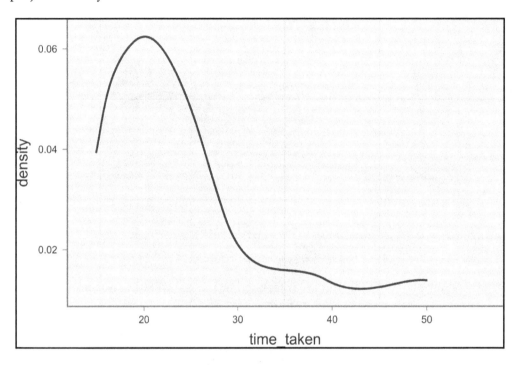

Figure 2: Histogram of the workout time (right-skewed)

Nevertheless, by removing the long tail, we cannot remove the imbalance completely. There is another workaround called outlier detection and removing those data points would be useful.

Moreover, we can also look at the box-plots for each individual feature. Where the box plot displays the data distribution based on five-number summaries: **minimum, first quartile,** median, **third quartile,** and **maximum,** as shown in *Figure 3*, where we can look for outliers beyond three (3) **Inter-Quartile Range (IQR):**

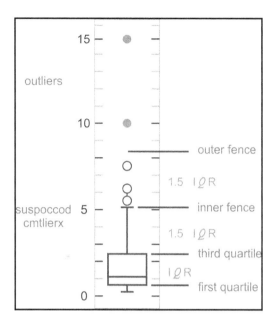

Figure 3: Outliers beyond three (3) Inter-Quartile Range (IQR)

Therefore, it would be useful to explore if removing the long tail could provide better predictions for supervised or unsupervised learning. But there is no concrete recommendation for this highly unbalanced dataset. In short, the skewness analysis does not help us in this regard.

Finally, if you observe your model cannot provide you the perfect classification but the **mean square error** (**MSE**) can provide some clue on finding the outlier or anomaly. For example, in our case, even if our projected model cannot classify your dataset into fraud and non-fraud cases but the mean MSE is definitely higher for fraudulent transactions than for regular ones. So even it would sound naïve, still we can identify outlier instances by applying an MSE threshold for what we can consider outliers. For example, we can think of an instance with an MSE > 0.02 to be an anomaly/outlier.

Now question would be how we can do so? Well, through this end-to-end project, we will see that how to use autoencoders and anomaly detection. We will also see how to use autoencoders to pre-train a classification model. Finally, we'll see how we can measure model performance on unbalanced data. Let's get started with some knowing about autoencoders.

Autoencoders and unsupervised learning

Autoencoders are artificial neural networks capable of learning efficient representations of the input data without any supervision (that is, the training set is unlabeled). This coding, typically, has a much lower dimensionality than the input data, making autoencoders useful for dimensionality reduction. More importantly, autoencoders act as powerful feature detectors, and they can be used for unsupervised pre-training of deep neural networks.

Working principles of an autoencoder

An autoencoder is a network with three or more layers, where the input layer and the output layer have the same number of neurons, and the intermediate (hidden) layers have a lower number of neurons. The network is trained to simply reproduce in output, for each input data, the same pattern of activity in the input. The remarkable aspect of the problem is that, due to the lower number of neurons in the hidden layer, if the network can learn from examples, and generalize to an acceptable extent, it performs data compression: the status of the hidden neurons provides, for each example, a compressed version of the input and output common states.

The remarkable aspect of the problem is that, due to the lower number of neurons in the hidden layer, if the network can learn from examples, and generalize in an acceptable extent, it performs *data compression*: the status of the hidden neurons provides, for each example, a *compressed version* of the *input* and *output common states*. Useful applications of autoencoders are **data denoising** and **dimensionality reduction** for data visualization.

The following schema shows how an autoencoder typically works. It reconstructs the received input through two phases: an encoding phase that corresponds to a dimensional reduction for the original input, and a decoding phase, capable of reconstructing the original input from the encoded (compressed) representation:

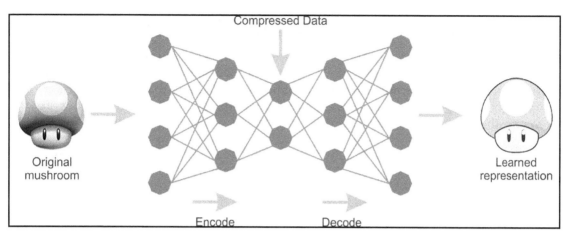

Figure 4: Encoder and decoder phases in autoencoder

As an unsupervised neural network, an autoencoders main characteristic is in its symmetrical structure. An autoencoder has two components: an encoder that converts the inputs to an internal representation, followed by a decoder that converts back the internal representation to the outputs. In other words, an autoencoder can be seen as a combination of an encoder, where we encode some input into a code, and a decoder, where we decode/reconstruct the code back to its original input as the output. Thus, a **Multi-Layer Perceptron** (**MLP**) typically has the same architecture as an autoencoder, except that the number of neurons in the output layer must be equal to the number of inputs.

As mentioned earlier, there is more than one way to train an autoencoder. The first one is by training the whole layer at once, similar to MLP. Although, instead of using some labeled output when calculating the cost function (as in supervised learning), we use the input itself. So, the `cost` function shows the difference between the actual input and the reconstructed input.

The second way is by greedy-training one layer at a time. This training implementation comes from the problem that was created by the backpropagation method in supervised learning (for example, classification). In a network with a large number of layers, the backpropagation method became very slow and inaccurate in gradient calculation. To solve this problem, Geoffrey Hinton applied some pretraining methods to initialize the classification weight, and this pretraining method was done to two neighboring layers at a time.

Efficient data representation with autoencoders

A big problem that plagues all supervised learning systems is the so-called **curse of dimensionality**: a progressive decline in performance while increasing the input space dimension. This occurs because the number of necessary samples to obtain a sufficient sampling of the input space increases exponentially with the number of dimensions. To overcome these problems, some optimizing networks have been developed.

The first are autoencoders networks: these are designed and trained for transforming an input pattern in itself, so that, in the presence of a degraded or incomplete version of an input pattern, it is possible to obtain the original pattern. The network is trained to create output data such as that presented in the entrance, and the hidden layer stores the data compressed, that is, a compact representation that captures the fundamental characteristics of the input data.

The second optimizing networks are **Boltzmann machines**: these types of networks consist of an input/output visible layer and one hidden layer. The connections between the visible layer and the hidden one are non-directional: data can travel in both directions, visible-hidden and hidden-visible, and the different neuronal units can be fully connected or partially connected.

Let's see an example. Decide which of the following series you think would be easier to memorize:

- 45, 13, 37, 11, 23, 90, 79, 24, 87, 47
- 50, 25, 76, 38, 19, 58, 29, 88, 44, 22, 11, 34, 17, 52, 26, 13, 40, 20

Seeing the preceding two series, it seems the first series would be easier for a human, because it is shorter, containing only a few numbers compared to the second one. However, if you take a careful look at the second series, you would find that even numbers are exactly two times the following numbers. Whereas the odd numbers are followed by a number times three plus one. This is a famous number sequence called the **hailstone sequence**.

However, if you can easily memorize long series, you can also recognize patterns in the data easily and quickly. During the 1970s, researchers observed that expert chess players were able to memorize the positions of all the pieces in a game by looking at the board for just five seconds. This might sound controversial, but chess experts don't have a more powerful memory than you and I do. The thing is that they can realize the chess patterns more easily than a non-chess player does. An autoencoder works such that it first observes the inputs, converts them to a better and internal representation, and can swallow similar to what it has already learned:

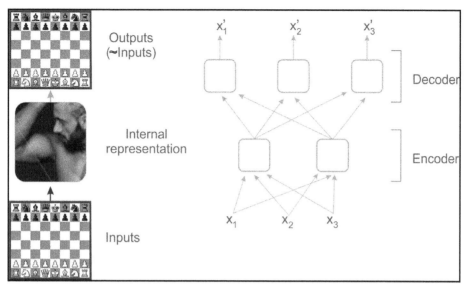

Figure 5: Autoencoder in chess game perspective

Take a look at a more realistic figure concerning the chess example we just discussed: the hidden layer has two neurons (that is, the encoder itself), whereas the output layer has three neurons (in other words, the decoder). Because the internal representation has a lower dimensionality than the input data (it is 2D instead of 3D), the autoencoder is said to be under complete. An under complete autoencoder cannot trivially copy its inputs to the coding, yet it must find a way to output a copy of its inputs.

It is forced to learn the most important features in the input data and drop the unimportant ones. This way, an autoencoder can be compared with **Principal Component Analysis** (**PCA**), which is used to represent a given input using a lower number of dimensions than originally present.

Up to this point, we know how an autoencoder works. Now, it would be worth knowing anomaly detection using outlier identification.

Developing a fraud analytics model

Before we fully start, we need to do two things: know the dataset, and then prepare our programming environment.

Description of the dataset and using linear models

For this project, we will be using the credit card fraud detection dataset from Kaggle. The dataset can be downloaded from `https://www.kaggle.com/dalpozz/creditcardfraud`. Since I am using the dataset, it would be a good idea to be transparent by citing the following publication:

- Andrea Dal Pozzolo, Olivier Caelen, Reid A. Johnson, and Gianluca Bontempi, *Calibrating Probability with Undersampling for Unbalanced Classification*. In Symposium on **Computational Intelligence and Data Mining (CIDM)**, IEEE, 2015.

The datasets contain transactions made by credit cards by European cardholders in September 2013 over the span of only two days. There is a total of 285,299 transactions, with only 492 frauds out of 284,807 transactions, meaning the dataset is highly imbalanced and the positive class (fraud) accounts for 0.172% of all transactions.

It contains only numerical input variables, which are the result of a PCA transformation. Unfortunately, due to confidentiality issues, we cannot provide the original features and more background information about the data. There are 28 features, namely `V1`, `V2`, ..., `V28`, that are principal components obtained with PCA, except for the `Time` and `Amount`. The feature `Class` is the response variable, and it takes value 1 in the case of fraud and 0 otherwise. We will see details later on.

Problem description

Given the class imbalance ratio, we recommend measuring the accuracy using the **Area Under the Precision-Recall Curve (AUPRC)**. Confusion matrix accuracy is not meaningful for imbalanced classification. Regarding this, use linear machine learning models, such as random forests, logistic regression, or support vector machines, by applying over-or under-sampling techniques. Alternatively, we can try to find anomalies in the data, since an assumption like only a few fraud cases being anomalies within the whole dataset.

When dealing with such a severe imbalance of response labels, we also need to be careful when measuring model performance. Because there are only a handful of fraudulent instances, a model that predicts everything as non-fraud will already achieve more than the accuracy of 99%. But despite its high accuracy, linear machine learning models won't necessarily help us find fraudulent cases.

Therefore, it would be worth exploring deep learning models, such as autoencoders. Additionally, we need to use anomaly detection for finding anomalies. In particular, we will see how to use autoencoders to pre-train a classification model and measure model performance on unbalanced data.

Preparing programming environment

In particular, I am going to use several tools and technologies for this project. The following is the list explaining each technology:

- **H2O/Sparking water**: For deep learning platform (see more in the previous chapter)
- **Apache Spark**: For data processing environment
- **Vegas**: An alternative to Matplotlib, similar to Python, for plotting. It can be integrated with Spark for plotting purposes
- **Scala**: The programming language for our project

Well, I am going to create a Maven project, where all the dependencies will be injected into the pom.xml file. The full content of the pom.xml can be downloaded from the Packt repository. So let's do it:

```
<dependencies>
   <dependency>
      <groupId>ai.h2o</groupId>
      <artifactId>sparkling-water-core_2.11</artifactId>
      <version>2.2.2</version>
   </dependency>
   <dependency>
      <groupId>org.vegas-viz</groupId>
      <artifactId>vegas_2.11</artifactId>
      <version>0.3.11</version>
   </dependency>
   <dependency>
      <groupId>org.vegas-viz</groupId>
      <artifactId>vegas-spark_2.11</artifactId>
      <version>0.3.11</version>
      </dependency>
</dependencies>
```

Now, Eclipse or your favorite IDE will pull all the dependencies. The first dependency will also pull all the Spark related dependencies compatible with this H2O version. Then, create a Scala file and provide a suitable name. Then we are ready to go.

Step 1 - Loading required packages and libraries

So let's start by importing required libraries and packages:

```
package com.packt.ScalaML.FraudDetection

import org.apache.spark.sql.SparkSession
import org.apache.spark.sql.functions._
import org.apache.spark.sql._
import org.apache.spark.h2o._
import _root_.hex.FrameSplitter
import water.Key
import water.fvec.Frame
import _root_.hex.deeplearning.DeepLearning
import _root_.hex.deeplearning.DeepLearningModel.DeepLearningParameters
import _root_.hex.deeplearning.DeepLearningModel.DeepLearningParameters.Activation
import java.io.File
import water.support.ModelSerializationSupport
import _root_.hex.{ ModelMetricsBinomial, ModelMetrics }
import org.apache.spark.h2o._
import scala.reflect.api.materializeTypeTag
import water.support.ModelSerializationSupport
import water.support.ModelMetricsSupport
import _root_.hex.deeplearning.DeepLearningModel
import vegas._
import vegas.sparkExt._
import org.apache.spark.sql.types._
```

Step 2 - Creating a Spark session and importing implicits

We then need to create a Spark session as the gateway of our program:

```
val spark = SparkSession
        .builder
        .master("local[*]")
        .config("spark.sql.warehouse.dir", "tmp/")
        .appName("Fraud Detection")
        .getOrCreate()
```

Additionally, we need to import implicits for spark.sql and h2o:

```
implicit val sqlContext = spark.sqlContext
import sqlContext.implicits._
val h2oContext = H2OContext.getOrCreate(spark)
```

```
import h2oContext._
import h2oContext.implicits._
```

Step 3 - Loading and parsing input data

We load and get the transaction. Then we get the distribution:

```
val inputCSV = "data/creditcard.csv"

val transactions = spark.read.format("com.databricks.spark.csv")
        .option("header", "true")
        .option("inferSchema", true)
        .load(inputCSV)
```

Step 4 - Exploratory analysis of the input data

As described earlier, the dataset contains numerical input variables V1 to V28, which are the result of a PCA transformation of the original features. The response variable Class tells us whether a transaction was fraudulent (value = 1) or not (value = 0).

There are two additional features, Time and Amount. The Time column signifies the time in seconds between the current transaction and the first transaction. Whereas the Amount column signifies how much money was transferred in this transaction. So let's see a glimpse of the input data (only V1, V2, V26, and V27 are shown, though) in *Figure 6*:

```
+----+-------------------+--------------------+--------------------+--------------------+------+-----+
|Time|                 V1|                  v2|                 V26|                 V27|Amount|Class|
+----+-------------------+--------------------+--------------------+--------------------+------+-----+
|   0|  -1.3598071336738| -0.0727811733098497|  -0.189114843888824|   0.133558376740387|149.62|    0|
|   0|   1.19185711131486|   0.26615071205963|   0.125894532368176| -0.00898309914322813|  2.69|    0|
|   1| -1.35835406159823|   -1.34016307473609|  -0.139096571514147| -0.0553527940384261|378.66|    0|
|   1|-0.966271711572087| -0.185226008082898|  -0.221928844458407|   0.0627228487293033| 123.5|    0|
|   2| -1.15823309349523|   0.877736754848451|   0.502292224181569|   0.219422229513348| 69.99|    0|
|   2|-0.425965884412454|   0.960523044882985|   0.105914779097957|   0.253844224739337|  3.67|    0|
|   4|   1.22965763450793|   0.141003507049326|  -0.257236845917139|   0.0345074297438413|  4.99|    0|
|   7|-0.644269442348146|   1.41796354547385| -0.0516342969262494|    -1.20692108094258|  40.8|    0|
|   7| -0.89428608220282|   0.286157196276544|  -0.384157307702294|   0.0117473564581996|  93.2|    0|
|   9| -0.33826175242575|   1.11959337641566|   0.0941988339514961|   0.246219304619926|  3.68|    0|
+----+-------------------+--------------------+--------------------+--------------------+------+-----+
only showing top 10 rows
```

Figure 6: A snapshot of the credit card fraud detection dataset

We have been able to load the transaction, but the preceding DataFrame does not tell us about the class distribution. So, let's compute the class distribution and think about plotting them:

```
val distribution = transactions.groupBy("Class").count.collect
Vegas("Class Distribution").withData(distribution.map(r => Map("class" ->
r(0), "count" -> r(1)))).encodeX("class", Nom).encodeY("count",
Quant).mark(Bar).show
>>>
```

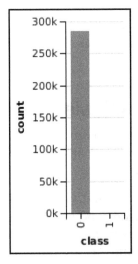

Figure 7: Class distribution in the credit card fraud detection dataset

Now, let's see if the time has any important contribution to suspicious transactions. The Time column tells us the order in which transactions were done, but doesn't tell us anything about the actual times (that is, time of day) of the transactions. Therefore, normalizing them by day and binning those into four groups according to time of day to build a Day column from Time would be useful. I have written a UDF for this:

```
val daysUDf = udf((s: Double) =>
if (s > 3600 * 24) "day2"
else "day1")

val t1 = transactions.withColumn("day", daysUDf(col("Time")))
val dayDist = t1.groupBy("day").count.collect
```

Now let's plot it:

```
Vegas("Day Distribution").withData(dayDist.map(r => Map("day" -> r(0),
"count" -> r(1)))).encodeX("day", Nom).encodeY("count",
Quant).mark(Bar).show
>>>
```

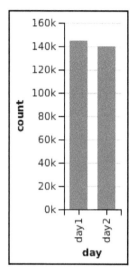

Figure 8: Day distribution in the credit card fraud detection dataset

The preceding graph shows that the same number of transactions was made on these two days, but to be more specific, slightly more transactions were made in day1. Now let's build the dayTime column. Again, I have written a UDF for it:

```
val dayTimeUDf = udf((day: String, t: Double) => if (day == "day2") t -
86400 else t)
val t2 = t1.withColumn("dayTime", dayTimeUDf(col("day"), col("Time")))

t2.describe("dayTime").show()
>>>
+-------+------------------+
|summary| dayTime |
+-------+------------------+
| count| 284807|
| mean| 52336.926072744|
| stddev|21049.288810608432|
| min| 0.0|
| max| 86400.0|
+-------+------------------+
```

Now that we need to get the quantiles (q1, median, q2) and building time bins (gr1, gr2, gr3, and gr4):

```
val d1 = t2.filter($"day" === "day1")
val d2 = t2.filter($"day" === "day2")
val quantiles1 = d1.stat.approxQuantile("dayTime", Array(0.25, 0.5, 0.75),
0)

val quantiles2 = d2.stat.approxQuantile("dayTime", Array(0.25, 0.5, 0.75),
0)

val bagsUDf = udf((t: Double) =>
    if (t <= (quantiles1(0) + quantiles2(0)) / 2) "gr1"
    elseif (t <= (quantiles1(1) + quantiles2(1)) / 2) "gr2"
    elseif (t <= (quantiles1(2) + quantiles2(2)) / 2) "gr3"
    else "gr4")

val t3 = t2.drop(col("Time")).withColumn("Time", bagsUDf(col("dayTime")))
```

Then let's get the distribution for class 0 and 1:

```
val grDist = t3.groupBy("Time", "class").count.collect
val grDistByClass = grDist.groupBy(_(1))
```

Now let's plot the group distribution for class 0:

```
Vegas("gr Distribution").withData(grDistByClass.get(0).get.map(r =>
Map("Time" -> r(0), "count" -> r(2)))).encodeX("Time",
Nom).encodeY("count", Quant).mark(Bar).show
>>>
```

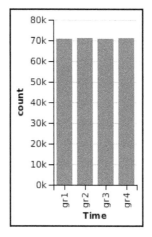

Figure 9: Group distribution for class 0 in the credit card fraud detection dataset

From the preceding graph, it is clear that most of them are normal transactions. Now let's see the group distribution for `class 1`:

```
Vegas("gr Distribution").withData(grDistByClass.get(1).get.map(r =>
Map("Time" -> r(0), "count" -> r(2)))).encodeX("Time",
Nom).encodeY("count", Quant).mark(Bar).show
>>>
```

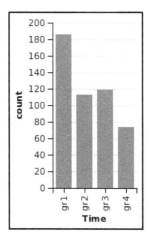

Figure 10: Group distribution for class 1 in the credit card fraud detection dataset

So, the distribution of transactions over the four **Time** bins shows that the majority of fraud cases happened in group 1. We can of course look at the distribution of the amounts of money that were transferred:

```
val c0Amount = t3.filter($"Class" === "0").select("Amount")
val c1Amount = t3.filter($"Class" === "1").select("Amount")

println(c0Amount.stat.approxQuantile("Amount", Array(0.25, 0.5, 0.75),
0).mkString(","))

Vegas("Amounts for class
0").withDataFrame(c0Amount).mark(Bar).encodeX("Amount", Quantitative, bin =
Bin(50.0)).encodeY(field = "*", Quantitative, aggregate =
AggOps.Count).show
>>>
```

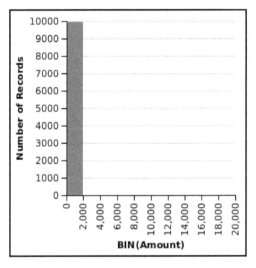

Figure 11: Distribution of the amounts of money that were transferred for class 0

Now let's plot the same for `class 1`:

```
Vegas("Amounts for class
1").withDataFrame(c1Amount).mark(Bar).encodeX("Amount", Quantitative, bin =
Bin(50.0)).encodeY(field = "*", Quantitative, aggregate =
AggOps.Count).show
>>>
```

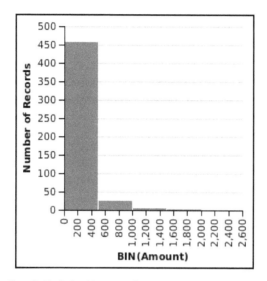

Figure 12: Distribution of the amounts of money that were transferred for class 1

So, from the preceding two graphs, it can be observed that fraudulent credit card transactions had a higher mean amount of money that was transferred, but the maximum amount was much lower compared to regular transactions. As we have seen in the `dayTime` column that we manually constructed, it is not that significant, so we can simply drop it. Let's do it:

```
val t4 = t3.drop("day").drop("dayTime")
```

Step 5 - Preparing the H2O DataFrame

Up to this point, our DataFrame (that is, `t4`) is in Spark DataFrame. But it cannot be consumed by the H2O model. So, we have to convert it to an H2O frame. So let's do it:

```
val creditcard_hf: H2OFrame = h2oContext.asH2OFrame(t4.orderBy(rand()))
```

We split the dataset to, say, 40% supervised training, 40% unsupervised training, and 20% test using H2O built-in splitter called FrameSplitter:

```
val sf = new FrameSplitter(creditcard_hf, Array(.4, .4),
            Array("train_unsupervised", "train_supervised", "test")
            .map(Key.make[Frame](_)), null)
```

```
water.H2O.submitTask(sf)
val splits = sf.getResult
val (train_unsupervised, train_supervised, test) = (splits(0), splits(1),
splits(2))
```

In the above code segment, `Key.make[Frame](_)` is used as a low-level task to split the frame based on the split ratio that also help attain distributed Key/Value pairs.

> Keys are very crucial in H2O computing. H2O supports a distributed Key/Value store, with exact Java memory model consistency. The thing is that Keys are a means to find a link value somewhere in the Cloud, to cache it locally, to allow globally consistent updates to a link Value.

Finally, we need to convert the `Time` column from String to Categorical (that is, **enum**) explicitly:

```
toCategorical(train_unsupervised, 30)
toCategorical(train_supervised, 30)
toCategorical(test, 30)
```

Step 6 - Unsupervised pre-training using autoencoder

As described earlier, we will be using Scala with the h2o encoder. Now it's time to start the unsupervised autoencoder training. Since the training is unsupervised, it means we need to exclude the `response` column from the unsupervised training set:

```
val response = "Class"
val features = train_unsupervised.names.filterNot(_ == response)
```

The next task is to define the hyperparameters, such as the number of hidden layers with neurons, seeds for the reproducibility, the number of training epochs and the activation function for the deep learning model. For the unsupervised pre-training, just set the autoencoder parameter to `true`:

```
var dlParams = new DeepLearningParameters()
    dlParams._ignored_columns = Array(response))// since unsupervised, we
ignore the label
    dlParams._train = train_unsupervised._key // use the train_unsupervised
frame for training
    dlParams._autoencoder = true // use H2O built-in autoencoder
    dlParams._reproducible = true // ensure reproducibility
    dlParams._seed = 42 // random seed for reproducibility
    dlParams._hidden = Array[Int](10, 2, 10)
    dlParams._epochs = 100 // number of training epochs
    dlParams._activation = Activation.Tanh // Tanh as an activation
function
    dlParams._force_load_balance = false

var dl = new DeepLearning(dlParams)
val model_nn = dl.trainModel.get
```

In the preceding code, we are applying a technique called **bottleneck** training, where the hidden layer in the middle is very small. This means that my model will have to reduce the dimensionality of the input data (in this case, down to two nodes/dimensions).

The autoencoder model will then learn the patterns of the input data, irrespective of given class labels. Here, it will learn which credit card transactions are similar and which transactions are outliers or anomalies. We need to keep in mind, though, that autoencoder models will be sensitive to outliers in our data, which might throw off otherwise typical patterns.

Once the pre-training is completed, we should save the model in the `.csv` directory:

```
val uri = new File(new File(inputCSV).getParentFile, "model_nn.bin").toURI
ModelSerializationSupport.exportH2OModel(model_nn, uri)
```

Reload the model and restore it for further use:

```
val model: DeepLearningModel = ModelSerializationSupport.loadH2OModel(uri)
```

Now let's print the model's metrics to see how the training went:

```
println(model)
>>>
```

```
Model Metrics Type: AutoEncoder
 Description: N/A
 model id: DeepLearning_model_1510425525966_1
 frame id: train_unsupervised.temporary.sample.8.78%
 MSE: 0.0016747947
 RMSE: 0.040924255
Variable Importances:
         Variable Relative Importance Scaled Importance Percentage
         Time.gr3            1.000000          1.000000   0.266028
         Time.gr1            0.834574          0.834574   0.222020
         Time.gr2            0.458785          0.458785   0.122050
              V13            0.380227          0.380227   0.101151
              V12            0.146439          0.146439   0.038957
         Time.gr4            0.098328          0.098328   0.026158
              V14            0.095269          0.095269   0.025344
               V9            0.068873          0.068873   0.018322
              V17            0.062106          0.062106   0.016522
              V11            0.051645          0.051645   0.013739
               V3            0.016222          0.016222   0.004316
              V22            0.016090          0.016090   0.004280
               V6            0.015982          0.015982   0.004252
              V19            0.015074          0.015074   0.004010
              V28            0.014994          0.014994   0.003989
              V18            0.014616          0.014616   0.003888
              V25            0.010810          0.010810   0.002876
               V1            0.010639          0.010639   0.002830
              V16            0.007121          0.007121   0.001894
Time.missing(NA)            0.000000          0.000000   0.000000
Status of Neuron Layers (auto-encoder, gaussian distribution, Quadratic loss, 776 weights/biases, 16.2 KB, 2,392,362
 Layer Units  Type Dropout       L1       L2 Mean Rate Rate RMS Momentum Mean Weight Weight RMS Mean Bias Bias RMS
     1    34 Input  0.00 %
     2    10  Tanh        0 0.000000 0.000000  0.549217 0.327317 0.000000   -0.040651   0.613107 -0.123076 0.560158
     3     2  Tanh        0 0.000000 0.000000  0.031482 0.060843 0.000000   -0.042979   0.266792  0.124719 0.119967
     4    10  Tanh        0 0.000000 0.000000  0.111525 0.151304 0.000000    0.287284   1.108348  0.023247 0.515582
     5    34  Tanh          0.000000 0.000000  0.252175 0.361352 0.000000    0.004365   0.602132  0.197952 0.758697
Scoring History:
         Timestamp   Duration  Training Speed   Epochs Iterations      Samples Training RMSE Training MSE
 2017-11-11 19:39:19  0.719 sec 0.00000 obs/sec  0.00000          0     0.000000       0.18766      0.03522
 2017-11-11 19:39:21  3.465 sec    42350 obs/sec  1.00000          1 113922.000000       0.04617      0.00213
 ...
 2017-11-11 19:40:16 57.972 sec    42616 obs/sec 21.00000         21 2392362.000000       0.04092      0.00167
```

Figure 13: Autoencoder model's metrics

Fantastic! The pre-training went very well, because we can see the RMSE and MSE are pretty low. We can also see that some features are pretty unimportant, such as `v16`, `v1`, `v25`, and so on. We will try to analyze it later on.

Step 7 - Dimensionality reduction with hidden layers

Since we used a shallow autoencoder with two nodes in the hidden layer in the middle, it would be worth using the dimensionality reduction to explore our feature space. We can extract this hidden feature with the `scoreDeepFeatures()` method and plot it to show the reduced representation of the input data.

The `scoreDeepFeatures()` method scores an auto-encoded reconstruction on-the-fly, and materialize the deep features of given layer. It takes the following parameters, frame Original data (can contain response, will be ignored) and layer index of the hidden layer for which to extract the features. Finally, a frame containing the deep features is returned. Where number of columns is the hidden [layer]

Now, for the supervised training, we need to extract the Deep Features. Let's do it from layer 2:

```
var train_features = model_nn.scoreDeepFeatures(train_unsupervised, 1)
train_features.add("Class", train_unsupervised.vec("Class"))
```

The plotting for eventual cluster identification is as follows:

```
train_features.setNames(train_features.names.map(_.replaceAll("[.]", "-")))
train_features._key = Key.make()
water.DKV.put(train_features)

val tfDataFrame = asDataFrame(train_features)
Vegas("Compressed").withDataFrame(tfDataFrame).mark(Point).encodeX("DF-L2-
C1", Quantitative).encodeY("DF-L2-C2", Quantitative).encodeColor(field =
"Class", dataType = Nominal).show
>>>
```

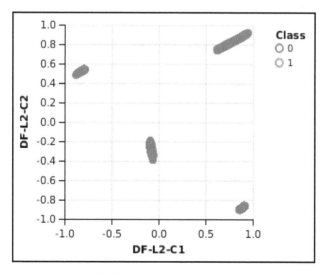

Figure 14: Eventual cluster for classes 0 and 1

From the preceding figure, we cannot see any cluster of fraudulent transactions that is distinct from non-fraudulent instances, so dimensionality reduction with our autoencoder model alone is not sufficient to identify fraud in this dataset. But we could use the reduced dimensionality representation of one of the hidden layers as features for model training. An example would be to use the 10 features from the first or third hidden layer. Now, let's extract the Deep Features from layer 3:

```
train_features = model_nn.scoreDeepFeatures(train_unsupervised, 2)
train_features._key = Key.make()
train_features.add("Class", train_unsupervised.vec("Class"))
water.DKV.put(train_features)

val features_dim = train_features.names.filterNot(_ == response)
val train_features_H2O = asH2OFrame(train_features)
```

Now let's do unsupervised DL using the dataset of the new dimension again:

```
dlParams = new DeepLearningParameters()
        dlParams._ignored_columns = Array(response)
        dlParams._train = train_features_H2O
        dlParams._autoencoder = true
        dlParams._reproducible = true
        dlParams._ignore_const_cols = false
        dlParams._seed = 42
        dlParams._hidden = Array[Int](10, 2, 10)
        dlParams._epochs = 100
        dlParams._activation = Activation.Tanh
        dlParams._force_load_balance = false

dl = new DeepLearning(dlParams)
val model_nn_dim = dl.trainModel.get
```

We then save the model:

```
ModelSerializationSupport.exportH2OModel(model_nn_dim, new File(new
File(inputCSV).getParentFile, "model_nn_dim.bin").toURI)
```

For measuring model performance on test data, we need to convert the test data to the same reduced dimensions as the training data:

```
val test_dim = model_nn.scoreDeepFeatures(test, 2)
val test_dim_score = model_nn_dim.scoreAutoEncoder(test_dim, Key.make(),
false)

val result = confusionMat(test_dim_score, test, test_dim_score.anyVec.mean)
println(result.deep.mkString("n"))
>>>
```

```
Array(38767, 29)
Array(18103, 64)
```

Now, this actually looks quite good in terms of identifying fraud cases: 93% of fraud cases were identified!

Step 8 - Anomaly detection

We can also ask which instances were considered outliers or anomalies within our test data. Based on the autoencoder model that was trained before, the input data will be reconstructed, and for each instance, the MSE between actual value and reconstruction is calculated. I am also calculating the mean MSE for both class labels:

```
test_dim_score.add("Class", test.vec("Class"))
val testDF = asDataFrame(test_dim_score).rdd.zipWithIndex.map(r =>
Row.fromSeq(r._1.toSeq :+ r._2))

val schema = StructType(Array(StructField("Reconstruction-MSE", DoubleType,
nullable = false), StructField("Class", ByteType, nullable = false),
StructField("idRow", LongType, nullable = false)))

val dffd = spark.createDataFrame(testDF, schema)
dffd.show()
>>>
```

```
+--------------------+-----+-----+
| Reconstruction-MSE|Class|idRow|
+--------------------+-----+-----+
|7.956054440127814E-7|    0|    0|
|6.106976382315064E-7|    0|    1|
|6.558716037639693E-6|    0|    2|
|8.753354094541301E-7|    0|    3|
|8.759964479355671E-7|    0|    4|
|5.720411000239647E-7|    0|    5|
|1.015871534556162E-6|    0|    6|
|1.110346446902160...|    1|    7|
|8.251552481892629E-7|    0|    8|
|4.216736950810848E-6|    0|    9|
|3.548204047963272...|    0|   10|
| 3.30049748192825E-7|    0|   11|
|4.504725850972922E-6|    0|   12|
| 5.81244841042056E-7|    0|   13|
|8.988460213316904E-7|    0|   14|
|4.308887907806179E-6|    0|   15|
| 7.33283846864895E-7|    0|   16|
|2.571894655334004...|    0|   17|
|2.341862714880748...|    0|   18|
|6.336200448585121E-7|    0|   19|
+--------------------+-----+-----+
only showing top 20 rows
```

Figure 15: DataFrame showing MSE, class, and row ID

Seeing this DataFrame, it's really difficult to identify outliers. But plotting them would provide some more insights:

```
Vegas("Reduced Test", width = 800, height =
600).withDataFrame(dffd).mark(Point).encodeX("idRow",
Quantitative).encodeY("Reconstruction-MSE", Quantitative).encodeColor(field
= "Class", dataType = Nominal).show
>>>
```

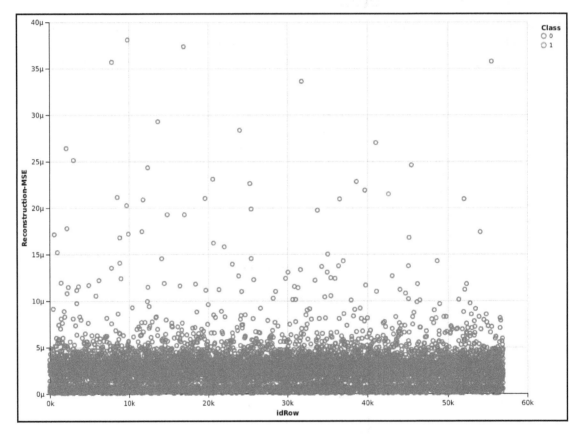

Figure 16: Distribution of the reconstructed MSE, across different row IDs

As we can see in the plot, there is no perfect classification into fraudulent and non-fraudulent cases, but the mean MSE is definitely higher for fraudulent transactions than for regular ones. But a minimum interpretation is necessary.

From the preceding figure, we can at least see that most of the **idRows** have an MSE of **5μ**. Or, if we extend the MSE threshold up to **10μ**, then the data points exceeding this threshold can be considered as outliers or anomalies, that is, fraudulent transactions.

Step 9 - Pre-trained supervised model

We can now try using the autoencoder model as a pre-training input for a supervised model. Here, I am again using a neural network. This model will now use the weights from the autoencoder for model fitting. However, transforming the classes from Int to Categorical in order to train for classification is necessary. Otherwise, the H2O training algorithm will treat it as a regression:

```
toCategorical(train_supervised, 29)
```

Now that the training set (that is, `train_supervised`) is ready for supervised learning, let's jump into it:

```
val train_supervised_H2O = asH2OFrame(train_supervised)
        dlParams = new DeepLearningParameters()
        dlParams._pretrained_autoencoder = model_nn._key
        dlParams._train = train_supervised_H2O
        dlParams._reproducible = true
        dlParams._ignore_const_cols = false
        dlParams._seed = 42
        dlParams._hidden = Array[Int](10, 2, 10)
        dlParams._epochs = 100
        dlParams._activation = Activation.Tanh
        dlParams._response_column = "Class"
        dlParams._balance_classes = true

dl = new DeepLearning(dlParams)
val model_nn_2 = dl.trainModel.get
```

Well done! We have now completed the supervised training. Now, to see the predicted versus actual classes:

```
val predictions = model_nn_2.score(test, "predict")
test.add("predict", predictions.vec("predict"))
asDataFrame(test).groupBy("Class", "predict").count.show //print
>>>
+-----+-------+-----+
|Class|predict|count|
+-----+-------+-----+
|    1|      0|   19|
|    0|      1|   57|
|    0|      0|56804|
|    1|      1|   83|
+-----+-------+-----+
```

Now, this looks much better! We did miss 17% of the fraud cases, but we also did not misclassify too many of the non-fraudulent cases. In real life, we would spend some more time trying to improve the model by example, performing grid searches for hyperparameter tuning, going back to the original features and trying different engineered features and/or trying different algorithms. Now, what about visualizing the preceding result? Let's do it using the `Vegas` package:

```
Vegas().withDataFrame(asDataFrame(test)).mark(Bar).encodeY(field = "*",
dataType = Quantitative, AggOps.Count, axis = Axis(title = "", format =
".2f"), hideAxis = true).encodeX("Class", Ord).encodeColor("predict",
Nominal, scale = Scale(rangeNominals = List("#EA98D2",
"#659CCA"))).configMark(stacked = StackOffset.Normalize).show
>>>
```

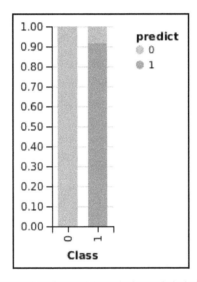

Figure 17: Predicted versus actual classes using the supervised trained model

Step 10 - Model evaluation on the highly-imbalanced data

Since the dataset is highly imbalanced towards non-fraudulent cases, using model evaluation metrics, such as accuracy or **area under the curve** (**AUC**), does not make sense. The reason is that these metrics would give overly optimistic results based on the high percentage of correct classifications of the majority class.

An alternative to AUC is to use the precision-recall curve, or the sensitivity (recall) - specificity curve. First, let's compute the ROC using the modelMetrics() method from the ModelMetricsSupport class:

```
val trainMetrics =
ModelMetricsSupport.modelMetrics[ModelMetricsBinomial](model_nn_2, test)
val auc = trainMetrics._auc
val metrics = auc._tps.zip(auc._fps).zipWithIndex.map(x => x match { case
((a, b), c) => (a, b, c) })

val fullmetrics = metrics.map(_ match { case (a, b, c) => (a, b, auc.tn(c),
auc.fn(c)) })
val precisions = fullmetrics.map(_ match { case (tp, fp, tn, fn) => tp /
(tp + fp) })

val recalls = fullmetrics.map(_ match { case (tp, fp, tn, fn) => tp / (tp +
fn) })
val rows = for (i <- 0 until recalls.length) yield r(precisions(i),
recalls(i))
val precision_recall = rows.toDF()
```

Now that we have the precision_recall DataFrame, it would be exciting to plot it. So let's do it:

```
Vegas("ROC", width = 800, height =
600).withDataFrame(precision_recall).mark(Line).encodeX("recall",
Quantitative).encodeY("precision", Quantitative).show
>>>
```

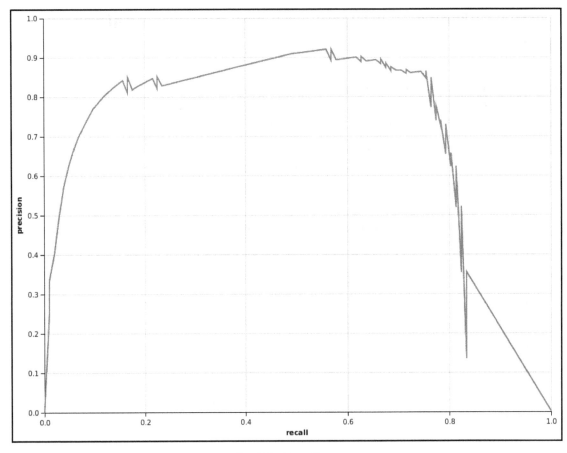

Figure 18: Precision-recall curve

 Precision is the proportion of test cases predicted to be fraudulent that were truly fraudulent, also called **true positive** predictions. On the other hand, recall, or sensitivity, is the proportion of fraudulent cases that were identified as fraudulent. And specificity is the proportion of non-fraudulent cases that are identified as non-fraudulent.

The preceding precision-recall curve tells us the relationship between actual fraudulent predictions and the proportion of fraudulent cases that were predicted. Now, the question is how to compute the sensitivity and specificity. Well, we can do it using standard Scala syntax and plot it using the `Vegas` package:

```
val sensitivity = fullmetrics.map(_
    match {
        case (tp, fp, tn, fn) => tp / (tp + fn) })
```

```
    val specificity = fullmetrics.map(_
    match {
        case (tp, fp, tn, fn) => tn / (tn + fp) })
        val rows2 =
        for (i <- 0 until specificity.length)
    yield r2(sensitivity(i), specificity(i))

val sensitivity_specificity = rows2.toDF
Vegas("sensitivity_specificity", width = 800, height =
600).withDataFrame(sensitivity_specificity).mark(Line).encodeX("specificity
", Quantitative).encodeY("sensitivity", Quantitative).show
>>>
```

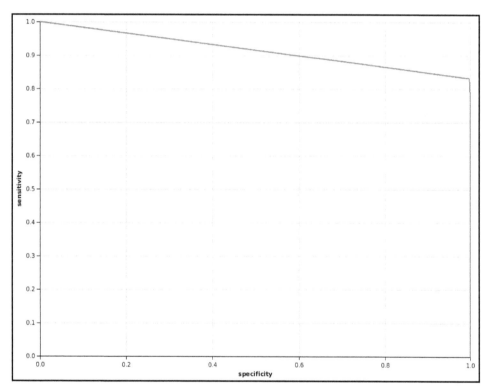

Figure 19: Sensitivity versus specificity curve

Now the preceding sensitivity-specificity curve tells us the relationship between correctly predicted classes from both labels—for example, if we have 100% correctly predicted fraudulent cases, there will be no correctly classified non-fraudulent cases, and vice versa).

Finally, it would be great to take a closer look at this a little bit differently, by manually going through different prediction thresholds and calculating how many cases were correctly classified in the two classes. More specifically, we can visually inspect true positive, false positive, true negative, and false negative over different prediction thresholds—for example, 0.0 to 1.0:

```
val withTh = auc._tps.zip(auc._fps)
        .zipWithIndex
        .map(x => x match { case ((a, b), c)
        => (a, b, auc.tn(c), auc.fn(c), auc._ths(c)) })
val rows3 = for (i <- 0 until withTh.length) yield r3(withTh(i)._1,
withTh(i)._2, withTh(i)._3, withTh(i)._4, withTh(i)._5)
```

First, let's draw the true positive one:

```
Vegas("tp", width = 800, height =
600).withDataFrame(rows3.toDF).mark(Line).encodeX("th",
Quantitative).encodeY("tp", Quantitative).show
>>>
```

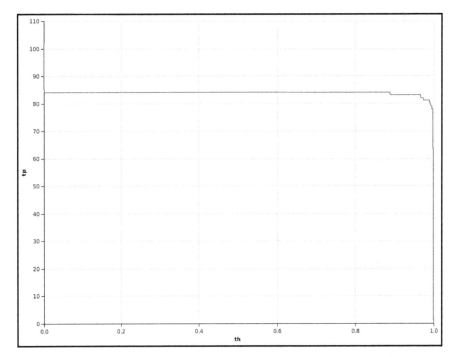

Figure 20: True positives across different prediction thresholds in [0.0, 1.0]

Secondly, let's draw the false positive one:

```
Vegas("fp", width = 800, height =
600).withDataFrame(rows3.toDF).mark(Line).encodeX("th",
Quantitative).encodeY("fp", Quantitative).show
>>>
```

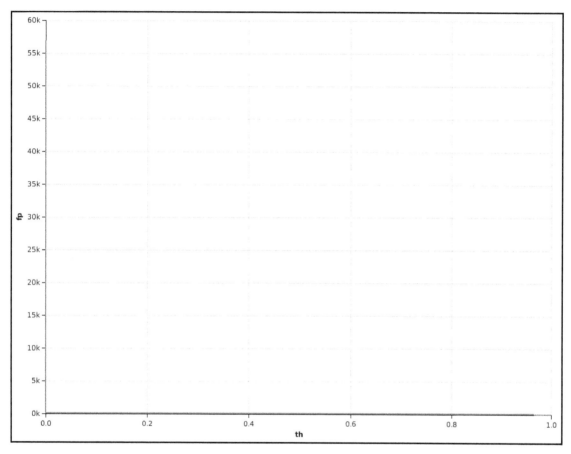

Figure 21: False positives across different prediction thresholds in [0.0, 1.0]

However, the preceding figure is not easily interpretable. So let's provide a threshold of 0.01 for the `datum.th` and then draw it again:

```
Vegas("fp", width = 800, height =
600).withDataFrame(rows3.toDF).mark(Line).filter("datum.th >
0.01").encodeX("th", Quantitative).encodeY("fp", Quantitative).show
>>>
```

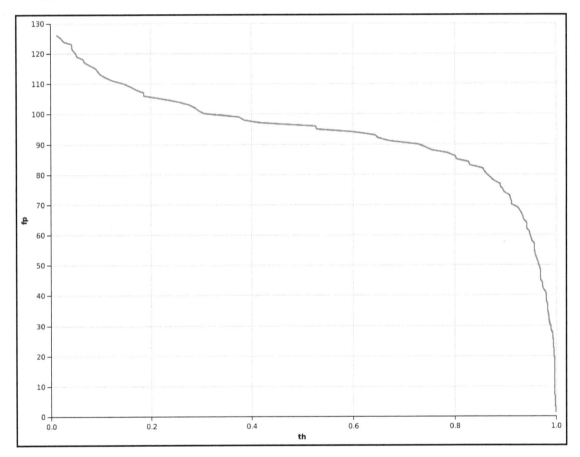

Figure 22: False positives across different prediction thresholds in [0.0, 1.0]

Then, it's the turn for the true negative one:

```
Vegas("tn", width = 800, height =
600).withDataFrame(rows3.toDF).mark(Line).encodeX("th",
Quantitative).encodeY("tn", Quantitative).show
>>>
```

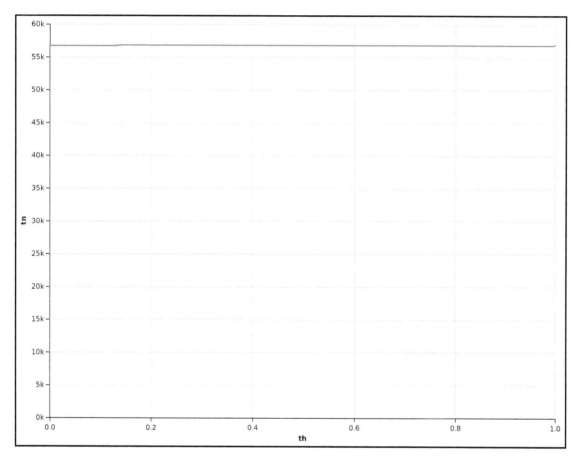

Figure 23: False positives across different prediction thresholds in [0.0, 1.0]

Finally, let's draw the false negative one, as follows:

```
Vegas("fn", width = 800, height =
600).withDataFrame(rows3.toDF).mark(Line).encodeX("th",
Quantitative).encodeY("fn", Quantitative).show
>>>
```

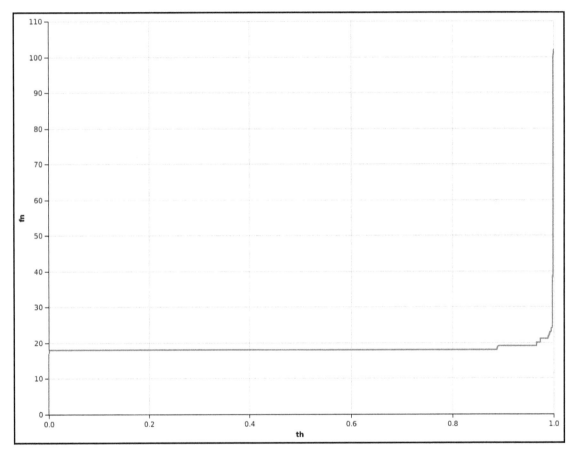

Figure 24: False positives across different prediction thresholds in [0.0, 1.0]

Therefore, the preceding plots tell us that we can increase the number of correctly classified non-fraudulent cases without losing correctly classified fraudulent cases when we increase the prediction threshold from the default 0.5 to 0.6.

Step 11 - Stopping the Spark session and H2O context

Finally, stop the Spark session and H2O context. The following `stop()` method invocation will shut down the H2O context and Spark cluster, respectively:

```
h2oContext.stop(stopSparkContext = true)
spark.stop()
```

The first one, especially, is more important, otherwise it sometimes does not stop the H2O flow but still holds the computing resources.

Auxiliary classes and methods

In the preceding steps, we have seen some classes or methods that we should describe here, too. The first method, named `toCategorical()`, converts the Frame column from String/Int to enum; this is used to convert `dayTime` bags (that is, `gr1`, `gr2`, `gr3`, `gr4`) to a factor-like type. This function is also used to convert the `Class` column to a factor type in order to perform classification:

```
def toCategorical(f: Frame, i: Int): Unit = {
    f.replace(i, f.vec(i).toCategoricalVec)
    f.update()
    }
```

This builds a confusion matrix for anomaly detection according to a threshold if an instance is considered anomalous (if its MSE exceeds the given threshold):

```
def confusionMat(mSEs:water.fvec.Frame,actualFrame:water.fvec.Frame,thresh:
Double):Array[Array[Int]] = {
    val actualColumn = actualFrame.vec("Class");
    val l2_test = mSEs.anyVec();
    val result = Array.ofDim[Int](2, 2)
    var i = 0
    var ii, jj = 0

    for (i <- 0 until l2_test.length().toInt) {
        ii = if (l2_test.at(i) > thresh) 1 else 0;
        jj = actualColumn.at(i).toInt
        result(ii)(jj) = result(ii)(jj) + 1
        }
    result
    }
```

Apart from these two auxiliary methods, I have defined three Scala case classes for computing precision, recall; sensitivity, specificity; true positive, true negative, false positive and false negative and so on. The signature is as follows:

```
caseclass r(precision: Double, recall: Double)
caseclass r2(sensitivity: Double, specificity: Double)
caseclass r3(tp: Double, fp: Double, tn: Double, fn: Double, th: Double)
```

Hyperparameter tuning and feature selection

Here are some ways of improving the accuracy by tuning hyperparameters, such as the number of hidden layers, the neurons in each hidden layer, the number of epochs, and the activation function. The current implementation of the H2O-based deep learning model supports the following activation functions:

- ExpRectifier
- ExpRectifierWithDropout
- Maxout
- MaxoutWithDropout
- Rectifier
- RectifierWthDropout
- Tanh
- TanhWithDropout

Apart from the Tanh one, I have not tried other activation functions for this project. However, you should definitely try.

One of the biggest advantages of using H2O-based deep learning algorithms is that we can take the relative variable/feature importance. In previous chapters, we have seen that, using the random forest algorithm in Spark, it is also possible to compute the variable importance. So, the idea is that if your model does not perform well, it would be worth dropping less important features and doing the training again.

Let's see an example; in *Figure 13*, we have seen the most important features in unsupervised training in autoencoder. Now, it is also possible to find the feature importance during supervised training. I have observed feature importance here:

```
INFO: Model Metrics Type: Binomial
INFO:  Description: Metrics reported on temporary training frame with 9975 samples
INFO:  model id: DeepLearning_model_1510449558864_3
INFO:  frame id: null
INFO:  MSE: 0.013227416
INFO:  RMSE: 0.11501051
INFO:  AUC: 0.99984205
INFO:  logloss: 0.04371999
INFO:  mean_per_class_error: 8.1103E-4
INFO:  default threshold: 0.06491753458976746
INFO:  CM: Confusion Matrix (Row labels: Actual class; Column labels: Predicted class):
INFO:           0      1    Error        Rate
INFO:     0  4924      8   0.0016    8 / 4,932
INFO:     1     0   5043   0.0000    0 / 5,043
INFO: Totals  4924   5051   0.0008    8 / 9,975
INFO: Gains/Lift Table (Avg response rate: 50.56 %):
INFO: Variable Importances:
INFO:          Variable Relative Importance Scaled Importance Percentage
INFO:               V10            1.000000          1.000000   0.054188
INFO:                V2            0.816018          0.816018   0.044218
INFO:               V27            0.729896          0.729896   0.039551
INFO:                V4            0.726038          0.726038   0.039342
INFO:               V12            0.717349          0.717349   0.038872
INFO:               V11            0.709694          0.709694   0.038457
INFO:                V9            0.658070          0.658070   0.035659
INFO:               V22            0.632086          0.632086   0.034251
INFO:                V1            0.624529          0.624529   0.033842
INFO:                V7            0.619922          0.619922   0.033592
INFO: ---
INFO:          Time.gr1            0.451975          0.451975   0.024492
INFO:               V14            0.450914          0.450914   0.024434
INFO:               V15            0.424829          0.424829   0.023021
INFO:               V13            0.397348          0.397348   0.021531
INFO:                V8            0.391477          0.391477   0.021213
INFO:                V6            0.383357          0.383357   0.020773
INFO:               V17            0.352461          0.352461   0.019099
INFO:               V21            0.339572          0.339572   0.018401
INFO:          Time.gr2            0.337747          0.337747   0.018302
INFO: Time.missing(NA)            0.000000          0.000000   0.000000
```

Figure 25: False positives across different prediction thresholds in [0.0, 1.0]

Therefore, from *Figure 25*, it can be observed that the features Time, V21, V17, and V6 are less important ones. So why don't you drop them and try training again and observe whether the accuracy has increased or not?

Nevertheless, grid searching or cross-validation techniques could still provide higher accuracy. However, I'll leave it up to you.

Summary

In this chapter, we have used a dataset having more than 284,807 instances of credit card use and for each transaction where only 0.172% transactions are fraudulent. We have seen how we can use autoencoders to pre-train a classification model and how to apply anomaly detection techniques to predict possible fraudulent transactions from highly imbalanced data—that is, we expected our fraudulent cases to be anomalies within the whole dataset.

Our final model now correctly identified 83% of fraudulent cases and almost 100% of non-fraudulent cases. Nevertheless, we have seen how to use anomaly detection using outliers, some ways of hyperparameter tuning, and, most importantly, feature selection.

A **recurrent neural network** (**RNN**) is a class of artificial neural network where connections between units form a directed cycle. RNNs make use of information from the past. That way, they can make predictions in data with high temporal dependencies. This creates an internal state of the network that allows it to exhibit dynamic temporal behavior.

An RNN takes many input vectors to process them and output other vectors. Compared to a classical approach, using an RNN with **Long Short-Term Memory cells** (**LSTMs**) requires almost no feature engineering. Data can be fed directly into the neural network, which acts like a black box, modeling the problem correctly. The approach here is rather simple in terms of how much of the data was preprocessed.

In the next chapter, we will see how to develop an machine learning project using an RNN implementation called **LSTM** for **human activity recognition** (**HAR**), using a smartphones dataset. In short, our machine learning model will be able to classify the type of movement from six categories: walking, walking upstairs, walking downstairs, sitting, standing, and laying.

10
Human Activity Recognition using Recurrent Neural Networks

A **recurrent neural network** (**RNN**) is a class of artificial neural network where connections between units form a directed cycle. RNNs make use of information from the past. That way, they can make predictions for data with high temporal dependencies. This creates an internal state of the network that allows it to exhibit dynamic temporal behavior.

An RNN takes many input vectors to process them and output other vectors. Compared to a classical approach, using an RNN with **Long Short-Term Memory** cells (**LSTMs**) requires no, or very little, feature engineering. Data can be fed directly into the neural network, which acts like a black box, modeling the problem correctly. The approach here is rather simple in terms of how much data is preprocessed.

In this chapter, we will see how to develop a machine learning project using RNN implementation, called LSTM for **human activity recognition** (**HAR**), using the smartphones dataset. In short, our ML model will be able to classify the type of movement from six categories: walking, walking upstairs, walking downstairs, sitting, standing, and lying down.

In a nutshell, we will learn the following topics throughout this end-to-end project:

- Working with recurrent neural networks
- Long term dependencies and drawbacks of RNN
- Developing an LSTM model for human activity recognition

- Tuning LSTM and RNN
- Summary

Working with RNNs

In this section, we will first provide some contextual information about RNNs. Then, we will highlight some potential drawbacks of classical RNNs. Finally, we will see an improved variation of RNNs called LSTM to address the drawbacks.

Contextual information and the architecture of RNNs

Human beings don't start thinking from scratch; the human mind has so-called **persistence of memory**, the ability to associate the past with recent information. Traditional neural networks, instead, ignore past events. For example, in a movie scenes classifier, it's not possible for a neural network to use a past scene to classify current ones. RNNs were developed to try to solve this problem:

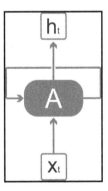

Figure 1: RNNs have loops

In contrast to conventional neural networks, RNNs are networks with a loop that allows the information to be persistent (*Figure 1*). In a neural network say, **A**: at some time **t**, input x_t and outputs a value h_t. So from *Figure 1*, we can think of an RNN as multiple copies of the same network, each passing a message to a successor. Now, if we unroll the previous network, what will we receive? Well, the following figure gives you some insight:

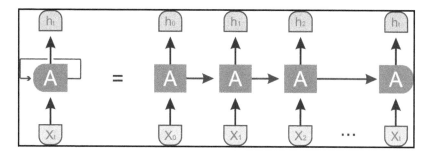

Figure 2: An unrolled representation of the same RNN represented in Figure 1

However, the preceding unrolled figure does not provide detailed information about RNNs. Rather, an RNN is different from a traditional neural network because it introduces a transition weight **W** to transfer information between times. RNNs process a sequential input one at a time, updating a kind of vector state that contains information about all past elements of the sequence. The following figure shows a neural network that takes as input a value of **X(t)**, and then outputs a value **Y(t)**:

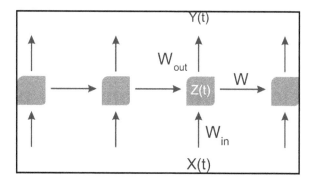

Figure 3: An RNN architecture can use the previous states of the network to its advantage

As shown in *Figure 1*, the first half of the neural network is characterized by the function $Z(t) = X(t) * W_{in}$, and the second half of the neural network takes the form $Y(t) = Z(t) * W_{out}$. If you prefer, the whole neural network is just the function $Y(t) = (X(t) * W_{in}) * W_{out}$.

At each time t, calls the learned model, this architecture does not take into account knowledge about the previous runs. It's like predicting stock market trends by only looking at data from the current day. A better idea would be to exploit overarching patterns from a week's worth or months worth of data:

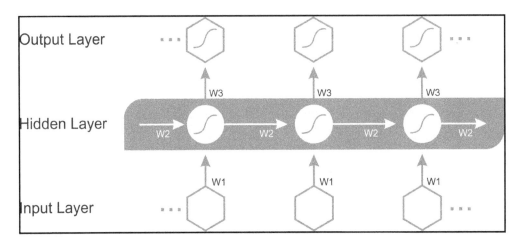

Figure 4: An RNN architecture where all the weights in all the layers have to be learned with time

A more explicit architecture can be found in *Figure 4*, where the temporally shared weights **w2** (for the hidden layer) must be learned in addition to **w1** (for the input layer) and **w3** (for the output layer).

Incredibly, over the last few years, RNNs have been used for a variety of problems, such as speech recognition, language modeling, translation, and image captioning.

RNN and the long-term dependency problem

RNNs are very powerful and popular too. However, often, we only need to look at recent information to perform the present task rather than information that was stored a long time ago. This is frequent in NLP for language modeling. Let's see a common example:

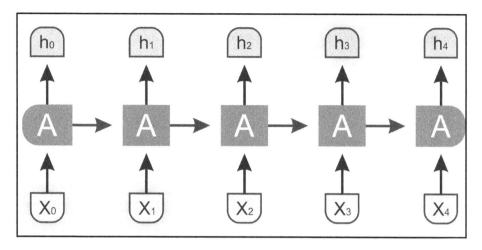

Figure 5: If the gap between the relevant information and the place that its needed is small, RNNs can learn to use past information

Suppose a language model is trying to predict the next word based on the previous words. As a human being, if we try to predict the last word in *the sky is blue*, without further context, it's most likely the next word that we will predict is *blue*. In such cases, the gap between the relevant information and the place is small. Thus, RNNs can learn to use past information easily.

But consider a longer sentence: *Asif grew up in Bangladesh... He studied in Korea... He speaks fluent Bengali* where we need more context. In this sentence, most recent information advises us that the next word will probably be the name of a language. However, if we want to narrow down which language, we need the context of *Bangladesh* from previous words:

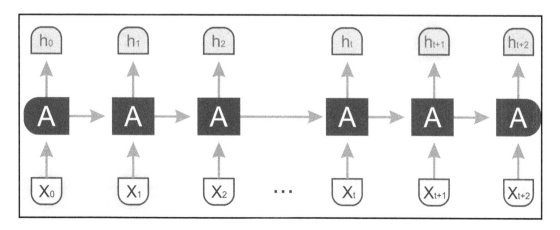

Figure 6: If the gap between the relevant information and the place that its needed is bigger, RNNs can't learn to use past information

Here, the gap is bigger so RNNs become unable to learn the information. This is a serious drawback of RNN. However, along comes LSTM to the rescue.

LSTM networks

One type of RNN model is an **LSTM**. The precise implementation details of LSTM are not within the scope of this book. An LSTM is a special RNN architecture, which was originally conceived by Hochreiter and Schmidhuber in 1997. This type of neural network has been recently rediscovered in the context of deep learning, because it is free from the problem of vanishing gradients, and offers excellent results and performance. LSTM-based networks are ideal for prediction and classification of temporal sequences, and are replacing many traditional approaches to deep learning.

It's a hilarious name, but it means exactly what it sounds. The name signifies that short-term patterns aren't forgotten in the long-term. An LSTM network is composed of cells (LSTM blocks) linked to each other. Each LSTM block contains three types of gate: input gate, output gate, and forget gate, respectively, that implement the functions of writing, reading, and resetting the cell memory. These gates are not binary, but analogical (generally managed by a sigmoidal activation function mapped in the range (0, 1), where 0 indicates total inhibition, and 1 shows total activation).

If you consider the LSTM cell as a black box, it can be used very much like a basic cell, except it will perform much better; training will converge faster, and it will detect long-term dependencies in the data. So how does an LSTM cell work? The architecture of a basic LSTM cell is shown in *Figure 7*:

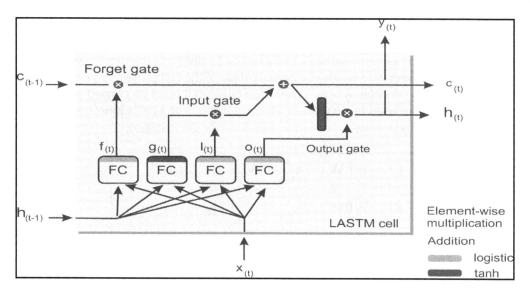

Figure 7: Block diagram of an LSTM cell

Now, let's see the mathematical notation behind this architecture. If we don't look at what's inside the LSTM box, the LSTM cell itself looks exactly like a regular memory cell, except that its state is split into two vectors, **h(t)** and **c(t)**:

- **c** is a cell
- **h(t)** is the short-term state
- **c(t)** is the long-term state

Now let's open the box! The key idea is that the network can learn what to store in the long-term state, what to throw away, and what to read from it. As the long-term state $c_{(t-1)}$ traverses the network from left to right, you can see that it first goes through a forget gate, dropping some memories, and then it adds some new memories via the addition operation (which adds the memories that were selected by an input gate). The resulting **c(t)** is sent straight out, without any further transformation.

So, at each timestamp, some memories are dropped and some memories are added. Moreover, after the addition operation, the long-term state is copied and passed through the **tanh** function, and then the result is filtered by the output gate. This produces the short-term state **h(t)** (which is equal to the cell's output for this time step **y(t)**). Now let's look at where new memories come from and how the gates work. First, the current input vector **x(t)** and the previous short-term state **h(t-1)** are fed to four different fully connected layers.

The presence of these gates allows LSTM cells to remember information for an indefinite time; if the input gate is below the activation threshold, the cell will retain the previous state, and if the current state is enabled, it will be combined with the input value. As the name suggests, the forget gate resets the current state of the cell (when its value is cleared to 0), and the output gate decides whether the value of the cell must be carried out or not. The following equations are used to do the LSTM computations of a cell's long-term state, its short-term state, and its output at each time step for a single instance:

$$\mathbf{i}_{(t)} = \sigma\left(\mathbf{W}_{xi}^{T} \cdot \mathbf{x}_{(t)} + \mathbf{W}_{hi}^{T} \cdot \mathbf{h}_{(t-1)} + \mathbf{b}_{i}\right)$$

$$\mathbf{f}_{(t)} = \sigma\left(\mathbf{W}_{xf}^{T} \cdot \mathbf{x}_{(t)} + \mathbf{W}_{hf}^{T} \cdot \mathbf{h}_{(t-1)} + \mathbf{b}_{f}\right)$$

$$\mathbf{0}_{(t)} = \sigma\left(\mathbf{W}_{xo}^{T} \cdot \mathbf{x}_{(t)} + \mathbf{W}_{ho}^{T} \cdot \mathbf{h}_{(t-1)} + \mathbf{b}_{o}\right)$$

$$\mathbf{g}_{(t)} = \tanh\left(\mathbf{W}_{xg}^{T} \cdot \mathbf{x}_{(t)} + \mathbf{W}_{hg}^{T} \cdot \mathbf{h}_{(t-1)} + \mathbf{b}_{g}\right)$$

$$\mathbf{c}_{(t)} = \mathbf{f}_{(t)} \otimes \mathbf{c}_{(t-1)} + \mathbf{i}_{(t)} \otimes \mathbf{g}_{(t)}$$

$$\mathbf{y}_{(t)} = \mathbf{h}_{(t)} = \mathbf{0}_{(t)} \otimes \tanh\left(\mathbf{c}_{(t)}\right)$$

In the preceding equation, W_{xi}, W_{xf}, W_{xo}, and W_{xg} are the weight matrices of each of the four layers for their connection to the input vector $x_{(t)}$. On the other hand, W_{hi}, W_{hf}, W_{ho}, and W_{hg} are the weight matrices of each of the four layers for their connection to the previous short-term state $h_{(t-1)}$. Finally, b_i, b_f, b_o, and b_g are the bias terms for each of the four layers.

Now that we know all that, how do both RNN and the LSTM network work? It's time to do some hands-on. We will start implementing an MXNet and Scala-based LSTM model for HAR.

Human activity recognition using the LSTM model

The **Human Activity Recognition** (**HAR**) database was built from the recordings of 30 study participants performing **activities of daily living** (**ADL**) while carrying a waist-mounted smartphone with embedded inertial sensors. The objective is to classify activities into one of the six activities performed.

Dataset description

The experiments have been carried out with a group of 30 volunteers within an age bracket of 19 - 48 years. Each person accomplished six activities, namely walking, walking upstairs, walking downstairs, sitting, standing, and laying by wearing a Samsung Galaxy S II smartphone on their waist. Using the accelerometer and gyroscope, the author captured 3-axial linear acceleration and 3-axial angular velocity at a constant rate of 50 Hz.

Only two sensors, that is, accelerometer and gyroscope, were used. The sensor signals were pre-processed by applying noise filters and then sampled in fixed-width sliding windows of 2.56 sec and 50% overlap. This gives 128 readings/window. The gravitational and body motion components from the sensor acceleration signal were separated via a Butterworth low-pass filter into body acceleration and gravity.

 For more information, please refer to this paper: Davide Anguita, Alessandro Ghio, Luca Oneto, Xavier Parra and Jorge L. Reyes-Ortiz. A Public Domain Dataset for *Human Activity Recognition Using Smartphones*. *21st European Symposium on Artificial Neural Networks, Computational Intelligence and Machine Learning, ESANN* 2013. Bruges, Belgium 24-26 April 2013.

For simplicity, the gravitational force is assumed to have only a few but low-frequency components. Therefore, a filter of 0.3 Hz cut-off frequency was used. From each window, a feature vector was found by calculating variables from the time and frequency domain.

The experiments have been video recorded to label the data manually. The obtained dataset has been randomly partitioned into two sets, where 70% of the volunteers were selected for generating the training data and 30% the test data. Now, when I explore the dataset, both the training and test set have the following file structure:

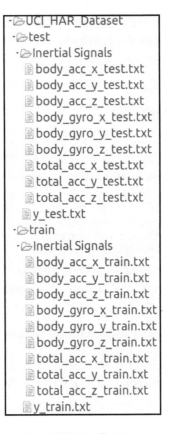

Figure 8: HAR dataset file structure

For each record in the dataset, the following is provided:

- Triaxial acceleration from the accelerometer and the estimated body acceleration
- Triaxial angular velocity from the gyroscope sensor
- A 561-feature vector with time and frequency domain variables
- Its activity label
- An identifier of the subject who carried out the experiment

Now we know the problem that needs to be addressed, it's time to explore the technology and related challenges. Well, as I already stated, we will be using an MXNet-based LSTM implementation. One question you may ask is: why aren't we using H2O or DeepLearning4j? Well, the answer is that both of them either do not have LSTM-based implementation, or cannot be applied to solve this problem.

Setting and configuring MXNet for Scala

Apache MXNet is a flexible and efficient library for deep learning. Building a high-performance deep learning library requires many system-level design decisions. In this design note, we share the rationale for the specific choices made when designing MXNet. We imagine that these insights may be useful to both deep learning practitioners and builders of other deep learning systems.

For this project, we will be needing different packages and libraries: Scala, Java, OpenBLAS, ATLAS, OpenCV, and overall, MXNet. Now let's start configuring these tools one by one. For Java and Scala, I am assuming that you already have Java and Scala configured. Now the next task is to install build tools and `git` since we will be using the MXNet from the GitHub repository. To do this, just execute the following commands on Ubuntu:

```
$ sudo apt-get update
$ sudo apt-get install -y build-essential git
```

Then we need to install OpenBLAS and ATLAS. These are required for linear algebra operations performed by MXNet. To install these, just execute the following command:

```
$ sudo apt-get install -y libopenblas-dev
$ sudo apt-get install -y libatlas-base-dev
```

We also need to install OpenCV for image processing. Let's install it by executing the following command:

```
$ sudo apt-get install -y libopencv-dev
```

Finally, we need to generate the prebuilt MXNet binary. To do this, we need to clone and build MXNet for Scala:

```
$ git clone --recursive https://github.com/apache/incubator-mxnet.git mxnet
--branch 0.12.0
$ cd mxnet
$ make -j $(nproc) USE_OPENCV=1 USE_BLAS=openblas
$ make scalapkg
$ make scalainsta
```

Now, if the preceding steps went smoothly, a prebuilt-binary for MXNet will be generated in `/home/$user_name/mxnet/scala-package/assembly/linux-x86_64-cpu` (or `linux-x86_64-gpu` with GPU configured on Linux, and `osx-x86_64-cpu` on macOS). Take a look at the following screenshot of the CPU on Ubuntu:

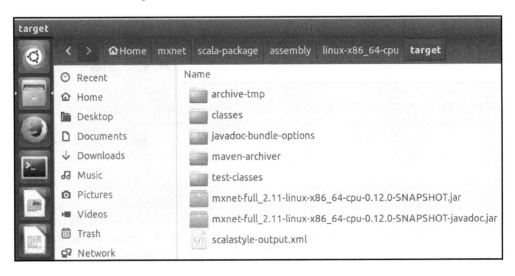

Figure 9: MXNet pre-built binary generated

Now, the next task before you start writing your Scala code on Eclipse (or IntelliJ) as a Maven (or SBT) project, is including this JAR in the build path. Additionally, we need some extra dependency for Scala plots and `args4j`:

```
<dependency>
    <groupId>org.sameersingh.scalaplot</groupId>
    <artifactId>scalaplot</artifactId>
    <version>0.0.4</version>
</dependency>
<dependency>
    <groupId>args4j</groupId>
    <artifactId>args4j</artifactId>
    <version>2.0.29</version>
</dependency>
```

Well done! All set and we're ready to go! Let's start coding.

Implementing an LSTM model for HAR

The overall algorithm (`HumanAR.scala`) has the following workflow:

- Loading the data
- Defining hyperparameters
- Setting up the LSTM model using imperative programming and the hyperparameters
- Applying batch wise training, that is, picking batch size data, feeding it to the model, then at some iterations evaluating the model and printing the batch loss and the accuracy
- Output the chart for the training and test errors

The preceding steps can be followed and constructed by way of a pipeline:

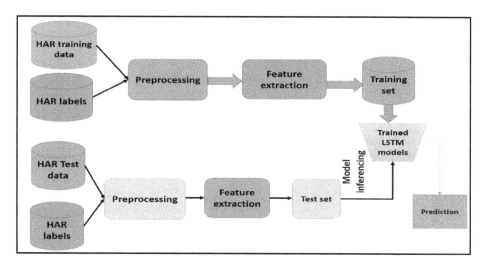

Figure 10: MXNet pre-built binary generated

Now let's start the implementation step-by-step. Make sure that you understand each line of code then import the given project in Eclipse or SBT.

Step 1 - Importing necessary libraries and packages

Let's start coding now. We start from the very beginning, that is, by importing libraries and packages:

```
package com.packt.ScalaML.HAR

import ml.dmlc.mxnet.Context
import LSTMNetworkConstructor.LSTMModel
import scala.collection.mutable.ArrayBuffer
import ml.dmlc.mxnet.optimizer.Adam
import ml.dmlc.mxnet.NDArray
import ml.dmlc.mxnet.optimizer.RMSProp
import org.sameersingh.scalaplot.MemXYSeries
import org.sameersingh.scalaplot.XYData
import org.sameersingh.scalaplot.XYChart
import org.sameersingh.scalaplot.Style._
import org.sameersingh.scalaplot.gnuplot.GnuplotPlotter
import org.sameersingh.scalaplot.jfreegraph.JFGraphPlotter
```

Step 2 - Creating MXNet context

Then we create an MXNet context for CPU-based computation. Since I am doing it by CPU, I instantiated for the CPU. Feel free to use the GPU if you have already configured it by providing the device ID:

```
// Retrieves the name of this Context object
val ctx = Context.cpu()
```

Step 3 - Loading and parsing the training and test set

Now let's load the dataset. I am assuming that you copied your dataset to the `UCI_HAR_Dataset/` directory. Then, also place the other data files as described previously:

```
val datasetPath = "UCI_HAR_Dataset/"
val trainDataPath = s"$datasetPath/train/Inertial Signals"
val trainLabelPath = s"$datasetPath/train/y_train.txt"
val testDataPath = s"$datasetPath/test/Inertial Signals"
val testLabelPath = s"$datasetPath/test/y_test.txt"
```

Now it's time to load the training and test set separately. To do this I wrote two methods called `loadData()` and `loadLabels()` that are in the `Utils.scala` file. These two methods and their signatures will be provided soon:

```scala
val trainData = Utils.loadData(trainDataPath, "train")
val trainLabels = Utils.loadLabels(trainLabelPath)
val testData = Utils.loadData(testDataPath, "test")
val testLabels = Utils.loadLabels(testLabelPath)
```

The `loadData()` method loads and maps the data from each `.txt` file based on the input signal type defined by the `INPUT_SIGNAL_TYPES` array in the `Array[Array[Array[Float]]]` format:

```scala
def loadData(dataPath: String, name: String): Array[Array[Array[Float]]] =
{
    val dataSignalsPaths = INPUT_SIGNAL_TYPES.map( signal =>
s"$dataPath/${signal}${name}.txt" )
    val signals = dataSignalsPaths.map { path =>
      Source.fromFile(path).mkString.split("n").map { line =>
        line.replaceAll("   ", " ").trim().split(" ").map(_.toFloat) }
    }

    val inputDim = signals.length
    val numSamples = signals(0).length
    val timeStep = signals(0)(0).length

    (0 until numSamples).map { n =>
      (0 until timeStep).map { t =>
        (0 until inputDim).map( i => signals(i)(n)(t) ).toArray
      }
    .toArray
    }
    .toArray
}
```

As stated earlier, the `INPUT_SIGNAL_TYPES` contains some useful constants: those are separate, normalized input features for the neural network:

```scala
private val INPUT_SIGNAL_TYPES = Array(
    "body_acc_x_",
    "body_acc_y_",
    "body_acc_z_",
    "body_gyro_x_",
    "body_gyro_y_",
    "body_gyro_z_",
    "total_acc_x_",
    "total_acc_y_",
```

```
                "total_acc_z_")
```

On the other hand, `loadLabels()` is also a user-defined method that is used to load only the labels in the training as well as the test set:

```
    def loadLabels(labelPath: String): Array[Float] = {
        Source.fromFile(labelPath).mkString.split("n").map(_.toFloat - 1)
        }
```

The labels are defined in another array as shown in the following code:

```
    // Output classes: used to learn how to classify
    private val LABELS = Array(
        "WALKING",
        "WALKING_UPSTAIRS",
        "WALKING_DOWNSTAIRS",
        "SITTING",
        "STANDING",
        "LAYING")
```

Step 4 - Exploratory analysis of the dataset

Now let's see some statistics about the number of training series (as described earlier, this is with 50% overlap between each series), number of test series, number of timesteps per series, and number of input parameters per timestep:

```
    val trainingDataCount = trainData.length // No. of training series
    val testDataCount = testData.length // No. of testing series
    val nSteps = trainData(0).length // No. of timesteps per series
    val nInput = trainData(0)(0).length // No. of input parameters per timestep

    println("Number of training series: "+ trainingDataCount)
    println("Number of test series: "+ testDataCount)
    println("Number of timestep per series: "+ nSteps)
    println("Number of input parameters per timestep: "+ nInput)
    >>>
```

The output is:

```
    Number of training series: 7352
    Number of test series: 2947
    Number of timestep per series: 128
    Number of input parameters per timestep: 9
```

Step 5 - Defining internal RNN structure and LSTM hyperparameters

Now, let's define the internal neural network structure and hyperparameters for the LSTM network:

```
val nHidden = 128 // Number of features in a hidden layer
val nClasses = 6 // Total classes to be predicted

val learningRate = 0.001f
val trainingIters = trainingDataCount * 100  // iterate 100 times on
trainset: total 7352000 iterations
val batchSize = 1500
val displayIter = 15000  // To show test set accuracy during training
val numLstmLayer = 3
```

Step 6 - LSTM network construction

Now, let's set up an LSTM model with the preceding parameters and structure:

```
val model = LSTMNetworkConstructor.setupModel(nSteps, nInput, nHidden,
nClasses, batchSize, ctx = ctx)
```

In the preceding line, setupModel() is the method that does the trick. The getSymbol() method actually constructs the LSTM cell. We will see its signature, too, later on. It accepts sequence length, number of input, number of hidden layers, number of labels, batch size, number of LSTM layers, dropout MXNet context, and constructs an LSTM model of type using the case class LSTMModel:

```
case class LSTMModel(exec: Executor, symbol: Symbol, data: NDArray, label:
NDArray, argsDict: Map[String,                 NDArray], gradDict:
Map[String, NDArray])
```

Now here's the signature of the setupModel():

```
def setupModel(seqLen: Int, nInput: Int, numHidden: Int, numLabel: Int,
batchSize: Int, numLstmLayer: Int = 1, dropout: Float = 0f, ctx: Context =
Context.cpu()): LSTMModel = {
//get the symbolic model
    val sym = LSTMNetworkConstructor.getSymbol(seqLen, numHidden, numLabel,
numLstmLayer = numLstmLayer)
    val argNames = sym.listArguments()
    val auxNames = sym.listAuxiliaryStates()
// defining the initial argument and binding them to the model
```

```
    val initC = for (l <- 0 until numLstmLayer) yield (s"l${l}_init_c",
(batchSize, numHidden))
    val initH = for (l <- 0 until numLstmLayer) yield (s"l${l}_init_h",
(batchSize, numHidden))
    val initStates = (initC ++ initH).map(x => x._1 -> Shape(x._2._1,
x._2._2)).toMap
    val dataShapes = Map("data" -> Shape(batchSize, seqLen, nInput)) ++
initStates
    val (argShapes, outShapes, auxShapes) = sym.inferShape(dataShapes)

    val initializer = new Uniform(0.1f)
    val argsDict = argNames.zip(argShapes).map { case (name, shape) =>
      val nda = NDArray.zeros(shape, ctx)
      if (!dataShapes.contains(name) && name != "softmax_label") {
        initializer(name, nda)
      }
      name -> nda
    }.toMap

    val argsGradDict = argNames.zip(argShapes)
        .filter(x => x._1 != "softmax_label" && x._1 != "data")
        .map( x => x._1 -> NDArray.zeros(x._2, ctx) ).toMap

    val auxDict = auxNames.zip(auxShapes.map(NDArray.zeros(_, ctx))).toMap
    val exec = sym.bind(ctx, argsDict, argsGradDict, "write", auxDict,
null, null)
    val data = argsDict("data")
    val label = argsDict("softmax_label")
    LSTMModel(exec, sym, data, label, argsDict, argsGradDict)
  }
```

In the preceding method, we obtained a symbolic model for the deep RNN using the
getSymbol() method that can be seen as follows. I have provided detailed comments and
believe that will be enough to understand the workflow of the code:

```
  private def getSymbol(seqLen: Int, numHidden: Int, numLabel: Int,
numLstmLayer: Int = 1,
                    dropout: Float = 0f): Symbol = {
            //symbolic training and label variables
            var inputX = Symbol.Variable("data")
            val inputY = Symbol.Variable("softmax_label")

            //the initial parameters and cells
            var paramCells = Array[LSTMParam]()
            var lastStates = Array[LSTMState]()
            //numLstmLayer is 1
            for (i <- 0 until numLstmLayer) {
```

```
                      paramCells = paramCells :+ LSTMParam(i2hWeight =
                      Symbol.Variable(s"l${i}_i2h_weight"),
                      i2hBias = Symbol.Variable(s"l${i}_i2h_bias"),
                      h2hWeight = Symbol.Variable(s"l${i}_h2h_weight"),
                      h2hBias = Symbol.Variable(s"l${i}_h2h_bias"))
                      lastStates = lastStates :+ LSTMState(c =
                      Symbol.Variable(s"l${i}_init_c"),
                      h = Symbol.Variable(s"l${i}_init_h"))
            }
        assert(lastStates.length == numLstmLayer)
        val lstmInputs = Symbol.SliceChannel()(inputX)(Map("axis"
        > 1, "num_outputs" -> seqLen,
        "squeeze_axis" -> 1))

        var hiddenAll = Array[Symbol]()
        var dpRatio = 0f
        var hidden: Symbol = null
//for each one of the 128 inputs, create a LSTM Cell
        for (seqIdx <- 0 until seqLen) {
                hidden = lstmInputs.get(seqIdx)
// stack LSTM, where numLstmLayer is 1 so the loop will be executed only
one time
                for (i <- 0 until numLstmLayer) {
                        if (i == 0) dpRatio = 0f else dpRatio = dropout
//for each one of the 128 inputs, create a LSTM Cell
                        val nextState = lstmCell(numHidden, inData =
hidden,
                          prevState = lastStates(i),
                          param = paramCells(i),
                          seqIdx = seqIdx, layerIdx = i, dropout =
                        dpRatio)
                    hidden = nextState.h // has no effect
                    lastStates(i) = nextState // has no effect
            }
// adding dropout before softmax has no effect- dropout is 0 due to
numLstmLayer == 1
            if (dropout > 0f) hidden = Symbol.Dropout()()(Map("data" ->
hidden, "p" -> dropout))
// store the lstm cells output layers
                hiddenAll = hiddenAll :+ hidden
    }
```

In summary, the algorithm uses 128 LSTM cells in parallel, and I concatenated all 128 cells and fed them to the output activation layer. Let's concatenate the cells, outputs:

```
val finalOut = hiddenAll.reduce(_+_)
```

Then we connect them to an output layer that corresponds to the 6 label:

```
val fc = Symbol.FullyConnected()()(Map("data" -> finalOut, "num_hidden" ->
numLabel))
//softmax activation against the label
Symbol.SoftmaxOutput()()(Map("data" -> fc, "label" -> inputY))
```

In the preceding code segment, `LSTMState` and `LSTMParam` are two case classes that used to define the state of each LSTM cell and the latter accepts the parameters needed to construct an LSTM cell. final case class `LSTMState(c: Symbol, h: Symbol)` final case class `LSTMParam(i2hWeight: Symbol, i2hBias: Symbol, h2hWeight: Symbol, h2hBias: Symbol)`.

Now it's time to discuss the most important step, which is LSTM cell construction. We will use some diagrams and legends as shown in the following diagram:

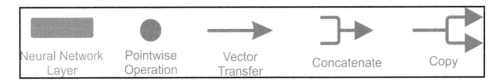

Figure 11: Legends used to describe LSTM cell in the following

The repeating module in an LSTM contains four interacting layers as shown in the following figure:

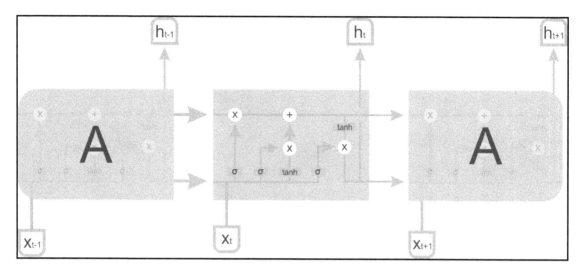

Figure 12: Inside an LSTM cell, that is the, repeating module in an LSTM contains four interacting layers

An LSTM cell is defined by its stats and parameters, as defined by the preceding two case classes:

- **LSTM state**: **c** is the cell stat (its memory knowledge) to be used during the training and **h** is the output
- **LSTM parameters**: To be optimized by the training algorithm
- **i2hWeight**: Input to hidden weight
- **i2hBias**: Input to hidden bias
- **h2hWeight**: Hidden to hidden weight
- **h2hBias**: Hidden to hidden bias
- **i2h**: An NN for input data
- **h2h**: An NN from the previous **h**

In the code, the two fully connected layers have been created, concatenated, and transformed to four copies by the following code. Let's add a hidden layer of size `numHidden * 4` (`numHidden` set to 28) that takes as input the `inputdata`:

```
val i2h =
Symbol.FullyConnected(s"t${seqIdx}_l${layerIdx}_i2h")()(Map("data" ->
inDataa, "weight" ->                 param.i2hWeight, "bias" ->
param.i2hBias, "num_hidden" -> numHidden * 4))
```

Then we add a hidden layer of size `numHidden * 4` (`numHidden` set to 28) that takes as input the previous output of the cell:

```
val h2h =
Symbol.FullyConnected(s"t${seqIdx}_l${layerIdx}_h2h")()(Map("data" ->
prevState.h,"weight" ->              param.h2hWeight,"bias" ->
param.h2hBias,"num_hidden" -> numHidden * 4))
```

Now let's concatenate them together:

```
val gates = i2h + h2h
```

Then let's make four copies of gates before we compute the gates:

```
val sliceGates =
Symbol.SliceChannel(s"t${seqIdx}_l${layerIdx}_slice")(gates)(Map("num_outpu
ts" -> 4))
```

Then we compute the gates:

```
val sliceGates =
Symbol.SliceChannel(s"t${seqIdx}_l${layerIdx}_slice")(gates)(Map("num_outpu
ts" -> 4))
```

Now the activation for the forget gate is represented by the following code:

```
val forgetGate = Symbol.Activation()()(Map("data" -> sliceGates.get(2),
"act_type" -> "sigmoid"))
```

We can see this in the following figure:

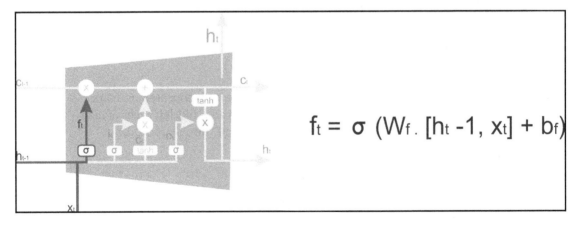

Figure 13: Forget gate in an LSTM cell

Now, the activation for the in gate and in transform are represented by the following code:

```
val ingate = Symbol.Activation()()(Map("data" -> sliceGates.get(0),
"act_type" -> "sigmoid"))
val inTransform = Symbol.Activation()()(Map("data" -> sliceGates.get(1),
"act_type" -> "tanh"))
```

We can also see this in *Figure 14*:

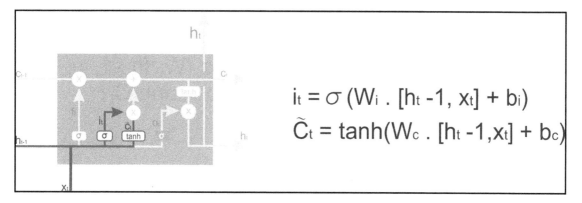

Figure 14: In gate and transform gate in an LSTM cell

The next state is defined by the following code:

```
val nextC = (forgetGate * prevState.c) + (ingate * inTransform)
```

The preceding code can be represented by the following figure too:

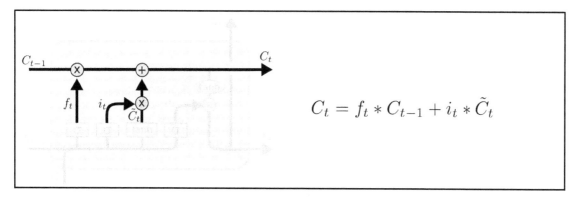

Figure 15: Next or transited gate in an LSTM cell

Finally, the output gate can be represented by the following code:

```
val nextH = outGate * Symbol.Activation()()(Map("data" -> nextC, "act_type"
-> "tanh"))
```

The preceding code can be represented by the following figure too:

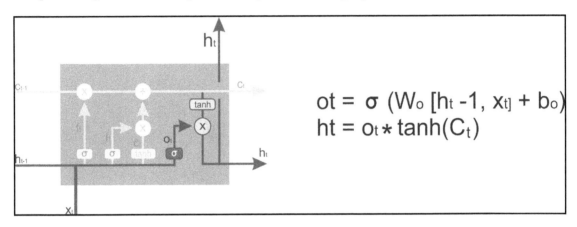

$$o_t = \sigma (W_o [h_{t}-1, x_t] + b_o)$$
$$h_t = o_t * \tanh(C_t)$$

Figure 16: Output gate in an LSTM cell

Too much of a mouthful? No worries, here I have provided the full code for this method:

```
// LSTM Cell symbol
private def lstmCell( numHidden: Int, inData: Symbol, prevState:
LSTMState, param: LSTMParam,
                    seqIdx: Int, layerIdx: Int, dropout: Float = 0f):
LSTMState = {
        val inDataa = {
            if (dropout > 0f) Symbol.Dropout()()(Map("data" -> inData,
"p" -> dropout))
            else inData
            }
        // add an hidden layer of size numHidden * 4 (numHidden set //to
28) that takes as input)
        val i2h =
Symbol.FullyConnected(s"t${seqIdx}_l${layerIdx}_i2h")()(Map("data" ->
inDataa,"weight"                          -> param.i2hWeight,"bias" ->
param.i2hBias,"num_hidden" -> numHidden * 4))
        // add an hidden layer of size numHidden * 4 (numHidden set to 28)
that takes output of the cell
        val h2h =
Symbol.FullyConnected(s"t${seqIdx}_l${layerIdx}_h2h")()(Map("data" ->
prevState.h,"weight" -> param.h2hWeight,"bias" ->
param.h2hBias,"num_hidden" -> numHidden * 4))
```

```
        //concatenate them
        val gates = i2h + h2h
        //make 4 copies of gates
        val
sliceGates=Symbol.SliceChannel(s"t${seqIdx}_l${layerIdx}_slice")(gates)(Map
("num_outputs"
        -> 4))
        // compute the gates
        val ingate = Symbol.Activation()()(Map("data" -> sliceGates.get(0),
"act_type" -> "sigmoid"))
        val inTransform = Symbol.Activation()()(Map("data" ->
sliceGates.get(1), "act_type" -> "tanh"))
        val forgetGate = Symbol.Activation()()(Map("data" ->
sliceGates.get(2), "act_type" -> "sigmoid"))
        val outGate = Symbol.Activation()()(Map("data" ->
sliceGates.get(3), "act_type" -> "sigmoid"))
        // get the new cell state and the output
        val nextC = (forgetGate * prevState.c) + (ingate * inTransform)
        val nextH = outGate * Symbol.Activation()()(Map("data" -> nextC,
"act_type" -> "tanh"))
        LSTMState(c = nextC, h = nextH)
    }
```

Step 7 - Setting up an optimizer

As suggested by many researchers, the RMSProp optimizer helps an LSTM network to converge quickly. Therefore, I have decided to use it here too:

```
val opt = new RMSProp(learningRate = learningRate)
```

Additionally, the model parameters to be optimized are its parameters, except the training data and the label (weights and biases):

```
val paramBlocks = model.symbol.listArguments()
    .filter(x => x != "data" && x != "softmax_label")
    .zipWithIndex.map { case (name, idx) =>
      val state = opt.createState(idx, model.argsDict(name))
      (idx, model.argsDict(name), model.gradDict(name), state, name)
    }
  .toArray
```

Step 8 - Training the LSTM network

Now we will start training the LSTM network. However, before getting started, let's try to define some variables to keep track of the training's performance:

```
val testLosses = ArrayBuffer[Float]()
val testAccuracies = ArrayBuffer[Float]()
val trainLosses = ArrayBuffer[Float]()
val trainAccuracies = ArrayBuffer[Float]()
```

Then, we start performing the training steps with `batch_size` iterations at each loop:

```
var step = 1
while (step * batchSize <= trainingIters) {
    val (batchTrainData, batchTrainLabel) = {
        val idx = ((step - 1) * batchSize) % trainingDataCount
        if (idx + batchSize <= trainingDataCount) {
          val datas = trainData.drop(idx).take(batchSize)
          val labels = trainLabels.drop(idx).take(batchSize)
          (datas, labels)
        } else {
          val right = (idx + batchSize) - trainingDataCount
          val left = trainingDataCount - idx
          val datas = trainData.drop(idx).take(left) ++
trainData.take(right)
          val labels = trainLabels.drop(idx).take(left) ++
trainLabels.take(right)
          (datas, labels)
    }
}
```

Don't get derailed but take a quick look at *step 6* previously, where we have instantiated the LSTM model. Now it's time to feed the input and labels to the RNN:

```
model.data.set(batchTrainData.flatten.flatten)
model.label.set(batchTrainLabel)
```

Then we do forward and backward passes:

```
model.exec.forward(isTrain = true)
model.exec.backward()
```

Additionally, we need to update the parameters using the `RMSProp` optimizer that we defined in *step 7*:

```
paramBlocks.foreach {
    case (idx, weight, grad, state, name) => opt.update(idx, weight, grad,
```

```
state)
   }
```

It would also be great to get metrics such as training errors—that is, loss and accuracy over the training data:

```
val (acc, loss) = getAccAndLoss(model.exec.outputs(0), batchTrainLabel)
      trainLosses += loss / batchSize
      trainAccuracies += acc / batchSize
```

In the preceding code segment, `getAccAndLoss()` is a method that computes the loss and accuracy and can be seen as follows:

```
def getAccAndLoss(pred: NDArray, label: Array[Float], dropNum: Int = 0):
(Float, Float) = {
    val shape = pred.shape
    val maxIdx = NDArray.argmax_channel(pred).toArray
    val acc = {
      val sum = maxIdx.drop(dropNum).zip(label.drop(dropNum)).foldLeft(0f){
case (acc, elem) =>
        if (elem._1 == elem._2) acc + 1 else acc
      }
      sum
    }
    val loss =
pred.toArray.grouped(shape(1)).drop(dropNum).zipWithIndex.map { case
(array, idx) =>
        array(maxIdx(idx).toInt)
      }.map(-Math.log(_)).sum.toFloat
  (acc, loss)
}
```

Additionally, it would be exciting to evaluate only the network at some steps for faster training:

```
if ( (step * batchSize % displayIter == 0) || (step == 1) || (step *
batchSize > trainingIters) ) {
        println(s"Iter ${step * batchSize}, Batch Loss =
${"%.6f".format(loss / batchSize)},
        Accuracy = ${acc / batchSize}")
    }

Iter 1500, Batch Loss = 1.189168, Accuracy = 0.14266667
 Iter 15000, Batch Loss = 0.479527, Accuracy = 0.53866667
 Iter 30000, Batch Loss = 0.293270, Accuracy = 0.83933336
 Iter 45000, Batch Loss = 0.192152, Accuracy = 0.78933334
 Iter 60000, Batch Loss = 0.118560, Accuracy = 0.9173333
 Iter 75000, Batch Loss = 0.081408, Accuracy = 0.9486667
```

```
Iter 90000, Batch Loss = 0.109803, Accuracy = 0.9266667
Iter 105000, Batch Loss = 0.095064, Accuracy = 0.924
Iter 120000, Batch Loss = 0.087000, Accuracy = 0.9533333
Iter 135000, Batch Loss = 0.085708, Accuracy = 0.966
Iter 150000, Batch Loss = 0.068692, Accuracy = 0.9573333
Iter 165000, Batch Loss = 0.070618, Accuracy = 0.906
Iter 180000, Batch Loss = 0.089659, Accuracy = 0.908
Iter 195000, Batch Loss = 0.088301, Accuracy = 0.87333333
Iter 210000, Batch Loss = 0.067824, Accuracy = 0.9026667
Iter 225000, Batch Loss = 0.060650, Accuracy = 0.9033333
Iter 240000, Batch Loss = 0.045368, Accuracy = 0.93733335
Iter 255000, Batch Loss = 0.049854, Accuracy = 0.96
Iter 270000, Batch Loss = 0.062839, Accuracy = 0.968
Iter 285000, Batch Loss = 0.052522, Accuracy = 0.986
Iter 300000, Batch Loss = 0.060304, Accuracy = 0.98733336
Iter 315000, Batch Loss = 0.049382, Accuracy = 0.9993333
Iter 330000, Batch Loss = 0.052441, Accuracy = 0.9766667
Iter 345000, Batch Loss = 0.050224, Accuracy = 0.9546667
Iter 360000, Batch Loss = 0.057141, Accuracy = 0.9306667
Iter 375000, Batch Loss = 0.047664, Accuracy = 0.938
Iter 390000, Batch Loss = 0.047909, Accuracy = 0.93333334
Iter 405000, Batch Loss = 0.043014, Accuracy = 0.9533333
Iter 420000, Batch Loss = 0.054124, Accuracy = 0.952
Iter 435000, Batch Loss = 0.044272, Accuracy = 0.95133334
Iter 450000, Batch Loss = 0.058916, Accuracy = 0.96066666
Iter 465000, Batch Loss = 0.072512, Accuracy = 0.9486667
Iter 480000, Batch Loss = 0.080431, Accuracy = 0.94733334
Iter 495000, Batch Loss = 0.072193, Accuracy = 0.9726667
Iter 510000, Batch Loss = 0.068242, Accuracy = 0.972
Iter 525000, Batch Loss = 0.057797, Accuracy = 0.964
Iter 540000, Batch Loss = 0.063531, Accuracy = 0.918
Iter 555000, Batch Loss = 0.068177, Accuracy = 0.9126667
Iter 570000, Batch Loss = 0.053257, Accuracy = 0.9206667
Iter 585000, Batch Loss = 0.058263, Accuracy = 0.9113333
Iter 600000, Batch Loss = 0.054180, Accuracy = 0.90466666
Iter 615000, Batch Loss = 0.051008, Accuracy = 0.944
Iter 630000, Batch Loss = 0.051554, Accuracy = 0.966
Iter 645000, Batch Loss = 0.059238, Accuracy = 0.9686667
Iter 660000, Batch Loss = 0.051297, Accuracy = 0.9713333
Iter 675000, Batch Loss = 0.052069, Accuracy = 0.984
Iter 690000, Batch Loss = 0.040501, Accuracy = 0.998
Iter 705000, Batch Loss = 0.053661, Accuracy = 0.96066666
ter 720000, Batch Loss = 0.037088, Accuracy = 0.958
Iter 735000, Batch Loss = 0.039404, Accuracy = 0.9533333
```

Step 9 - Evaluating the model

Well done! We have finished the training. How about now evaluating the test set:

```
val (testLoss, testAcc) = test(testDataCount, batchSize, testData,
testLabels, model)
  println(s"TEST SET DISPLAY STEP:  Batch Loss =
${"%.6f".format(testLoss)}, Accuracy = $testAcc")
      testAccuracies += testAcc
      testLosses += testLoss
    }
    step += 1
  }
val (finalLoss, accuracy) = test(testDataCount, batchSize, testData,
testLabels, model)
  println(s"FINAL RESULT: Batch Loss= $finalLoss, Accuracy= $accuracy")
```

```
TEST SET DISPLAY STEP: Batch Loss = 0.065859, Accuracy = 0.9138107
 TEST SET DISPLAY STEP: Batch Loss = 0.077047, Accuracy = 0.912114
 TEST SET DISPLAY STEP: Batch Loss = 0.069186, Accuracy = 0.90566677
 TEST SET DISPLAY STEP: Batch Loss = 0.059815, Accuracy = 0.93043774
 TEST SET DISPLAY STEP: Batch Loss = 0.064162, Accuracy = 0.9192399
 TEST SET DISPLAY STEP: Batch Loss = 0.063574, Accuracy = 0.9307771
 TEST SET DISPLAY STEP: Batch Loss = 0.060209, Accuracy = 0.9229725
 TEST SET DISPLAY STEP: Batch Loss = 0.062598, Accuracy = 0.9290804
 TEST SET DISPLAY STEP: Batch Loss = 0.062686, Accuracy = 0.9311164
 TEST SET DISPLAY STEP: Batch Loss = 0.059543, Accuracy = 0.9250085
 TEST SET DISPLAY STEP: Batch Loss = 0.059646, Accuracy = 0.9263658
 TEST SET DISPLAY STEP: Batch Loss = 0.062546, Accuracy = 0.92941976
 TEST SET DISPLAY STEP: Batch Loss = 0.061765, Accuracy = 0.9263658
 TEST SET DISPLAY STEP: Batch Loss = 0.063814, Accuracy = 0.9307771
 TEST SET DISPLAY STEP: Batch Loss = 0.062560, Accuracy = 0.9324737
 TEST SET DISPLAY STEP: Batch Loss = 0.061307, Accuracy = 0.93518835
 TEST SET DISPLAY STEP: Batch Loss = 0.061102, Accuracy = 0.93281305
 TEST SET DISPLAY STEP: Batch Loss = 0.054946, Accuracy = 0.9375636
 TEST SET DISPLAY STEP: Batch Loss = 0.054461, Accuracy = 0.9365456
 TEST SET DISPLAY STEP: Batch Loss = 0.050856, Accuracy = 0.9290804
 TEST SET DISPLAY STEP: Batch Loss = 0.050600, Accuracy = 0.9334917
 TEST SET DISPLAY STEP: Batch Loss = 0.057579, Accuracy = 0.9277231
 TEST SET DISPLAY STEP: Batch Loss = 0.062409, Accuracy = 0.9324737
 TEST SET DISPLAY STEP: Batch Loss = 0.050926, Accuracy = 0.9409569
 TEST SET DISPLAY STEP: Batch Loss = 0.054567, Accuracy = 0.94027823
 FINAL RESULT: Batch Loss= 0.0545671,
 Accuracy= 0.94027823
```

Yahoo! We have managed to achieve 94% accuracy, which is really outstanding. In the previous code, `test()` is the method used for evaluating the performance of the model.

The signature of the model is given in the following code:

```
def test(testDataCount: Int, batchSize: Int, testDatas:
Array[Array[Array[Float]]],
    testLabels: Array[Float], model: LSTMModel): (Float, Float) = {
  var testLoss, testAcc = 0f
  for (begin <- 0 until testDataCount by batchSize) {
    val (testData, testLabel, dropNum) = {
      if (begin + batchSize <= testDataCount) {
        val datas = testDatas.drop(begin).take(batchSize)
        val labels = testLabels.drop(begin).take(batchSize)
        (datas, labels, 0)
      } else {
        val right = (begin + batchSize) - testDataCount
        val left = testDataCount - begin
        val datas = testDatas.drop(begin).take(left) ++
testDatas.take(right)
        val labels = testLabels.drop(begin).take(left) ++
testLabels.take(right)
        (datas, labels, right)
      }
    }
    //feed the test data to the deepNN
    model.data.set(testData.flatten.flatten)
    model.label.set(testLabel)
    model.exec.forward(isTrain = false)
    val (acc, loss) = getAccAndLoss(model.exec.outputs(0), testLabel)
    testLoss += loss
    testAcc += acc
  }
  (testLoss / testDataCount, testAcc / testDataCount)
}
```

When done, it's good practice to destroy the model to release resources:

```
model.exec.dispose()
```

We saw earlier that we achieved up to 93% accuracy on the test set. How about seeing the previous accuracy and errors in a graph:

```
// visualize
val xTrain = (0 until trainLosses.length * batchSize by
batchSize).toArray.map(_.toDouble)
val yTrainL = trainLosses.toArray.map(_.toDouble)
val yTrainA = trainAccuracies.toArray.map(_.toDouble)
val xTest = (0 until testLosses.length * displayIter by
displayIter).toArray.map(_.toDouble)
val yTestL = testLosses.toArray.map(_.toDouble)
```

```
val yTestA = testAccuracies.toArray.map(_.toDouble)
var series = new MemXYSeries(xTrain, yTrainL, "Train losses")
val data = new XYData(series)
series = new MemXYSeries(xTrain, yTrainA, "Train accuracies")
data += series
series = new MemXYSeries(xTest, yTestL, "Test losses")
data += series
series = new MemXYSeries(xTest, yTestA, "Test accuracies")
data += series
val chart = new XYChart("Training session's progress over iterations!",
data)
chart.showLegend = true
val plotter = new JFGraphPlotter(chart)
plotter.gui()
>>>
```

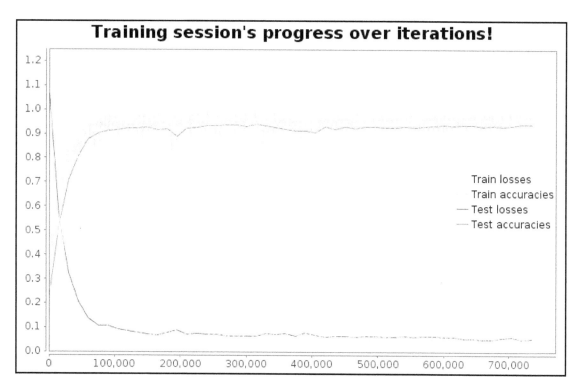

Figure 17: Training and test losses and accuracies per iteration

From the preceding graph, it is clear that with only a few iterations, our LSTM converged well and produced very good classification accuracy.

Tuning LSTM hyperparameters and GRU

Nevertheless, I still believe it is possible to attain about 100% accuracy with more LSTM layers. The following are the hyperparameters that I would still try to tune to see the accuracy:

```
// Hyper parameters for the LSTM training
val learningRate = 0.001f
val trainingIters = trainingDataCount * 1000 // Loop 1000 times on the
dataset
val batchSize = 1500 // I would set it 5000 and see the performance
val displayIter = 15000 // To show test set accuracy during training
val numLstmLayer = 3 // 5, 7, 9 etc.
```

There are many other variants of the LSTM cell. One particularly popular variant is the **Gated Recurrent Unit** (**GRU**) cell, which is a slightly dramatic variation on the LSTM. It also merges the cell state and hidden state and makes some other changes. The resulting model is simpler than standard LSTM models and has been growing increasingly popular. This cell was proposed by Kyunghyun Cho et al. in a 2014 paper that also introduced the encoder-decoder network we mentioned earlier.

For this type of LSTM, interested readers should refer to the following publications:

- *Learning Phrase Representations using RNN Encoder-Decoder for Statistical Machine Translation*, K. Cho et al. (2014).
- A 2015 paper by Klaus Greff et al., *LSTM: A Search Space Odyssey*, seems to show that all LSTM variants perform roughly the same.

Technically, a GRU cell is a simplified version of an LSTM cell, where both the state vectors are merged into a single vector called **h(t)**. A single gate controller controls both the forget gate and the input gate. If the gate controller outputs a 1, the input gate is open and the forget gate is closed:

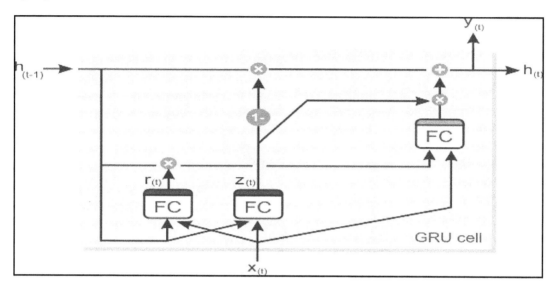

Figure 18: Internal structure of a GRU cell

On the other hand, if it outputs a 0, the opposite happens. Whenever a memory must be stored, the location where it will be stored is erased first, which is actually a frequent variant to the LSTM cell in and of itself. The second simplification is that since the full state vector is output at every time step, there is no output gate. However, there is a new gate controller introduced that controls which part of the previous state will be shown to the main layer. The following equations are used to do the GRU computations of a cell's long-term state, its short-term state, and its output at each time step for a single instance:

$$\mathbf{z}_{(t)} = \sigma\left(\mathbf{W}_{xz}^{T} \cdot \mathbf{x}_{(t)} + \mathbf{W}_{hz}^{T} \cdot \mathbf{h}_{(t-1)}\right)$$

$$\mathbf{r}_{(t)} = \sigma\left(\mathbf{W}_{xr}^{T} \cdot \mathbf{x}_{(t)} + \mathbf{W}_{hr}^{T} \cdot \mathbf{h}_{(t-1)}\right)$$

$$\mathbf{g}_{(t)} = \tanh\left(\mathbf{W}_{xg}^{T} \cdot \mathbf{x}_{(t)} + \mathbf{W}_{hg}^{T} \cdot \left(\mathbf{r}_{(t)} \otimes \mathbf{h}_{(t-1)}\right)\right)$$

$$\mathbf{h}_{(t)} = \left(1 - \mathbf{z}_{(t)}\right) \otimes \mathbf{h}_{(t-1)} + \mathbf{z}_{(t)} \otimes \mathbf{g}_{(t)}$$

The LSTM and GRU cells are one of the main reasons for the success of RNNs in recent years, in particular for applications in NLP.

Summary

In this chapter, we have seen how to develop an ML project using the RNN implementation, and called LSTM for HAR using the smartphones dataset. Our LSTM model has been able to classify the type of movement from six categories: walking, walking upstairs, walking downstairs, sitting, standing, and lying. In particular, we have achieved up to 94% accuracy. Later on, we discussed some possible ways to improve the accuracy further using GRU cell.

A **convolutional neural network** (**CNN**) is a type of feedforward neural network in which the connectivity pattern between its neurons is inspired by the animal visual cortex. Over the last few years, CNNs have demonstrated superhuman performance in complex visual tasks such as image search services, self-driving cars, automatic video classification, voice recognition, and **natural language processing** (**NLP**).

Considering these, in the next chapter we will see how to develop an end-to-end project for handling a multi-label (that is, each entity can belong to multiple classes) image classification problem using CNN based on the Scala and Deeplearning4j framework on real Yelp image datasets. We will also discuss some theoretical aspects of CNNs before getting started. Furthermore, we will discuss how to tune hyperparameters for better classification results.

11
Image Classification using Convolutional Neural Networks

So far, we haven't developed any **machine learning** (**ML**) projects for image processing tasks. Linear ML models and other regular **deep neural network** (**DNN**) models, such as **Multilayer Perceptrons** (**MLPs**) or **Deep Belief Networks** (**DBNs**), cannot learn or model non-linear features from images.

On the other hand, a **convolutional neural network** (**CNN**) is a type of feedforward neural network in which the connectivity pattern between its neurons is inspired by the animal visual cortex. In the last few years, CNNs have demonstrated superhuman performance in complex visual tasks such as image search services, self-driving cars, automatic video classification, voice recognition, and **natural language processing** (**NLP**).

In this chapter, we will see how to develop an end-to-end project for handling multi-label (that is, each entity can belong to multiple classes) image classification problems using CNN based on the Scala and **Deeplearning4j** (**DL4j**) framework with real **Yelp** image datasets. We will also discuss some theoretical aspects of CNNs and how to tune hyperparameters for better classification results before getting started.

In a nutshell, we will learn the following topics throughout this end-to-end project:

- The drawbacks of regular DNNs
- CNN architectures: convolution operations and pooling layers
- Image classification using CNNs
- Tuning CNN hyperparameters

Image classification and drawbacks of DNNs

Before we start developing the end-to-end project for image classification using CNN, we need some background studies, such as the drawbacks of regular DNNs, suitability of CNNs over DNNs for image classification, CNN constructions, CNN's different operations, and so on. Although regular DNNs work fine for small images (for example, MNIST, CIFAR-10), it breaks down for larger images because of the huge number of parameters it requires. For example, a 100 x 100 image has 10,000 pixels, and if the first layer has just 1,000 neurons (which already severely restricts the amount of information transmitted to the next layer), this means a total of 10 million connections. And that's just for the first layer.

CNNs solve this problem using partially connected layers. Because consecutive layers are only partially connected and because it heavily reuses its weights, a CNN has far fewer parameters than a fully connected DNN, which makes it much faster to train, reduces the risk of overfitting, and requires much less training data. Moreover, when a CNN has learned a kernel that can detect a particular feature, it can detect that feature anywhere on the image. In contrast, when a DNN learns a feature in one location, it can detect it only in that particular location. Since images typically have very repetitive features, CNNs are able to generalize much better than DNNs for image processing tasks, such as classification, using fewer training examples.

Importantly, DNN has no prior knowledge of how pixels are organized; it does not know that nearby pixels are close. A CNN's architecture embeds this prior knowledge. Lower layers typically identify features in small areas of the images, while higher layers combine the lower-level features into larger features. This works well with most natural images, giving CNNs a decisive head start compared to DNNs:

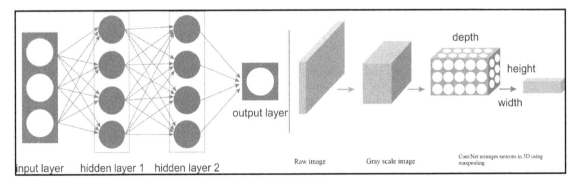

Figure 1: Regular DNN versus CNN

For example, in *Figure 1*, on the left, you can see a regular three-layer neural network. On the right, a ConvNet arranges its neurons in three dimensions (width, height, and depth), as visualized in one of the layers. Every layer of a ConvNet transforms the 3D input volume to a 3D output volume of neuron activations. The red input layer holds the image, so its width and height would be the dimensions of the image, and the depth would be three (red, green, and blue channels).

So, all the multilayer neural networks we looked at had layers composed of a long line of neurons, and we had to flatten input images or data to 1D before feeding them to the neural network. However, what happens once you try to feed them a 2D image directly? The answer is that, in CNN, each layer is represented in 2D, which makes it easier to match neurons with their corresponding inputs. We will see examples of it in upcoming sections.

Another important fact is all the neurons in a feature map share the same parameters, so it dramatically reduces the number of parameters in the model, but, more importantly, it means that once the CNN has learned to recognize a pattern in one location, it can recognize it in any other location. In contrast, once a regular DNN has learned to recognize a pattern in one location, it can recognize it only in that particular location.

CNN architecture

In multilayer networks, such as MLP or DBN, the outputs of all neurons of the input layer are connected to each neuron in the hidden layer, so the output will again act as the input to the fully-connected layer. In CNN networks, the connection scheme that defines the convolutional layer is significantly different. The convolutional layer is the main type of layer in CNN, where each neuron is connected to a certain region of the input area called the **receptive field**.

In a typical CNN architecture, a few convolutional layers are connected in a cascade style, where each layer is followed by a **rectified linear unit** (**ReLU**) layer, then a pooling layer, then a few more convolutional layers (+ReLU), then another pooling layer, and so on.

The output from each convolution layer is a set of objects called **feature maps** that are generated by a single kernel filter. The feature maps can then be used to define a new input to the next layer. Each neuron in a CNN network produces an output followed by an activation threshold, which is proportional to the input and not bound:

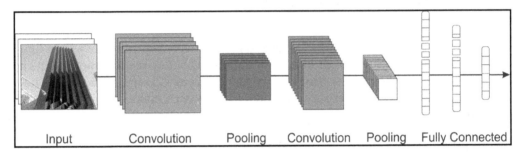

Figure 2: A conceptual architecture of CNN

As you can see in *Figure 2*, the pooling layers are usually placed after the convolutional layers. The convolutional region is then divided by a pooling layer into sub-regions. Then, a single representative value is selected using either a max-pooling or average pooling technique to reduce the computational time of subsequent layers.

This way, the robustness of the feature with respect to its spatial position gets increased too. To be more specific, when the image properties, as feature maps, pass through the image, they get smaller and smaller as they progress through the network, but they also typically get deeper and deeper, since more feature maps will be added. At the top of the stack, a regular feedforward neural network is added, just like an MLP, which might compose of a few fully connected layers (+ReLUs), and the final layer outputs the prediction, for example, a softmax layer that outputs estimated class probabilities for a multiclass classification.

Convolutional operations

A convolution is a mathematical operation that slides one function over another and measures the integral of their pointwise multiplication. It has deep connections with the Fourier transform and the Laplace transform and is heavily used in signal processing. Convolutional layers actually use cross-correlations, which are very similar to convolutions.

Thus, the most important building block of a CNN is the convolutional layer: neurons in the first convolutional layer are not connected to every single pixel in the input image (as they were in previous chapters), but only to pixels in their receptive fields—see *Figure 3*. In turn, each neuron in the second convolutional layer is connected only to neurons located within a small rectangle in the first layer:

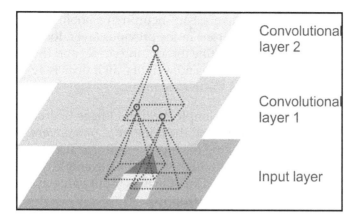

Figure 3: CNN layers with rectangular local receptive fields

This architecture allows the network to concentrate on low-level features in the first hidden layer, and then assemble them into higher-level features in the next hidden layer, and so on. This hierarchical structure is common in real-world images, which is one of the reasons why CNNs work so well for image recognition.

Pooling layer and padding operations

Once you understand how convolutional layers work, the pooling layers are quite easy to grasp. A pooling layer typically works on every input channel independently, so the output depth is the same as the input depth. You may alternatively pool over the depth dimension, as we will see next, in which case the image's spatial dimensions (height and width) remain unchanged, but the number of channels is reduced. Let's see a formal definition of pooling layers from a well-known TensorFlow website:

"The pooling ops sweep a rectangular window over the input tensor, computing a reduction operation for each window (average, max, or max with argmax). Each pooling op uses rectangular windows of size called ksize separated by offset strides. For example, if strides are all ones, every window is used, if strides are all twos, every other window is used in each dimension, and so on."

Therefore, just like in convolutional layers, each neuron in a pooling layer is connected to the outputs of a limited number of neurons in the previous layer, located within a small rectangular receptive field. You must define its size, the stride, and the padding type, just like before. However, a pooling neuron has no weights; all it does is aggregate the inputs using an aggregation function such as the max or mean.

Well, the goal of using pooling is to subsample the input image in order to reduce the computational load, the memory usage, and the number of parameters. This helps to avoid overfitting in the training stage. Reducing the input image size also makes the neural network tolerate a little bit of image shift. In the following example, we use a 2 x 2 pooling kernel and a stride of 2 with no padding. Only the max input value in each kernel makes it to the next layer since the other inputs are dropped:

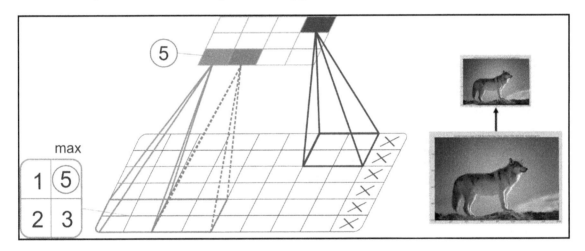

Figure 4: An example using max pooling, that is, subsampling

Usually, *(stride_length)* x + filter_size <= input_layer_size* is recommended for most CNN-based network development.

Subsampling operations

As stated earlier, a neuron located in a given layer is connected to the outputs of the neurons in the previous layer. Now, in order for a layer to have the same height and width as the previous layer, it is common to add zeros around the inputs, as shown in the diagram. This is called **SAME** or **zero padding**.

The term SAME means that the output feature map has the same spatial dimensions as the input feature map. Zero padding is introduced to make the shapes match as needed, equally on every side of the input map. On the other hand, VALID means no padding and only drops the right-most columns (or bottom-most rows):

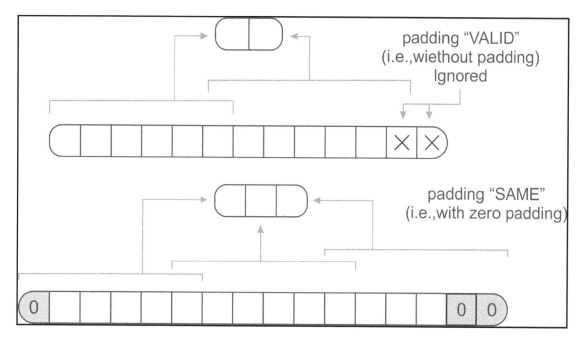

Figure 5: SAME versus VALID padding with CNN

Now we have the minimum theoretical knowledge about CNNs and their architectures, it's time to do some hands-on work and create convolutional, pooling, and subsampling operations using Deeplearning4j (aka. DL4j), which is one of the first commercial-grade distributed open source deep-learning libraries written for Java and Scala. It also provides integrated support for Hadoop and Spark. DL4j is designed to be used in business environments on distributed GPUs and CPUs.

Convolutional and subsampling operations in DL4j

Before getting started, setting up our programming environment is a prerequisite. So let's do that first.

Configuring DL4j, ND4s, and ND4j

The following libraries can be integrated with DL4j. They will make your JVM experience easier, whether you're developing your ML application in Java or Scala:

- **DL4j**: Neural net platform
- **ND4J**: NumPy for the JVM
- **DataVec**: Tool for ML ETL operations
- **JavaCPP**: The bridge between Java and native C++
- **Arbiter**: Evaluation tool for ML algorithms
- **RL4J**: Deep reinforcement learning for the JVM

ND4j is just like NumPy for JVM. It comes with some basic operations of linear algebra, such as matrix creation, addition, and multiplication. ND4S, on the other hand, is a scientific computing library for linear algebra and matrix manipulation. Basically, it supports n-dimensional arrays for JVM-based languages.

If you are using Maven on Eclipse (or any other editor—that is, IntelliJ IDEA), use the following dependencies in the `pom.xml` file (inside the `<dependencies>` tag) for dependency resolution for DL4j, ND4s, and ND4j:

```
<dependency>
    <groupId>org.deeplearning4j</groupId>
    <artifactId>deeplearning4j-core</artifactId>
    <version>0.4-rc3.9</version>
</dependency>
<dependency>
    <artifactId>canova-api</artifactId>
    <groupId>org.nd4j</groupId>
    <version>0.4-rc3.9</version>
</dependency>
<dependency>
    <groupId>org.nd4j</groupId>
    <artifactId>nd4j-native</artifactId>
    <version>0.4-rc3.9</version>
</dependency>
<dependency>
    <groupId>org.nd4j</groupId>
    <artifactId>canova-api</artifactId>
    <version>0.0.0.17</version>
</dependency>
```

I used old versions since I was facing some compatibility issues, and it is still under active development. But feel free to adopt the latest upgrades. I believe readers can do it with minimal efforts.

Additionally, if a native system BLAS is not configured on your machine, ND4j's performance will be reduced. You will experience a warning once you execute simple code written in Scala:

```
**************************************************************
WARNING: COULD NOT LOAD NATIVE SYSTEM BLAS
ND4J performance WILL be reduced
**************************************************************
```

However, installing and configuring BLAS such as OpenBLAS or IntelMKL is not that difficult; you can invest some time and do it. Refer to the following URL for details: `http://nd4j.org/getstarted.html#open`. It is also to be noted that the following are prerequisites when working with DL4j:

- Java (developer version) 1.8+ (only 64-bit versions supported)
- Apache Maven for automated build and dependency manager
- IntelliJ IDEA or Eclipse
- Git

Well done! Our programming environment is ready for a simple deep learning application development. Now it's time to get your hands dirty with some sample code. Let's see how to construct and train a simple CNN, using the CIFAR-10 dataset. CIFAR-10 is one of the most popular benchmark datasets and has thousands of labelled images.

Convolutional and subsampling operations in DL4j

In this subsection, we will see an example of how to construct a CNN for MNIST data classification. The network will have two convolutional layers, two subsampling layers, one dense layer, and the output layer as the fully connected layer. The first layer is a convolutional layer followed by a subsampling layer, which is again followed by another convolutional layer. Then, a subsampling layer is followed by a dense layer, which is followed by an output layer.

Let's see how these layers would look like using DL4j. The first convolution layer with ReLU as activation function:

```
val layer_0 = new ConvolutionLayer.Builder(5, 5)
    .nIn(nChannels)
    .stride(1, 1)
    .nOut(20)
    .activation("relu")
    .build()
```

The following activation functions are currently supported in DL4j:

- ReLU
- Leaky ReLU
- Tanh
- Sigmoid
- Hard Tanh
- Softmax
- Identity
- **ELU (Exponential Linear Units)**
- Softsign
- Softplus

The second layer (that is, the first subsampling layer) is a subsampling layer with pooling type MAX, with kernel size 2 x 2 and stride size of 2 x 2 but no activation function:

```
val layer_1 = new
SubsamplingLayer.Builder(SubsamplingLayer.PoolingType.MAX)
    .kernelSize(2, 2)
    .stride(2, 2)
    .build()
```

The third layer (2nd convolution layer) is a convolutional layer with ReLU as activation function, 1*1 stride:

```
val layer_2 = new ConvolutionLayer.Builder(5, 5)
    .nIn(nChannels)
    .stride(1, 1)
    .nOut(50)
    .activation("relu")
    .build()
```

The fourth layer (that is, the second subsampling layer) is a subsampling layer with pooling type MAX, with kernel size 2 x 2, and stride size of 2 x 2 but no activation function:

```
val layer_3 = new
SubsamplingLayer.Builder(SubsamplingLayer.PoolingType.MAX)
    .kernelSize(2, 2)
    .stride(2, 2)
    .build()
```

The fifth layer is a dense layer with ReLU as an activation function:

```
val layer_4 = new DenseLayer.Builder()
    .activation("relu")
    .nOut(500)
    .build()
```

The sixth (that is, the final and fully connected layer) has Softmax as the activation function with the number of classes to be predicted (that is, 10):

```
val layer_5 = new
OutputLayer.Builder(LossFunctions.LossFunction.NEGATIVELOGLIKELIHOOD)
    .nOut(outputNum)
    .activation("softmax")
    .build()
```

Once the layers are constructed, the next task is to construct and build the CNN by chaining all the layers. Using DL4j, it goes as follows:

```
val builder: MultiLayerConfiguration.Builder = new
NeuralNetConfiguration.Builder()
    .seed(seed)
    .iterations(iterations)
    .regularization(true).l2(0.0005)
    .learningRate(0.01)
    .weightInit(WeightInit.XAVIER)
    .optimizationAlgo(OptimizationAlgorithm.STOCHASTIC_GRADIENT_DESCENT)
    .updater(Updater.NESTEROVS).momentum(0.9)
    .list()
        .layer(0, layer_0)
        .layer(1, layer_1)
        .layer(2, layer_2)
        .layer(3, layer_3)
        .layer(4, layer_4)
        .layer(5, layer_5)
    .backprop(true).pretrain(false) // feedforward and supervised so no
pretraining
```

Finally, we set up all the convolutional layers and initialize the network as follows:

```
new ConvolutionLayerSetup(builder, 28, 28, 1) //image size is 28*28
val conf: MultiLayerConfiguration = builder.build()
val model: MultiLayerNetwork = new MultiLayerNetwork(conf)
model.init()
```

Conventionally, to train a CNN, all images need to be the same shape and size. So I placed the dimension as 28 x 28 in the preceding lines for simplicity. Now, you may be thinking, how do we train such a network? Well, now we will see this but, before that, we need to prepare the MNIST dataset, using the `MnistDataSetIterator` () method, as follows:

```
val nChannels = 1 // for grayscale image
val outputNum = 10 // number of class
val nEpochs = 10 // number of epoch
val iterations = 1 // number of iteration
val seed = 12345 // Random seed for reproducibility
val batchSize = 64 // number of batches to be sent
log.info("Load data....")
val mnistTrain: DataSetIterator = new MnistDataSetIterator(batchSize, true,
12345)
val mnistTest: DataSetIterator = new MnistDataSetIterator(batchSize, false,
12345)
```

Now let's start training the CNN, using the train set and iterate for each epoch:

```
log.info("Model training started...")
model.setListeners(new ScoreIterationListener(1))
var i = 0
while (i <= nEpochs) {
    model.fit(mnistTrain);
    log.info("*** Completed epoch {} ***", i)
    i = i + 1
    }
var ds: DataSet = null
var output: INDArray = null
```

Once we have trained the CNN, the next task is to evaluate the model on the test set, as follows:

```
log.info("Model evaluation....")
val eval: Evaluation = new Evaluation(outputNum)
while (mnistTest.hasNext()) {
    ds = mnistTest.next()
    output = model.output(ds.getFeatureMatrix(), false)
    }
eval.eval(ds.getLabels(), output)
```

Finally, we compute some performance matrices, such as `Accuracy`, `Precision`, `Recall`, and `F1 measure`, as follows:

```
println("Accuracy: " + eval.accuracy())
println("F1 measure: " + eval.f1())
println("Precision: " + eval.precision())
println("Recall: " + eval.recall())
println("Confusion matrix: " + "n" + eval.confusionToString())
log.info(eval.stats())
mnistTest.reset()
>>>
==========================Scores========================================
 Accuracy: 1
 Precision: 1
 Recall: 1
 F1 Score: 1
========================================================================
```

For your ease, here I provided the full source code for this simple image classifier:

```
package com.example.CIFAR

import org.canova.api.records.reader.RecordReader
import org.canova.api.split.FileSplit
import org.canova.image.loader.BaseImageLoader
import org.canova.image.loader.NativeImageLoader
import org.canova.image.recordreader.ImageRecordReader
import org.deeplearning4j.datasets.iterator.DataSetIterator
import org.canova.image.recordreader.ImageRecordReader
import org.deeplearning4j.datasets.canova.RecordReaderDataSetIterator
import org.deeplearning4j.datasets.iterator.impl.MnistDataSetIterator
import org.deeplearning4j.eval.Evaluation
import org.deeplearning4j.nn.api.OptimizationAlgorithm
import org.deeplearning4j.nn.conf.MultiLayerConfiguration
import org.deeplearning4j.nn.conf.NeuralNetConfiguration
import org.deeplearning4j.nn.conf.Updater
import org.deeplearning4j.nn.conf.layers.ConvolutionLayer
import org.deeplearning4j.nn.conf.layers.DenseLayer
import org.deeplearning4j.nn.conf.layers.OutputLayer
import org.deeplearning4j.nn.conf.layers.SubsamplingLayer
import org.deeplearning4j.nn.conf.layers.setup.ConvolutionLayerSetup
import org.deeplearning4j.nn.multilayer.MultiLayerNetwork
import org.deeplearning4j.nn.weights.WeightInit
import org.deeplearning4j.optimize.listeners.ScoreIterationListener
import org.nd4j.linalg.api.ndarray.INDArray
import org.nd4j.linalg.api.rng.Random
import org.nd4j.linalg.dataset.DataSet
```

```
import org.nd4j.linalg.dataset.SplitTestAndTrain
import org.nd4j.linalg.lossfunctions.LossFunctions
import org.slf4j.Logger
import org.slf4j.LoggerFactory
import java.io.File
import java.util.ArrayList
import java.util.List

object MNIST {
    val log: Logger = LoggerFactory.getLogger(MNIST.getClass)
    def main(args: Array[String]): Unit = {
    val nChannels = 1 // for grayscale image
    val outputNum = 10 // number of class
    val nEpochs = 1 // number of epoch
    val iterations = 1 // number of iteration
    val seed = 12345 // Random seed for reproducibility
    val batchSize = 64 // number of batches to be sent

    log.info("Load data....")
    val mnistTrain: DataSetIterator = new MnistDataSetIterator(batchSize,
true, 12345)
    val mnistTest: DataSetIterator = new MnistDataSetIterator(batchSize,
false, 12345)

    log.info("Network layer construction started...")
    //First convolution layer with ReLU as activation function
    val layer_0 = new ConvolutionLayer.Builder(5, 5)
        .nIn(nChannels)
        .stride(1, 1)
        .nOut(20)
        .activation("relu")
        .build()

    //First subsampling layer
    val layer_1 = new
SubsamplingLayer.Builder(SubsamplingLayer.PoolingType.MAX)
        .kernelSize(2, 2)
        .stride(2, 2)
        .build()

    //Second convolution layer with ReLU as activation function
    val layer_2 = new ConvolutionLayer.Builder(5, 5)
        .nIn(nChannels)
        .stride(1, 1)
        .nOut(50)
        .activation("relu")
        .build()
```

```
    //Second subsampling layer
    val layer_3 = new
SubsamplingLayer.Builder(SubsamplingLayer.PoolingType.MAX)
        .kernelSize(2, 2)
        .stride(2, 2)
        .build()

    //Dense layer
    val layer_4 = new DenseLayer.Builder()
        .activation("relu")
        .nOut(500)
        .build()

    // Final and fully connected layer with Softmax as activation function
    val layer_5 = new
OutputLayer.Builder(LossFunctions.LossFunction.NEGATIVELOGLIKELIHOOD)
        .nOut(outputNum)
        .activation("softmax")
        .build()

    log.info("Model building started...")
    val builder: MultiLayerConfiguration.Builder = new
NeuralNetConfiguration.Builder()
        .seed(seed)
        .iterations(iterations)
        .regularization(true).l2(0.0005)
        .learningRate(0.01)
        .weightInit(WeightInit.XAVIER)
.optimizationAlgo(OptimizationAlgorithm.STOCHASTIC_GRADIENT_DESCENT)
        .updater(Updater.NESTEROVS).momentum(0.9)
        .list()
            .layer(0, layer_0)
            .layer(1, layer_1)
            .layer(2, layer_2)
            .layer(3, layer_3)
            .layer(4, layer_4)
            .layer(5, layer_5)
    .backprop(true).pretrain(false) // feedforward so no backprop

// Setting up all the convlutional layers and initialize the network
new ConvolutionLayerSetup(builder, 28, 28, 1) //image size is 28*28
val conf: MultiLayerConfiguration = builder.build()
val model: MultiLayerNetwork = new MultiLayerNetwork(conf)
model.init()

log.info("Model training started...")
model.setListeners(new ScoreIterationListener(1))
    var i = 0
```

```
while (i <= nEpochs) {
    model.fit(mnistTrain);
    log.info("*** Completed epoch {} ***", i)
    i = i + 1
    var ds: DataSet = null
    var output: INDArray = null
    log.info("Model evaluation....")
    val eval: Evaluation = new Evaluation(outputNum)

    while (mnistTest.hasNext()) {
        ds = mnistTest.next()
        output = model.output(ds.getFeatureMatrix(), false)
            }
    eval.eval(ds.getLabels(), output)
    println("Accuracy: " + eval.accuracy())
    println("F1 measure: " + eval.f1())
    println("Precision: " + eval.precision())
    println("Recall: " + eval.recall())
    println("Confusion matrix: " + "n" + eval.confusionToString())
    log.info(eval.stats())
    mnistTest.reset()
            }
log.info("***************Example finished********************")
        }
    }
```

Large-scale image classification using CNN

In this section, we will show a step-by-step example of developing a real-life ML project for image classification. However, we need to know the problem description first, to learn what sort of image classification needs to be done. Moreover, learning about the dataset is a mandate before getting started.

Problem description

Nowadays, food selfies and photo-centric social storytelling are becoming social trends. Food lovers willingly upload an enormous amount of selfies taken with food and a picture of the restaurant to social media and respective websites. And, of course, they also provide a written review that can significantly boost the popularity of the restaurant:

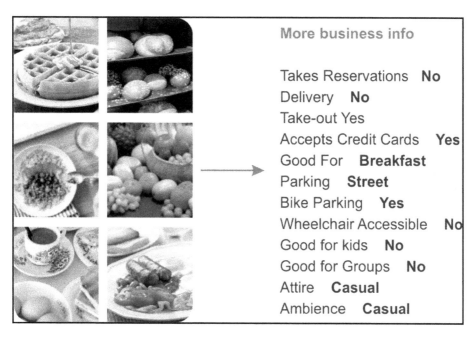

Figure 6: Mining some insights about business from Yelp dataset

For example, millions of unique visitors visit Yelp and have written more than 135 million reviews. There are lots of photos and lots of users who are uploading photos. Business owners can post photos and message their customers. This way, Yelp makes money by **selling ads** to those local businesses. An interesting fact is that these photos provide rich local business information across categories. Thus, training a computer to understand the context of these photos is not a trivial one and also not an easy task (see *Figure 6* to get an insight).

Now, the idea of this project is a challenging one: how can we turn those pictures into words? Let's give it a try. More specifically, you are given photos that belong to a business. Now we need to build a model so that it can tags restaurants with multiple labels of the user-submitted photos automatically—that is, to predict the business attributes.

Description of the image dataset

For such a challenge we need to have a real dataset. Don't worry, there are several platforms where such datasets are publicly available or can be downloaded with some terms and conditions. One such platform is **Kaggle**, which provides a platform for data analytics and ML practitioners to try ML challenges and win prizes. The Yelp dataset and the description can be found at: `https://www.kaggle.com/c/yelp-restaurant-photo-classification`.

The labels of the restaurants are manually selected by Yelp users when they submit a review. There are nine different labels annotated by the Yelp community associated in the dataset:

- `0: good_for_lunch`
- `1: good_for_dinner`
- `2: takes_reservations`
- `3: outdoor_seating`
- `4: restaurant_is_expensive`
- `5: has_alcohol`
- `6: has_table_service`
- `7: ambience_is_classy`
- `8: good_for_kids`

So we need to predict these labels as accurately as possible. One thing to be noted is that since Yelp is a community-driven website, there are duplicated images in the dataset for several reasons. For example, users can accidentally upload the same photo to the same business more than once, or chain businesses can upload the same photo to different branches. There are six files in the dataset, as follows:

- `train_photos.tgz`: Photos to be used as the training set (234,545 images)
- `test_photos.tgz`: Photos to be used as the test set (500 images)
- `train_photo_to_biz_ids.csv`: Provides the mapping between the photo ID to business ID (234,545 rows)
- `test_photo_to_biz_ids.csv`: Provides the mapping between the photo ID to business ID (500 rows)

- `train.csv`: This is the main training dataset including business IDs, and their corresponding labels (1996 rows)
- `sample_submission.csv`: A sample submission—reference correct format for your predictions including `business_id` and the corresponding predicted labels

Workflow of the overall project

In this project, we will see how to read images from `.jpg` format into a matrix representation in Scala. Then, we will further process and prepare those images feedable by the CNNs. We will see several image manipulations, such as squaring all the images and resizing every image to the same dimensions, before we apply a grayscale filter to the image:

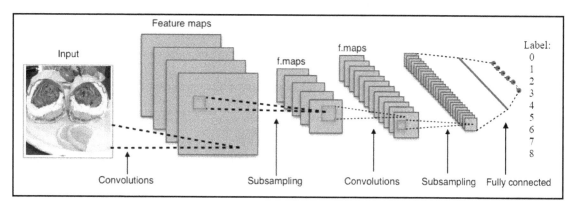

Figure 7: A conceptualize view of a CNN for image classification

Then we train nine CNNs on training data for each class. Once the training is completed, we save the trained model, CNN configurations and parameters, so that they can be restored later on, and then we apply a simple aggregate function to assign classes to each restaurant, where each one has multiple images associated with it, each with its own vector of probabilities for each of the nine classes. Then we score test data and finally, evaluate the model using test images.

Now let's see the structure of each CNN. Each network will have two convolutional layers, two subsampling layers, one dense layer, and the output layer as the fully connected layer. The first layer is a convolutional layer followed by a subsampling layer, which is again followed by another convolutional layer, then a subsampling layer, then a dense layer, which is followed by an output layer. We will see each layer's structure later on.

Implementing CNNs for image classification

The Scala object containing the `main()` method has the following workflow:

1. We read all the business labels from the `train.csv` file
2. We read and create a map from image ID to business ID of form `imageID →` `busID`
3. We get a list of images from the `photoDir` directory to load and process and, finally, get the image IDs of 10,000 images (feel free to set the range)
4. We then read and process images into a `photoID →` vector map
5. We chain the output of *step 3* and *step 4* to align the business feature, image IDs, and label IDs to get the feature extracted for the CNN
6. We construct nine CNNs.
7. We train all the CNNs and specify the model savings locations
8. We then repeat *step 2* to *step 6* to extract the features from the test set
9. Finally, we evaluate the model and save the prediction in a CSV file

Now let's see how the preceding steps would look in a high-level diagram:

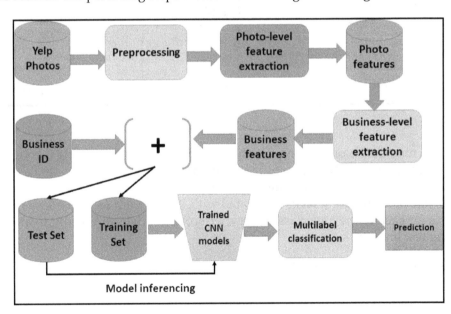

Figure 8: DL4j image processing pipeline for image classification

Programmatically, the preceding steps can be represented as follows:

```
val labelMap = readBusinessLabels("data/labels/train.csv")
val businessMap =
readBusinessToImageLabels("data/labels/train_photo_to_biz_ids.csv")
val imgs = getImageIds("data/images/train/", businessMap,
businessMap.map(_._2).toSet.toList).slice(0,100) // 20000 images

println("Image ID retreival done!")
val dataMap = processImages(imgs, resizeImgDim = 128)
println("Image processing done!")
val alignedData = new featureAndDataAligner(dataMap, businessMap,
Option(labelMap))()

println("Feature extraction done!")
val cnn0 = trainModelEpochs(alignedData, businessClass = 0, saveNN =
"models/model0")
val cnn1 = trainModelEpochs(alignedData, businessClass = 1, saveNN =
"models/model1")
val cnn2 = trainModelEpochs(alignedData, businessClass = 2, saveNN =
"models/model2")
val cnn3 = trainModelEpochs(alignedData, businessClass = 3, saveNN =
"models/model3")
val cnn4 = trainModelEpochs(alignedData, businessClass = 4, saveNN =
"models/model4")
val cnn5 = trainModelEpochs(alignedData, businessClass = 5, saveNN =
"models/model5")
val cnn6 = trainModelEpochs(alignedData, businessClass = 6, saveNN =
"models/model6")
val cnn7 = trainModelEpochs(alignedData, businessClass = 7, saveNN =
"models/model7")
val cnn8 = trainModelEpochs(alignedData, businessClass = 8, saveNN =
"models/model8")

val businessMapTE =
readBusinessToImageLabels("data/labels/test_photo_to_biz.csv")

val imgsTE = getImageIds("data/images/test//", businessMapTE,
businessMapTE.map(_._2).toSet.toList)

val dataMapTE = processImages(imgsTE, resizeImgDim = 128) // make them
128*128

val alignedDataTE = new featureAndDataAligner(dataMapTE, businessMapTE,
None)()
val Results = SubmitObj(alignedDataTE, "results/ModelsV0/")
val SubmitResults = writeSubmissionFile("kaggleSubmitFile.csv", Results,
thresh = 0.9)
```

Too much of a mouthful? Don't worry, we will now see each step in detail. If you look at the preceding steps carefully, you'll see *steps 1* to *step 5* are basically image processing and feature constructions.

Image processing

When I tried to develop this application, I found that the photos are of different size and shape: some images are tall, some of them are wide, some of them are outside, some images are inside, and most of them are pictures of food. However, some are other, random things too. Another important aspect is, while training images varied in portrait/landscape and the number of pixels, most were roughly square, and many of them were exactly 500 x 375:

Figure 9: Resized figure (left the original and tall one, right the squared one)

As we have already seen, CNN cannot work with images with a heterogeneous size and shape. There are many robust and efficient image processing techniques to extract only the **region of interest** (**ROI**). But, honestly, I am not an image processing expert, so I decided to keep this resizing step simpler.

CNN has a serious limitation as it cannot address the orientational and relative spatial relationships. Therefore, these components are not very important to a CNN. In short, CNN is not that suitable for images having heterogeneous shape and orientation. For why, people are now talking about the Capsule Networks. See more at the original paper at https://arxiv.org/pdf/1710.09829v1.pdf and https://openreview.net/pdf?id=HJWLfGWRb.

Naively, I made all the images square, but still, I tried to preserve the quality. The ROIs are centered in most cases, so capturing only the center-most square of each image is not that trivial. Nevertheless, we also need to convert each image to a grayscale image. Let's make irregularly shaped images square. Take a look at the following image, where the original one is on the left and the right is the square one (see *Figure 9*).

Now we have generated a square one, how did we achieve this? Well, I checked first if the height and the width are the same, if so, no resizing takes place. In the other two cases, I cropped the center region. The following method does the trick (but feel free to execute the SquaringImage.scala script to see the output):

```scala
def makeSquare(img: java.awt.image.BufferedImage):
java.awt.image.BufferedImage = {
    val w = img.getWidth
    val h = img.getHeight
    val dim = List(w, h).min
    img match {
        case x
            if w == h => img // do nothing and returns the original one
        case x
            if w > h => Scalr.crop(img, (w - h) / 2, 0, dim, dim)
        case x
            if w < h => Scalr.crop(img, 0, (h - w) / 2, dim, dim)
    }
}
```

Well done! Now that all of our training images are square, the next import preprocessing task is to resize them all. I decided to make all the images 128 x 128 in size. Let's see how the previous (the original) one looks after resizing:

Figure 10: Image resizing (256 x 256, 128 x 128, 64 x 64 and 32 x 32 respectively)

The following method did the trick (but feel free to execute the `ImageResize.scala` script to see a demo):

```
def resizeImg(img: java.awt.image.BufferedImage, width: Int, height: Int) =
{
    Scalr.resize(img, Scalr.Method.BALANCED, width, height)
}
```

By the way, for the image resizing and squaring, I used some built-in packages for image reading and some third-party packages for processing:

```
import org.imgscalr._
import java.io.File
import javax.imageio.ImageIO
```

To use the preceding packages, add the following dependencies in a Maven-friendly `pom.xml` file:

```
<dependency>
    <groupId>org.imgscalr</groupId>
    <artifactId>imgscalr-lib</artifactId>
    <version>4.2</version>
</dependency>
<dependency>
    <groupId>org.datavec</groupId>
    <artifactId>datavec-data-image</artifactId>
    <version>0.9.1</version>
</dependency>
<dependency>
    <groupId>com.sksamuel.scrimage</groupId>
    <artifactId>scrimage-core_2.10</artifactId>
    <version>2.1.0</version>
</dependency>
```

Although DL4j-based CNNs can handle color images, it's better to simplify the computation with grayscale images. Although color images are more exciting and effective, this way we can make the overall representation simpler and space efficient.

Let's give an example of our previous step. We resized each image to a 256 x 256 pixel image represented by 16,384 features, rather than 16,384 x 3 for a color image having three RGB channels (execute `GrayscaleConverter.scala` to see a demo). Let's see how the converted image would look:

Figure 11: Left - original image, right the grayscale one RGB averaging

The preceding conversion is done using two methods called `pixels2Gray()` and `makeGray()`:

```
def pixels2Gray(R: Int, G: Int, B: Int): Int = (R + G + B) / 3
def makeGray(testImage: java.awt.image.BufferedImage):
java.awt.image.BufferedImage = {
    val w = testImage.getWidth
    val h = testImage.getHeight
        for {
        w1 <- (0 until w).toVector
        h1 <- (0 until h).toVector
        }
    yield
    {
    val col = testImage.getRGB(w1, h1)
    val R = (col & 0xff0000) / 65536
    val G = (col & 0xff00) / 256
    val B = (col & 0xff)
    val graycol = pixels2Gray(R, G, B)
testImage.setRGB(w1, h1, new Color(graycol, graycol, graycol).getRGB)
    }
testImage
}
```

So what happens under the hood? We chain the preceding three steps: make all the images square, then convert all of them to 25 x 256, and finally convert the resized image into a grayscale one:

```
val demoImage = ImageIO.read(new File(x))
    .makeSquare
    .resizeImg(resizeImgDim, resizeImgDim) // (128, 128)
    .image2gray
```

So, in summary, we now have all the images in gray after squaring and resizing. The following image gives some sense of the conversion step:

Figure 12: Resized figure (left the original and tall one, right the squared one)

The following chaining also comes with some additional effort. Now we put these three steps together in the code, and we can finally prepare all of our images:

```
import scala.Vector
import org.imgscalr._

object imageUtils {
    implicitclass imageProcessingPipeline(img:
java.awt.image.BufferedImage) {
    // image 2 vector processing
    def pixels2gray(R: Int, G:Int, B: Int): Int = (R + G + B) / 3
    def pixels2color(R: Int, G:Int, B: Int): Vector[Int] = Vector(R, G, B)
    private def image2vec[A](f: (Int, Int, Int) => A ): Vector[A] = {
        val w = img.getWidth
        val h = img.getHeight
        for {
            w1 <- (0 until w).toVector
            h1 <- (0 until h).toVector
```

```
        }
    yield {
        val col = img.getRGB(w1, h1)
        val R = (col & 0xff0000) / 65536
        val G = (col & 0xff00) / 256
        val B = (col & 0xff)
    f(R, G, B)
            }
        }

def image2gray: Vector[Int] = image2vec(pixels2gray)
def image2color: Vector[Int] = image2vec(pixels2color).flatten

// make image square
def makeSquare = {
    val w = img.getWidth
    val h = img.getHeight
    val dim = List(w, h).min
    img match {
        case x
            if w == h => img
        case x
            if w > h => Scalr.crop(img, (w-h)/2, 0, dim, dim)
        case x
            if w < h => Scalr.crop(img, 0, (h-w)/2, dim, dim)
        }
    }

// resize pixels
def resizeImg(width: Int, height: Int) = {
    Scalr.resize(img, Scalr.Method.BALANCED, width, height)
        }
    }
}
```

Extracting image metadata

Up too this point, we have loaded and pre-processed raw images, but we have no idea about the image metadata that we need to make our CNNs learn. Thus, it's time to load the CSV files that contain metadata about each image.

I wrote a method to read such metadata in CSV format, called `readMetadata()`, which is used later on by two other methods called `readBusinessLabels` and `readBusinessToImageLabels`. These three methods are defined in the `CSVImageMetadataReader.scala` script. Here's the signature of the `readMetadata()` method:

```
def readMetadata(csv: String, rows: List[Int]=List(-1)): List[List[String]]
= {
    val src = Source.fromFile(csv)

    def reading(csv: String): List[List[String]]= {
        src.getLines.map(x => x.split(",").toList)
            .toList
        }
    try {
        if(rows==List(-1)) reading(csv)
        else rows.map(reading(csv))
        }
    finally {
        src.close
        }
    }
```

The `readBusinessLabels()` method maps from business ID to labels of the form businessID → Set (labels):

```
def readBusinessLabels(csv: String, rows: List[Int]=List(-1)): Map[String,
Set[Int]] = {
    val reader = readMetadata(csv)
    reader.drop(1)
        .map(x => x match {
        case x :: Nil => (x(0).toString, Set[Int]())
        case _ => (x(0).toString, x(1).split(" ").map(y => y.toInt).toSet)
        }).toMap
    }
```

The `readBusinessToImageLabels ()` method maps from image ID to business ID of the form `imageID → businessID`:

```
def readBusinessToImageLabels(csv: String, rows: List[Int] = List(-1)):
Map[Int, String] = {
    val reader = readMetadata(csv)
    reader.drop(1)
        .map(x => x match {
        case x :: Nil => (x(0).toInt, "-1")
        case _ => (x(0).toInt, x(1).split(" ").head)
        }).toMap
}
```

Image feature extraction

So far we have seen how to preprocess images so that features from those images can be extracted and fed into CNNs. Additionally, we have seen how to extract and map metadata and link it with the original images. Now it's time to extract features from those preprocessed images.

We also need to keep in mind the provenance of the metadata of each image. As you can guess, we need three map operations for feature extractions. Essentially, we have three maps. For details see the `imageFeatureExtractor.scala` script:

1. Business mapping with the form `imageID → businessID`
2. Data map of the form `imageID →` image data
3. Label map of the form `businessID →` labels

We first define a regular expression pattern to extract the `.jpg` name from the CSV `ImageMetadataReader` class, which is used to match against training labels:

```
val patt_get_jpg_name = new Regex("[0-9]")
```

Then we extract all the image IDs associated with their respective business ID:

```
def getImgIdsFromBusinessId(bizMap: Map[Int, String], businessIds:
List[String]): List[Int] = {
    bizMap.filter(x => businessIds.exists(y => y == x._2)).map(_._1).toList
    }
```

Now we need to load and process all the images that are already preprocessed to extract the image IDs by mapping with the IDs extracted from the business IDs, as shown earlier:

```
def getImageIds(photoDir: String, businessMap: Map[Int, String] = Map(-1 ->
"-1"), businessIds:
    List[String] = List("-1")): List[String] = {
    val d = new File(photoDir)
    val imgsPath = d.listFiles().map(x => x.toString).toList
    if (businessMap == Map(-1 -> "-1") || businessIds == List(-1)) {
        imgsPath
    }
    else {
        val imgsMap = imgsPath.map(x =>
patt_get_jpg_name.findAllIn(x).mkString.toInt -> x).toMap
        val imgsPathSub = getImgIdsFromBusinessId(businessMap, businessIds)
        imgsPathSub.filter(x => imgsMap.contains(x)).map(x => imgsMap(x))
        }
    }
```

So far, we have been able to extract all the image IDs that are somehow associated with at least one business. The next move would be to read and process these images into an imageID → vector map:

```
def processImages(imgs: List[String], resizeImgDim: Int = 128, nPixels: Int
= -1): Map[Int,Vector[Int]]= {
    imgs.map(x => patt_get_jpg_name.findAllIn(x).mkString.toInt -> {
        val img0 = ImageIO.read(new File(x))
        .makeSquare
        .resizeImg(resizeImgDim, resizeImgDim) // (128, 128)
        .image2gray
    if(nPixels != -1) img0.slice(0, nPixels)
    else img0
        }
    ).filter( x => x._2 != ())
    .toMap
    }
```

Well done! We are just one step behind to extract required to train our CNNs. The final step in feature extraction is to extract the pixel data:

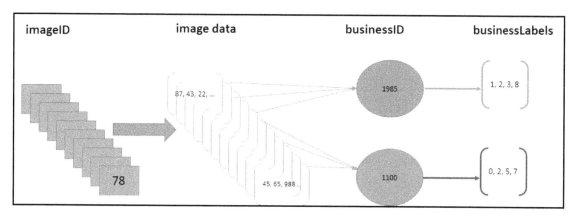

Figure 13: Image data representation

In summary, we need to keep track of four pieces of the object for each image—that is, `imageID`, `businessID`, labels, and pixel data. Thus, as shown in the preceding figure, the primary data structure is constructed with four data types (four tuples)—`imgID`, `businessID`, pixel data vector, and labels:

```
List[(Int, String, Vector[Int], Set[Int])]
```

Thus, we should have a class containing all pieces of these objects. Don't worry, everything we need is defined in the `featureAndDataAligner.scala` script. Once we have instantiated an instance of `featureAndDataAligner` using the following line of code in the `Main.scala` script (under the `main` method), the `businessMap`, `dataMap`, and `labMap` are provided:

```
val alignedData = new featureAndDataAligner(dataMap, businessMap,
Option(labelMap))()
```

Here, the option type for `labMap` is used since we don't have this information when we score on test data—that is, `None` is used for that invocation:

```
class featureAndDataAligner(dataMap: Map[Int, Vector[Int]], bizMap:
Map[Int, String], labMap: Option[Map[String, Set[Int]]])(rowindices:
List[Int] = dataMap.keySet.toList) {
    def this(dataMap: Map[Int, Vector[Int]], bizMap: Map[Int,
String])(rowindices: List[Int]) =          this(dataMap, bizMap,
None)(rowindices)
```

```scala
    def alignBusinessImgageIds(dataMap: Map[Int, Vector[Int]], bizMap:
Map[Int, String])
        (rowindices: List[Int] = dataMap.keySet.toList): List[(Int, String,
Vector[Int])] = {
        for {
            pid <- rowindices
            val imgHasBiz = bizMap.get(pid)
            // returns None if img doe not have a bizID
            val bid = if(imgHasBiz != None) imgHasBiz.get
            else "-1"
            if (dataMap.keys.toSet.contains(pid) && imgHasBiz != None)
        }
        yield {
        (pid, bid, dataMap(pid))
        }
    }
def alignLabels(dataMap: Map[Int, Vector[Int]], bizMap: Map[Int, String],
labMap: Option[Map[String,    Set[Int]]])(rowindices: List[Int] =
dataMap.keySet.toList): List[(Int, String, Vector[Int], Set[Int])] = {
    def flatten1[A, B, C, D](t: ((A, B, C), D)): (A, B, C, D) = (t._1._1,
t._1._2, t._1._3, t._2)
        val al = alignBusinessImgageIds(dataMap, bizMap)(rowindices)
        for { p <- al
        }
        yield {
            val bid = p._2
            val labs = labMap match {
            case None => Set[Int]()
            case x => (if(x.get.keySet.contains(bid)) x.get(bid)
        else Set[Int]())
            }
            flatten1(p, labs)
        }
    }
    lazy val data = alignLabels(dataMap, bizMap, labMap)(rowindices)
    // getter functions
    def getImgIds = data.map(_._1)
    def getBusinessIds = data.map(_._2)
    def getImgVectors = data.map(_._3)
    def getBusinessLabels = data.map(_._4)
    def getImgCntsPerBusiness =
getBusinessIds.groupBy(identity).mapValues(x => x.size)
}
```

Excellent! Up to this point, we have managed to extract the features to train our CNNs. However, the feature in current form is still not suitable to feed into the CNNs, because we only have the feature vectors without labels. Thus, we need an intermediate conversion.

Preparing the ND4j dataset

As I said, we need an intermediate conversion and pre-process to get the training set to contain feature vectors as well as labels. The conversion is pretty straightforward: we need the feature vector and the business labels.

For this, we have the `makeND4jDataSets` class (see `makeND4jDataSets.scala` for details). The class creates a ND4j dataset object from the data structure from the `alignLables` function in the form of `List[(imgID, bizID, labels, pixelVector)]`. First, we prepare the dataset using the `makeDataSet()` method:

```
def makeDataSet(alignedData: featureAndDataAligner, bizClass: Int): DataSet
= {
    val alignedXData = alignedData.getImgVectors.toNDArray
    val alignedLabs = alignedData.getBusinessLabels.map(x =>
    if (x.contains(bizClass)) Vector(1, 0)
    else Vector(0, 1)).toNDArray
    new DataSet(alignedXData, alignedLabs)
    }
```

Then we need to convert the preceding data structure further, into `INDArray`, which can then be consumed by the CNNs:

```
def makeDataSetTE(alignedData: featureAndDataAligner): INDArray = {
    alignedData.getImgVectors.toNDArray
    }
```

Training the CNNs and saving the trained models

So far, we have seen how to prepare the training set; now we have a challenge ahead. We have to train 234,545 images. Although the testing phase would be less exhaustive with only 500 images, it's better to train each CNN using batch-mode using DL4j's `MultipleEpochsIterator`. Here's a list of important hyperparameters and their details:

- **Layers**: As we have already observed with our simple 5 layers MNIST, we received outstanding classification accuracy, which is very promising. Here I will try to construct a similar network having.

- **The number of samples**: If you're training all the images, it will take too long. If you train using the CPU, not the GPU, it will take days. When I tried with 50,000 images, it took one whole day for a machine with an i7 processor and 32 GB of RAM. Now you can imagine how long it would take for the whole dataset. In addition, it will require at least 256 GB of RAM even if you do the training in the batch model.
- **Number of epochs**: This is the number of iterations through all the training records.
- **Number of output feature maps (that is, nOut)**: This is the number of feature maps. Take a closer look at other examples in the DL4j GitHub repository.
- **Learning Rate**: From the TensorFlow-like framework, I got some insights. In my opinion, it would be great to set a learning rate of 0.01 and 0.001.
- **Number of batch**: This is the number of records in each batch—32, 64, 128, and so on. I used 128.

Now, with the preceding hyperparameters, we can start training our CNNs. The following code does the trick. At first, we prepare the training set, then we define the required hyperparameters, then we normalize the dataset so the ND4j data frame is encoded and any labels that are considered true are 1s and the rest are zeros. Then we shuffle both the rows and labels of the encoded dataset.

Now we need to create epochs for the dataset iterator using the `ListDataSetIterator` and `MultipleEpochsIterator` respectively. Once the datasets are converted into batch-model, we are then ready to train the constructed CNNs:

```
def trainModelEpochs(alignedData: featureAndDataAligner, businessClass: Int
= 1, saveNN: String = "") = {
    val ds = makeDataSet(alignedData, businessClass)
    val nfeatures = ds.getFeatures.getRow(0).length // Hyperparameter
    val numRows = Math.sqrt(nfeatures).toInt //numRows*numColumns ==
data*channels
    val numColumns = Math.sqrt(nfeatures).toInt //numRows*numColumns ==
data*channels
    val nChannels = 1 // would be 3 if color image w R,G,B
    val outputNum = 9 // # of classes (# of columns in output)
    val iterations = 1
    val splitTrainNum = math.ceil(ds.numExamples * 0.8).toInt // 80/20
training/test split
    val seed = 12345
    val listenerFreq = 1
    val nepochs = 20
    val nbatch = 128 // recommended between 16 and 128
```

```
    ds.normalizeZeroMeanZeroUnitVariance()
    Nd4j.shuffle(ds.getFeatureMatrix, new Random(seed), 1) // shuffles rows
in the ds.
    Nd4j.shuffle(ds.getLabels, new Random(seed), 1) // shuffles labels
accordingly

    val trainTest: SplitTestAndTrain = ds.splitTestAndTrain(splitTrainNum,
new Random(seed))

    // creating epoch dataset iterator
    val dsiterTr = new ListDataSetIterator(trainTest.getTrain.asList(),
nbatch)
    val dsiterTe = new ListDataSetIterator(trainTest.getTest.asList(),
nbatch)
    val epochitTr: MultipleEpochsIterator = new
MultipleEpochsIterator(nepochs, dsiterTr)

    val epochitTe: MultipleEpochsIterator = new
MultipleEpochsIterator(nepochs, dsiterTe)
    //First convolution layer with ReLU as activation function
    val layer_0 = new ConvolutionLayer.Builder(6, 6)
        .nIn(nChannels)
        .stride(2, 2) // default stride(2,2)
        .nOut(20) // # of feature maps
        .dropOut(0.5)
        .activation("relu") // rectified linear units
        .weightInit(WeightInit.RELU)
        .build()

    //First subsampling layer
    val layer_1 = new
SubsamplingLayer.Builder(SubsamplingLayer.PoolingType.MAX)
        .kernelSize(2, 2)
        .stride(2, 2)
        .build()

    //Second convolution layer with ReLU as activation function
    val layer_2 = new ConvolutionLayer.Builder(6, 6)
        .nIn(nChannels)
        .stride(2, 2)
        .nOut(50)
        .activation("relu")
        .build()

    //Second subsampling layer
    val layer_3 = new
SubsamplingLayer.Builder(SubsamplingLayer.PoolingType.MAX)
        .kernelSize(2, 2)
```

```
            .stride(2, 2)
            .build()

    //Dense layer
    val layer_4 = new DenseLayer.Builder()
            .activation("relu")
            .nOut(500)
            .build()

    // Final and fully connected layer with Softmax as activation function
    val layer_5 = new
OutputLayer.Builder(LossFunctions.LossFunction.MCXENT)
            .nOut(outputNum)
            .weightInit(WeightInit.XAVIER)
            .activation("softmax")
            .build()

    val builder: MultiLayerConfiguration.Builder = new
NeuralNetConfiguration.Builder()
            .seed(seed)
            .iterations(iterations)
            .miniBatch(true)
.optimizationAlgo(OptimizationAlgorithm.STOCHASTIC_GRADIENT_DESCENT)
            .regularization(true).l2(0.0005)
            .learningRate(0.01)
            .list(6)
                .layer(0, layer_0)
                .layer(1, layer_1)
                .layer(2, layer_2)
                .layer(3, layer_3)
                .layer(4, layer_4)
                .layer(5, layer_5)
        .backprop(true).pretrain(false)

    new ConvolutionLayerSetup(builder, numRows, numColumns, nChannels)
    val conf: MultiLayerConfiguration = builder.build()
    val model: MultiLayerNetwork = new MultiLayerNetwork(conf)

    model.init()
    model.setListeners(Seq[IterationListener](new
ScoreIterationListener(listenerFreq)).asJava)
    model.fit(epochitTr)

    val eval = new Evaluation(outputNum)
    while (epochitTe.hasNext) {
        val testDS = epochitTe.next(nbatch)
        val output: INDArray = model.output(testDS.getFeatureMatrix)
        eval.eval(testDS.getLabels(), output)
```

```
        }
    if (!saveNN.isEmpty) {
        // model config
        FileUtils.write(new File(saveNN + ".json"),
model.getLayerWiseConfigurations().toJson())
        // model parameters
        val dos: DataOutputStream = new
DataOutputStream(Files.newOutputStream(Paths.get(saveNN + ".bin")))
        Nd4j.write(model.params(), dos)
        }
    }
```

In the preceding code, we also save a `.json` file containing all the network configurations and a `.bin` file for holding all the weights and parameters of all the CNNs. This is done by two methods; namely, `saveNN()` and `loadNN()` that are defined in the `NeuralNetwok.scala` script. First, let's see the signature of the `saveNN()` method that goes as follows:

```
def saveNN(model: MultiLayerNetwork, NNconfig: String, NNparams: String) =
{
    // save neural network config
    FileUtils.write(new File(NNconfig),
model.getLayerWiseConfigurations().toJson())
    // save neural network parms
    val dos: DataOutputStream = new
DataOutputStream(Files.newOutputStream(Paths.get(NNparams)))
    Nd4j.write(model.params(), dos)
}
```

The idea is visionary as well as important since, as I said, you wouldn't train your whole network for the second time to evaluate a new test set—that is, suppose you want to test just a single image. We also have another method named `loadNN()` that reads back the `.json` and `.bin` file we created earlier to a `MultiLayerNetwork` and is used to score new test data. The method goes as follows:

```
def loadNN(NNconfig: String, NNparams: String) = {
    // get neural network config
    val confFromJson: MultiLayerConfiguration =
    MultiLayerConfiguration.fromJson(FileUtils.readFileToString(new
File(NNconfig)))

    // get neural network parameters
    val dis: DataInputStream = new DataInputStream(new
FileInputStream(NNparams))
    val newParams = Nd4j.read(dis)
```

```
    // creating network object
    val savedNetwork: MultiLayerNetwork = new
MultiLayerNetwork(confFromJson)
    savedNetwork.init()
    savedNetwork.setParameters(newParams)
    savedNetwork
    }
```

Evaluating the model

The scoring approach that we're going to use is pretty simple. It assigns business-level labels by averaging the image-level predictions. I know I did it naively, but you can try a better approach. What I have done is assign a business with label 0 if the average of the probabilities across all of its images that it belongs to class 0 is greater than 0.5:

```
def scoreModel(model: MultiLayerNetwork, ds: INDArray) = {
    model.output(ds)
}
```

Then we collect the model predictions from the `scoreModel()` method and merge with `alignedData`:

```
def aggImgScores2Business(scores: INDArray, alignedData:
featureAndDataAligner ) = {
    assert(scores.size(0) == alignedData.data.length, "alignedData and
scores length are different. They     must be equal")

def getRowIndices4Business(mylist: List[String], mybiz: String): List[Int]
= mylist.zipWithIndex.filter(x     => x._1 == mybiz).map(_._2)

def mean(xs: List[Double]) = xs.sum / xs.size
    alignedData.getBusinessIds.distinct.map(x => (x, {
    val irows = getRowIndices4Business(alignedData.getBusinessIds, x)
    val ret =
    for(row <- irows)
        yield scores.getRow(row).getColumn(1).toString.toDouble
        mean(ret)
        }))
    }
```

Finally, we can restore the trained and saved models, restore them back, and generate the submission file for Kaggle. The thing is that we need to aggregate image predictions to business scores for each model.

Wrapping up by executing the main() method

Let's wrap up the overall discussion by watching the performance of our model. The following code is an overall glimpse:

```scala
package Yelp.Classifier
import Yelp.Preprocessor.CSVImageMetadataReader._
import Yelp.Preprocessor.featureAndDataAligner
import Yelp.Preprocessor.imageFeatureExtractor._
import Yelp.Evaluator.ResultFileGenerator._
import Yelp.Preprocessor.makeND4jDataSets._
import Yelp.Evaluator.ModelEvaluation._
import Yelp.Trainer.CNNEpochs._
import Yelp.Trainer.NeuralNetwork._

object YelpImageClassifier {
    def main(args: Array[String]): Unit = {
        // image processing on training data
        val labelMap = readBusinessLabels("data/labels/train.csv")
        val businessMap =
readBusinessToImageLabels("data/labels/train_photo_to_biz_ids.csv")
        val imgs = getImageIds("data/images/train/", businessMap,
        businessMap.map(_._2).toSet.toList).slice(0,20000) // 20000 images
        println("Image ID retreival done!")
        val dataMap = processImages(imgs, resizeImgDim = 256)
        println("Image processing done!")

        val alignedData =
            new featureAndDataAligner(dataMap, businessMap,
Option(labelMap))()
        println("Feature extraction done!")

        // training one model for one class at a time. Many hyperparamters
hardcoded within
        val cnn0 = trainModelEpochs(alignedData, businessClass = 0, saveNN
= "models/model0")
        val cnn1 = trainModelEpochs(alignedData, businessClass = 1, saveNN
= "models/model1")
        val cnn2 = trainModelEpochs(alignedData, businessClass = 2, saveNN
= "models/model2")
        val cnn3 = trainModelEpochs(alignedData, businessClass = 3, saveNN
= "models/model3")
```

```
        val cnn4 = trainModelEpochs(alignedData, businessClass = 4, saveNN
= "models/model4")
        val cnn5 = trainModelEpochs(alignedData, businessClass = 5, saveNN
= "models/model5")
        val cnn6 = trainModelEpochs(alignedData, businessClass = 6, saveNN
= "models/model6")
        val cnn7 = trainModelEpochs(alignedData, businessClass = 7, saveNN
= "models/model7")
        val cnn8 = trainModelEpochs(alignedData, businessClass = 8, saveNN
= "models/model8")

    // processing test data for scoring
        val businessMapTE =
readBusinessToImageLabels("data/labels/test_photo_to_biz.csv")
        val imgsTE = getImageIds("data/images/test//", businessMapTE,
        businessMapTE.map(_._2).toSet.toList)

        val dataMapTE = processImages(imgsTE, resizeImgDim = 128) // make
them 256x256
        val alignedDataTE = new featureAndDataAligner(dataMapTE,
businessMapTE, None)()

        // creating csv file to submit to kaggle (scores all models)
        val Results = SubmitObj(alignedDataTE, "results/ModelsV0/")
        val SubmitResults = writeSubmissionFile("kaggleSubmitFile.csv",
Results, thresh = 0.9)
        }
    }
>>>
==========================Scores==========================================
 Accuracy: 0.6833
 Precision: 0.53
 Recall: 0.5222
 F1 Score: 0.5261
==========================================================================
```

So, what's your impression? It's true that we haven't received outstanding classification accuracy. But we can still try with tuned hyperparameters. The next section provides some insight.

Tuning and optimizing CNN hyperparameters

The following hyperparameters are very important and must be tuned to achieve optimized results.

- **Dropout**: Used for random omission of feature detectors to prevent overfitting
- **Sparsity**: Used to force activations of sparse/rare inputs
- **Adagrad**: Used for feature-specific learning-rate optimization
- **Regularization**: L1 and L2 regularization
- **Weight transforms**: Useful for deep autoencoders
- **Probability distribution manipulation**: Used for initial weight generation
- Gradient normalization and clipping

Another important question is: when do you want to add a max pooling layer rather than a convolutional layer with the same stride? A max pooling layer has no parameters at all, whereas a convolutional layer has quite a few. Sometimes, adding a local response normalization layer that makes the neurons that most strongly activate inhibit neurons at the same location but in neighboring feature maps, encourages different feature maps to specialize and pushes them apart, forcing them to explore a wider range of features. It is typically used in the lower layers to have a larger pool of low-level features that the upper layers can build upon.

One of the main advantages observed during the training of large neural networks is overfitting, that is, generating very good approximations for the training data but emitting noise for the zones between single points. In the case of overfitting, the model is specifically adjusted to the training dataset, so it will not be used for generalization. Therefore, although it performs well on the training set, its performance on the test dataset and subsequent tests is poor because it lacks the generalization property:

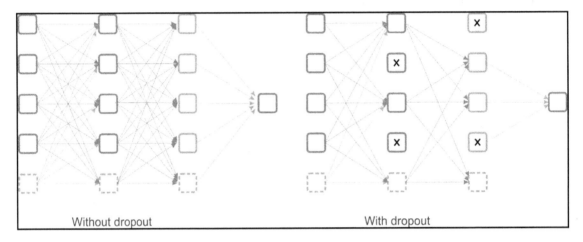

Figure 14: Dropout versus without dropout

The main advantage of this method is that it avoids all neurons in a layer to synchronously optimize their weights. This adaptation made in random groups avoids all the neurons converging on the same goals, thus de-correlating the adapted weights. A second property discovered in the dropout application is that the activation of the hidden units becomes sparse, which is also a desirable characteristic.

Since in CNN, one of the objective functions is to minimize the evaluated cost, we must define an optimizer. The following optimizers are supported by DL4j:

- SGD (learning rate only)
- Nesterovs momentum
- Adagrad
- RMSProp
- Adam
- AdaDelta

In most of the cases, we can adopt the implemented RMSProp, which is an advanced form of gradient descent, if the performance is not satisfactory. RMSProp performs better because it divides the learning rate by an exponentially decaying average of squared gradients. The suggested setting value of the decay parameter is 0.9, while a good default value for the learning rate is 0.001.

More technically, by using the most common optimizer, such as **Stochastic Gradient Descent** (**SGD**), the learning rates must scale with 1/T to get convergence, where T is the number of iterations. RMSProp tries to overcome this limitation automatically by adjusting the step size so that the step is on the same scale as the gradients. So, if you're training a neural network, but computing the gradients is mandatory, using RMSProp would be the faster way of learning in a mini-batch setting. Researchers also recommend using a Momentum optimizer while training a deep CNN or DNN.

From the layering architecture's perspective, CNN is different compared to DNN; it has a different requirement as well as tuning criteria. Another problem with CNNs is that the convolutional layers require a huge amount of RAM, especially during training, because the reverse pass of backpropagation requires all the intermediate values computed during the forward pass. During inference (that is, when making a prediction for a new instance), the RAM occupied by one layer can be released as soon as the next layer has been computed, so you only need as much RAM as required by two consecutive layers.

However, during training, everything computed during the forward pass needs to be preserved for the reverse pass, so the amount of RAM needed is (at least) the total amount of RAM required by all layers. If your GPU runs out of memory while training a CNN, here are five things you could try to solve the problem (other than purchasing a GPU with more RAM):

- Reduce the mini-batch size
- Reduce dimensionality using a larger stride in one or more layers
- Remove one or more layers
- Use 16-bit floats instead of 32-bit floats
- Distribute the CNN across multiple devices

Summary

In this chapter, we have seen how to use and build real-life applications using CNNs, which are a type of feedforward artificial neural network in which the connectivity pattern between neurons is inspired by the organization of the animal visual cortex. Our image classifier application using CNN can classify real-life images with an acceptable level of accuracy, although we did not achieve higher accuracy. However, readers are encouraged to tune hyperparameters in the code and also try the same approach with another dataset.

Nevertheless, and importantly since the internal data representation of a convolutional neural network does not take into account important spatial hierarchies between simple and complex objects, CNN has some serious drawbacks and limitation for certain instances. Therefore, I would suggest you take a look at the recent activities around capsule networks on GitHub at `https://github.com/topics/capsule-network`. Hopefully, you can get something useful out from there

This is, more-or-less, the end of our little journey in developing ML projects using Scala and different open source frameworks. Throughout the chapters, I tried to provide you with several examples of how to use these wonderful technologies efficiently for developing ML projects. During the writing of this book, I had to keep many constraints in my mind, for example, the page count, API availability, and my expertise. But I tried to make the book more-or-less simple, and I also tried to avoid details on the theory, as you can read about that in many books, blogs, and websites on Apache Spark, DL4j, and H2O itself.

I will also keep the code of this book updated on my GitHub repo at: `https://github.com/PacktPublishing/Scala-Machine-Learning-Projects`. Feel free to open a new issue or any pull request for improving this book and stay tuned.

Finally, I did not write this book to earn money but a major portion of the royalties will be spent for the child education in the rural areas of my home district in Bangladesh. I would like to say thanks and express my sincere gratitude for buying and enjoying this book!

Other Books You May Enjoy

If you enjoyed this book, you may be interested in these other books by Packt:

Scala for Machine Learning, Second Edition
Patrick R. Nicolas

ISBN: 978-1-78712-238-3

- Build dynamic workflows for scientific computing
- Leverage open source libraries to extract patterns from time series
- Write your own classification, clustering, or evolutionary algorithm
- Perform relative performance tuning and evaluation of Spark
- Master probabilistic models for sequential data
- Experiment with advanced techniques such as regularization and kernelization
- Dive into neural networks and some deep learning architecture
- Apply some basic multiarm-bandit algorithms
- Solve big data problems with Scala parallel collections, Akka actors, and Apache Spark clusters
- Apply key learning strategies to a technical analysis of financial markets

Mastering Scala Machine Learning
Alex Kozlov

ISBN: 978-1-78588-088-9

- Sharpen your functional programming skills in Scala using REPL
- Apply standard and advanced machine learning techniques using Scala
- Get acquainted with Big Data technologies and grasp why we need a functional approach to Big Data
- Discover new data structures, algorithms, approaches, and habits that will allow you to work effectively with large amounts of data
- Understand the principles of supervised and unsupervised learning in machine learning
- Work with unstructured data and serialize it using Kryo, Protobuf, Avro, and AvroParquet
- Construct reliable and robust data pipelines and manage data in a data-driven enterprise
- Implement scalable model monitoring and alerts with Scala

Leave a review - let other readers know what you think

Please share your thoughts on this book with others by leaving a review on the site that you bought it from. If you purchased the book from Amazon, please leave us an honest review on this book's Amazon page. This is vital so that other potential readers can see and use your unbiased opinion to make purchasing decisions, we can understand what our customers think about our products, and our authors can see your feedback on the title that they have worked with Packt to create. It will only take a few minutes of your time, but is valuable to other potential customers, our authors, and Packt. Thank you!

Index